THE POLITICS OF
THE REFORMATION
IN GERMANY

THE POLITICS OF THE REFORMATION IN GERMANY:

JACOB STURM (1489–1553) OF STRASBOURG

Thomas A. Brady, Jr.

HUMANITIES PRESS
NEW JERSEY

First published in 1997 by
Humanities Press International, Inc.,
165 First Avenue, Atlantic Highlands, New Jersey 07716.

Library of Congress Cataloging-in-Publication Data
Brady, Thomas A.
    The politics of the Reformation in Germany : Jacob Sturm
  (1489–1553) of Strasbourg / Thomas A. Brady, Jr.
       p.   cm.
    Includes bibliographical references (p.   ) and index.
    ISBN 0–391–04004–9 (pbk.)
    1. Sturm, Jakob, 1489–1553.   2. Reformation—France—Strasbourg—
  Biography.   3. Reformation—Germany.   4. Germany—Church
  history—16th century.   5. Strasbourg (France)—Biography.
  6. Strasbourg (France)—Church history—16th century.   I. Title.
  BR350.S78B72   1996
  944'.38353028'092—dc20
    [B]   96–26855
                                                               CIP

Printed in the United States of America

10 9 8 7 6 5 4 3 2

To Arthur J. Quinn, a friend beyond compare

One friend in a lifetime is much.
—Henry Adams

Many shall run to and fro, and knowledge
shall be increased.
—Daniel 12:4

CONTENTS

LIST OF MAPS

PREFACE

This book grew out of a project I began nearly thirty years ago, the full scholarly fruits of which appeared in 1995 as *Protestant Politics: Jacob Sturm (1489–1553) and the German Reformation* (Humanities Press). During its completion I reflected on the fact that the most recent English-language account of German history in the age of the Reformation appeared in 1959 and rested on pre-1933 scholarship. It therefore occurred to me to prepare a shorter, more accessible account of the subject for people who read history but are not specialists in the field. This led to an entirely rewritten and much shortened text, of which one version appeared in German from Siedler Verlag in early 1996 and another, revised once more, is offered here. These versions begin with two new chapters—on the Holy Roman Empire and on Strasbourg and the Upper Rhine region—which provide context for the nonspecialist. I also pruned away most of the scholarly apparatus, leaving only citations of the sources of direct quotes, and replaced the full bibliography with suggestions of further readings in English. I hope that the result will prove interesting to those who want to know more about earlier German history and the history of the Protestant Reformation, and that it will give pleasure to all those who love history.

Some peculiarities of usage in this book need to be explained. I have treated personal names as seemed best, giving the rulers English forms and leaving most of the others alone. I call the other Sturm "Jean" to emphasize his distinctness from his (unrelated) namesake and patron, the subject of this book. For place names I have used English forms where they are well established and unconfusing, such as "Brunswick" for "Braunschweig" and "Hanover" for "Hannover," but not where they are peculiar to British English, such as "Bale" or "Basle" for "Basel." I have avoided some anglicized gallicisms, such as "Mayence" for "Mainz" and "Ratisbon" for "Regensburg," and accepted others, such as "Munich" for "München." My rule of thumb was to choose the form that sounded best to me, so long as the choice introduced no confusion. I have also tried to put the institutional names into English, though occasionally, notably with "ammeister" and "stettmeister," I simply gave up. Most of them appear in the glossary.

Some other usages require a bit of explanation. I have used for Germany's Protestants the name they used for themselves, "Evangelicals," and reserved "Protestant" for the rulers and urban regimes that adhered to the Reformation's cause, a practice which also follows their usage. All Protestants were

Evangelicals, but not all Evangelicals were Protestants. I have also capitalized "Empire" and "Imperial" when they refer to the Holy Roman Empire, and "Reformation" when it refers to the Protestant Reformation as a single process, but not when it refers to reformations in particular places.

The principal unit of coinage is the Rhenish gulden, also called a florin, and a few sums are given in Strasbourg pounds, worth about half a florin each. In this book, the two monetary units are abbreviated rhfl. and lbs. respectively.

The map of "Germany in 1547" is reprinted with permission from Random House, Inc.

LIST OF ABBREVIATIONS

AGBR.	Emil Dürr and Paul Roth, eds. *Aktensammlung zur Geschichte der Basler Reformation.* 6 vols. Basel, 1921–50.
AMS.	Archives Municipales de Strasbourg.
"Ann. Brant."	*Annales de Sébastien Brant.* Edited by Léon Dacheux. In *BSCMHA,* n.s., 15 (1892): 211–79; n.s., 19 (1899): 33–260.
ARC.	Georg Pfeilschifter, ed. *Acta reformationis catholicae ecclesiae Germaniae concernantia saeculi XVI: Die Reformverhandlungen des deutschen Episkopats von 1520 bis 1570.* 6 vols. Regensburg, 1959–74.
ARG.	*Archiv für Reformationsgeschichte.*
AST.	Archives du Chapître de St.-Thomas de Strasbourg.
BDS.	Martin Bucer. *Deutsche Schriften.* Edited by Robert Stupperich et al. Gütersloh, 1964–.
BOSS.	Ekkehart Fabian, ed. *Die Beschlüße der oberdeutschen schmalkaldischen Städtetage.* 3 vols. SKRG, vols. 9/10, 14/15, 21/24. Tübingen, 1959–60.
BSCMHA.	*Bulletin de la Société pour la Conservation des Monuments Historiques de l'Alsace.*
CR.	*Corpus Reformatorum.* Vols. 1–29, Philip Melanchthon, *Opera quae supersunt omnia,* edited by Carl Gottlieb Bretschneider et al. (Halle a. d. S., 1834–60). Vols. 30–89, John Calvin, *Ioannis Calvini opera quae supersunt omnia,* edited by Johann Wilhelm Baum et al. (Brunswick, 1863–1900).
EA.	*Amtliche Sammlung der älteren eidgenössischen Abschiede.* Vols. 3–4. Zurich and Lucerne, 1858–86.
ELJb.	*Elsaß-Lothringisches Jahrbuch.*
JWOS.	Jacob Wimpfeling. *Opera Selecta.* Edited by Otto Herding and Dieter Mertens. Munich, 1965–.
Lenz.	Max Lenz, ed. *Briefwechsel Landgraf Philipps des Großmüthigen von Hessen mit Bucer.* 3 vols. Publicationen aus den K. Preussischen Staatsarchiven, 5, 28, 47. Stuttgart, 1880–91; reprint, Osnabrück, 1965.

PC.	*Politische Correspondenz der Stadt Straßburg im Zeitalter der Reformation.* 5 vols. Edited by Hans Virck et al. Strasbourg, 1882–99; Heidelberg, 1928–33.
RTA, jR.	*Deutsche Reichstagsakten, jüngere Reihe.*
SBA.	Ekkehart Fabian, ed. *Die Schmalkaldischen Bundesabschiede 1530–1536.* 2 vols. SKRG, vols. 7–8. Tübingen, 1958.
Specklin.	Daniel Specklin, "Les collectanées." Edited by Rodolphe Reuss, in *BSCMHA*, 2d ser., 13 (1888): 157–360, nos. 600–1299; 14 (1889): 1–178, 201–404, nos. 1300–2561.
TAE.	*Elsaß*, pts. 1–4, *Stadt Straßburg 1522–52*. Edited by Manfred Krebs et al. Quellen zur Geschichte der Täufer, vols. 7–8, 15–16. Gütersloh, 1959–88.
WA.	*Luthers Werke: Kritische Gesamtausgabe.* 60 vols. Weimar, 1883–1988.
WA Br.	*Luthers Werke: Kritische Gesamtausgabe. Briefe.* 17 vols. Weimar, 1930–85.
ZW.	Emil Egli et al., eds. *Huldrych Zwinglis sämtliche Werke.* 24 vols. Corpus Reformatorum, 88–101. Berlin and Zurich, 1905–91.

MAP 1

Sturm's House

St. Stephen

JEWS STREET

St. Nicolaus-
in-Undis

Rhine →

Williamites

inicans

Cathedral

Bishop's Palace

Pfalz
(City Hall)

Butchers'
Gate

N

Hospital

Colmar

Strasbourg

around 1500

0   100 m

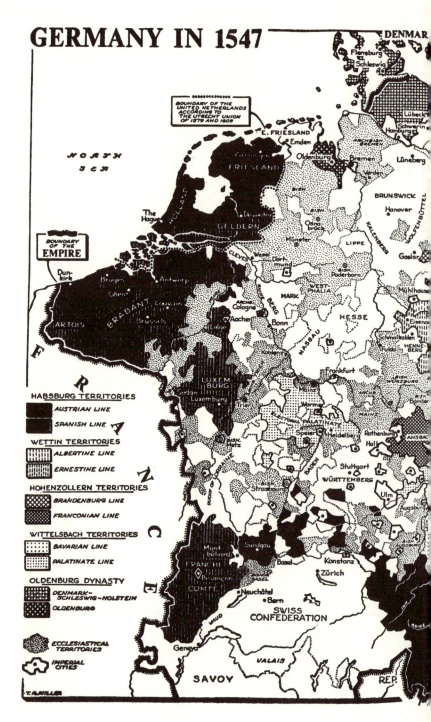

GERMANY IN 1547

BOUNDARY OF THE UNITED NETHERLANDS ACCORDING TO THE UTRECHT UNION OF 1579 AND 1609

NORTH SEA

BOUNDARY OF THE EMPIRE

HABSBURG TERRITORIES
- AUSTRIAN LINE
- SPANISH LINE

WETTIN TERRITORIES
- ALBERTINE LINE
- ERNESTINE LINE

HOHENZOLLERN TERRITORIES
- BRANDENBURG LINE
- FRANCONIAN LINE

WITTELSBACH TERRITORIES
- BAVARIAN LINE
- PALATINATE LINE

OLDENBURG DYNASTY
- DENMARK–SCHLESWIG–HOLSTEIN
- OLDENBURG

ECCLESIASTICAL TERRITORIES

IMPERIAL CITIES

T.A.MILLER

DENMARK · Flensburg · Schleswig · Lübeck · Schwerin · Hamburg · Lüneberg

E. FRIESLAND · Emden · Oldenburg · Bremen · Verden

FRIESLAND

BRUNSWICK · Hanover · WOLFENBÜTTEL · Goslar

The Hague · HOLLAND · GELDERN · Münster · LIPPE · Paderborn · KALENBERG · Mühlhause

Dunkirk · Bruges · Ghent · Antwerp · Louvain · Brussels · CLEVES · Wesel · Dortmund · WEST-PHALIA · BERG · Cologne · Aachen · Bonn · MARK · NASSAU · HESSE · Eisen · Schmalkalden · Fulda · HENNE-BERG

ARTOIS · BRABANT · LIÈGE · Frankfurt · BISH WÜRZBURG · Bambe

LUXEMBURG · Sedan · Luxemburg · Trier · Worms · PALATINATE · Speier · Heidelber · MAINZ · Rothenburg · ANSBAC · Hall

FRANCE · BISH METZ · LORRAINE · Strasbourg · BADEN · Stuttgart · WÜRTTEMBERG · Ulm · Augsburg · BISH

Mont-béliard · Besançon · FRANCHE COMTÉ · Sundgau · Basel · Konstanz · Zürich

Neuchâtel · Bern · SWISS CONFEDERATION · ADIGE

Geneva · VAUD · VALAIS · REP.

SAVOY

MAP 2

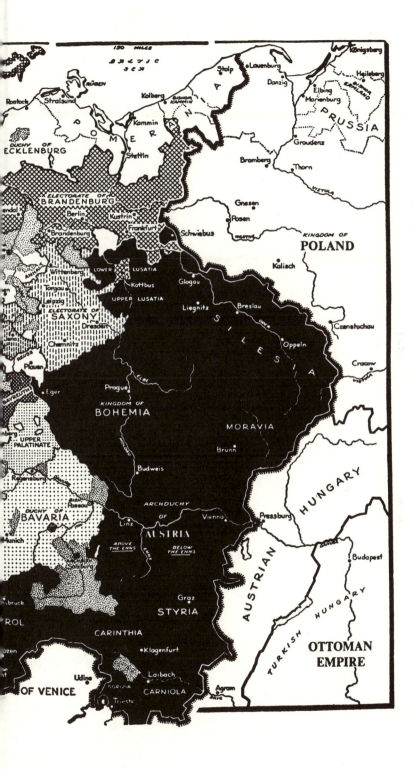

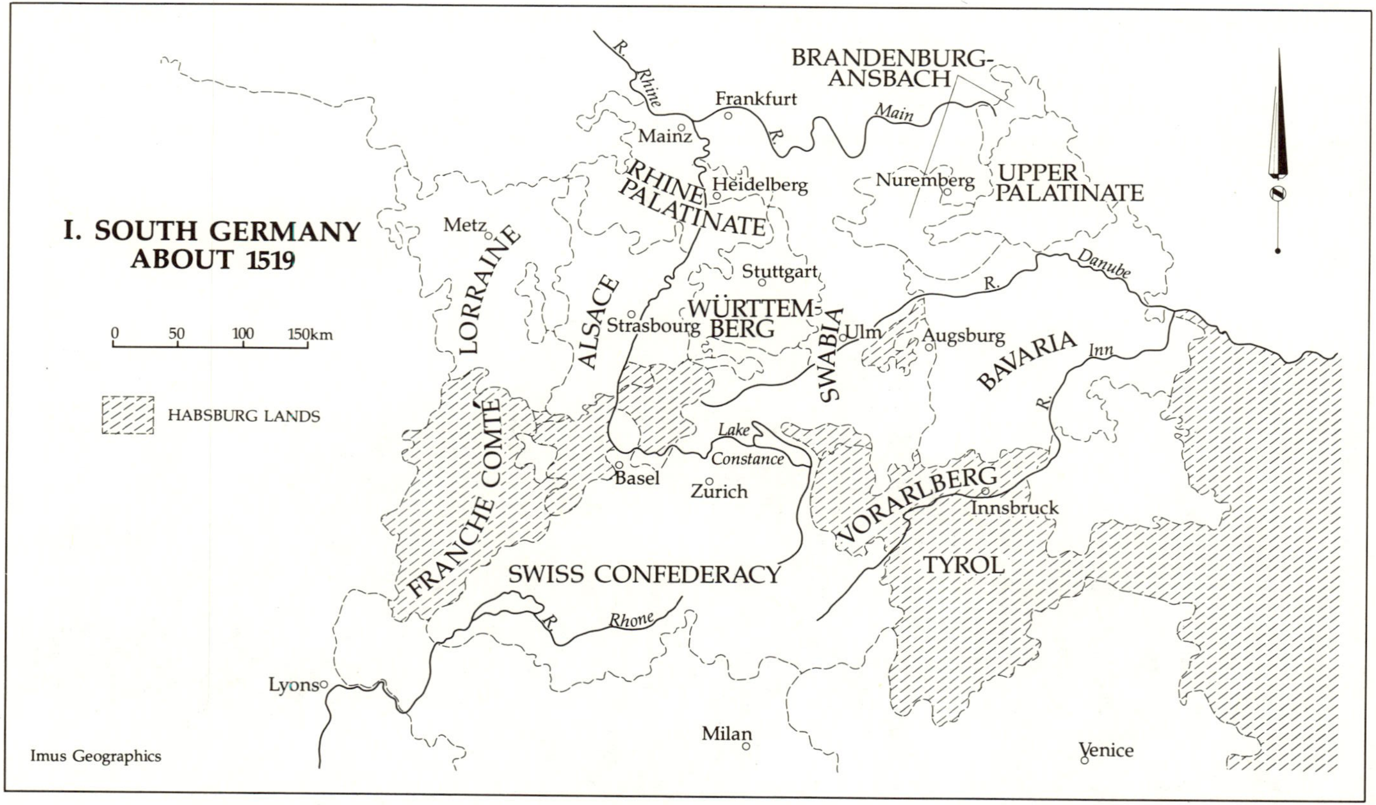

I. SOUTH GERMANY
ABOUT 1519

0   50   100   150km

HABSBURG LANDS

MAP 3

Imus Geographics

BRANDENBURG-
ANSBACH

UPPER
PALATINATE

BAVARIA

VORARLBERG

TYROL

Venice

SWABIA

WÜRTTEM-
BERG

RHINE
PALATINATE

ALSACE

SWISS CONFEDERACY

LORRAINE

FRANCHE COMTÉ

Nuremberg

Augsburg

Innsbruck

Ulm

Frankfurt

Heidelberg

Stuttgart

Mainz

Strasbourg

Basel

Zürich

Lake Constance

Milan

Lyons

Metz

Danube

Inn

Main

Rhine

R.

R.

R.

Rhine

R.

Rhone

R.

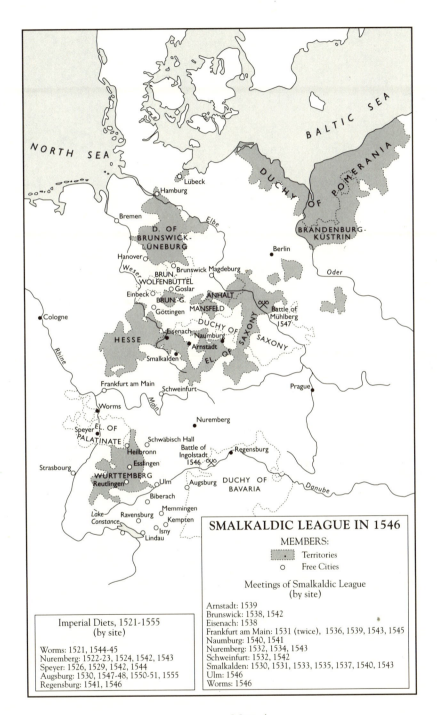

NORTH SEA

BALTIC SEA

Lübeck
Hamburg

DUCHY OF POMERANIA

Bremen

Elbe

D. OF BRUNSWICK-LÜNEBURG

BRANDENBURG-KÜSTRIN

Hanover

Berlin

Weser

Oder

Brunswick Magdeburg
BRUN.-WOLFENBÜTTEL
Goslar
Einbeck BRUN.-G.
ANHALT
MANSFELD
Göttingen
Battle of Mühlberg 1547

Cologne

DUCHY OF SAXONY

EL. OF SAXONY

Rhine

HESSE
Eisenach Naumburg
Arnstadt
Smalkalden

Frankfurt am Main
Schweinfurt
Prague

Worms
Main
Nuremberg

Speyer EL. OF PALATINATE
Schwäbisch Hall
Battle of Ingolstadt 1546
Regensburg

Heilbronn

Strasbourg
Esslingen
WÜRTTEMBERG
Reutlingen Ulm Augsburg
DUCHY OF BAVARIA
Danube

Biberach
Memmingen
Lake Constance Ravensburg Kempten
Isny
Lindau

SMALKALDIC LEAGUE IN 1546

MEMBERS:

▪ Territories

○ Free Cities

Meetings of Smalkaldic League
(by site)

Arnstadt: 1539
Brunswick: 1538, 1542
Eisenach: 1538
Frankfurt am Main: 1531 (twice), 1536, 1539, 1543, 1545
Naumburg: 1540, 1541
Nuremberg: 1532, 1534, 1543
Schweinfurt: 1532, 1542
Smalkalden: 1530, 1531, 1533, 1535, 1537, 1540, 1543
Ulm: 1546
Worms: 1546

Imperial Diets, 1521-1555
(by site)

Worms: 1521, 1544-45
Nuremberg: 1522-23, 1524, 1542, 1543
Speyer: 1526, 1529, 1542, 1544
Augsburg: 1530, 1547-48, 1550-51, 1555
Regensburg: 1541, 1546

MAP 4

INTRODUCTION

This is a book about the place of the Protestant Reformation in German history. It aims to show how the Reformation affected, and was shaped by, the political structure of the Holy Roman Empire, a country so different in its governance from modern European states that the historian's customary method—tracking modern institutions back into the past—is unhelpful, even distorting.

The need for a new treatment of this subject arises from the fact that, outside the circle of specialists, modern conceptions of the deeper German past are often fragmentary, confused, or altogether lacking. For this state of affairs the twentieth century is to blame. Laying aside the propagandistic grotesqueries that attended the two world wars—such as the defense of Western civilization versus Prussian militarism and the slogan "From Luther to Hitler"—the main traditional explanation of the connection between the Protestant Reformation and modern Germany suffered mortal injury in 1918 and death in 1945, and nothing has taken its place. This explanation or interpretation, which arose in the early nineteenth century and became canonical by midcentury, held that the Protestant Reformation represented the spiritual birth of modern Germany. Its chief fashioner was the founder of modern historical scholarship in Germany, Leopold von Ranke (1795–1886), who portrayed Martin Luther's reformation as a national event, the religious side of "[the German] nation's need to consolidate itself into a certain unity."[1] The satisfaction of this need, according to Ranke, was well under way by 1524, when it mysteriously began to be disrupted by a Catholic resistance that split the nation for three hundred years and prevented it from achieving national statehood. He believed, as did many others, that Protestantism was both a superior form of Christianity and the proper, even destined, religion of a modern German nation. This is the essence of the confessional-national view of the Protestant Reformation, which Ranke and his disciples made canonical in German historical writing.[2] It long held a position in German historiography, as Jaroslav Pelikan has written, which was "analogous in some ways to that of the Civil War in American historiography, as the crucial and (in a quite literal sense of the term) epoch-making event by which the nature of an entire national community and of its history has been defined."[3]

Ranke's view of the Reformation came to be seen as prophetic after the new Germany was created under Prussian hegemony in 1871. In 1883, when German Protestants celebrated Luther's four-hundredth birthday, Ranke's heirs raised aloud their hopes that their one nation, now united under one state (Austria was dismissed), would soon possess one faith.

1

These hopes were dashed forever by World War I and the collapse of the Bismarckian state. The turning point came in 1917, the depths of the Great War, when one of Ranke's disciples, the historian Erich Marcks (1861–1938), turned his back on the Rankean conception of a Protestant German nation.[4] "The internal difference between the confessions has survived," he wrote, "and will remain." The confessions, "these two old, greater—perhaps greatest—spiritual parties" represented "the permanent co-existence and antagonism of two spiritual tendencies within a single whole, the people and the nation. They have always been forces of struggle, but also of vitality, and so they will remain in our future—with and against one another!" Marcks went on to argue that although the Reformation had divided Germany, it also united the Germans in a new way. The confessional rift "went right across both North and South and brought together Protestants from all over Germany and Catholics from all over Germany and thus became, as surprising as this may sound, a unifying force. Württemberg and Saxony, Bavaria and Cologne, now stood inseparably connected to one another, and in every division—old and new—there was also a new association." Furthermore, if the Germans received a more modern culture from Luther's hands, "the modern state came to us from the Latin South and especially the West," and it is difficult to say whether Lutheranism or Catholicism contributed more to German development. For Marcks, therefore, the religious division of the Holy Roman Empire meant not a destruction of German unity but "a doubling of German life."

The old confessional-national vision of German history lived on into the interwar era, albeit in such crippled forms as the "From Luther to Hitler" slogan, but the defeat of 1945 effectively killed the Rankean view of the German past. Indeed, in the postwar era there arose interpretations of modern German history in which the entire earlier history—the Middle Ages, the Protestant Reformation, the Thirty Years' War, and the Austro-Prussian dualism— were simply blanked out, and the story was begun de nuovo with the nineteenth century. The late Thomas Nipperdey had something like this in mind when he began his account of Germany in the first half of the nineteenth century with the words "In the beginning was Napoleon."[5]

Nowadays, before any relevance to modern times can be claimed for the earlier epochs, they must be extricated from the husks of old dreams and dead narratives and reevaluated in terms of their own times, to begin with, apart from all evolutionary stories. This book aims to contribute to the task of reevaluation. It profits immensely from a generation's work, both in and outside Germany, that has laid the foundations for a new way to see German history in the age of the Protestant Reformation. Two aspects of the new approach have special relevance to the task. In the first place, we have come to understand that the German Reformation, which was undoubtedly a movement of religious ideas, was also a social movement. This discovery began in the 1960s with work on the cities, especially the Imperial free cities, which led the English historian A. G. Dickens to write in 1974 that "the Reformation was an urban event."[6] It continued during the 1970s with work on and around the Peasants' War, which prompted the German historian Hans-Christoph Rublack to assert in 1987 that "the Reformation . . . was also much more than an urban event."[7] Peter Blickle then crowned the edifice by unifying the urban and rural movements under the rubric of the "communal reformation."[8] Each stage pushed us forward to the conclusion that the decisive force in making Luther's movement into the German Reformation was not his message's content and not his alliance with the princes but the brief, tumultuous involvement of very large numbers of ordinary urban and rural folk.

The second step forward is the appearance a new interpretation of the Holy Roman Empire as a system of governance. Long despised as a political monstrosity (in Samuel Pufendorf's famous bon mot) because it could not be fitted into theories of the state based on sovereignty, for most of the time between the fifteenth and the end of the eighteenth century the Empire was in fact a durable, relatively effective structure of governance. In this long sight, indeed, "Germany's position in central Europe makes the political solution which the old empire comprised appear far from inappropriate."[9] Freed from anachronistic political ideas, such as the sovereignty of the state and the nineteenth-century distinction between state and society, the Empire has come to be understood on its own terms as a vast network of dispersed, multicentered, and multilayered structures of authority and power. Unlike the centralized kingdoms of western Europe, "it was built not on internally developed force but on a remarkable mechanism for the restraint and limitation of force; its stability came from the perpetual frustration of disruptive energy and aggressive power."[10] The Empire's distinctive mark was the long duration of small and very small units and of parliamentary and other dispersed institutions within the units. Its "distinctive genius," the American historian Mack Walker has written, "was that, in practice as well as in law, to preserve the powerless was to defend one's interests and to uphold the imperial constitution."[11] The Empire had no sovereign and no center, and its governance operated on many different levels and in many different configurations. Its history, therefore, always unfolds as a tale braided of Imperial, territorial, and local stories, events, and figures. This is the truth, as we see it now, behind the famous problem of what has been called German "particularism" or "parcellized sovereignty," but which is perhaps better described by the phrase "dispersed governance."

These two breakthroughs—the Reformation as a social movement and the Holy Roman Empire as dispersed governance—enable us to build a new, post-Rankean and postnational account of the German Reformation in the space created by the collapse of the confessional-national story. We now know that in this age the common people were historically present in an especially intense way, for the German Reformation, unlike the Protestant Reformations in other countries, was characterized in the early stages by a very high level of popular involvement. The possibility for this involvement arose from the Empire's late medieval dispersal of authority and from the appearance of a novel instrument for mobilizing and molding public opinion, printing. They allowed a public role in one or another forum to some of the Empire's common folk—those (mostly men) who lacked power and status but who, under certain circumstances, came to voice. The early urban reform movements and the Peasants' War of 1524–25 came, more than any previous events in German or European history, "from below," both in the sense that the commitment of common people made the Protestant Reformation into a political issue and in the sense that the movement became a local issue before it became a regional or Imperial one.

Yet the Protestant Reformation was but partly successful in Germany, and its political impact tended to confirm and strengthen dispersed governance, particularism, rather than to disrupt it in a revolutionary or a centralizing direction. For most of a generation, it unhinged traditional relationships among the levels of Imperial political life but did not permanently change them. This unsettlement nonetheless allowed the Reformation movement the freedom of action to create lasting centers within an Imperial system it could not dominate. Any other outcome would have required German Protestantism to create a new type of political community, something it had no power to do.

The second shift, recognizing the Empire's dispersed governance, requires the story of the Reformation to be pursued simultaneously on Imperial, regional, provincial, and local levels. In the sixteenth century "Imperial" means the Holy Roman Empire as a state or country, "regional" the broad sections of south and north (dividing roughly at the Main basin), "provincial" such parts of regions as Bavaria, Swabia, Alsace, Saxony, and the Lower Rhine, and "local" a town and its environs in which people could know one another. None of these levels was more or less "German" or "national" than any other, and nothing recommends that the history be viewed in terms of national interest or national development. The aims of the Habsburg emperors were not "foreign," because Austrian and dynastic, nor those of the princes "national," any more than German Protestantism was more or less national than German Catholicism.

These are the principles of a book that seeks to contribute to a new political history of the German Reformation. The book's perspective is that of an inverted pyramid, which rests its point at Strasbourg and mounts in ever larger layers—Lower Alsace, the Upper Rhine, South Germany, the Protestant alliance known as the Smalkaldic League—to the Empire. The point is more solidly fixed than are the other layers, for the documents on Strasbourg's political relations in this era are accessible to a unique degree. Much of the Smalkaldic League's history remains in darkness, but progress in publication of the acts of the Imperial Diets have made the completion of this book less daunting than it seemed at the outset, a quarter of a century ago. It has become a contribution to the story of the interaction between the structures of the Empire and the agency of the Reformation movement.

Ranke saw the German Reformation in terms of both a confessional teleology (Protestantism as a more advanced type of Christianity than Catholicism) and a national teleology (the Germans' need for a centralized nation-state). The collapse of his vision allows us to see the relationship between the Protestant Reformation and German history as more complex and more varied than the old history believed, just as the Holy Roman Empire was more complex and more varied than any subsequent German state has been, and just as the Protestant Reformation was more complex and more varied than was its image as the heroic national work of Martin Luther. The real reformation, the enduring reformation, occurred not on a national level but on a local one, and its success was both enabled and highly qualified by its fusion with the structures of German particularism. For that reason, it is proper that we read this story through the life not of an emperor, or even of a great territorial prince, but of a local magistrate who became a statesman of Imperial stature.

NOTES

1. Leopold von Ranke, *Deutsche Geschichte im Zeitalter der Reformation*, ed. Willy Andreas, 2 vols. (Wiesbaden, 1957), 1:142.
2. In the German-speaking world, "confession" is a name for a politically established religious body.
3. Jaroslav Pelikan, "Leopold von Ranke as Historian of the Reformation: What Ranke Did for the Reformation—What the Reformation Did for Ranke," in *Leopold von Ranke and the Shaping of the Historical Discipline*, ed. Georg G. Iggers and James Powell (Syracuse, N.Y., 1990), 90.
4. Erich Marcks, *Luther und Deutschland: Eine Reformationsrede im Kriegsjahr 1917* (Leipzig, 1917).
5. Thomas Nipperdey, *Deutsche Geschichte 1800–1860: Bürgerwelt und starker Staat* (Munich, 1983), 11.
6. A. G. Dickens, *The German Nation and Martin Luther* (London, 1974), 182.
7. Hans-Christoph Rublack, "Is There a 'New History' of the Urban Reformation?" in *Politics and Society in Reformation Europe: Essays for Sir Geoffrey Elton on His Sixty-Fifth Birthday*, ed. E. I. Kouri and Tom Scott (London, 1987), 121–41, here at 122.
8. Peter Blickle, *The Communal Reformation: The Quest for Salvation in Sixteenth-Century Germany*, trans. Thomas Dunlap (Atlantic Highlands, N.J., 1992).
9. Volker Press, "The Holy Roman Empire in German History," in *Politics and Society in Reformation Europe*, ed. E. I. Kouri and Tom Scott, 51–77, here at 51.
10. Mack Walker, *German Home Towns: Community, State, and General Estate, 1648–1871* (Ithaca, N.Y., 1971), 12.
11. Ibid., 16.

1

THE HOLY ROMAN EMPIRE

I am a king of kings, whose subjects do as they please, whereas the king of France is a king of animals, whose subjects must obey him.
—Emperor Maximilian I

Emperor Maximilian's joke about kings and animals alludes to a fact well known to his contemporaries: France had a strong monarchy, the Empire a weak one. Niccolò Machiavelli (1469–1527), his Florentine contemporary, made the same point more bluntly: "Germany . . . abounds in men, riches, and arms, . . . but [this power] is such that it is of little use to the emperor."[1] True enough, and the Venetians, who knew a great deal about men, riches, and arms, snidely called this most grandiosely ambitious of emperors "Maximilian Empty-Pockets" (*Massimiliano pocchi denari*).

Maximilian I (r. 1493–1519), sometimes called "the last knight," in fact presided in the Empire over the very end of Christendom's long late medieval agony: the failed crusades, the papacy's removal to Avignon, the Black Death, the double papal election and the schism, the Bohemian Hussites' revolt against church and Empire, and the century-long economic depression. The last great blow had come in 1453 with the news that the "Grand Turk," Mehmed II (r. 1451–81), called "the Conqueror," had taken Constantinople, the Arabs' "Red Apple" and the center of Latin Christendom's Byzantine sibling. Thereafter came the rising time, when populations, princes, and states began to recover, and Eurasia's far westerners began to venture out into the great ocean. One year before Maximilian ascended the Imperial throne, Christopher Columbus sailed westward to Asia and found the Americas; three years thereafter, Vasco da Gama sailed eastward to Asia and found India's Malabar Coast. It was the autumn of the Middle Ages; it was the springtime of the Renaissance.

THE EMPIRE'S SHAPES

The Holy Roman Empire was the largest and most varied country in late medieval Latin Christendom.[2] Its boundary ran from the North Sea coast between the Low Countries (except Flanders) and France, then southward between France

7

and the old Imperial provinces of Lorraine, Imperial Burgundy (the Franche-Comté), and Savoy; the line then crossed Italy north of the Papal State, taking in Lombardy but not Venice, to the shore of the Adriatic Sea; it moved around Carniola (roughly modern Slovenia) and Carinthia (now southern Austria) and northward between Austria and Hungary; a final great loop to the northeast separated Bohemia and Moravia (the modern Czech Republic), the Silesian principalities (now southwestern Poland), Brandenburg, and Pomerania (now northwestern Poland) from the Polish kingdom and ran down to the Baltic Sea west of Danzig/Gdansk.

Within these boundaries, the Empire stretched from highly urbanized northern Italy across the Alps into the pastoral and farming landscapes of South Germany, then over the central highlands, which dribble across modern Germany's waist, and on down across the northern plain, on the western edge of which, facing the sea, lay the seventeen provinces of the Low Countries. Great river systems flowed out of the Empire's mountainous heartlands into the wider world: the Rhone came tumbling westward out of the central Alps and then turned southward toward the Mediterranean Sea; the Po drained the southern flank of the central Alps into the Adriatic Sea below Venice; the Danube rose in southwestern Germany and ran down through Bavaria and Austria into Hungary, headed for the Black Sea; the Rhine took the waters from the central Alps' northern flank, flowed through Lake Constance, and then, turning at Basel, gathered streams from the Empire's western regions and ran northward down to the Netherlands and the North Sea; and to the east, the Rhine's parallel companions—the Weser, the Elbe, and the Oder—drained the Bohemian basin and the great northern plain into the North and Baltic Seas. Compared to the fertile lands of northwestern Europe, many of the Empire's soils were poor, except along the rivers and on the northern plain, and its forests had been thinned by centuries of colonization; but its many rivers and its low relief made the Empire's interior relatively easy to cross, right up to the great Alpine wall. How easy, of course, also depended on how one traveled. In the mid-fifteenth century, the journey from Lübeck on the Baltic Sea to the Imperial court at Vienna required an average of forty-three days, but the Imperial post, organized in 1489–90, could move letters by mounted courier from Brussels to Innsbruck in five and a half days in summer and six and a half days in winter.

In the Empire's German-speaking heartlands lived and labored about seventeen million people in perhaps 130,000 settled places—among them about 2,800 cities, towns, and market places—covering the land in densities ranging from about fifteen to eighteen persons/per square kilometer in the west to much lower levels in the east. All of them, except for the fewer than one hundred thousand Jews—who were much rarer in the north than in the south, where they may have reached 15 percent of the population of the city of Regensburg—were in some respect Latin Christians, and except for the Bohemian schismatics and separatists, they were more or less willing members of the Roman communion. They prayed in Latin, but they worked and loved in many other tongues: in the heartlands, dozens of forms of German, of which the southern and the northern were mutually unintelligible; along the western and southern margins, many different Romance languages related to modern French and Italian; and down the eastern margins, South and West Slavic tongues. The Empire was polyglot but not multinational, for it contained many peoples but no nations.

Besides the Empire as a jurisdiction, contemporaries also recognized a country called "Germany," which meant roughly the lands where forms of German were spoken. No one, however, could say definitively where Germany's limits lay, and as late as the second half of the sixteenth century, the Flemish cartographer Abraham Ortelius (1527–98) gave up in disgust the task of defining them, because "her [Germany's] boundaries have been given differently by the various authors."[3] The lack of a precise distinction between the Empire as a state and Germany as a country of German-speakers is confirmed by a comment of the Strasbourg politician Jacob Sturm (1489–1553), who once referred to the francophone Imperial chancellor, a Burgundian, as "by heritage a German."[4] He meant, of course, not a German-speaker but an Imperial subject.

Wherever the legal boundaries lay, the late fifteenth-century Empire was becoming in effect a smaller country. It was shrinking back on its German-speaking core, as its heavily non-German-speaking borderlands began to drift out of Imperial political life. In the Northwest, the succession of the House of Austria to the House of Valois seemed to strengthen Netherlandish community rather than Imperial patriotism. In the Northeast, German-colonized and -ruled lands of the Teutonic Order came under Polish feudal suzerainty by the Peace of Torún/Thorn (1466). In the South, Imperial authority in Italy had long been nebulous at best, and from the time of the Swabian War in 1499 the Empire began to lose its grip on the Swiss Confederacy, whose free rural federations and city-states professed Imperial loyalty but did pretty much as they pleased. In the East, many decades of revolt and practical autonomy had loosened Bohemia's ties to the Empire, even though the Golden Bull of 1356 had named its king as one of the seven Imperial electors. Only in the far Southeast did the Empire's practical boundary run with the legal one between the Austrian lands and the Hungarian kingdom, though King Matthias Corvinus (r. 1458–90) of Hungary had more than once grabbed off chunks of Austria. One consequence of this shrinkage was a sense of decline. "Must we continue in this way," lamented Elector Berthold of Mainz in 1497, "seeing how the empire has declined and still declines from day to day? . . . It has come to this, that if we continue in our present path, we may soon see a foreigner appear in our lands, ruling us with iron rods."[5]

Yet in the Empire's weakness was also strength, for as the edges unraveled, the German-speaking core assumed greater definition and profile. The new quality appears in a new title, "the Holy Roman Empire of the German Nation," first attested in 1486. It appears, too, in the growing supremacy of a common written High German over all other competitors for vernacular expression in writing and print; in the construction from the 1480s of a refurbished Imperial constitution based on the collaboration of emperor and Imperial Estates; and in the Imperial governing classes' skeptical attitude toward Emperor Maximilian's adventures in far places, especially Italy. Each of these tendencies reflected, in its own way, the recovery of populations and economies from the long late medieval depression.

THE RECOVERY OF POPULATION AND ECONOMIES

POPULATIONS

Behind the broad tendencies of Imperial life—eroding edges, strengthening core— lay the large forces that were reshaping the Empire's social landscapes around 1500. Since around the mid-fifteenth century, the growth of population, production, and trade had gradually brought an end to the late medieval depression. The demographic growth, which reached its peak rate during the first third of the sixteenth century, filled up the villages—earlier and more rapidly in the South and West than in the East—and revived land hunger among the peasants, who made up about 85 percent of the Empire's population. The fifteen villages of Saxony's Pirna District, for example, rose from 125 households in 1450 to 201 a century later. Such growth exaggerated distinctions between inheriting and non-inheriting peasants and so packed the villages with people that Sebastian Münster (1499–1543) judged—after the Peasants' War of 1525—that southwestern Germany "is so full of people that there is room for no more."[6] Rising commodity prices helped the fortunate, but they also sparked a revival of servile dues, as the lords competed with the territorial governments for the peasants' surplus. Such rural changes placed new strains on the communal institutions that had spread across southern Germany since the early fourteenth century, based on headman and court, unwritten customary laws (*Weistümer*), and sometimes communally endowed parishes. In the face of a growing population, the villages had either to export young people or to suffer their communities to be increasingly divided between fortunate, inheriting farmers and unfortunate, landless ones. Either way, growth increased tensions.

Some of the surplus men went off to war. Emperor Maximilian contributed to this relief of rural population pressure by creating in the 1490s a new type of German infantry, called lansquenets (*Landsknechte*), who were drilled, equipped, and deployed in the Swiss manner, and whose bodies he left on his battlefields from Brabant to Tuscany. Most of the countryside's unneeded mouths and hands, however, flowed not to the wars but to the cities. The Empire's core contained no true metropolis—in 1500 only Cologne ranked among Christendom's twenty-three leading cities (over forty thousand population)—but many important towns with populations between fifteen and twenty thousand, such as Ulm, Strasbourg, Augsburg, Nuremberg, Frankfurt am Main in the South, and Brunswick, Hamburg, Bremen, and Lübeck in the North. These and a host of smaller towns absorbed the land's surplus and converted farmers into burghers. The burghers' slowly growing numbers—by 1600 they would make up a full quarter of all German-speakers—by no means exhausted their superiority to the rural folk, for they also included the vast majority of the 5 percent of German-speakers who commanded the one skill that distinguished the age, the ability to read.

ECONOMIES

If city air did not always grant freedom, it often offered opportunity. Migrants from the villages and small towns found the greatest chances for employment in the major centers of production for international and interregional trade. Cloth, the most important branch, concentrated in the Lower Rhenish region, Upper Swabia, and Saxony, while mining and smelting was more scattered: iron in the Upper Palatinate, eastern Austria, and southern Westphalia; copper and silver in the Tyrol, Carinthia, Bohemia, Silesia, and the Harz. Products of these industries and other, including foreign, goods moved across the northern seas, controlled by the urban federation known as the Hansa, and along the roads that formed nodes at Augsburg, Nuremberg, Frankfurt, Leipzig, and Cologne. The quickening of trade and production after 1450 depended in turn on the growing engagement of the South German trading houses at Venice and Antwerp, metropoles of Europe's two richest urban zones and gateways to the worlds beyond Christendom.

In the cities, as on the land, the upswing tended to benefit the "haves" rather than the "have-nots" (*habenitse*), because the value of human labor was falling, just as it had risen during the late medieval depression. Around 1500 the possession of property worth 25–30 rhfl. or an income of 15 rhfl. per year—the absolute minimum for a single person and about a third of the wage of an artisan master—meant true poverty. Property worth 100 rhfl. meant modest prosperity, those who possessed 500 rhfl. were rich, and more than 5,000 rhfl. made one the late medieval equivalent of a millionaire. A nest egg of 200 rhfl. was considered "quite a lot of money."[7] The general upswing of commodity prices—grain prices had begun to rise around 1450—increased both profits and poverty, more so in the major manufacturing centers than in the older trading cities. The differential effects may be illustrated by comparing figures for Augsburg in 1475 with those for 1460 at Lübeck, a northern trade entrepot which manufactured little for export. In these two cities, the rich and upper middle classes made up, respectively, 18 and 4.9 percent; the middling ones, 68 and 27 percent; and the poor, 14 and 66 percent. Debasements of coinage—

the widely used Rhenish gold florin lost almost a third of its gold content during the fifteenth century—further accelerated the fall of real wages, which continuously made the potentially poor into the actually poor, a process which took the steam out of the artisans' political movements.

The recovery encouraged analogous social changes in the great mining districts, which around 1500 were approaching the peak of their output. In the mines the transfer of control from the miners to urban firms, chiefly Nurembergers and Augsburgers, was encouraged by three things: the introduction of modern smelters, which greatly boosted the need for capital; the possession of the right to mine, originally a regalian right, in princely hands; and the absence of guilds and corporate political traditions among the miners. From the building of the first smelters in Thuringia (1450) and around Goslar (1478) to the development of the silver bonanzas of the Ore Mountains (*Erzgebirge*) at Annaberg and Schneeberg, the urban capitalists gained control by buying up shares in the highly fragmented mining syndicates and protected it through monopolistic contracts for delivery of metals to the princes.[8] The system worked much the same way in Tyrol, where silver production tripled and copper more than doubled between 1470 and 1520, and where, in return for monopolies of the sale of metals and foodstuffs, the Augsburg firms lent gigantic sums to the ruling prince, Emperor Maximilian.

It is common practice to call the bankers, merchants, and investors of this age "capitalists" and to call their promotion of market forces in the distribution of money and goods "capitalistic." In the stricter sense, Karl Marx's sense, only a few special branches, such as mining, developed genuinely capitalistic organization, defined by separation of a commoditized (i.e., "free") labor from the means of production, and nowhere did capitalism in this sense become, nor would it yet for centuries, the dominant economic mode. And whereas the German burghers of that age may be called in English a bourgeoisie, they are more accurately seen as an integral element of the late medieval social scene than as precursors of the bourgeoisie in the modern sense. As for the economy in which they operated, its free paths were few and narrow, and most of its processes of production and distribution were heavily regulated, constrained, and directed.

In some sectors the Empire's economies nevertheless created institutions which pointed in a new direction. One of them was the large-scale trading firm. The long-term, highly capitalized firm, which dealt in both money and commodities and possessed an extensive network of agents, emerged in the South German cities during the fifteenth century. In the Hanseatic cities of the North, by contrast, merchants preferred to stick to the old ways, which included Roman numerals, single-entry bookkeeping, and small, short-term partnerships engaged in general trade but not in banking. Their conservatism was protected, as yet, by the fleets and diplomacy of the great Hanseatic federation, though by the late fifteenth century the Hansa merchants were fighting for their economic lives against Netherlandish competition across the whole zone organized along the axis Novgorod-Reval-Visby-Lübeck-Hamburg-Bruges-London.

Meanwhile, the South German merchants were creating powerful, long-lasting firms, often around a single family, in which the principal partners supplied both capital and management skills, for an average of four to six years, often renewed. The Nurembergers operated in this way, and so did the Great Ravensburg Company, established by three Swabian merchant families in 1380, which expanded from its base around Lake Constance to monopolize the linen trade all the way to Barcelona. Meanwhile, since the fourteenth century the Nurembergers had been expanding their operations through the area bounded by the line Rome-Seville-Lisbon-Toulouse-Paris-Antwerp-London-Lübeck-Cracow-Lwów/ Lemberg-Constantinople. The firms spread the techniques they learned from the Italians, such as double-entry bookkeeping (introduced by Praun and Tucher at Nuremberg in 1476/84) and the bill of exchange, and they codified their knowledge in books modeled on Francesco Balducci Pegolotti's *La practica della mercatura* (1337/40).

Where Nurembergers pioneered, Augsburgers followed, and from about 1470 the great Augsburg firms began to outstrip all competitors. Greatest of all was Jakob Fugger (1459–1525), who ran his family-based firm with an iron hand, pursued both trade and finance, and over the years 1484 to 1524 made 15 to 20 percent per year to the Ravensburgers' 7.5 percent. By 1510, when his firm was worth about 245,000 rhfl., Fugger was cock of the walk in South German commerce and banking. He linked his firm's fortunes in a special way to the House of Austria, becoming lord of the mines and smelters of Hungary and the Tyrol and chief creditor to the free-spending Emperor Maximilian. Fugger backed Maximilian through the terrible Venetian War in 1508–17 and supplied the fabulous sum—900,000 rhfl. at least—that assured the Imperial succession to his grandson, Charles V (r. 1519–56). "I am rich by the grace of God," Fugger once said, but ordinary folk considered him the worst of those "sores on body politic," who, as Johann Geiler von Kaysersberg (1445–1510) thundered from his Strasbourg pulpit, ought to "be cut away and entirely removed," for they "stand alone in the trough like an old sow who won't let the other hogs in."[9] Individual good fortune versus the common good, the clash of new values with old.

SOCIAL CONSEQUENCES

Geiler's suspicions were well placed, for the general social effect of the economic recovery was not to improve the lot of most people but to concentrate wealth and power. The recovery increased the pressure of men on the available land and depressed real wages; it increased stratification in the villages and accumulation of wealth in the towns; it fostered oligarchy in village communes, urban magistracies, and guilds and shops; it reduced the political voice of lesser artisans and shopkeepers; it worsened the conditions for journeymen and women in the workplace; and its depression of wages made more lives more precarious. If the appreciation of human labor had made the late Middle Ages the "golden age of the artisans," in Wilhelm Abel's phrase, by the years after 1500 the common people in town and countryside were facing an age of iron. Strong voices now spoke for stronger hands at the reins and for the exclusion from political life of the artisans, miners, and farmers whom contemporary usage lumped together as the Common Man. Dr. Christoph Scheurl of Nuremberg spoke for the ruling classes in 1516: "The common folk [*das gemain völklein*] have no authority, as they properly should have none, for all authority comes from God, and governance is granted to only those few who are specially gifted by the special wisdom of Him who created nature and all things."[10] As if to confirm this wisdom, rural revolts flared after 1475 in an unbroken chain from the Fifer of Niklashausen's movement in 1476 to the great Peasants' War of 1525; and the incidence of urban revolts jumped from ten in the 1490s to eighteen in the 1510s and forty-five in the 1520s.

These signs of conflict and dislocation swelled the ranks of those who believed that the Empire needed to be more strongly governed. This belief, however, ran straight against the condition of dispersed governance, which set severe limits to the possibilities for reforming the Empire.

THE EMPIRE'S GOVERNANCE

THE MONARCHY

The Empire resembled no other state in European history. Its king, elected by seven princely electors as "King of the Romans" and emperor-elect, became through papal coronation (Holy) Roman emperor and titular lord of Christendom.[11] This ancient office, now more than five hundred years old, adorned a dynasty called Habsburg or, from their principal hereditary holdings, the House of Austria, whose colors—red-white-red—were to adorn, with one brief break, the black, double-headed Imperial eagle's breast until the end of the Holy Roman Empire. Long ago, in 1282, the Habsburgs had migrated from east-central Switzerland to rule the Austrian duchy (then a margraviate) in the Danube Valley.[12] In those days they had supplied the Empire with only one emperor, the able Rudolph I (r. 1273–92), but since the accession of Albert II in 1438 their grip on the elective Imperial throne was becoming semihereditary. His successor, Frederick III (r. 1440–93), reigned more than he ruled, rusticating for much of his long reign in the princely residences of his hereditary lands, Wiener Neustadt and Graz, while the Hungarians chewed at his eastern lands and the Empire's governance drifted slowly toward the electors and princes. Yet the House of Austria's stock was rising. During the 1470s Habsburg forces joined the southwestern powers against the armies of Burgundy, and they and their Swiss and Upper Rhenish allies smashed three Burgundian armies and killed the last Valois duke, Charles the Bold, at Nancy in Lorraine in January 1477. A decade later, in 1488, a Habsburg agent organized the Swabian League, a peace-keeping alliance of South German free cities, nobles, and princes, whose main initial object was to block the westward expansion of Bavaria. In 1499 Maximilian, now king-emperor in his own right, roused Imperial forces to defend his western Austrian lands against the Swiss Confederates in the Swabian War, and five years later he took the field to force a settlement between the two lines of the House of Wittelsbach, the Palatine line at Heidelberg and the Bavarian line at Munich, in the War of the Bavarian Succession in 1504.

By 1500 the Austrian hereditary lands formed a solid belt from the Hungarian border to the Rhine Valley above Lake Constance—nearly the extent of the Austrian Republic today—and continued in a broken but respectable arc across southwestern Germany through Swabia and across the Rhine below Basel to the gates of Burgundy. By this time, too, the prospective union of the Austrian lands with the Burgundian lands—Imperial Burgundy and the seventeen provinces of the Netherlands—in the hands of a single heir, Prince Philip (1482–1506), called "the Handsome," threatened to give the House of Austria a truly commanding position on the southern and western sides of the Empire. Philip, however, who was the only son of Maximilian and his first wife, Duchess Mary of Burgundy, and the husband of Princess Juana of Castile and Aragon, died two years later, and his father's lament on hearing the news—"My God! My God! Why has Thou forsaken me," he immodestly quoted—drew extra intensity from the smashing of best-laid plans. Still, the House of Austria stood at a summit of its power in the Empire during the years just after 1500. When Maximilian, victor over the Palatine Wittelsbachs and soon to be a hammer of Hungary, came to Cologne to preside over the Imperial Diet in 1505, he marched into the Empire's greatest city on foot, pike on shoulder, at head of his beloved lansquenets, the modern, Swiss-style infantry he had created. "The king's power in the Empire is so great," the Venetian envoy wrote home, "that no one dares any longer to oppose him."[13]

The rise of the House of Austria in the late fifteenth and early sixteenth centuries thus recapitulated a common European theme, the reconstruction of central government in royal hands. The Empire's failure to continue on the path to royal centralism is to be explained by its political past, very different from those of France, England, and the other kingdoms of Europe's western tier. Late medieval central Europe had experienced not only a demographic and economic depression but also a "political depression" in the sense that, coming on the heels of the thirteenth-century collapse of royal authority, the fourteenth-century catastrophes promoted a massive intensification of de facto governance at the local and regional levels. During the long depression, the princes and prince-bishops began to reshape their temporal holdings into organized territorial states, the free cities fleshed out their autonomies and even took over parts of the countryside, and within the towns and the villages the task of regulating local life often passed into local hands. The economic recovery after 1450 did not halt this process, but it hardened the depression's creations into relatively stable units ranging from near-sovereign princely states to self-administering villages. The traditional name for this condition of dispersed governance is "particularism," though some authors have called it "parcellized sovereignty." It is the general background to the rise of parliamentary governance in the Empire in general and the emergence, during the later fifteenth century, of the Imperial Estates in particular.

THE IMPERIAL ESTATES

The Imperial Estates comprised all those who by customary right were called to give the king advice and consent. All were direct Imperial subjects, though many were not the emperor's feudal vassals, and some of the emperor's direct subjects—the Imperial knights and the Imperial peasants—were not Imperial Estates. When sitting as the Imperial Parliament, or Diet, the Estates divided into three chambers, or houses. In the first, the Electoral House, sat the six Imperial electors: the prince-archbishops of Mainz, Cologne, and Trier, and the lay princes of the Rhine Palatinate, Saxony, and Brandenburg.[14] In the Princes' House sat the other princes spiritual and temporal. The former included fifty prince-bishops, headed by the archbishops of Salzburg and Magdeburg and ranging from such leading bishops as Würzburg, Bamberg, Strasbourg, and Münster downward to fairly minor ones, such as Chur and Minden, plus two representatives of the Imperial abbots and abbesses. The lords temporal ranged from the heads of great lay dynasties—the Bavarian Wittelsbachs, the Welfs of Brunswick, and the Saxon Wettins—downward through middling princes, such as Hesse, Mecklenburg, Pomerania, Baden, and Anhalt, to two representatives of the Imperial counts. In the third chamber, the Cities' House, sat fifty-five or so Imperial free cities, which owed their liberties either to royal charter or to their ancestors' having wrested self-rule from their lords, usually prince-bishops. Collectively, all of these powers—from the prince-archbishop of Mainz down to the tiny free city of Zell am Harmersbach, a couple of hundred souls tucked into a creek valley in the Black Forest—counted among the Imperial Estates that represented "the Empire" in the increasingly common, dualistic formula for the rulers of the Empire, "Emperor and Empire."

The Imperial Diet convened at the king's call to give him advice and to consent to his proposals for new taxes and new laws. By the 1480s and 1490s the Diet's form was becoming fixed, though some issues, notably the cities' possession of equal voting rights, were still contested. As Strasbourg's Hans von Seckingen (d. 1509) growled in 1481, the electors and princes sat in their chambers and voted taxes, "while the townsmen sit outside the door like snuffling dogs."[15] But at least they sat outside the door, while other direct subjects of the Empire, such as the Imperial free knights, who were numerous in the Danube and Rhine basins but not elsewhere, and Imperial free peasants, who were rare everywhere, were not Estates of the Empire at all and were, therefore, unrepresented in the Diet. Imperial free peasants, such as the thirty-nine free villages and hamlets on the Leutkirch Heath in Upper Swabia, whose folk until 1803 appointed their sheriffs and judges and owned no lord but the emperor, belonged to the Empire's cabinet of political curiosities, along with Imperial free abbesses and prince-provosts, the heads of military-religious orders, and the Imperial free knights. Their liberties all rested on the same principle, their direct relationship to emperor and Empire, but this did not make them the political equals of the great princes and prelates.

Except for the Cities' House, the Diet was in effect an assembly of the Imperial aristocracy, headed by the great princely dynasties—the Wittelsbachs of Bavaria and the Palatinate, the Wettins of Saxony, the Welfs of Brunswick, and the Hohenzollerns of Brandenburg and Franconia, plus the princes of Württemberg, Hesse, and perhaps Baden in the South and Mecklenburg and Pomerania in the North. Denmark's king and Savoy's duke were also Imperial princes, but neither took a regular seat in the Diet, nor did the princes of Imperial Italy.

The weight of the great lay dynasties was even greater in the Imperial Diet than the precedence lists suggest, because they often dominated prince-bishoprics and important Imperial abbeys through the appointment of their own kinsmen to these benefices. The prince-bishoprics varied in desirability, of course, with poor Regensburg, Freising, and Constance ranking as far less desirable than rich Speyer, Würzburg, Cologne, Strasbourg, and Salzburg, while appointees to Mainz, Trier, and Cologne became electors of the Empire. The scramble for bishoprics formed but the fastest lane in the race to grab the choicest grass in the great pasture of the Imperial church, where aristocratic lineages and lesser nobles alike grazed their children with ever greater intensity. Four contemporary princes of the Palatine lines of the Wittelsbachs, a son and three nephews of Elector Louis III (r. 1410–36), collected one archbishopric and five bishoprics, and in the following generation five clerical siblings accumulated seven bishoprics, the provostship of Ellwangen, and an important abbacy, plus numerous cathedral canonries.[16] The margraves of Baden kept step, as two children and six grandchildren (including three women) of Margrave Charles I (r. 1453–75) made a rich haul of benefices.[17] These tendencies cemented the community of lords spiritual and lords temporal with mutual interest and obligation, making the bishops more secular in commitments than they were elsewhere in Latin Christendom and the princes more open to helping the church by helping themselves. This integration also made the Imperial Diet a far less heterogeneous parliamentary assembly than it superficially appeared to be.

Yet for all of its integrating tendencies, the Imperial Diet did not *represent* the Empire in any but the most general sense. For one thing, it was heavily weighted to the more densely populated, old-settled Imperial lands of the West and the South and against the more sparsely populated, newly settled lands of the North and East. Partly this was so because the East and North had fewer and larger territorial states and many fewer Imperial free cities. Then, too, the southern and western dynasties were wealthier than the northern and eastern ones, a point which is made by a glance at some rulers' revenues around 1500.[18] The richest lay prince, the Elector Palatine, took in 90,000 rhfl. per year, and his Bavarian kinsman about 65,000 rhfl. per year. These are respectable sums compared to the Empire—22.5 and 16.3 percent, respectively—but not compared to the revenues of the Venetian Republic, which collected some 1.3 million rhfl. per year. Even so, the Bavarian duke took in more than twice as much as the elector of Brandenburg, who got a paltry 33,000 rhfl. per year, which was only a little more than the free city of Basel, only two-thirds (64.7 percent) as much as Nuremberg, and a measly 19 percent as much as Augsburg. The richest Imperial prince, in fact, took in only about half of Augsburg's annual revenue of 176,000 rhfl. The western and southern princes nonetheless outclassed the northerners, with the sole exception of the electors and dukes of Saxony, whose lands, straddling the border zones between North and South, were yielding tremendous sums from the silver and copper mines of the Ore Mountains in this era. The partition of Saxony by two Wettin princes in 1485, however, created two second-rate principalities out of a first-rate one. Nor did the new wealth make the Saxons feel more central to the Empire, for sixteenth-century Saxon travelers westward into the older Imperial lands commonly said that they were going "into the Empire."[19]

The old Imperial heartlands in the Danube and Rhine Valleys also gained weight from their abutment on the Habsburgs' lands—Austria and the Netherlands—and their lesser powers supplied most of the House of Austria's political clientele. The sites of Imperial governance mirrored this Imperial concentration in the older lands, especially the South. Only three of Maximilian's twenty-four Diets (in thirty-four years) and none of Charles V's sixteen (in thirty-seven years) met in the North, and between 1512 and 1803, the Imperial Diet never sat outside the South.[20] The new organs of Imperial government, too, which the Imperial Reform of 1495–1512 created, all had their seats in southern free cities—Nuremberg, Frankfurt am Main, Esslingen, and Speyer. The Imperial Reform thus intensified the southern-centeredness of Imperial governance, which is one reason why, in the following decades, the Protestant Reformation won its greatest successes in the newer lands of the North and East. The reform also interleaved with the general intensification of governance at the local level in the Empire's older regions.

COMMUNAL GOVERNMENTS

One of the most characteristic changes in the late medieval Empire was the growth of local self-government through communes—sworn associations of householders and their elected magistrates—in the towns and also in the villages. Although in some respects opposed to aristocratic rule, the rise of the communes contributed to the general strengthening of governance, for by the fifteenth century the free cities were pioneering some of the greatest advances in governmental technique. The magistrates' dependence on the written word made possible the articulation of urban government into small bodies, such as privy councils, supervisory boards over schools, tax collection, coinage, markets, poor relief, and so on, and ad hoc committees, and the transfer of many functions to paid city employees, beginning with town clerks and university-trained lawyers. Nuremberg, which appointed its first attorney in 1366, retained ten by 1516. A third area in which the towns pioneered was financial management, one of the two central pillars—the other was military organization—of central European state building. In the large towns were created or adapted from Italian models all of the instruments for the passage of public finance from a cash to a credit basis. The two main such instruments were taxes, direct and indirect, and the sale of annuities, which accounted for 43 and 34 percent, respectively, of Nuremberg's incomes between 1431 and 1444. Some cities, such as Constance, Schwäbisch Hall, and Basel, were able to preserve a balance between incomes and outlays over the longer run; others, notably Mainz and Mühlhausen (Thuringia), spent their ways into bankruptcy. But on the whole the towns proved better at finance than any other type of regime in the fifteenth-century Empire.

The urban advantage in governance largely explains why cities were able to maintain large political federations, of which the most successful was the Hansa, the tremendous federation of coastal and inland towns across the basin of the North and Baltic Seas, with its center at Lübeck. It policed the trade of member towns, negotiated with kings and princes, and, until the rise of the Netherlanders in the fifteenth century, beat down all rivals. Urban leagues also operated in late medieval Swabia and the Rhine Valley, though after their defeat by the princes in the Cities' War of 1449–53, the southern free cities tended to ally with nobles and princes in such federations as the Swabian League (1488–1534) and the Protestant League of Smalkalden (1531–47). The most remarkable federation, however, was also the longest lived. The Swiss Confederacy combined free cities with free rural communities, the only such formation in Christendom. By the fifteenth century it had evolved a government which possessed no permanent central organs. In its assembly (*Tagsatzung*), which rotated its frequent sessions among a group of centrally located towns, sat two envoys (*Boten*) from each of the confederacy's thirteen full members (*Orte*) and one each from the three related members (*zugewandte Orte*). Despite its lack of central organs, this structure proved strong enough to withstand urban-rural conflicts following the Burgundian Wars of the 1470s and the civil strife aroused by the Protestant Reformation in 1529–31.

Rural communes, the basis of the Swiss Confederacy's rural members, existed through much of the Empire. These late medieval formations resembled urban communes in that they were sworn associations of adult male householders, who elected and obeyed a headman and a village court. These officials exercised jurisdiction over village spaces, including roads, churchyard, bathhouse, fields, pastures, woods, and waters, and policed both the village's bounds and its residents and visitors. In only a few places did federated rural communes become strong enough to organize territorial governments, and, as Martin Luther noted, only in Switzerland and Ditmarsh, on the North Sea coast, did there exist "democracy, where many of the Common Man rule."[21] Although the Frisian farmers of Ditmarsh later lost their liberties to neighboring princes, in the central Alpine lands, by contrast, self-government without princes and in disregard of kings continued to flourish, not least because in this age of the renaissance of heavy infantry, the Swiss, as Machiavelli remarked, "are best armed and most free."[22] Their demonstration effect on the peasants and small townsmen of neighboring lands—the Upper Rhine Valley both above and below Lake Constance, the Allgäu, Vorarlberg, and Tyrol—had often evoked a powerful urge to "turn Swiss," a phrase defined by one poet as trying "to become their own lords."[23]

Most of the Empire's peoples enjoyed far lower levels of self-government than did the free cities' burghers and the free peasants of the Empire's south-western corner. The process of emancipation, which had created such local zones of liberty, had exhausted itself by 1500. Thereafter, the benefit of rising grain prices tended to be captured more and more by the seigneurs, who in some regions consolidated their large estates on the basis of more or less bound labor. This "second serfdom," as it is called, divided the Empire into two major zones of structures governing rural life, a western zone of relatively high and an eastern zone of relatively low levels of self-government. In both regions, however, the dominant form of government was the territorial principality.

TERRITORIAL PRINCIPALITIES

Like a massive archipelago, the large territorial states rose out of the vast political sea of dispersed government that was the late medieval Empire. By the fifteenth century the German territorial princes enjoyed a high degree of autonomy across the whole space from Württemberg to Pomerania on the Baltic Sea and from Austria to Cleves-Jülich on the Lower Rhine. In many ways they were the largest and strongest of all those local powers who developed more effective institutions of governance during the later Middle Ages. The princes were not simply dependents of the emperor, though they were all his feudal vassals and were invested by him with their lands. They did not rule alone but in cooperation with their two- to four-chambered territorial parliaments, whose estates included the territorial nobility, the prelates, the towns, and, in Pomerania, Tyrol, and Berchtesgaden, sometimes the peasants. The territory was the seedground of German parliamentary life, which was quite well established on this level before the Imperial Diet took shape in the 1480s.

Parliaments sat infrequently and irregularly, and the prince's ordinary instrument was the regime that governed in his name. By 1500 the formation of such regimes out of the prince's household was well advanced, and most princely courts, spiritual as well as temporal, began with the traditional offices of marshal, steward, butler, and treasurer or chamberlain.[24] How these offices grew into the departments of a precocious territorial regime is illustrated by a Bavarian ordinance of 1511–12, which describes the departments of the chancellery, the household, the treasury, the court of justice, and the prince's council. There were still many overlapping functions, of course, and the traditional household officers outweighed experts and administration, but the entire body was small, numbering some fifty men with the rank of councilor and fifteen others. Nobles still held most high offices at most courts, but the number of legally trained commoners was growing, earliest at the courts in Stuttgart and Munich, more slowly at those of Hesse and Saxony.

For the prince to be transformed from a territorial lord into a lord over his territory, the territorial states had to become less vulnerable to the practice of partitioning lands among the prince's male heirs. The desirability of unity was already enshrined in the Greater Privilege, a mid-fourteenth-century forgery for the duchy of Austria: "These lands shall forever have as their ruler the eldest of the dukes of Austria, to whose eldest son the rule shall pass by the law of inheritance, though without leaving this lineage. And at no time shall the duchy of Austria be divided."[25] The principles of primogeniture and indivisibility nonetheless proved quite difficult to establish in practice. In the vanguard stood Bavaria, where in 1506 Duke Albert IV (1465–1508), backed by his estates, made primogeniture and indivisibility the law. Around the same time, King Maximilian united the western lands—the Tyrol, Vorarlberg, and western Austria—with the five eastern duchies—Upper and Lower Austria, Styria, Carinthia, and Carniola—under a central administration at Innsbruck.[26]

Further northward, princely dynasties continued to create divisions that endured for very long periods or even became permanent. The Welfs of Brunswick divided and subdivided their lands with abandon; Hesse split in 1567 into four territories; a testamentary division in 1515 permanently converted Baden from a second-class power into two third-class powers; and Saxony, once after Habsburg Austria the Empire's greatest power, was partitioned in 1485 by the two brothers of the House of Wettin, Elector Ernest (r. 1464–86) and Duke Albert (r. 1464–1500), who thereby made Saxony far weaker in Imperial affairs than its population (ca. 400,000) and its silver mines warranted.

Effective territorial regimes required both a functional articulation of departments and a centralization of judicial powers.[27] The dominant tendencies around 1500 were to distinguish governmental functions—justice, chancellery, finance, audit, and household—to allot them to collegially organized bodies of nobles and learned councilors, and to require much more record keeping. Bavaria had by 1520 a centralized judicial system based on Roman legal (i.e., written) procedures; Baden acquired its first chancellery regulations in 1504 and a central court in 1509; in Hesse the high court was finally separated in 1500 from both the state council and the chancellery; and in Mecklenburg Duke Magnus II (r. 1477–1503) created a regime which lasted until the nineteenth century. The territorial parliaments often supported centralization, especially if it helped to reduce princely debts, but at the same time they often expressed strong reservations against the growing use of Roman law. Although the Diet in 1495 named it "the Empire's common law" and prescribed it for the new Imperial Chamber Court (*Reichskammergericht*), many people saw in the learned, Roman law an engine of novelty, disruption of ancient custom, suppression of privilege, and even tyranny.[28]

ECCLESIASTICAL PRINCIPALITIES

Such changes, which around 1500 were transforming a Bavaria, a Brandenburg, or a Württemberg into recognizable examples of the early modern European state, were also at work in the ecclesiastical states, the almost fifty prince-bishoprics and the great Imperial abbeys. These states, in which a prince-prelate united spiritual office with temporal jurisdiction, had formed around 1000 A.D. and remained one of the Empire's great peculiarities.[29] The fusion of spiritual and temporal authority had important implications for both offices. A diocese stood under the bishop's sacral powers but under an ecclesiastical administration shared between him and the cathedral chapter, which in most cases had elected him bishop.[30] Under them stood the rural archdeaconries and the parishes, though in fact nominations to most parish benefices were either controlled by monasteries ("incorporation") or by lay nobles ("advowson" or "lay patronage"). Throughout the diocese, except for chartered immunities, the bishop's court exercised its authority over the clergy in all matters and the laity in specific ones, such as marriage litigation and some moral offenses.

In their role as temporal lords, the bishops had to share authority with territorial estates, just as other princes did. Most of the fifteenth-century bishops were aristocrats born, such as Elector Berthold of Mainz (ca. 1442–1504), who was by birth a count of Henneberg and by accomplishment Emperor Maximilian's bitterest enemy. Still, the late fifteenth century witnessed the rise of several commoners who became great Imperial prelates: Matthäus Lang (1468–1540), an Augsburg boy who rose to be prince-archbishop of Salzburg, cardinal, and Maximilian's closest advisor; Matthäus Schiner (ca. 1469–1522) from a Valaisian stockmen's family, who became bishop of Sitten, cardinal, and the most power-ful German-speaker in Rome; and Adriaan Floriszn (1459–1523) of Utrecht, who became rector of the University of Louvain, tutor to the young Charles V, and pope as Adrian VI (r. 1522–23).

The conditions of the late-fifteenth-century Empire made it difficult for prince-bishops to be either strong princes or good bishops. They stood at a great disadvantage in dealing with their more powerful subjects, especially the burghers. Most of the cathedral towns in the Rhine Valley—Constance, Basel, Stras-bourg, Worms, Speyer, Mainz, and Cologne—freed themselves from the bish-op's temporal authority and forced the bishops to take up residence in smaller towns. Often as at Salzburg and Würzburg, the bishops stayed in cities in which they held great fortresses. Other episcopal cities, such as Mainz and Erfurt, gained their liberty only to lose it again later. Such frictions fueled the enmity between burghers and their bishops, who were pushed into the hands of their territorial nobles. The Nuremberg patrician Willibald Pirckheimer (1470–1530) lamented that "the free cities used to be great in number and power, but . . . most of them have fallen, . . . [and] especially they have suffered from this all-consuming flame, the arrogance and greed of the bishops."[31]

Pirckheimer raged not because the bishops were more predatory than other princes, but because they were not less so. The fusion of spiritual and tempo-ral jurisdictions, which five hundred years before had seemed so useful, now prompted reformers to insist on the incompatibility between the two offices, bishop and prince. "Take a good look at how bishops act nowadays," lamented the author of *The Reformation of Emperor Sigmund* around 1438:

> They make war and cause unrest in the world; they behave like secular lords, which is, of course, what they are. And the money for this comes from pious donations that ought to go to honest parish work, and not be spent on war. I agree with a remark made by Duke Frederick [of the Tyrol] to the Emperor Sigmund in Basel: "Bishops are blind; it is up to us to open their eyes."

"No bishop should own a castle," and every bishop should reside permanently in the principal church of his diocese "and lead a spiritual life there. He should be an example to the clerics in his bishopric. But nowadays bishops ride about like lords in secular states. Change this wicked practice and you will have greatly increased the chances of peace."[32]

The central problem was that, by the end of the Middle Ages, a man who made a good bishop would probably be a poor prince, and the importance of temporal lordship to law and order and of the church's wealth to aristocratic well-being assured that many bishops would be better princes than they were bishops. The Christians of the late medieval Empire had grown so enured to this situation that some dioceses had forgotten what it was like to have a bishop who was a vigorous spiritual leader. When Bishop William von Honstein

(r. 1506–41) of Strasbourg celebrated Mass in his own cathedral on 22 June 1508, one observer remarked that this astonishing act "had been performed by no bishop in a hundred and fifty years, and it seemed marvelous to the people. . . . Such things were done in olden times."[33]

The jurisdictional situation in the Empire made it nearly impossible for a bishop to function as both an effective spiritual lord and as a good prince. Consider, in this light, the prince-archbishop of Trier's position. His spiritual authority extended over lands which lay principally under the counts of Nassau, the Electors Palatine, the dukes of Lorraine and Luxembourg, and the prince-archbishop of Cologne, in the midst of which his own temporal lands formed a central spine about a third the size of his archdiocese. But some of his territory lay spiritually in the archdiocese of Cologne, and other small chunks in the dioceses of Liège and Metz. The fit was even worse for the prince-archbishop of Mainz, whose small temporal territories lay strewn from one end of his enormous archdiocese to the other. Consider, then, the same problem from the lay princes' point of view. Before the Protestant Reformation, the lands of the Saxon House of Wettin lay in ten different spiritual jurisdictions, those of the Brandenburg Hohenzollerns in eight, and those of the very compact Bavarian duchy in seven. Such conditions made a collaboration of temporal and spiritual authorities—the key to any effective religious reform—impossible, because while reform under episcopal authority met resistance from the many temporal lords in a diocese, reform under princely authority provoked opposition from at least some of the bishops in whose dioceses his lands lay. This deadlock was general, and it is the main reason why ecclesiastical issues became bound up in the reform of Imperial governance.

THE IMPERIAL REFORM

The prince-bishops, and to a lesser degree the abbots and the abbesses, lived in the fracture zone where aristocratic norms of living overlapped and clashed with spiritual duties. Some bishops resorted to violence, and abbots could be, as the Imperial abbots of Kempten were around 1500, extremely harsh against their own peasants. As a whole, however, the prelates of the Empire had far more to gain—for themselves, their subjects, and their flocks—from better government than from the continuation of legal violence embodied in the right to feud. Their support was therefore vital to the movement among the Imperial Estates for a central but nonroyal government of the Empire.

The urban merchants, too, wanted stronger government and more law and order. Several years after Maximilian's death, a group of merchants gathered at Frankfurt begged his grandson and successor, Charles V, to make the roads safe for traders, especially those traveling to and from the great Frankfurt Fair. "Despite all assurances, protection, safe conducts, and toll payments," they complained, we are arrested, kidnapped, stopped, plagued, held to impossibly high ransoms, and sold by our captors to third parties; our goods by land and by water are confiscated, attacked, seized, burned, and ruined; and we are treated tyrannically to a degree that is horrifying to many people, but especially to all obedient subjects of the Empire, and that brings the German name and the reputations of the Empire's rulers to ridicule, mockery, and diminution in foreign lands.[34]

By that time, yet other arguments for more law and order arose from the fear of rural unrest, which was was erupting more and more frequently and taking larger and more dangerous forms. In 1514, when the common people rose in Württemberg against new consumption taxes, a poor boy of Beutelsbach, named Gailspeter, set the tone by tossing the new, falsified weights into the Rems River with the cry, "If the prince's action is just and right, let the weights float up and swim; if the peasants are right, let them sink to the bottom!"[35] Three years later, Joss Fritz reorganized the secret rural league called the *Bundschuh*, named after the peasant's laced boot, which stretched from Strasbourg to the Black Forest and to the Vosges and drew into its ranks veteran lansquenets, itinerant craftsmen, beggars, and peasants. This *Bundschuh* showed a new and ominous face, for its economic and social demands were justified not by the customary appeal to ancient tradition but by a new religious ideal of an absolute godly law. The conspirators demanded the establishment of a just society, no matter what rights and obligations were sanctioned by customary law or stipulated by charters. And yet, when this movement rose to its climax in the great Peasants' War of 1525, its principal voices demanded not weaker but stronger and more responsive states or, where the land was deeply fragmented, the formation of new territorial states. This is hardly surprising, for more regulation was universally believed to be the best solution not only to endemic violence but also to the economic hardship caused by rising prices. As the Bavarian estates complained in 1510, "all the grain and other things, which the peasant must sell to pay his taxes, are in little demand now; but the things he must buy in the town do not fall in price and are not regulated by law, but they cost ever more."[36]

Not everyone wanted stronger government. The lesser nobles' incomes had plunged during the depression, and they were in many areas being pushed to the political and economic margins by the consolidations of the territorial states. The situation hit especially hard the Imperial free knights, so numerous in Franconia and on the Rhine, who felt especially injured and poured forth their grievances into whatever ears were handy. They complained of being treated like common lawbreakers and denied the ancient right of feud and the freedom to assemble. "We consider it unjust," the Franconian free knights told the Imperial Diet in 1522, "that while all the other Estates of the Holy Roman Empire are wont to meet at times for deliberation and consideration of their grievances, the nobility has been prevented by certain princes and sovereign authorities from meeting and consulting together."[37] The knights felt that the princes were trying to make them subjects, and in a petition of 1523 they complained that "in these times some princes bind a nobleman in such a way as to prevent him from speaking or making complaint, either within or outside the law, against his pledge [*Urfehde*], on pain of heavy penalties, regardless of the fact that this violates all law, reason, and honor."[38]

Spurred by their sense of grievance, many nobles resorted to self-help, and the early sixteenth century became a golden age of the noble brigands. One such was the Franconian thug Cuntz Schott, who collected hands from the Nurembergers he kidnapped for ransom. Another was the infamous Franconian free knight Götz von Berlichingen (1480/81–1562), who complained in 1513 that "it seems to me, that I just move from one war to another. Only yesterday I made peace with Nuremberg; today it begins again [with Mainz]."[39] Even more destructive was Götz's kinsman, Franz von Sickingen (1481–1523), whose three-year (1514–17) feud against the city of Worms disrupted trade along the Rhine. Finally, in 1522–23, the Franconian free knights formed a general conspiracy, only to be crushed by the neighboring princes.

Under these circumstances, a broad consensus existed among the Empire's governing classes, right down to the local level, that stronger governance was needed. It was not the monarch, however, who put himself at the head of the movement in this direction, but Archbishop Berthold of Henneberg (r. 1484–1504) of Mainz, and it was his hand rather than the king's that lay behind the great reform laws of 1495: the Perpetual Public Peace which suppressed the right of feud; the law which created a new supreme court of justice called the Imperial Chamber Court; the creation of the Common Penny, the Empire's first general property tax; and the creation of regional executive organs in the form of the Imperial Circles. Five years later at the Diet of Augsburg in 1500, Berthold's reform party even managed to transfer the entire royal executive to an Imperial Governing Council, which, though headed by the king or his representative, was controlled by the Imperial Estates. Maximilian's refusal to cooperate killed this council, just as the lack of an effective means of collection killed the Common Penny, but the Chamber Court and the Circles—six, eventually ten, regional peace-keeping districts—wobbled into existence and became functioning organs of Imperial governance, though their main period of effectiveness began after 1555. When Berthold of Henneberg died in 1504, it seemed as if Maximilian had defeated the movement for a central regime in which the small royal share contrasted dramatically with the large parliamentary one. But some of the reforms survived, and the reformed Imperial constitution endured in roughly this shape until 1803.

THE REFORM OF THE CHURCH

Freed from the Protestant reformers' polemics, the condition of the late medieval church in the Empire has gradually come to reveal some of its true contours. One of the truly striking features of this landscape is the powerful upsurge of religious sentiment and practice among the Empire's peoples around 1500. It was a high point, perhaps, in the thousand-year effort of the church to embed this non-European religion, Christianity, in these northern lands. In earlier times, the urban-bred structures of ancient Christianity had been forced to adapt to the poor, rural world of medieval Europe. Just as the great rural abbeys had formed the chief instruments for that missionary effort, so, in later centuries, this role had fallen to the parish. New parishes were still being founded around 1500 in remoter, poorer villages, sometimes by popular initiative. They had long been fully formed, extremely active institutions, however, in the towns and cities, which had become the nodal points of late medieval religion.

The burghers played a central role in the religious intensification around 1500. For generations a generous laity had built the larger German-speaking cities into veritable monuments to the faith, especially in the ecclesiastical centers, those "German Romes," over whose rooftops spires sprouted like barley in the fields: Cologne had 11 collegiate chapters, 20 religious houses, 19 parishes, 24 autonomous and 20 other chapels, and 62 houses of beguines and beghards; and Erfurt, the most churched town in central Europe, possessed 2 chapters, 22 monasteries, 23 other churches, 36 chapels, and 6 hospitals, plus 28 parishes. There were no signs around 1500 that the church at this level was losing its grip. Besides the endless stream of young men into the priesthood—Breslau counted 414 priests serving 322 altars—and avid donations of altars and retables (a measly 2 percent of them survive), popular new pilgrimages appeared. The most successful of them brought the devout to the chapel Zur Schönen Maria at Regensburg, which arose on the site of Regensburg's synagogue after the city's huge Jewish community was expelled in 1519; in three years, 25,374 Masses were read here, and in 1520 alone there were 109,198 lead and 9,763 silver pilgrim's badges sold. In South Germany and Switzerland, a wave of endowments by rural communes of village churches created pressure for the repatriation of tithes, which threatened long-held property rights, and for a whole new localization of the control of parish life. At the local level, indeed, it is easy to see that the custody of religion by no means belonged to the clergy alone. The Ulmers, for example, took pride in having acquired the patronage rights to their parish, which embraced the whole commune.

Many of those who could helped to endow the elaborate arrays of religious institutions. The urban rich endowed by family, the middling folk by confraternity, a kind of "consensual parish" that boomed in such cities as Lübeck (over seventy) and Cologne (eighty) around 1350 and Hamburg (ninety-nine) around

1520—and sometimes grew to enormous size. Ulm's Rosary Confraternity (est. 1483) grew to four thousand members. Their caritative activities swelled the flow of prayers and wealth to the hospitals and poorhouses, the most important of which was Cologne's great Hospital of the Holy Spirit, where seven hundred poor folk ate each day. Most such foundations drew their resources from donations by burghers, such as Cologne's Dr. Peter Rynck, who in 1500 left forty-three hundred marks to clothe and feed "the poor foundlings, who are cared for as abandoned and unwanted children."[40]

Amid the warmth of such devotion, all the more remarkable seem the severe structural limits to the church's ability to change with the times by redeploying its resources toward new demands from the laity. The specific reasons for the Imperial church's immobility are illuminated by conditions in the diocese of Strasbourg, the one Imperial diocese that has been well studied. On the eve of the Reformation, this small southwestern diocese had probably the best educated clergy in its history. Their energies were ensnared, however, in an immense network of property management, which depended legally on the benefice system and financially on the clergy's role as creditors of the peasants and traders in foodstuffs. Each monastery and collegial chapter thus formed a microcosm of the union of spiritual and temporal functions in the prince-bishoprics, and the canon law, which in principle protected the priests, monks, and nuns from lay intervention, also protected them from their own bishops and provincials.

Caged by an immense web of property rights, the traditional bonds between clergy and laity seem to have been disintegrating. "You laymen hate us priests," Geiler preached in 1508, "and it is an old hatred that separates us. Whence comes your hatred for us? I believe from our insane way of life and that we live so evilly and create such scandal."[41] It is doubtful, in fact, that the clergy were living more or less immoral lives than they had in preceding centuries. What is not doubtful is that great struggle was developing over the immense, poorly guarded, and anachronistically deployed resources of the church. Many laymen benefited from clerical property rights and privileges, and, as the experience of the diocese of Strasbourg shows, every episcopal or monastic reform program met with fierce resistance by entrenched lay interests. Many, perhaps even more, laymen, however, coveted those same rights and the resources to which they gave access. And still others believed that a church freed of its bondage to property rights, chiefly the prince-bishoprics and the benefice system, could become more spiritual and more pastoral. None of these interests aimed to overturn the world in a revolutionary way, so all of them faced the same dilemma: How to free the church from its cage of property rights, or the properties from the grip of the priests, without endangering all property rights? Johann Geiler, writing around 1508, warned that if the laity should begin to expropriate the clergy, "because they have too much, . . . I don't know where it would end."[42] Thirteen years later, Desiderius Erasmus repeated Geiler's warning: "For if they think it lawful to lay hands on the property of priests, just because some of them use their resources for a life of luxury or for purposes which are unworthy in other ways, many of our burghers and nobles alike will find that their hold on their possessions is precarious."[43] Yet the presentiment of radical change was also strong. In 1482 Geiler had warned the diocesan synod of Strasbourg that "Jesus Christ is sending other reformers, who will understand the task better than I do." Though he would not live to see them, "many of you will see and experience what is coming. Then you'll want to heed and obey me, but then it will be too late."[44]

Only one class of persons, the rulers themselves, could effect change without revolution, for they could alter property relations in particular without threatening property rights in general. Medieval constitutional principles dictated that the prince's duty to protect and safeguard the church placed the clergy and their properties under his advocacy as part of his "treasury" (*Kammer*), and that for this protection the clergy would, naturally, render him aid and counsel. It was via this principle that in many fifteenth-century territories the upper clergy became incorporated as an estate and sat in the territorial parliaments. But the rights of protection were also an invitation to financial exploitation, and the fifteenth-century Habsburgs set a very high standard as exploiters of the church in the Austrian lands. "What the priests have, belongs to our treasury," ran Emperor Frederick III's maxim[45]—and many other dynasties followed his prompt. When, for example, Margrave Albert Achilles of Brandenburg-Ansbach decided in 1480 to make his clergy help pay the Imperial tax against the Turks, the bishops of Würzburg and Bamberg stood helplessly by, powerless to stop him. "A new Pharaoh," the clergy's spokesman railed at the margrave, "a new Sennacherib, a new Antiochus, a new Nero, a new Diocletian"—but they paid nonetheless.[46]

The predatory prince was one side of a coin, the obverse of which bore the likeness of the reforming prince. The Wettin princes of Saxony, for example, whose lands were divided among seven different dioceses, chose to promote the monastic reform movement known as the Observance. Here, and in other territories, long before Luther's reformation the foundations of the post-Reformation fusion of territorial state and reformed church were being laid.

The princes were by no means the sole practitioners or even the pioneers of domestication, that is, the establishment of greater local control over the church. The real vanguard here, once again, was played by the cities, especially the free cities, who for many decades strove to bring the local church, both seculars and regulars, under magisterial authority. Nowhere, perhaps, did this effort succeed more spectacularly than in the Upper Swabian city of Ulm. In 1376–77, with the approval of its patron and its bishop, the abbot of Reichenau and the bishop of Constance, Ulm tore down its single parish church outside the walls and laid the foundations within the walls of a church large enough to contain the whole commune. It became the largest parish church in the German-speaking world, and in 1446 the magistrates paid the abbot the immense sum of twenty-five thousand gulden for the patronage rights, making Ulm the extreme example of church-state fusion in the fifteenth-century Empire. Similar, if less spectacular, purchases were made by Nuremberg from the bishop and chapter of Würzburg and by other cities, while the supervision of parish finances and properties came into the hands of churchwardens (*Pfleger*), selected sometimes by the parishioners and sometimes by the magistrates. As for the regular clergy, the magistrates tended to leave the older monasteries, many of which had papal or Imperial immunities, alone, but they made frequent use of and intervened frequently in the affairs of the mendicant convents, which became, in one formulation, "quasi-municipal institutions."[47] Mendicant houses even sometimes served as temporary townhalls, notably at Frankfurt until 1504, and at Basel, Speyer, and Brunswick.

The movement for closer local control of the clergy, clerical property, and clerical services reached all the way down to the villages. In many parts of southern Germany and Switzerland, too, local concern for religion prompted rural communes to establish and endow parishes in their own villages. In two districts of the prince-bishopric of Speyer, for example, more than a third (seventeen of forty-six) of the village pastorates had been founded by village communes. Communalization of religion challenged existing property relations, especially with respect to tithes, and already a few parishes were demanding the right to approve and depose pastors. Shortly after 1500, the relatively new idea of the "godly law" began to be called upon to justify such changes and to breach the historic structures of benefices, patronage rights, and impropriated tithes. When Luther's reformation came, it initially, but very briefly, empowered this local domestication in communal hands. The shock of the Peasants' War changed all that, and except in a few favored places, such as the Graubünden, the Protestant Reformation simply completed the process of reshaping the church by fusing it with temporal governance.

INSTRUMENTS OF REFORM? BOOKS AND IDEAS

The truism that the church, like the individual Christian's life, always needed reform did not neutralize the feeling around 1500 that things were coming to a head. Or so it seemed. When a writer known to us only as the "Upper Rhenish Revolutionary" came to the Diet of Worms in 1495 to convince the mighty that unless they strengthened the monarchy, reformed abuses in church and society, and persuaded the people to lead Christian lives, a terrible punishment awaited the Germans, Elector Berthold sent him away. Eventually, as he wrote, "I stopped this bustling around, when I saw that none of the mighty cared a bit for the correct path."[48]

PRINTING AND LANGUAGE

The preservation of the "correct path" in a unique manuscript reminds us that the replication of the word through print had not yet revolutionized lettered culture by 1500, even though the Alsatian humanist Jakob Wimpheling (1450–1528) celebrated printing as the "German art." "Of no other invention or fruit of the spirit should we Germans be prouder than of the printing of books," he wrote in 1507, "which has elevated us to the new bearers of Christian doctrine and worldly learning and to benefactors of all mankind."[49] And the response was so great, as an anonymous clergyman wrote, that "in these days everyone wants to read and write, which is fine and good when the books are good, but not so fine when the books are wicked ones which stir you up to false desires and immorality."[50] By 1500 something between twenty-seven thousand and forty thousand titles, mostly on secular subjects, had been printed to serve the Empire's forty thousand or so literate people.

The relationship of print to culture was complicated by the existence around 1500 of not one, not two, but three cultures of print: High German, Latin, and Low German, which was still a written language from the Lower Rhine Valley and Westphalia across Brandenburg to Prussia and Livonia.[51] The linguistic future among literate German-speakers, true, belonged to Early New High German, which had long been taking shape in the east-central and southeastern parts of the Empire. The triumph of High over Low German, however, and the consequent simplification of print culture into two sectors, German and Latin, became definitive only with the Reformation. "Common German" was first so called in 1464 at the Imperial chancellery resident in Austria, whence it spread through the southern printing centers, especially Nuremberg and Augsburg, until by 1500 the forms of German printed in the South had become nearly unified. Important differences nonetheless remained between the southern printed language and the "Meissen tongue" used in Saxony. Although Martin Luther was able to assume the role of a linguistic unifier, supplementing and consolidating the Imperial chancellery's work in Maximilian's time, still, his German New Testament had to be glossed for southern readers. When Luther's translation of the New Testament was printed at Basel in 1523, his *flehen* (plead) became *bitten*, his *Lippe* (lip) became *Lefze*, and his *Ziege* (goat) became *Geiss*.

From a modern perspective the most difficult thing to grasp about the cultures of that time is the complicated interpenetration of German and Latin in both writing and speech. A great deal of translation went on, both from Latin into German and from more technical to more popular levels in the form, for example, of vernacular handbooks on the civil and canon laws, and Latin exercised a powerful influence on written German in both lexicon and syntax. From the international Latin culture, too, translations made works of theology, law, philosophy, and medicine available to those who read only German, and the expansion of the vernacular reading public opened ever wider publics to those who could write both languages. "I used to write in Latin," wrote Ulrich von Hutten in 1520, "which not everyone could understand, but now I cry to the fatherland, the German nation, in its own tongue."[52]

EDUCATION

Education in German was acquired in the town schools, in Latin in the civic and monastic Latin schools and in the universities. It is easy to imagine the typical situation as far less chaotic and ineffective than it in fact was. Some important cities, notably Strasbourg, had no decent schools until well into the Reformation generation, and many pupils wandered about from school to school, their attention taken more by the need to stay alive than by the desire for letters. A very clear picture of this fruitless wandering of pupils emerges from the famous authobiography of Thomas Platter (1499–1582), a poor herding family's boy from high in the Goms, the Upper Valais, which a generation before had produced Matthäus Cardinal Schiner. Platter went on the roads as a boy and wandered for years from town to town before coming to the famous Latin school at Sélestat/Schlettstadt in central Alsace. Here, he tells us, he first mastered Donatus's grammar, which means that after nearly twelve years of "studying," Platter did not yet have the elements of Latin grammar. That he went on to learn Hebrew well enough to teach it to others, speaks more for his tenacity and fervor than for the quality of the schools of his day. In the light of his experience, it is hardly surprising that most of the age's scholars were town boys who had access to regular schooling in their hometowns.

Inefficient its educational institutions may have been, but the Empire's nine universities were instructing steadily rising numbers of students. The earliest universities had been founded in the Empire in the fourteenth century, and around 1500 new inscriptions totaled about 1,820 per year and ranged from a high of 455 at Cologne to a low of 59 at Greifswald. University instruction followed, though with great variety, normal scholastic curricula and methods in all faculties, and although there was nothing especially retrograde about the Empire's universities, the awareness of success encouraged by their rising popularity tended to reinforce resistance to pedagogical reform. Although the universities were still clerical institutions, the proportion of lay students was rising, and, perhaps more significantly, the mendicant friars were gaining ground over those headed for careers as secular priests and, most of them, parish clergy.

Since the middle years of the fifteenth century, a wave of criticism had risen around the prevailing methods of instruction, standard texts, and curricula that had grown up since the twelfth century in the universities and the schools of the mendicant orders. Scholasticism, as this common academic culture is called in modern times, had long been the common ground of discourse of Catholic Christendom in philosophy and theology and, to lesser but important degrees, in medicine and law. The new learning, humanism, took its rise in the north-ern and central Italian cities, not in Paris, and insisted on placing language, not philosophy, at the center of the curriculum. Since the 1450s and 1460s Italians and Italian-educated Germans (teaching in a number of the Empire's universities) and others, such as wandering poets, had been contributing to the luster of "good letters"—humanism, to us. In the Empire, the most important agents of the new learning were those who practiced it alongside the old. All of the really influential German-speaking humanists down to the 1510s were men of this mixed intellectual and scholarly type. This reception phase of hu-manism in the Empire lasted from the mid-fifteenth century until around 1510, when the influence of Desiderius Erasmus (1469?–1536), the great Dutch hu-manist, became paramount, and when the fiercest battles between the old learning and the new really began. Finally, during the two decades between 1515 and 1535, the new learning came to supremacy in the Empire's universities, a bene-ficiary of the Protestant Reformation, though not invariably its ally.

SCHOLASTICISM AND HUMANISM

It is a common error to see in scholaticism and humanism two utterly irrecon-cilable intellectual cultures, the incompatibility of which led to constant, sometimes titanic, literary battles for supremacy over the schools. The progress of "good letters" was slow and indirect, not least because of the complicated attitudes toward Italy through which it had to be filtered. Italy was not only the home of humanism, which many men of traditional learning despised, it was also the home of papalism, which many Imperial churchmen, most of whom were conciliarists, rejected or at least criticized. The Viennese theologian Konrad Säldner, for example, who rejected "the poets [rightly] said to be dilettantes," also commented that "in our days since the overthrow of the General Coun-cils, Italian authors have shown me little expertise in the higher learning or in morals conducive to the building up of Holy Church."[53] Not all Germans, however, felt scandalized, repelled, or humiliated by Italians and Italian learn-ing—Martin Luther's disdain and Hutten's brutal chauvinism were by no means typical—and some Germans, such as the Nuremberg artist Albrecht Dürer, found Italy exhilarating. "Here I am a gentleman," he wrote in 1506, "at home a sponger."[54]

More important than either praise or blame, however, was the call for Ger-man-speaking scholars to imitate the Italians' reputation for learning and to expunge thereby the Germans' own reputation for laziness, drunkenness, and ignorance. In 1425 the Florentine Gian Francesco Poggio Bracciolini (1380–1459) had discovered at Fulda the only surviving manuscript of Tacitus's *Germania*, and after the work was brought to Rome in 1455, Enea Silvio Piccolomini (1405–64) spread its fame to the Empire. The *Germania*'s recovery embold-ened German scholars to provide their people with an ancient past that would both awaken pride in their Germanic ancestors and desire in themselves to emulate and surpass the Italians. This essential program of German humanism received its most important formulation by Conrad Bickel, or "Celtis" (1459–1508), son of a Franconian vintner, who on 31 August 1492 delivered an inaugural lecture at Ingolstadt, in which he called the Germans to learn about the ancient world and their own land: "Shame on you, who are ignorant of Greek and Latin history, but far more of the rivers, mountains, monuments, and peoples of our own land. . . . Take up again that spirit, you German men, which once made you the nemesis of the Romans. . . . Now turn, turn, o you Germans, to more peaceful studies and win thereby immortality and your country's eternal praise!"[55]

Patriotic pride and individual reputation, such were the ideals the German humanists were spreading through the educated world of the Empire around 1500. And they did so by and large without opposition, for humanist studies gradually found a place both in informal arrangements around the universities and in burghers' literary circles. The movement's leading figures, such as Celtis and Wimpheling, campaigned for better Latin and for the humanities (*bonae litterae*) but did not attack scholastic learning as such. That would come later, around 1510, when the influence of Desiderius Erasmus over the German-speaking humanists became paramount. Nor, for that matter, did the humanists yet scorn to write also in the common tongue. That, too, would come later. Around 1500 the spirit was different, more relaxed and more in tune with traditional culture. The writers of this age possessed a confidence in the tested value of the genres and themes of older vernacular literature. Thus, when the Franconian nobleman Ludwig von Eyb sought to fashion the biography of the Franconian knight Wilwolt von Schaumburg into a manual of behavior for the young noblemen of his age, he drew freely from the well of traditional chivalric literature and twined its materials around the thread of Schaumburg's own deeds. And Sebastian Brant, a Basel-trained lawyer and humanist who became city secretary in his native Strasbourg, achieved his greatest fame through a satirical work in German, his *Ship of Fools* of 1494, in which he pilloried the world's follies in around seven thousand verses about more than a hundred kinds of fools. Brant drew entirely from vernacular traditions, both for the chief figure of the fool, which came from indigenous carnival culture, and for the principle theme of wisdom versus human folly, which Heinrich von Wittenwiller's *Ring* had treated nearly a century before. What a contrast to Erasmus's *Praise of Folly* of 1508, which took up the same theme and made Brant instantly obsolete, at least among the humanists and their fans. The great Dutch humanist cast the same theme in elegant Latin and made folly not the foe of wisdom but its embodiment. It was indeed Erasmus's influence, which soon became paramount among fashionable young men of letters, which sounded the death knell of this old-fashioned vernacular literature by insisting on neoclassical Latin as the only fitting vehicle of good letters. The standards of Latinity escalated enormously, and during the 1510s the older writers, such as Jakob Wimpheling and Johannes Reuchlin, stood aside as their juniors plunged into fierce literary battles against traditional academic learning and the mendicant orders. This development came to a head during the "Reuchlin affair" in the hilariously savage *Letters of Obscure Men* (1515–17), which attacked scholastic theology, bad Latin, and the friars.

It is nonetheless easy to overestimate the genuinely critical edge of the humanist movement. Its representatives in the Empire displayed little interest in politics, except for their devout flattery of the House of Austria and their bombastic defenses of German virtue and pride against the pope and the French, and even less for practical social questions. Those who wrote on such questions—witchcraft, usury, and tithing—were not humanists but university scholars trained in scholastic philosophy, theology, and law.

Through the medium of the printed word, some of the new ideas reached audiences outside the academically trained clergy and lawyers and fed a convergence of opinions, formerly separated by language and geography, into a broadly based public opinion. A new level of such opinion was forming in the Empire before Martin Luther became a public figure, and its earliest forum was the Imperial Diet. Antipapal pamphleteering fueled the Diet's compilation at Augsburg in 1518 of a long, detailed catalogue of "grievances" [*gravamina*] against the clergy and especially the papacy. Yet many of those who came to Augsburg had no awareness of having witnessed a sea change. Emperor Maximilian, mired deep in his negotiations with the electors for his grandson's sucession, had neither time for nor interest in this new coagulation of public opinion. He had little time left, and the portrait Albrecht Dürer painted of him at Augsburg did not hide the fact that years of stress and of hard, strenuous living had made him look older than his sixty years. He was old, and when the Diet rose, Maximilian headed for Tyrol and then to Castle Wels on Upper Austria's Traun River. His death there on 12 January 1519 marked the end of the Empire's Middle Ages and the beginning of its Reformation era.

The ten years between Maximilian's death and the birth of Protestantism may well have been the most turbulent decade the Holy Roman Empire ever knew. His reign nonetheless made life for most people in the Empire a bit more secure than it had been during the long late medieval depression. The new security, the economic recovery, and a long respite from protracted wars encouraged a flowering of the arts and crafts and vernacular culture around 1500, and nowhere more vitally than in the Empire's southern free cities. It was the age of Memmingen fustians and Constance linens, of Augsburg armor and Strasbourg cannon, of Nuremberg clocks and Esslingen silverware, of the Great Ravensburg Company and the mighty Fugger firm, of Swiss infantry and German lansquenets, of Dürer's paintings and Riemenschneider's limewood sculptures, of Hartmann Schedel's *World Chronicle* and Sebastian Brant's *Ship of Fools*, of Conrad Celtis's chorography and Wimpheling's patriotic histories, of Geiler's sermons and the Nuremberg mastersingers, and of Behaim's globe and Waldseemüller's world map. At least one witness believed that these proud communes, which lie sprinkled across our historical maps of the Empire like red islets in the green territorial seas, could compare themselves with the nonpareil among Christendom's autonomous cities, the mighty Republic of Saint Mark:

> Venice's might,
> Augsburg's splendor,
> Nuremberg's brains,
> Strasbourg's cannon,
> And Ulm's money,
> Rule the world—
> Sic transit gloria mundi![56]

NOTES

1. Niccolo Machiavelli, "Rittrato della cose della Magna," in *Arte della guerra et scritti politici minori*, ed. Sergio Bertelli (Milan, 1961), 209, 213.
2. The largest, that is, until the formation of the Commonwealth of Poland-Lithuania in 1569.
3. Quoted by Gerald Strauss, *Sixteenth-Century Germany: Its Topography and Topographers* (Madison, 1959), 40.
4. Lenz 1:156 n. 8.
5. Gerald Strauss, ed. and trans., *Manifestations of Discontent in Germany on the Eve of the Reformation* (Bloomington, 1971), 32–33.
6. Heinz Schilling, *Aufbruch und Krise: Deutschland 1517–1648* (Berlin, 1988), 55.
7. Walter Jacob, *Politische Führungsschicht und Reformation: Untersuchungen zur Reformation in Zürich 1519–1528*, Zürcher Beiträge zur Reformationsgeschichte, 1 (Zurich, 1970), 102–3.
8. The shares, syndicates, and contracts were called, respectively, *Kuxen, Gewerke,* and *Käufe.*
9. Hermann Wiesflecker, *Kaiser Maximilian I: Das Reich, Österreich und Europa an der Wende zur Neuzeit,* 5 vols. (Munich, 1971–86), 5:584; Thomas A. Brady, Jr., *Turning Swiss: Cities and Empire, 1450–1550,* Cambridge Studies in Early Modern History (Cambridge, 1981), 122.
10. Christoph Scheurl, "Epistel über die Verfassung der Reichsstadt Nürnberg," in *Die Chroniken der fränkischen Städte. Nürnberg,* vol. 5 (= Chroniken der deutschen Städte, vol. 11) (Leipzig, 1874; reprint, Göttingen, 1961), 791.
11. An emperor-elect was sometimes elected during the emperor's reign, as Maximilian I was. Before coronation he was called "King of the Romans." Frederick III, Maximilian's father, was the last emperor to be crowned in Rome, and only one other emperor, Charles V, was crowned by a pope—at Bologna in 1529. Maximilian himself unilaterally appropriated the Imperial title during a ceremony in Trent Cathedral in 1507.

12. These odd German noble titles—margrave, landgrave, palsgrave, and burggrave—originally specified types of comital functions. A margraviate, for example, was a marcher or border county, while a palsgrave or count palatine was a royal castellan. By the end of the Middle Ages these supercomital titles had become simply titles. That they had not always been so is demonstrated by the fact that the famous charter called the "Privilegium maius," forged in Austria in 1368–69 but purporting to be a charter of the Emperor Frederick I Barbarossa, raised Austria from a margraviate to a duchy. The ruler of Hesse was a landgrave, and the Brandenburg princes were margraves, but some such titles—the landgraves of Alsace and of Thuringia—designated offices not fixed to hereditary rule over particular lands.

13. Quoted by Wiesflecker, *Kaiser Maximilian I.* 3:205.

14. The seventh elector, the king of Bohemia, participated only in the election of king-emperors but not in the governance of the Empire.

15. Brady, *Turning Swiss*, 47.

16. Heribert Raab, "Die oberdeutschen Hochstifte zwischen Habsburg und Wittelsbach in der frühen Neuzeit," *Blätter für deutsche Landesgeschichte* 109 (1973): 69–101, here at 80–85.

17. Wilhelm Karl von Isenburg, *Europäische Stammtafeln: Stammtafeln zur Geschichte der europäischen Staaten*, 2d ed. (Marburg, 1956), tables 82, 84.

18. Hartmut Boockmann, *Stauferzeit und spätes Mittelalter: Deutschland 1125–1517* (Berlin, 1987), 320; Wiesflecker, *Kaiser Maximilian I.* (Austria); Hermann Kellenbenz, "Wirtschaftsleben der Blütezeit," in G. Gottlieb et al., eds.; *Augsburg: Geschichte einer Stadt*, 288 (Augsburg); Hans Mauersberg, *Wirtschafts- und Sozialgeschichte zentraleuropäischer Städte* (Göttingen, 1960), 438 (Basel), 443 (Hamburg); Dieter Kreil, *Der Stadthaushalt von Schwäbisch Hall im 15./16. Jahrhundert: Eine finanzgeschichtliche Untersuchung* (Schwäbisch Hall, 1967), 274 (Schwäbisch Hall). Sums are converted to Rhenish gulden (rhfl.) based on Peter Spufford, *A Handbook of Medieval Exchange* (London, 1986).

19. Karlheinz Blaschke, *Sachsen im Zeitalter der Reformation*, Schriften des Vereins für Reformationsgeschichte, no. 185 (Gütersloh, 1970), 126.

20. Gerhard Benecke, *Maximilian I, 1459–1519: An Analytical Biography* (London, 1982), 139; and see the map in Thomas A. Brady, Jr., *Protestant Politics: Jacob Sturm (1489–1553) and the German Reformation* (Atlantic Highlands, N.J., 1995), xix.

21. Martin Luther, *D. Martin Luthers Gesammelte Werke: Tischreden* (Weimar, 1916), 4:240, lines 43–44, no. 4342.

22. Machiavelli, *The Prince*, ch. 12.

23. Rochus Freiherr von Liliencron, ed., *Die historischen Volkslieder der Deutschen*, 5 vols. (Leipzig, 1865–96), 3:448, stanza 6.

24. The German terms are, respectively, *Marschall, Truchsess, Schenk,* and *Kammerer.*

25. Lorenz Weinrich, ed., *Quellen zur Verfassungsgeschichte des Römisch-Deutschen Reiches im Spätmittelalter (1250–1500)*, Ausgewählte Quellen zur deutschen Geschichte des Mittelalters, vol. 33 (Darmstadt, 1983), 399, no. 95.

26. His grandson, Emperor Ferdinand I (r. 1556–64), partitioned Austria among his three sons, whose capitals lay at Vienna, Graz, and Innsbruck, and the lands were not reunited until after the Thirty Years' War.

27. It has frequently been held that the Burgundian-style reforms introduced by King Maximilian in his hereditary lands were the models for the German territorial regimes, but the point remains unproved. On this controversial point, see Wiesflecker, *Kaiser Maximilian I.* 1:237–38, 5:205–10.

28. Karl Zeumer, ed., *Quellensammlung zur Geschichte der Deutschen Reichsverfassung in Mittelalter und Neuzeit*, 2d ed. (Tübingen, 1913), 2:174

29. Of the sixty-eight dioceses in the Empire, twenty had no temporal lordship and were therefore not prince-bishops. Almost all of them lay in the eastern tier of the Empire: the northeastern and Baltic lands, Bohemia, and Austria.

30. The chapter's rights in territorial government varied. The chapter had permanent rights of co-governance at Würzburg, but only while the see was vacant at Mainz.

31. Quoted by Brady, *Turning Swiss*, 19.

32. Strauss, *Manifestations of Discontent*, 11.

33. Matern Berler, "Chronik," in Louis Schneegans, ed., *Code historique et diplomatique de la Ville de Strasbourg*, 2 vols. (Strasbourg, 1845–47), 2:110–11.

34. Quoted by Brady, *Turning Swiss*, 243.

35. Günther Franz, ed., *Quellen zur Geschichte des Bauernkrieges* (Darmstadt, 1963), 37.

36. Quoted in ibid., 131 n. 1.

37. Strauss, *Manifestations of Discontent*, 181. One reason why Franconia was a major center of noble resistance was that in this region, uniquely in the Empire, territorial rule had devolved upon possessors of low justice and not, as was normal, on the possessors of high justice (i.e., for blood crimes) alone.

38. Hanns Hubert Hofmann, ed., *Quellen zum Verfassungsorganismus des Heiligen Römischen Reiches Deutscher Nation 1495–1815* (Darmstadt, 1976), 72, lines 8–11.

39. Götz von Berlichingen, *Mein Fehd und Handlungen*, ed. Helgard Ulmschneider, Forschungen aus Württembergisch Franken, vol. 17 (Sigmaringen, 1981), 106.

40. Franz Irsigler and Arnold Lassotta, *Bettler und Gaukler, Dirnen und Henker* (Cologne, 1985), 47.

41. Johann Geiler von Kaysersberg, *Die Emeis: Dis ist das buch von der Omeissen, und auch Herr der könnig ich diente gern* (Strasbourg, Johann Grüninger, 1516), fol. 28ᵛ; and the following quote is at ibid., fol. 22ʳ.

42. Geiler, *Die Emeis*, fol. 28ᵛ.

43. Erasmus to Justus Jonas, Louvain/Leuven, 10 May 1521, in *Collected Works of Erasmus*, vol. 8, *The Correspondence of Erasmus, 1520–1521*, trans. R. A. B. Mynors (Toronto, 1988), 206, lines 180–84, no. 202.

44. Specklin, no. 2167.

45. Wiesflecker, *Kaiser Maximilian I.* 1:79, 5:156.

46. Julius von Minutoli, ed., *Das kaiserliche Buch des Markgrafen Albrecht Achilles: Kurfürstliche Periode 1470–1486* (1850; reprint, Osnabrück, 1984), 382.

47. Eberhard Isenmann, *Die deutsche Stadt im Spätmittelalter 1250–1500: Stadtgestalt, Recht, Stadtregiment, Kirche, Gesellschaft, Wirtschaft* (Stuttgart, 1988), 220.

48. *Deutsche Reichstagsakten, mittlere Reihe*, 5:1171, no. 1597.

49. Quoted by Heinrich Lutz, *Das Ringen um deutsche Einheit und kirchliche Erneuerung: Von Maximilian I. bis zum Westfälischen Frieden 1490 bis 1648* (Berlin, 1983), 81.

50. Ibid., 82–83.

51. As with geographical names, "high" and "low" refer not to cultural or social distinctions but to altitude. High German is spoken in the South, Low German in the North, and Central German in the middle. The zones are defined by sets of sound shifts that spread through some German-speaking regions but not others during the Middle Ages. Early New High German is the early modern (since ca. 1350) form of modern standard German.

52. Lutz, *Das Ringen um deutsche Einheit*, 80.

53. Heinz-Otto Burger, *Renaissance, Humanismus, Reformation: Deutsche Literatur im*

europäischen Kontext (Bad Homburg v.d.H., Berlin, and Zurich, 1969), 146; Lutz, *Das Ringen um deutsche Einheit*, 88.

54. Peter Burke, *The Italian Renaissance: Culture and Society in Italy* (Princeton, 1986), 76.

55. Burger, *Renaissance, Humanismus, Reformation*, 244–45.

56. Brady, *Turning Swiss*, 9.

2

STRASBOURG AND
THE UPPER RHINE

In all of Germany no land is to be compared with Alsace.
—Sebastian Münster

One of the most important characteristics of all the Germanies of modern times is the representation of their continuities with earlier times not by a central state or a capital city but by regions, some of which descend from very remote eras. This principle—German history is regional and local history—was enunciated a hundred years ago by Karl Lamprecht (1856–1915). Today it is the immovable foundation of all German social and political history.

THE UPPER RHINE VALLEY

The region of the Upper Rhine Valley is best imagined from a point high above Basel, where the Rhine breaks through the ancient Jura Mountains and turns to begin its long run to the North Sea. From this imaginary roost a bird's-eye view looks northward down a great trench or graben, which formed when the earth's crust rose and collapsed remote ages ago. It lies between two mountain walls, the higher Black Forest to the east and the gentler Vosges to the west, both younger than the eroded Jura. These natural walls protect the Upper Rhine without in the least isolating it from the higher, cooler, and poorer uplands on its flanks, Swabia to the east and Lorraine to the west. At the region's two ends, the river leads away to different landscapes, downstream to the Middle and the heavily urbanized Lower Rhine and to the sea, and upstream to the pre-alpine terraces of Switzerland, the passes of the Central Alps, and the sunny plains of Lombardy.

Shifting to other vantage points atop the conifer-clad crests of the Black Forest and the Vosges, the gaze tumbles down toward the Rhine, past the spurs and ridges on which perched the nobles' castles, over the foothills clad in vineyards and orchards, down to the alluvial plain, densely speckled with villages and dotted with small towns and an occasional city. The Rhine of 1500

40

was not the tamed, canalized river of recent times but a braided stream full of twists and meanders, offering destruction and death in the spring floods and swift passage downstream for people and goods in other seasons. Along its margins lay marshes, mostly still unsettled in that era, while higher up the great alluvial plain, which is broader on the western (Alsatian) bank than on its eastern counterpart, forms one of Europe's most fruitful lands. It is riven and sustained by the smaller streams that flow down to spill their waters into the mighty Rhine: the Kandel, Dreisam, Elz, Kinzig, Rench, and Murg out of the Black Forest; the Ill, Fecht, Leber, Breusch, Moder, and Sauer out of the Vosges.

At the end of the Middle Ages, the Upper Rhine's abundant water and deep, fertile soils supported the rich mixed agriculture—grain, orchards, and vineyards—that nourished its towns and cities, with their solid, familiar manufactures—cloth, metalwares, and books—and their well balanced combinations of local and long-distance trade. Goods had to be moved along safe and established ways, and at Strasbourg the region's major trade routes crossed: the north-south route that linked Europe's two richest regions, northern Italy and the Netherlands, and the east-west route that linked South Germany and lands further east to Lorraine, Burgundy, and the kingdom of France. The chief trading axis, however, was the great river itself, a highway but no boundary. Both banks spoke the same language, Alemannic German, and in the northern sector both banks belonged to the same ecclesiastical dioceses, Strasbourg and Speyer, though upstream the river divided the diocese of Basel from that of Constance. Politically, the Rhine formed the spine of the German Southwest, where the brilliant growth of late medieval particularism had shaped a rich and varied region which contained no major territorial powers. Its leading princes were the margraves of Baden, whose lands lay on the Rhine's east bank; western Austria, then governed from Ensisheim in Alsace rather than, as later, from Freiburg im Breisgau; and further downstream the prince-bishop of Strasbourg, whose lands also straddled the river. The rest of the region was ruled by a large and varied corps of Imperial counts, barons, knights, and abbeys, plus the free cities, ranging from Basel and Strasbourg, both stretching upward toward twenty thousand souls, down through the middling towns of four to eight thousand persons—Colmar, Sélestat, Offenburg, and Hagenau—to tiny Zell am Harmersbach, whose eighty-five citizens huddled in a creek valley in the Black Forest. Great, middling, and small, the Upper Rhenish towns kept close ties to the land. Some very small ones, such as Zell, had mostly farmers for burghers, and others housed whole guilds of agricultural workers, such as truck gardeners and vinedressers, while their nobles commonly maintained both town houses and rural chateaux.

Not that relations between town and countryside always ran smoothly, for although the region was sharing in the general economic recovery around 1500, troubling signs were appearing in the villages. Borne on a wave of rising population, the upswing created strain that sharpened the farmers' grievances against their economic superiors—the noble seigneurs, the clergy, and the Jews—whose customary incomes and usury held the countryside in what seemed, to the farmers, to be a hostile and greedy grip. Grievances led to actions, and in 1493 on the Upper Rhine's west bank arose the rural conspiracy called the *Bundschuh*. The farmers sensed opportunity for improvement, for grain prices were reviving, and further southward, the "peasants"—a noble epithet for all Swiss—had already "become their own lords."

In many respects, the Upper Rhine Valley around 1500 looked like a wealthier, and perhaps more sedate, counterpart to the Swiss Confederacy. Since the collapse of royal power in Germany after 1250, the peoples of both of these political landscapes had grown accustomed to maintaining law and order by means of self-help. Their primary instruments were federations of small powers, for, like Switzerland, the Upper Rhine lacked dominant princes, and its powerful neighbors—the Elector Palatine and the dukes of Lorraine and Württemberg—maintained interests in the region but did not dominate its political life. Only one power in living memory had seriously threatened the region's richly articulated local liberties. This was Charles the Bold (r. 1467–77), the last Valois duke of Burgundy, who in the 1470s had tried to seize both Lorraine and the Upper Rhine to fill the gap between his Burgundian and his Netherlandish possessions. He reaped a whirlwind, as the whole region exploded in his face. The Upper Rhenish powers mobilized their Lower Union and, allied with the Upper Union (i.e., the Swiss Confederacy), took, tried, and executed the Burgundian governor. They then smashed three Burgundian armies, and in January 1477 they left Duke Charles's frozen, naked corpse on the field of Nancy. The Burgundian Wars brought the age of Upper Rhenish particularism to a brilliant climax, in which the black bull of Uri fluttered beside Strasbourg's red-and-white, Zurich's blue-and-white beside Hagenau's Imperial eagle, and Schwyz's crossed red banner beside Basel's black-and-white bishop's crozier. Together the allies—farmers, burghers, and knights—smashed the expansive "Latin tyranny" of the Burgundian state. It was the greatest, most splendid vindication of local autonomy, of particularism.

By the end of the fifteenth century, the whole region north of the Swiss Confederacy nevertheless seemed to become ever riper for consolidation under a major dynasty. For one thing, the ties between the Swiss and the Upper Rhenish powers were broken by the Swabian War of 1499, and although Swiss victories in the field brought two more Rhenish powers into the Confederacy, Basel and Schaffhausen in 1501, there Swiss expansion stopped—approximately along the present boundary between Switzerland and Germany. The niche left by this separation was filled by the House of Austria, whose prestige in the Southwest the Bavarian War of 1504 brought to new heights. In that year King Maximilian's spokesmen on the Upper Rhine promised the small powers that their monarch would "plant a rose garden around them with his own gracious hands and protect them with both wings of the eagle."[1] A whole generation of Upper Rhenish publicists—humanists mostly—rushed in to glorify the House of Austria and the monarchy, and when the emperor in 1512 pressured many of the region's powers into the Swabian League, the chief instrument of Habsburg influence in South Germany, the black eagle soared even higher over the Southwest. Maximilian, however, had become too deeply enmired in the Italian Wars to cultivate his German clientele, and his grandson and successor, Charles V, never appreciated the region's possibilities. When the Swabian League conquered the duchy of Württemberg in 1519 and offered it to Charles in return for the members' war costs, a councilor, the Brabanter Maximiliaan van Bergen urged that "this land of Württemberg is a large and important territory," the key to control of the Southwest,

> and Your Royal Majesty can procure no greater advantage than to bring it into Your Majesty's hands. This is so, because it lies in the middle of the Holy Empire and borders on some of Your Royal Majesty's hereditary Austrian lands. . . . Your Majesty should also consider that he could thus all the better maintain law and order in the Holy Empire.[2]

The House of Austria was deeply engaged elsewhere, and though Charles took Württemberg, the Habsburgs did not hold it long. The Protestant Reformation both benefited from and hardened this deep fragmentation of the Southwest.

THE CITY OF STRASBOURG

The relative weakness of the princely dynasties on the Upper Rhine magnified the influence of its cities, especially Strasbourg and Basel. Strasbourg, the larger of the two, was the metropolis of the Upper Rhine. It lay out on the plain, just below where the River Ill, Alsace's lifeline, receives the Breusch before running down to the Rhine. Strasbourg also sat at the crossroads of the Ill route with the great east-west road, which came over the pontoon Rhine Bridge the city owned, maintained, and guarded. The city's walls, last widened in 1441, embraced about 620 acres and sheltered some twenty thousand souls, more than three thousand of whom were full citizens—adult male heads of household who had inherited, married into, or purchased rights of citizenship. Their city was guarded by a tremendous circuit of walls, studded with towers and bastions and pierced by ten gates and a massively fortified water gate through which the combined Ill and Breusch flowed into the city's numerous and busy canals. Church spires dominated the city's skyline: the wondrous thirteenth-century cathedral with its characteristic profile dominated by two towers and a single spire, then the tallest in Europe; six other parish churches, most of them served by collegiate chapters; the houses and churches of nine male religious orders and nine women's convents (of which two had double communities);

and several dozen chapels. To the welfare of citizens and strangers alike ministered the great hospital, founded in 1315, several other hospices, a hospital for syphilitics, a lazar house, a poorhouse, an orphanage, and a dozen or more public bathhouses. Over all ruled the secular and temporal authorities, civic magistrates, and bishop.

CONSTITUTION

From its basis in the commune conceived essentially as a "fraternity of fathers,"[3] that is, adult male heads of household, Strasbourg's regime had gradually evolved a corporately constituted oligarchy which, in normal times, made up in local wisdom and proximity for its lack of formal legitimacy. Measured against Italy, where communal regimes had evolved into true states, the regime of every Imperial free city, Strasbourg included, remained small in size, uncomplicated in structure, and relatively close to its communal roots. No German-speaking city ever lived for long under the rule of a single lineage, as Florence did under the Medici and Milan under the Visconti and the Sforza. This difference of political fates owed less to differences in size or wealth than it did to the Empire's vast networks of military federations, which provided regionally based security under the umbrella of Imperial political legitimacy and dampened the scale and frequency of both external wars and internal factional strife. The latter, according to Italian writers, formed the two principal reasons why the Italian path of communal liberty produced dynastic despotism.

When Strasbourg's constitutional evolution came to a close in 1482, its regime represented a common type of urban government in the Empire, the "guild regime," based on the representations of a noble minority and a majority of merchants and artisans organized corporately in guilds. Such regimes normally had a large council composed of all burghers or of the officials of their guilds, a small council of representatives of the nobles and the guilds, and even smaller privy councils, filled for life terms by cooptation. Once evolved, these last became the regime's core and the city's true rulers. They operated through the small council, which exercised the city's judicial authority and fell heir to the powers of the largely atrophied larger councils.

Like the Roman Republic, Strasbourg created new institutions but rarely abolished the old ones. Its regime contained two structures of authority, each of which preserved one stage of the commune's evolution: the older Master and Council referred to the noble stettmeister and the small council, while the younger Schöffen and Ammeister designated the three hundred ruling officials of the city's twenty guilds and their president, the ammeister, who was by law a guildsman.

All strings in both structures led into the combined small council and privy councils, called the Senate & XXI, whose normal complement of fifty-one or fifty-two came one-third from the nobility and two-thirds from the guilds. The small council's members—six nobles and twenty guildsmen—sat for two-year terms, while the privy councilors, whose ranks included the stettmeister and ammeister, were coopted for life. These magistrates ruled over a citizenry organized into two noble societies (*Constoffeln*) and twenty guilds, through which the entire economic life of the city was regulated under the watchful gaze of the privy council called the XV. Another such council, the XIII, called "the old gentlemen" [*die alten Herren*], dealt with diplomacy and war.[4]

Male citizens were eligible for magistracies at age twenty-five if married, thirty if single. Most magistrates came either from the noble families—who barely managed to fill their allotted one-third of magistracies—or from the wealthy merchants and rentiers who clustered in the richer guilds. Since around 1450 a firm solidarity had developed between nobles and wealthy commoners, cemented by frequent intermarriage, common patterns of property ownership, and a common culture. This social merger and political alliance was fairly typical of the free cities of the Southwest, though it differed markedly from Nuremberg's mercantile patriciate, from the rentier patriciates of the francophone free cities to the west—Metz and Besançon—and from the purely mercantile elites of the northern Hanseatic cities.

Strasbourg's prince-bishop, whose predecessors had long ago removed their residence to Saverne, a small town at the foot of the Vosges, no longer ruled the city. He was nonetheless still head of the church, and much of his diocesan administration (*Offizialat*) remained at Strasbourg. The cathedral chapter, which was wholly immune from civic jurisdiction and quite independent of the bishop, consisted of twenty-four beneficed aristocratic canons whose religious duties were performed by paid deputies, and like the other collegiate churches—St. Thomas, Old St. Peter, and New St. Peter—the cathedral also housed one of the city's parishes. Most of the collegiate churches' beneficed canons were not Strasbourgeois, and many were not natives of the Upper Rhine. Not only did the cathedral chapter require such elaborate proofs of lineage that, as Erasmus once joked, Jesus Christ could not have joined their ranks, but the other collegiate churches' canonries and the convents—except for the mendicant women—had come into the possession of outsiders, chiefly Swabians, who flocked from the poorer neighboring dioceses into this rich one. This clerical invasion fostered a growing sense of strangeness between laity and clergy which, though not yet divisive, would soon become so.

The common foundations of church and commune were the several thousand burghers' households, linked by kinship, friendship, shop, neighborhood, guild, parish, and confraternity. The male heads of most of them belonged among the three thousand members of the twenty guilds, six hundred in the huge Gardeners' Guild alone. Some households were headed by women, and so were some shops, mostly widows of masters, for at Strasbourg women did not belong to the guilds, much less possess whole guilds of their own, as they did at Cologne. They suffered, too, from the general tendency around 1500 to place women under closer supervision, and the cathedral preacher, Johann Geiler von Kaysersberg, protested in vain that a law of 1501, which required all single women to have male guardians, violated sound custom. Many women belonged to the work force, of course, and much of the city's regulating and supervising activities directly concerned women, but the regulators and supervisors themselves were all men.

The burghers' ideal householder was an adult male who kept "fire and smoke," that is, maintained himself and his wife, children, and servants—perhaps six to seven persons on average. Once admitted to a guild, he became a full, active citizen and a member of the commune, bound to pay taxes, to help guard the walls, and to serve in the guild militia, which would soon be made obsolete by the rise of the German mercenaries, the lansquenets.

Strasbourg's political body, the commune, paraded in the flesh once a year, on *Schwörtag*, the first Tuesday of January, when the burghers assembled to witness the installation of new magistrates and renew the civic oath which specified their rights and their duties to one another. To witness the commune assembled on *Schwörtag* was to view the city as its ruling magistrates wished the world to see it. In the cold light of early morning the burghers gathered by corporation, the fifty to eighty male patricians at their two clubs (*Constoffeln*), Zum Mühlstein and Zum Hohen Steg, and the guildsmen at their respective guildhalls strewn across the city. Then, arrayed behind its president (*Oberherr*) and fourteen other officials (*Schöffen*), each guild filed through the streets toward the cathedral, the glory of the Upper Rhine, which stood at the city's heart. In Cathedral Square, below the single spire, the twin towers, and the great rose window, and before the great west portal, studded with the entire Christian faith carved in stone, a high wooden scaffold stood. On it were arrayed the magistrates, while the guildsmen and the nobles moved into their accustomed places in the square to witness the installation of magistrates and to renew their own oath of citizenship. The commune here on view was not the city, but its official body, which, although its ranks excluded the young, the women, the journeymen, and all noncitizens, was held to represent them all, for the commune consisted not of individuals but of households. The corporate character of the city thus embraced all who enjoyed its protections and who shared its burdens.

POLITICAL CULTURE

Strasbourg in 1500 was a very large and very successful example of the guild-based city-state of late medieval South Germany. Its political stability rested on two zones of trust. The first zone lay between the nobles and the leading families of the guilds. Following social struggles around 1420, the noble lineages had come to accept sharing power with the guilds and intermarriage and even economic cooperation with the merchants; in return, they retained one-third of the magistracies, a share which allowed the commune to take advantage of the nobles' wealth, leisure, and experience in government and war, without running the risk of restoring noble political domination. This arrangement was tolerable because only twenty or so noble lineages remained in the city, and in each generation they could at best produce around eighty adult males to serve the commune "with word and deed" [*mit Rat und Tat*]—in peace by means of their counsels and diplomatic service, in war by means of their swords.

The second zone of trust lay between the magistrates and the ordinary guildsmen. They were linked, of course, by the intermediary offices of the three hundred Schöffen, fifteen per guild, who comprised the infrequently consulted large council or assembly of the commune, but who also governed their respective guilds under a president, who was invariably a magistrate. In 1500 this structure also still furnished the commune's military power, a guild militia armed from the civic arsenal, though the rich of all guilds were obliged to keep horses in the civic stable and serve as cavalry, along with the nobles. The chief social fact that guarded this system was the distribution of wealth in the taxpaying body of citizens, which resembled not a pyramid, as in modern class societies, but a turban or an onion, with its largest layers in the bulging middle. At Strasbourg, as in all city-states, political stability and civic unity depended on the trust between the ruling elite and this bulge of middling citizens, who at all costs had to be prevented from siding with the much smaller class of poor citizens below them. That this could be maintained, at least in ordinary times, is illustrated by Strasbourg's tax system. The direct tax (*Stallgeld*) was levied on all property except for exemptions. The rate was fixed by the regime, but the taxpayers calculated their own assessments, and no record was kept of the sums they paid. In fact, the three collectors (*Stallherren*) were forbidden by law to make any record of payments, which is why, unlike some other cities, such as Augsburg and Constance, Strasbourg left no tax registers. With all allowance for evasion, this system suggests a high level of voluntary compliance, else the city would have been bankrupt, and this in turn suggests a relatively strong degree of political trust between the regime and the citizens who counted. This solid structure acquired its ultimate form in 1482, when Ammeister Peter Schott (1427–1504) presided over the final revision of the *Schwörbrief,* Strasbourg's constitution and the pact on which the burghers annually swore.

ECONOMY

At Strasbourg the constitution and the economy complemented one another relatively well, for the manufacturing and trading economy of Strasbourg around 1500 possessed deep roots in a rich hinterland, and the city lacked the sort of dominant export industry, which elsewhere—at Augsburg, for example—swelled a few guilds at the expense of others and magnified the gap between rich and poor. Strasbourg had its important commercial firms, true, but none to rival the Great Ravensburg Company or the firms of Nuremberg, much less the Fuggers and Welsers of Augsburg. And although the city produced some goods that commanded respect abroad, notably its cannon, it had no export product to rival Memmingen's fustians, Constance's linens, and Nördlingen's lodens. Its cloth, "Strasbourg gray," was stout stuff, but not fine.

Its great range of crafts made Strasbourg a broadly important center of artisanal organizations, both of masters and of journeymen. It was the headquarters, for example, of a stonemasons federation that stretched across the whole southern half of the Holy Roman Empire, and its journeymen's organizations were noted for their strength and forwardness in the defense of their rights. Then, too, the city's ties to a rich, densely populated hinterland swelled the victualing trades— gardeners, butchers, and bakers—while the immense volume of the transit commerce both helped to fill the civic treasury and supported a large number of retailers and service trades. Taken together, the various aspects of the civic economy reinforced a balance among the many trades, and therefore among the guilds, and kept the gap between extremes of wealth and poverty relatively modest.

Not that the city lacked poor and unfortunate people, for the general recovery of population and economy also swelled the numbers and the mobility of the poor. So much so that an investigation in 1523 turned up about four hundred destitute persons, and the gap between their needs, reckoned at 2,311 rhfl. per year, and the welfare fund's income, about 419 rhfl., prompted the magistrates to organize a new, civic system of poor relief. They also forbade public begging, because "a great number of beggars have come from many lands to live at Strasbourg, and many take alms illicitly, lead shameless lives, send their children begging, and give bad example by letting their children stand freezing before the churches in the winter."[5]

The fear of unrestricted begging was surely intensified by the spread of a new disease, syphilis, which appeared at Strasbourg in 1495 and, under the local name of "the French disease" ('s *Französel*), quickly became a major object of official concern. The numbers of victims, whose affliction aroused such terror that even the lepers, themselves largely segregated in the Good People's House outside the walls, would have nothing to do with them, rapidly outstripped every possible accommodation. The houses set aside for syphilitics were soon full, and the physicians to treat them too few, so that Geiler had to complain in 1501 of the inadequate care. The magistrates' solution was to install a good-hearted merchant, Caspar Hoffmeister (ca. 1466–1532), as protector of the victims of syphilis, but to give him no funds, so that his wards had to be supported through charity. The good man himself bought a house for them in the Finkweiler district and renovated it at his own expense. The credit for the establishment of a civic hospital for this purpose (*Blatterhaus*), therefore, belonged not to the magistrates but to Hoffmeister and to his mentor, Geiler the preacher.

EXTERNAL RELATIONS

Its extensive trading relations and the geographical discrepancy between its economic hinterland and the city's own territory meant that Strasbourg, like all city-states, kept a sharp eye on its external relations. The city's traditional foreign policy rested on two pillars, friendships with the Swiss Confederacy to the south and with the Elector Palatine to the north. This policy had reached its grand peak in the Burgundian Wars, when Old Peter Schott had raised the war cry against Burgundy and the Strasbourgeois had fought and died alongside their allies. Then, at the turn of the century, the two pillars crumbled. The Swabian War of 1499 smashed the old friendship with the Swiss, who routed their former comrades in the Battle of Dornach,[6] and the Bavarian War of 1504 crushed the Palatine power and with it the head of the German princely opposition to the emperor. Into the vacated political space flowed, though temporarily, the revived Austrian power under Maximilian, which forced itself dramatically on the Strasbourgeois in the summer of 1504. The king, who had brought his army westward from Swabia to make war on the Palatine elector, entered the city by torchlight one night to see and be seen in the region's metropolis. He lodged with the Knights of St. John, received praises and presents, toured the treasury and the arsenal, and rode away to finish reducing the Palatine fortresses in the region. With the war over and the king at the peak of his power, Austrian influence flowed into the Upper Rhine, and for a time Strasbourg even joined the Habsburg-sponsored Swabian League.

The Austrian surge brought into its service the pens of Strasbourg's devotees of the new Italianate learning, humanism, who quickly turned their talents from the praise of old friends, the Swiss, to the king and his dynasty. One such man was Strasbourg's town clerk, Sebastian Brant (1457–1521), a former employee of the now-Swiss city of Basel and a graduate of its university. King Maximilian's largesse evoked a stream of pro-Austrian propaganda from Brant and others of this first generation of Alsatian humanists, who defended the German monarchy's legitimate claim to the Roman *imperium* and gnashed their teeth at the "Latins," chiefly the French. The pacesetter was Jacob Wimpheling (1450–1528) of Sélestat, who had owed his Heidelberg professorship to Palatine patronage before he came to Strasbourg in 1501 to live by tutoring upperclass boys. Wimpheling turned his wrath on the French and the Swiss former comrades alike, attacking the latter as rebels against those he called their "natural lords."[7] At Strasbourg this pro-Austrian turn of sentiment ran against the city's long-established political traditions, which were particularist and federal, pro-Swiss and pro-Palatine. The turn offered one more sign that the old late medieval order was changing.

Maximilian's appearances in 1504 and again in 1507 at Strasbourg, where no reigning king had been seen for many decades, reminded the Strasbourgeois of the powers that ruled the world beyond the borders of their own Upper Rhine. The free cities, including Strasbourg, stood more steadfastly to the king than the princes and nobles did, and they viewed with great suspicion the efforts, which the reform party among the Imperial Estates initiated in 1495, to give the Empire a new central, but not royal government. Their merchants, true, shared the deep longing for more law and order and security of travel, but the urban regimes were wary of central institutions controlled by the princes, which might mean heavier taxes and new tolls. The cities preferred to serve the Empire by serving the king, which they did in many ways—with credit, cash, troops, guns, officials, and hospitality. Strasbourg was no exception, although, conforming to its economy, situation, and traditions, the city maintained a more independent attitude than did Nuremberg or Augsburg.

THE CITY AND THE BISHOP

The free cities' support and the favorable situation after the Bavarian War presented the possibility of a political consolidation of the Upper Rhine Valley under Austrian rule. Maximilian's gaze, however, moved in other directions, toward Hungary and Italy, and he was willing to live and let live in the West. Strasbourg gained proof of this benign royal attitude in the next episcopal election. The late Bishop Albert (d. 1506) had been a Wittelsbach prince of the Heidelberg line, just like his predecessor and first cousin, Bishop Robert (r. 1439–78). In 1506 Count Palatine Frederick tried to become the third consecutive Wittelsbach in the see, and, despite his house's disaster in the war of 1504, he failed by only one vote. The successful candidate, a Thuringian count named William of Honstein (ca. 1470–1541), was a client of the Hennebergs, whose head, the late Elector Berthold of Mainz (r. 1484–1504), had since 1495 usually led the Estates' opposition to Maximilian. If not an Austrian partisan, William was at least a neutral, and he chose to be consecrated on Laetare Sunday 1507 in his own cathedral, where no bishop had been consecrated since 1353 and, some said, probably since 1260. Odder still, he took Holy Orders and said his first Mass, something Bishop Robert, his predecessor but one, had never done. When the consecration Mass reached the Gloria, a sensation occurred, as the royal chaplain stopped the Mass, and an hour later strode in King Maximilian himself, dressed in black—his son and heir, Philip the Handsome (d. 1506), had died in Spain the previous September—and wearing the collar of the Order of the Golden Fleece. The king had often visited Strasbourg, where he had many clients and many debts, but this visit was a great surprise. After Mass he hustled the young bishop off to dinner, leaving the latter's guests, the magistrates, in the lurch. They had to return that evening, and after Stettmeister Ott Sturm (d. 1518) presented the city's congratulations and gifts, William "promised the city much, how he would be their good neighbor and friend." Indeed, some weeks later, noted City Secretary Sebastian Brant, William requested that the Senate & XXI "support him in both his ecclesiastical power and watch over his lands and people and loyally protect them. For his part, if something threatens the city, he will aid them with life, land, and people." "This is what he said," Brant mused, "but it is not what he meant."

A BISHOP'S ENTRY

Nothing confirmed and displayed Strasbourg's serene security on the Upper Rhine so much as did the regime's relations with its new bishop. William had been elected on 9 September 1506 by the cathedral's canons, nobles all, who gathered in the cathedral's choir under the eyes of the city's magistrates. The latter stood in their customary position atop the great stone rood screen that divided the cathedral's dark, Romanesque choir—the clergy's cathedral—from the light, Gothic nave—the burghers' church.[8] Down below, the door guards let "very many folk into the choir," and more than two hundred pushed their way into the adjoining Carthusian cloister. After Mass the canons retired to perform their one indispensable function: to elect the next bishop of the diocese and lord of the entire region between the crest of the Vosges Mountains and the summit of the Black Forest, and from just below Colmar nearly to the northern borders of Alsace. Shortly after noon, the canons escorted their choice, Count William of Honstein, into the cathedral and moved to lift him, as customary, onto the high altar to be seen by all, "but as he was a vigorous man, he jumped onto the altar without help." After the Te Deum, the guards were dismissed, the ammeister lunched with his colleagues at his guildhall, and by midafternoon Strasbourg drifted off into the normal sounds of a late summer afternoon, the snores of the after-dinner nap. As the bishop-elect rode away, "some said that his words suggest that he won't come back very soon." Return he did, however, on 4 October 1507 for his solemn entry and enthronement.

At the Cronenbourg Gate early on 4 October gathered the civic escort, sixty mounted and armored nobles and wealthy guildsmen, at their head two stettmeisters and two ammeisters. Seventy more magistrates and patricians waited with the ruling stettmeister and ruling ammeister at the Horse Market, where they would receive the bishop in his own cathedral city. Everywhere, wrote Sebastian Brant, "there was a wondrous number of people to be seen, for though many stood to in armor or were arrayed along the barricades, all the houses and their windows were stuffed with people." All the streets were filled with people, "for an uncountable number of country folk from all quarters came to town early that morning in order to see this grand entry."

His was indeed a grand entry, for Bishop William was bringing six hundred mounted dignitaries, about a thousand horses in all, but the magistrates refused him permission to enter their city until he had sworn to respect its liberties. Even then, they took plenty of precautions. They marked out his route—through the Cronenbourg Gate and along Cronenbourg Street to the Bishop's Castle Gate and then into the Wine Market, eastward along the High Bridge into the Small Horse Market and then into the Horse Market proper to be greeted by the official civic party, then southward through Cathedral Street to the open area around the cathedral—and closely guarded all the other gates but one. Inside the city, nearly half the guildsmen were mustered in two parties, 530 receiving body armor and "good poleaxes, long pikes, or guns," and the other 980 getting what was left. They were joined by 500 armed peasants from the civic territory and the patricians' country estates. When the villagers arrived in the evening before the bishop's entry, they made a deep impression on the burghers. "Many were very pleased," records Sebastian Brant, "that these loyal folk had come so far on such short notice, that they arrived so well armed and ready for action, and that they were so loyal and obedient, so that the city of Strasbourg could justly regard them with all the more affection and trust." Some of these "loyal and obedient" folk came, in fact, from villages which had been involved in the conspiratorial movement "to establish a *Bundschuh*, so that everyone would join them and strive to become masters of this land."[9] On this day the armed peasants made a fine impression, especially the Kentzingers and Ettenheimers from across the Rhine, who landed and marched in through the Butchers' Gate to the beat of their own drums, then moved over the Hangman's Bridge and past the great slaughterhouse to the guildhall Zur Möhrin. They and the other peasants stacked arms at three designated guildhalls, got their suppers, and settled down for the night.

On the morning of entry day, the armed guildsmen and villagers—2,071 men in all—split into six bands commanded by magistrates—one of them, old Bartholomäus Barpfennig (d. 1518), had more than thirty years ago marched off to fight the Burgundians—stiffened by guns and gunners. Bearing banners that showed the city's holy patrons, the Madonna and Child, the bands guarded the vulnerable points, especially the canal bridges over which the bishop's riders might try to veer southward into the city's heart.

The city's clergy remained out of sight until the cathedral's bells pealed for the bishop's approach, whereupon they poured out of the cathedral and into Cathedral Street, which ran northward from the cathedral to the Horse Market. When they pushed beyond their assigned places to crowd in among the burghers, the angry ammeister decided not to make a scene: "But we should see to it in the future that the barrier is not raised for them. And we should tell the priests what they are to do and that they should stick to the old ways." That was the Strasbourg way, telling the priests "what they are to do" and to "stick to the old ways." This time, however, the clergy were allowed to rush forward down Cathedral Street and over the Stone Bridge, eager to see their new lord. In the van came the canons of the city's three principal collegiate churches, Old St. Peter, New St. Peter, and St. Thomas, with crosses and banners. Though less aristocratic than the cathedral canons, they were the cream of the city's own clergy, among them prominent burghers' sons and some accomplished, if few renowned, scholars. After them came their schools' pupils—Strasbourg had no civic schools yet—followed by the aristocratic Knights of St. John and the Teutonic Knights, the mendicant friars, and the Williamite monks. Back at the cathedral's west portal stood the diocese's auxiliary bishop, who was flanked by the cathedral's canons, vicars, and chaplains, plus visiting abbots and other prelates. Civic magistrates guarded the doors into the cathedral's choir, and once the approaching dignitaries slipped through and into their places, the great west doors were to be flung open, "and everyone would be allowed into the cathedral." The rite of entry was at once Imperial, princely, episcopal, clerical, and civic.

When, near ten o'clock, the bishop's party finally appeared before the Cronenbourg Gate, Stettmeister Ott Sturm dismounted to greet Strasbourg's titular lord on behalf of its true lords. "Worthy prince and gracious lord," this armored veteran of the Burgundian Wars intoned in broad and melodious Alemannic, "the stettmeister and Senate of Strasbourg humbly receive Your Princely Grace and rejoice at Your Princely Grace's arrival, and they declare themselves Your Princely Grace's servants." Then Sturm's party remounted to escort the visitors through the Cronenbourg Gate into the city. Straight across the old suburb called "in Stone Street" and through the Bishop's Castle Gate they rode, more than a thousand riders between the solid lines of armored and armed men. At the Wine Market the procession turned left past the Almshouse and moved eastward with Tanners' Ditch (*Gerbergraben*) at its right hand. Soon it came to the High Bridge, past one of the city's oldest noble clubs, called At the High Bridge (*Zum Hohen Steg*)—where the Sturms and other noble lineages belonged—to Treasury Bridge, at the south end of which stood the Treasury, called the Pennytower. Coming now into the Horse Market, the escort joined the waiting ammeister's party to make a single rank of armored horsemen, about 140 strong, with upright lances braced on their saddles' bows. Before them sat their mounted bishop, a proud, erect, young man in a long black coat and white choir robe, on his head a black beret. This scene posed less a confrontation of church and state than of territorial power and city-state, for at William's sides sat his territorial officials—counts of Hanau-Lichtenberg, Bitsch, and Fürstenberg—the Imperial vicar, and an agent of the metropolitan, the archbishop of Mainz.

Across from these great lords, the ammeister, stettmeister, and other officials, who had been waiting for about four hours, bared their heads to honor the bishop, then quickly covered again. All the city's bells now rang out, as the bishop and his party turned right to mount the Stone Bridge and to approach the cathedral, turning right once more to gain Cathedral Square before the great west portal. There William dismounted and donned the cap and mantle of a canon—marking his metamorphosis from a prince into a bishop—while the clergy streamed into the cathedral, followed by the bishop with miter and crozier. Meanwhile, the ammeister and other councilors, who had trailed him to the cathedral's north portal, gave the password—"St. Anne"—and slipped into the church to take their places atop the rood screen.

While the armed burghers and villagers retired for their dinners, inside the cathedral the great organ intoned "Come, Holy Ghost," as the chapter's dean led William into the festively draped choir. Then, after a Te Deum to the accompaniment of all the city's bells, the Mass began. Johann Geiler was to give the sermon, as was his right, from the great stone pulpit built expressly for him, but instead the Mass rushed on to its end, and William hurried out without waiting to give the blessing. It was an inauspicious beginning of what was to be a very troubled episcopacy.

After Mass, Bishop William gave the magistrates a disastrous dinner. Ceremonial dining was taken with utmost seriousness in the German-speaking world, where dining "in the German manner" could take up to seven or eight hours. On this occasion nothing went right, for the food wasn't ready, and when it did come to table, Brant writes, "most of it was cold and tasted bad." There were many entrees for show (schauweszen), he joked, few edible ones (dauweszen), and, alas, no women (frouwenweszen).[10] Truly, Brant remembered with a shudder, "if at a princely meal one intended to present something really vile or horrible to eat, it could scarcely have been done with more skill." Some of the magistrates simply excused themselves and wandered off to find their suppers elsewhere, and next day, as if to repay their bishop in kind, only two local nobles appeared at the Horse Market to joust in his honor.

. Before leaving town, the newly enthroned bishop complained to the civic regime, the Senate & XXI, that he had never intended to bring armed infantry into their city, and that yesterday he had been surprised "to see such a large mobilization of armed citizens and country folk, which need not have taken place on his account." Their numbers "also dishonored the princes and lords who rode in with him as vassals, for the senators willy-nilly showed them a hostile face." The bishop's complaint "displeases the Senate," came the magistrates' icy reply, for "it pertains to the Senate of the city of Strasbourg to order, mobilize, command, and forbid in their city, just as they please. Enough said." And so he rode away, leaving behind a very bad impression. He was, after all, a "foreigner"—in good Alemannic a hergloffner—and "though he has repeatedly said that he wants to be a good neighbor," noted Brant, "one can't much trust the slick ways of this Thuringian." The weary militiamen turned in their arms and went home to sleep in their own beds; the country folk returned to their villages; and the magistrates returned to the everyday business of the town—getting after loose dogs, loose tongues, butchers who gave short weight, and burghers who dumped garbage into the streets. The entry had cost them, to be sure, 700 pounds from the civic treasury, plus a good many senatorial digestions, but in return they had taught their new bishop a 250-year-old lesson: within the walls of Strasbourg they, not he, were the lords.

THE PROBLEM OF REFORM

The new bishop proved to be full of surprises. At Corpus Christi (22 June) 1508, to universal astonishment, he celebrated Mass in his cathedral, the first bishop to do so, Brant's researches revealed, since John of Lichtenberg (r. 1353–65), "who was so humble and serious about divine services that he consecrated his priests and churches himself and did other things a bishop should do, but which normally other bishops refuse, out of arrogance, to perform and leave to their auxiliary bishops." Thus, sighed Brant, "are Christ's sheep treated throughout the world, for the proper shepherds have become lords and give their sheep over to the care of hirelings. The sheep are accustomed to fleeing when they see the wolf, so that the faith is going down the drain." The astonishing news spread far and wide, and a Ruffach priest named Matern Berler (d. after 1555) noted that William's act "awakened in his subjects a great respect, favor, and love toward their pastor. Such things were done in olden times," but nowadays the bishops "want to be princes and not pastors or shepherds to their flocks. Therefore they will meet the wrath of God, and the saying of Ezechiel 34[:2] will be fulfilled: 'Woe be to the shepherds of Israel that do feed themselves.' I fear that in time the sheep will flee their shepherds."[11]

The worldly young bishop had more pastoral surprises in store, for in Holy Week 1508 he blessed the oils and led in the penitents on Holy Thursday (5 April 1508) and conferred minor and major orders on Holy Saturday. On Easter Sunday he sang High Mass "and acted so properly [*wesenlich*] and nobly that everyone was pleased." Perhaps, just perhaps, this vigorous young bishop, who was so anxious to show himself more bishop than prince, might turn to the problem that had defeated his predecessors for sixty years, the reform of the clergy in the diocese of Strasbourg. And, truly, on 9 March 1509 William published his reform ordinance, which he hoped would supply the point of departure for a great effort to reform the diocesan clergy. It aimed to turn the church's resources, now locked up in livings, other incomes, monastic houses, and Mass stipends, to the recruitment and training of a clerical corps capable of meeting effectively the laity's spiritual needs. His two Wittelsbach predecessors had failed miserably at this task of redeployment, which had formed the heart of reform programs from the anonymous author of the *Reformation of Emperor*

Sigmund (1437) to Nicholas of Cusa (1401–64) to the anonymous Alsatian who authored the unpublished *Book of the Hundred Chapters and the Forty Articles.*

The problem of pre-Reformation clerical reform is better understood for the diocese of Strasbourg than for any other part of the Holy Roman Empire. The essential difficulty was that the church had not adapted to the changed situation and needs of the laity since the beginnings of the late medieval depression around 1350. In Lower Alsace the clerical corporations, collegiate chapters, and monasteries and convents had responded to the ensuing agrarian depression by investing their capital in rural debt and entering the wholesale trade in grain and wine. The move succeeded, though at the price of immobilizing the church's resources, on the one hand, and fueling anticlericalism among the farmers and craftsmen, on the other. At the same time, the encroachment of lay elites on the powers of the bishop, abbots, and other prelates—in the early fifteenth century Strasbourg's bankers tried to take over the diocese's finances—crippled the capacity for reform of even the most conscientious bishop. "The church" was rich on the Upper Rhine, but only in the sense that many of its highly protected and independent-minded corporate bodies were wealthy. The protection of clerical wealth by the temporal authorities, who, either privately or officially, benefited greatly from it, frustrated all major programs for reform.

The church's wealth had the added effect of drawing clerical entrepreneurs and graziers from poorer regions, especially Swabia across the Black Forest. Such outsiders contributed to a deteriorating familiarity between clergy and people and helped to fuel the traffic in benefices, which reached a peak of commercialization in the pre-Reformation decades—not least because the papal chamberlain at Rome was Johann Burckhard (1450–1506), a local Alsatian boy made good. On every hand, religious houses and corporations, protected by the civil authorities or powerful nobles, often with the connivance of Rome or the emperor, soaked up the church's substance, and when temporal authority backed clerical resistance to reform, as Strasbourg's Senate & XXI did against Bishop William's reform ordinance in 1509, episcopal reform was doomed, especially when Rome sided, as it did in this case, with the resisters and their lay friends and supporters. The solution, which all the fifteenth-century reform writers recognized—a pastoral, salaried (and perhaps married) clergy and learned, pastorally mind bishops—could not be supplied if the current patterns of property relations and clerical recruitment were not changed.

At Strasbourg no one diagnosed this situation better, or spent himself more freely trying to remedy it, than did Johann Geiler, who for a generation censored the city's morals from his pulpit in the cathedral. Geiler was a man of the free cities, born and bred. Born at Schaffhausen on the Rhine above Basel, he grew up at Kaysersberg in central Alsace, studied philosophy at Freiburg and theology at Basel, and taught theology at Freiburg for a short while before coming to Strasbourg. Though he was called and sponsored by Ammeister Peter Schott (1427–1504) and his fellow magistrates, Geiler believed the keys to reform lay with the bishop and the clergy. From 1492, as episcopal reform faltered, he turned his unflagging energy to the censorship of the burghers' morals and to their religious instruction. For his wit, wisdom, and austere life, Geiler was admired and loved by people, high and low, at Strasbourg, in Alsace, and all over South Germany.[12] King Maximilian, who esteemed him "on account of his teaching and his holy life," heard Geiler preach in 1504 about the coming cataclysm. "If the pope, bishops, emperor, and king do not reform our unspiritual, insane, godless way of life," Geiler preached, "God will raise up someone who can do it and who will restore our fallen religion. I wish I could see that day and be his disciple, but I am too old. Many of you will see him."[13]

Geiler's late medieval Catholic revivalism dramatized the importance of collaboration between human striving and God's grace. In the memorable phrase of nominalist theology, "facientibus quod in se est Deus non denegat gratiam," in effect, "do your best, God will do the rest."[14] He embodied this earnest, easy doctrine of salvation in a moralistic monastic ideal cut to the laity's cloth, ascetic in spirit, mystical in piety, but worldly in context. As he once said, "We are all one order, and Christ is our abbot."[15] Geiler thought of the church as he thought of the commune, a social body in which laity and clergy mutually supported each other with material and spiritual goods respectively. In his sermon cycle called "The Ants," which compares human society to a well-ordered anthill, Geiler affirms that the working folk "pack the wine and corn into our cellars, so that we might celebrate the Mass and do our other duties, not so that we can collect three or four whores apiece, as the proud college boys at the bishop's court do."[16] If the clergy are nourished "by your labor," he told his congregation,

> we should repay spiritual goods for these material ones. But to have a lot of property, rents and dues, wine and corn, and to neglect our spiritual duties, this makes people mad. I don't say this so that you will exclaim: "We should take half the priests' goods away from them, for why should they have so much? They have too much." That is surely true, many a priest has too much, but you shouldn't therefore take it away from him. I don't know what would happen if everyone who has too much should have it taken away.

He wanted his listeners to regard the church as a universal spiritual community, so that "when a priest in Rome reads a Mass in a state of grace, you here in Strasbourg benefit therefrom, and when you here pray the Our Father in a state of grace, the priest in Rome benefits therefrom." It was not an easy idea for the burghers to grasp, for the intensification of local autonomy and communal pride was making distant Rome more distant yet.

For thirty years, Geiler preached this communal-universal gospel of service and spiritual mutuality from the splendidly ornate Gothic pulpit, which Hans Hammerer, at Old Peter Schott's order, had carved for Geiler on one of the cathedral's great pillars. To imagine there Geiler's ascetic face and warning voice is to re-create a religious world deceptively intact, as the man's ornate and mystical moralism fits without seam the pulpit's complexly framed figures.

And yet Geiler could find no lever with which to start this world moving together toward reform. The most pressing need, the redeployment of the church's substance and personnel toward a more intense pastoral program, seemed, absent a revolutionary intervention, hopeless, and it was further frustrated by the clergy's increasing disintegration from civic society and declining respect from the laity. Young Peter Schott (1460–90), the ammeister's only son and himself a future priest, when a schoolboy turned into Latin the Alsatian rhyme: "There are three things you should never let in the door—an old ape, a young priest, and wild bears."[17]

Geiler, Schott's mentor and friend to his parents, recognized that the sense of trust, on which the entire structure depended, was breaking down. Geiler admitted this, when he preached "You laymen hate us priests."[18] What could be done about it? By this time, probably nothing. In 1508, two years before his death, Geiler gave vent to his despair: "The best thing to do is to sit in one's own corner and stuff one's head into a hole, seeking only to follow God's commandments, to do good, and thereby to gain eternal salvation."[19]

On the surface, nothing had changed. The great families continued to endow the convents with their goods and their daughters; creative work went on in the churches, notably the splendid Mount of Olives at St. Thomas; and bells rang out, Masses were sung, and on feast days processions filed through the city's streets. Official piety flourished in the form of civic Masses, such as the Bridge Mass, which commemorated a bishop's attack on the Rhine Bridge in 1392, and in 1513 the magistrates ordered that the greatest civic event, *Schwörtag*, should be blessed by the Mass of the Holy Spirit. Strasbourg around 1500 witnessed innumerable acts of private and public piety, such as the new hospital for victims of syphilis and the hanging of the great "St. Mary's bell" in the cathedral belfry at great risk and expense in 1520. Despite the tensions between clergy and laity, the city of Strasbourg remained, as it ever had been, "ever loyal to the church of Rome." On its banner and on its coins appeared for all to see the city's motto of supplication to its patroness: "O Virgin Mary, please beg your Son to save our city and its people."[20]

During the years around 1500 the Upper Rhine Valley's myriad small powers basked in peace, security, and a self-satisfied enjoyment of traditional liberties. Even more than among their Swiss neighbors, whose autonomies were qualified by their confederacy, on the Upper Rhine the political miracle of particularism had borne its most luxuriant fruits. This lack of effective larger powers, the late Middle Ages' gift to the region, also made it vulnerable to movements and intrusions. During the early 1520s the Reformation movement would sweep in gusts through the region's cities, while in 1525 the great Peasants' War would begin to rage across the land like an avenging, purifying, and heartening storm. These events initiated the Upper Rhine's passage from the age of Christendom into that of Europe of the great powers. By midcentury this once-secure region would become a borderland between the spheres of interest of two great dynasties, Habsburg and Valois, and two great realms, the Holy Roman Empire and the Kingdom of France. At the region's center lay the city of Strasbourg, where all the great forces of this turbulent era—humanism and printing, rural insurrection and urban revolt, Zwinglian militance and Lutheran solidarity, Anabaptist agitation and Protestant intolerance, pedagogical innovation and ecclesiastical reconstruction, and Imperial tradition and French expansionism—struck with special force. Within a few decades, these forces thrust a thriving provincial city into what Lucien Febvre, in a happy phrase, called "the religious heart of the sixteenth century."[21] The city made this passage under the guidance of one man, Stettmeister Jacob Sturm, who led Strasbourg out of its comfortable past as a provincial metropolis and into a troubled future in a world of religious division and of conflict among the great powers.

NOTES

1. Quoted by Wiesflecker, *Kaiser Maximilian I.* 3:185, trans. in Brady, *Turning Swiss*, 78.
2. Hauptstaatsarchiv Marburg, PA 389, fol. 81ʳ, quoted by Brady, *Turning Swiss*, 107–8.
3. I borrow this apt term from Richard Trexler.
4. There were also several "simple members of the XXI," so that the XXI normally numbered around thirty men, including the four stettmeisters (who rotated quarterly) and the six ammeisters (who served in a six-year rotation). No one has solved the riddle of why they were called "the XXI."
5. "Ordnung des gemeinen Almusens auf Michaelis [29 Sept.] anno 1523 angefangen," in Otto Winckelmann, *Das Fürsorgewesen der Stadt Straßburg vor und nach der Reformation bis zum Ausgang des sechzehnten Jahrhunderts: Ein Beitrag zur deutschen Kultur- und Wirtschaftsgeschichte*, 2 vols., Quellen und Forschungen zur Reformationsgeschichte, vol. 5 (Leipzig, 1922), 2:97, no. 43.
6. The Strasbourg banner captured at the Battle of Dornach is still displayed in the Schweizerisches Landesmuseum in Zurich.
7. Guy P. Marchal, "Bellum justum contra judicium belli. Zur Interpretation von Jakob Wimpfelings antieidgenössischer Streitschrift 'Soliloquium pro Pace Christianorum et pro Helvetiis ut respiscant...,' (1505)," in *Gesellschaft und Gesellschaften: Festschrift zum 65. Geburtstag von Professor Dr. Ulrich Im Hof*, ed. Nicolai Bernard and Quirinus Reichen (Bern, 1982), 114–37.
8. The roodscreen was torn down long ago. All following quotes, unless otherwise

identified, are from Sebastian Brant, "Bischoff Wilhelm von Hoensteins waal und einritt: Anno 1506 et 1507," in *Code historique et diplomatique de la Ville de Strasbourg,* ed. Louis Schnéegans (Strasbourg, 1845–47), 2:239–99.

9. Franz, ed., *Quellen zur Geschichte des Bauernkrieges,* 69.
10. The joke, of course, only works in German.
11. Matern Berler, "Chronik," in *Code historique,* 2:110–11.
12. Ibid., 113–14.
13. Specklin, no. 2190.
14. Heiko A. Oberman, "Facientibus Quod in se est Deus non denegat gratiam: Robert Holcot, O.P., and the Beginnings of Luther's Theology," in his *The Dawn of the Reformation: Essays in Late Medieval and Early Reformation Thought* (Edinburgh, 1986), 84–103.
15. Quoted without source by Richard Newald, "Elsässische Charakterköpfe aus dem Zeitalter des Humanismus: Johann Geiler von Kaisersberg, Jakob Wimpfeling, Sebastian Brant, Thomas Murner, Matthias Ringman," in idem, *Probleme und Gestalten des deutschen Humanismus* (Berlin, 1963), 339.
16. Geiler, *Die Emeis,* fol. 28[b].
17. Peter Schott, *Works of Peter Schott (1460–1490),* ed. Murray A. Cowie and Marian L. Cowie, 2 vols., Univ. of North Carolina Studies in the Germanic Languages and Literatures, vols. 41, 71 (Chapel Hill, N.C. 1963–71), 1:226.
18. Geiler, *Emeis,* fol. 28[b].
19. Ibid., fol. 22[a].
20. Francis Rapp, "Préréformes et humanisme: Strasbourg et l'Empire (1482–1520)," in *Histoire de Strasbourg des origines à nos jours,* ed. Georges Livet and Francis Rapp (Strasbourg, 1981), 2:205.
21. The title of Febvre's collected articles, *Au coeur religieux du XVIe siècle,* 2d ed. (Paris, 1968), and of a symposium in his memory held at Strasbourg in June 1975. The symposium's papers were edited by Georges Livet, Francis Rapp, and Jean Rott, *Strasbourg au coeur religieux du XVIe siècle: Hommage à Lucien Febvre,* Société Savante d'Alsace et des Régions de l'Est, Collection "Grandes publications," vol. 12 (Strasbourg, 1977).

3

A MAN OF THE CITY

It is a very miserable thing to feel ashamed of home.
—Charles Dickens, *Great Expectations*

In the ardently localized societies of late medieval Europe, hardly anyone had occasion to be ashamed of home. Even cardinals and eminent courtiers remembered the places of their birth. Cardinal Nicholas of Cusa, the fifteenth-century philosopher and churchman, founded a hospice in his native town of Cues in the Mosel Valley. It exists to this day. In the Empire, when a student registered in the university, he was identified by place or diocese of origin. A birthplace was a signature, an identity card, a point of reference for self-definition; and except perhaps for the emperor himself, Imperial political life was as much a matter of places as it was of persons.

The life of Jacob Sturm began, as it would end, in an intensely local context, the city in which his family had flourished for nearly 250 years. Strasbourg was his place of origin, his point of identity, his home.

HERITAGES

At the end of the 1480s, the small world in and around Strasbourg basked in the afterglow of the Burgundian Wars. Jacob Sturm was born there on 10 August 1489, the second son among the eight or more children of Martin Sturm and Ottilia von Köllen. The Sturms, who had crossed the Rhine from the little free city of Offenburg around 1250, had been ennobled by Emperor Rudolph I in the late thirteenth century. Thereafter the male Sturms often served in civic magistracies, and they remained loyal to the city in 1419, when many noble lineages abandoned the city. Martin Sturm, Jacob's father, served from 1506 to 1521 as a member of the privy council of the XV, and two of his brothers also held magistracies: Ludwig as a patrician senator and Ott as a stettmeister for twenty annual terms between 1484 and 1512.

The Sturms also belonged to the landed nobility. On the Upper Rhine, as in much of South Germany and also in Italy, it was by no means unusual for noblemen to be citizens and even magistrates of free cities. Like many of their

61

kinfolk the Sturm brothers were simultaneously urban patricians and landed nobles, and they held fiefs of the Holy Roman emperor, the Elector Palatine, the bishop of Strasbourg, and lesser Alsatian lords. They also owned an allodial seigneury at Breuschwickersheim, a village located just southwest of Strasbourg.[1]

The Sturms also served the church. Jacob's Uncle Leonhard was a monk of Alpirsbach, a Benedictine abbey at the head of the Kinzig Valley, high in the central Black Forest, and his cousins Ott and Stephan, Uncle Ott's boys, entered the church and got good benefices—livings endowed from ecclesiastical incomes—in local collegiate churches around 1508. The family's special affection nonetheless attached to the local Dominican women, whose many convents were generally favored by local families of the better sort. Margarethe Sturm, Martin's sister and Jacob's aunt, was a nun in the convent of St. Nicolaus in Undis in the suburb called "the Krutenau." Local tongues unused to Latin jokingly called this convent *zu den Hunden*, that is, "among the dogs."[2] Jacob's sister, Clara, was placed in 1508 in the Dominican convent of SS. Margaret and Agnes; and his cousin Magdalene, Uncle Ott's daughter, joined the same house. When possible, the Sturms had themselves interred in the churches belonging to the same order.

To their venerable lineage and their traditions of service and piety, the Sturms united wealth. Martin Sturm owned property in the city and allodial lands at Düttelnheim and Achenheim, and he shared with Ludwig, his brother, the allodial seigneury of Breuschwickersheim, the buildings and incomes from which were estimated later in the century to be worth about 4,800 rhfl. On the whole, the Sturms stuck to the traditional investments of Strasbourg's nobles, land and usury. They owned a number of houses at Strasbourg, but the bulk of their wealth lay in interest-bearing debts, mainly small sums lent to little people, mostly peasants. They did not invest in trade, but neither did they disdain to intermarry with families which did, such as the Wurmsers and the Miegs. Indeed, the close social and economic links between long-established noble lineages, such as the Sturms, and newly made commercial families in the guilds, such as the Wurmsers and Ottilia von Köllen's maternal grandparents, the Schotts, were characteristic of Strasbourg's upper ranks.

Ottilia's grandparents, Peter Schott and Susanna von Köllen, were two of Strasbourg's most remarkable personalities. Old Peter Schott had come to Strasbourg in 1449. He acquired citizenship through his marriage to Susanna, entered the magistracies in 1465, and became late-fifteenth-century Strasbourg's greatest statesman. During the Burgundian Wars of the 1470s, Schott's leadership anchored Strasbourg's place in a strong provincial federation, the Lower Union, which joined the Upper Union (another name for the Swiss Confederacy) to smash the Burgundian power on the Upper Rhine. As ruling ammeister, head of the regime, Schott also presided in 1482 over the ultimate constitutional revision, which secured Strasbourg's internal peace by ending the guild revolts. The atmosphere of peace and civic security, in which Jacob Sturm grew to maturity, owed very much to his great-grandfather's political leadership.

As new in Strasbourg as the Sturms were old, the Schotts floated up on the tide of economic recovery since the mid-fifteenth century. Old Peter was a grain merchant who married into a minor noble family, and his rise reaped clear social benefits for their children. Three of his and Susanna's daughters made good matches with noblemen or rich merchants; Anna, who could write German and Latin, lived as a nun in the Dominican community of SS. Margaret and Agnes; and Young Peter (1460–90), their only son, became a learned priest and gentleman-lawyer. These children were nurtured in a domestic atmosphere of learning and fervent piety, to which Susanna gave the tone. Her hand reached beyond their home into the convents of Dominican women, of whom the Schotts, like the Sturms, were especially fond, and into the commune. Angered by the poor quality of preaching in the cathedral parish, the story goes, Old Peter Schott in the early 1480s brought the great Alsatian preacher Johann Geiler von Kaysersberg to fill the preaching post in Strasbourg's cathedral. Not only did the Schotts endow the cathedral's pulpit to the tune of 2,230 rhfl., but as ammeister Peter also ordered to be built a magnificent stone pulpit, carved with nearly fifty saints, from which Geiler censored Strasbourg's morals for the next thirty years.

Two distinct streams thus formed Jacob Sturm's heritage: from the noble Sturms came lineage, connections to the church, seigneurial status, landed wealth, and a tradition of magisterial service; from the commoner Schotts came connections to the city's vibrant merchant community, great political prestige, a fervent familial piety, and dedication to learning. Equally embedded in their native city and region, both families lived, worked, and died within sight of waters that flowed down to form the Upper Rhine. This local centeredness, as intense and as rich as were to be found in Europe's other zones of vibrant urban life—Italy and the Netherlands—characterized the Strasbourg, the Alsace, the Upper Rhine, and the German Southwest into which Jacob Sturm was born.

CHILDHOOD

At Jacob's birth in late summer 1489, Martin Sturm and Ottilia von Köllen had been married for about five years. He and his siblings—despite chronic ill health, Ottilia von Köllen lived another twenty years and bore at least three more children—probably grew up in a house in Peacock Lane, near St. Martin's Church[3] and near Uncle Ott's mansion called At the Large Camel. From the beginning, Jacob's life was marked by an event just after his birth, the death in 1490 of his great-uncle, Young Peter Schott, at the age of thirty. This scholarly young priest had stirred great hopes in his doting parents, who had managed their son's life "with over-much indulgence and affection," and in the teachers who hoped that he would make Strasbourg a center of learning and piety.[4] To make good this grievous loss, the elder Schotts and Jacob Sturm's parents and tutors collaborated to fashion the boy in the idealized image of his dead kinsman, the learned clergyman cut down in his prime. One guardian of this image was Great-Aunt Anna, Young Peter's sister and a learned Dominican nun, who in 1499 had the ten-year-old Jacob copy out a letter in which her late brother had once sent her some religious counsels. Another was Johann Geiler, a familiar of the Schott household and, probably, of the Sturms' as well.

A further strong push in this direction came from Jakob Wimpheling (1450–1528), whose arrival at Strasbourg in 1501 intensified the project for making a scholarly clergyman of Jacob Sturm. A native of Sélestat/Schlettstadt, a middling free city south of Strasbourg, and a former professor and rector of the University of Heidelberg, Wimpheling settled in with the Williamite monks on the southern arm of the Ill River and began lobbying Strasbourg's magistrates to establish a civic Latin school. When this project failed, he earned his keep by preparing boys of good family, among them Jacob Sturm and Peter, his brother, for the university.

Wimpheling had known about these Sturm lads before he arrived at Strasbourg. A principal patron of Young Peter Schott, whose writings he prepared for a posthumous edition, in 1499 Wimpheling had sent a composite volume of ancient and modern (mostly Italian) texts on education, which he inscribed "to Jacob Sturm, son of Martin Sturm." The boy added below—the first lines that survive in his hand—"this volume belongs to the grandnephew of the most venerable gentleman, Peter Schott, burgher of Strasbourg 1499."[5] At the age of ten, therefore, well before he came under Wimpheling's direct influence, Jacob Sturm identified himself—and presumably his future—with his family's plan to groom as successor of and replacement for that "most venerable gentleman," his great-uncle. Jacob's parents were heart and soul for this project, reported Wimpheling, who soon became a familiar in their home and later, when Jacob was studying at Freiburg, resided in the Sturms' mansion and took his leisure at their country seat in Breuschwickersheim.

As mentor to promising young scholars, Wimpheling employed dedicatory letters to his books as a means for pressing his counsels upon them. In one such letter of 17 November 1501, he reminded Jacob Sturm of his chosen path. "You know," the mentor wrote, "that I prefer you to study theology and that both God and serious men hold the study and practice of law in low esteem." "I therefore urge and exhort you," he continued, "to prefer the love of God, the friendship of those around you, good reputation, the honor of your entire family, and the health of your own soul, to all of which the study of theology conduces."[6] "Consider," Wimpheling drove the point home, "that Peter Schott, the brother of your maternal grandmother, regretted that he did not dedicate himself at an earlier age to the study of true learning," that is, theology. Ever and again, Wimpheling strove to keep the boy on this path, and always with the same arguments. "You once said," he reminisced later, while Sturm was studying theology at Freiburg, "that your ultimate wish is to begin the study of sacred things." And Wimpheling knew how to neutralize Sturm's sense of familial obligation, for "since you have brothers, who *deo volente* can continue your lineage, you can aspire to the priesthood and to celibacy." He praised the boy for "openly displaying your intention of following the example of Peter Schott, your grandmother's brother, for chastity and modesty," and asked, "what could be more pleasing, what could be dearer to me, than to see you imitate in manly way the noble conduct and great learning of Peter Schott?"[7] Jacob's decision for the priesthood, Wimpheling testified, was also "your father's fondest wish" and "your mother's strongest desire."[8] This barrage of reinforcing counsel helped to shape Sturm's trajectory until his collision with the Protestant Reformation.

FORMATIONS

AT THE UNIVERSITY

An aspirant to the life of a learned clergyman might acquire an education at home, as Jacob Sturm did, but he needed the polish and learning of a university education to move among important men and, not incidentally, to win out in the competition for benefices, endowed ecclesiastical offices. In Sturm's youth the surest path to clerical preferment ran through the universities, and in his native region the schools of choice were Basel, Freiburg, and Heidelberg.[9] On Wimpheling's advice, twelve-year-old Jacob was sent in 1501 to study at Heidelberg, the capital of the Rhine Palatinate, where his mother's people had relations. There he was admitted to the arts faculty on 29 September. The faculties were still divided, as they had been for generations, into two philosophical traditions, called the "old way," or *via antiqua*, and the "new way," or *via moderna*. These traditions owed allegiance to the great scholastic doctors of the past, respectively to Thomas Aquinas and Duns Scotus and to William of Ockham. Although Geiler and Wimpheling were *moderni*, Jacob Sturm enrolled as a "Scotist" (i.e., follower of Duns Scotus) in the *via antiqua*.[10]

Wimpheling, less concerned about in which faculty his boys enrolled than about how they might spend their spare time, bombarded Sturm and his other Heidelberg pupils with exhortations to industry and virtue. "Some people want great riches," he wrote during Sturm's first semester, "they would gaze on gold, drink out of silver, don bright silks, take delight in spectacles, rage after love, . . . languish from the pleasures of the flesh, waste time in gambling, reek of wine, rush to Rome, look around that city, and accumulate benefices." His own pupils, he hoped, would scorn such temptations and pursue philosophy out of a desire to have time for the study of wisdom, to pursue virtue, to become involved in humane studies, to learn agreeable habits and detest vices, to become accustomed to morality in all things, . . . to persevere in good letters and virtues, to bear all things with equanimity, to restrain passions and motions of the soul, to quarrel with no one, to love chastity, to fear God, to love parents and friends, to reflect on the immortality of the soul, to dread the inextinguishable fire of hell, and never to lose sight of the hour of death, . . . so that God, our Creator and Redeemer . . . may receive you at last into His eternal kingdom among the blessed.[11]

Whether such exhortations kept his boys from catching songbirds, going about in disguise, or poaching in the elector's fishponds—all pleasures forbidden by university statutes—we do not know.

Jacob Sturm's studies at Heidelberg ended abruptly in the summer of 1504, when a Hessian army, allied to King Maximilian against the Elector Palatine in the War of the Bavarian Succession, appeared before the city's gates. "At that time," Wimpheling later recalled, "Sir Martin Sturm and Matthias Pauwel . . . , my very good friends, asked me what would happen to their sons, whom at my advice they had sent to Heidelberg three years before. Then they recalled the boys."[12] Now fifteen years old, Sturm was sent to continue his studies at Freiburg im Breisgau, which lay on the Rhine's right bank between Strasbourg and Basel. He registered at Freiburg on 27 July 1504, which means that he just missed King Maximilian and Queen Bianca Maria, who entered Strasbourg by torchlight on 9 August 1504. He also missed Geiler's sermon a week later, in which the great moralist warned the crowned heads that one day God would raise up a prophet "who will restore our fallen religion."[13]

Wimpheling visited Jacob at Freiburg and brought Peter Sturm there to study in 1506, though the choice of Freiburg for Jacob still sat poorly with Martin Sturm's Dominican relatives, who wanted him sent to the Dominican theological faculty at Cologne. "But I said," Wimpheling commented, "that whatever Jacob might learn at Cologne, he can also learn at Freiburg."[14] At Freiburg Sturm enrolled not in law, where the great Ulrich Zasius (1461–1535) held sway, but in theology in the five-year preliminary course of biblical studies (*cursus biblicus*) for theologians. He lectured simultaneously as a Scotist in the arts faculty, giving Aristotle's "De generatione animalium" in 1505 and the "Nicomachean Ethics" in 1506–7 and 1508. He probably received minor orders by 6 May 1507, when he preached a Latin sermon to the theological faculty assembled in the Dominican church. Among his fellow students were several who were headed for distinguished clerical careers, such as the Swabian Johann Eck (1486–1543), three years Sturm's senior and also a Wimpheling protégé, and two Alsatians, Mathis Zell (1477–1548) from Kaysersberg and Wolfgang Capito (1472–1541) from Hagenau, both future Protestant reformers at Strasbourg.

In 1508, for unknown reasons, Peter Sturm shifted to Heidelberg and the law, and Jacob left the university for good. He came home from Freiburg without a theological degree, though in later years he was acknowledged an adept student of the Bible. Jacob was now twenty years old, time to begin a career, and he probably hoped to get a benefice, as two of his first cousins, Uncle Ott's sons, recently had. The world he had known as a boy was passing. On 10 March 1510 Jacob stood at Geiler's deathbed, and next day he looked on as magistrates and burghers packed the cathedral to bid farewell to the man who had worn himself out in the cause of their reformation.

POSSIBLE FUTURES

Jacob Sturm came home from Freiburg in 1508 at the right moment, and he was of the right age, background, and disposition to be caught up in the cultural movement known to its devotees as "good letters" and to history as "humanism." The terms refer to the literary culture which since the 1450s had been streaming over the Alps from Italy. This new fashion promoted the study of classical Latin and (later and less successfully) Greek and urged concentration on grammar and rhetoric rather than logic and philosophy. Down to the 1510s, when Erasmus's influence spread through the Empire, the German humanists were neither very productive nor very militant. Nothing was further from their minds than reform of the church, and they quickly swelled the ranks of benefice-hunting place-seekers in the church. When Jacob Sturm joined it in 1508, the circle around Jakob Wimpheling at Strasbourg contained a number of young men who had precisely this goal in mind.

In adopting the life of a gentleman-clergyman, Sturm completed his own fashioning after the model of his late kinsman, Young Peter Schott. Not the Schott of sentimental family memory, nor the Schott of later legend—a reforming humanist poisoned in his prime by "the priests"[15]—but the real Peter Schott, who had been a pampered only son of a doting family and a fashionable, well-educated clergyman of leisure. After the best education money could buy—private tuition, the famous Latin school at Sélestat, philosophy at Paris, and law at Bologna—Schott had returned to Strasbourg, secured a prebend at New St. Peter's, and announced that "as soon as I have satisfied the mandatory year of residence for my canonry at New St. Peter's, God willing, I shall study theology at Paris."[16] Somehow, the right moment for Paris and theology never came, as Schott settled into a gentleman's life in his parents' home at Strasbourg, toured the spas of the Black Forest, and visited his sister Ottilia in her chateau at Wasselonne. It was a fine way of life, devoted to family, friends, parties, and "good letters," all supported by the church, that milch cow of local aristocracies.

Wimpheling's circle contained a number of ambitious young men, mostly Strasbourgeois and other Alsatians, who had flocked to what has justly been called his "mediocre program."[17] It rested on two pillars: mildly Italianate learning, which Wimpheling retailed as the best preparation for the professions, and moral self-discipline, which he drummed into his pupils from an early age. The latter began with the simple precepts he drew up for young Peter Sturm in 1499: "Love God. Honor your parents. Get up at dawn. Make the sign of the cross. Put on your clothes. Wash your hands and dry them. Wash your mouth, but not with water that is too cold, which will damage your teeth."[18] Older boys received the advice Wimpheling gave to the twelve-year-old Jacob Sturm in 1501 against the three vices to which he with some reason thought students might be especially vulnerable—drunkenness, gambling, and fornication. On the positive side, Wimpheling taught his boys a combination of Christian and burgher values—frugality; constancy; perseverance in learning and virtue; equanimity; self-control; modesty; love of God, parents, and friends; and concern for one's immortal soul—which ought to lead them to ecclesiastical preferment, scholarly eminence, and everlasting salvation. Wimpheling's program thus drew on personal and social resources to promote mainly individual benefits; he did not much think of its wider consequences for the church and the problem of clerical reform. Reform to Wimpheling meant chiefly that the church ought to prefer the learned and deserving ahead of the merely well born.

If one of Sturm's mentors, Wimpheling, taught that the church's substance ought to nourish the friends of "good letters," another, Johann Geiler, taught that the clergyman's ideal ought to be a life of service to the laity. "The Son of Man," he once preached, "is not come to be ministered to, but to minister. All rulers, temporal and spiritual, should hear this and should believe not that the community belongs to them, but they to the community. The community exists not for their sake, but they for its sake. They are the community's servants."[19] This was Geiler's way, framed in the spirit of the great reform tracts of the previous century, such as the famous *Reformation of the Emperor Sigmund*, which had called for an end to the benefice system and for refashioning the clergy from lords into servants, "for the meanest parish church is worth more than the grandest of monasteries."[20]

Between these two notions of clerical life, Wimpheling's scholarship and Geiler's pastoral service, Sturm chose the former. He did not seek ordination as a priest, but he did seek from the church a living to support his life as a literary gentlemen. It was for such a life, after all, that he had been fashioned since boyhood.

A GENTLEMAN CLERGYMAN

Humanism spread along networks of friendships and alliances, nourished by frequent correspondence. Sturm's preparation for this world had begun during his Freiburg days, when Wimpheling had taken him to meet influential friends of good letters, such as the publisher Johannes Amerbach (1444–1513) at Basel and the great humanist and Hebraist Johannes Reuchlin (1455–1522), who had known Young Peter Schott. Back home, Sturm made himself useful in modest ways, such as helping Sebastian Brant see one of Wimpheling's own books through the press, and began to establish his own reputation for learning. When, for example, a Swabian scholar wrote to ask about an Augsburg woman who allegedly lived without eating, Sturm replied—based on the opinion of Gianfrancesco Pico della Mirandola (1469–1533), who had visited Strasbourg in 1505—that the phenomenon was natural rather than miraculous.

Sociability formed a very important part of humanist culture, and Wimpheling and the other friends of good letters gathered occasionally to dine, drink, declaim, and discuss. Their ranks included some gifted young scholars, such as the Lorraine schoolteacher Matthias Ringmann (1482–1511), called "Philesius," who in 1507 helped to prepare the great Waldseemüller world map for the press, and also some opportunists. One of the latter was Thomas Wolf, Sr. (d. 1511), the son of a rich Eckbolsheim farmer and a Strasbourgeoise, who became a gentleman-clergyman and pluralist at Strasbourg and headed the notorious Wolf clan. He had four nephews, of whom two, Cosmas and Johann Andreas, ranked among the most notorious clerical seducers of young women at Strasbourg. Wimpheling, a strong critic of concubinage and sexual impropriety in others, corrected the Wolfs privately but maintained their friendship. The remainder of Wimpheling's circle, which a contemporary called "learned and virtuous," was more respectable than the Wolfs, but not much more distinguished. A list composed around 1514 of a "literary sodality of the city of Strasbourg" mentions "the four noble Sturms"—Jacob, Peter, their elder brother Friedrich, and either their youngest brother Stephan or their father—and some others who fit more closely the Wimpheling mold: ambitious, well-educated men from modest backgrounds in provincial towns.[21]

The amusements of this circle were as modest as their attainments. We see them as early as 1505, when Martin Sturm invited Wimpheling and friends to his chateau at Breuschwickersheim, where they amused themselves by examining a Roman cult object, which a farmer's plough had turned up in a local field. We see them, too, in the memorial volume they prepared for Amandus Wolf (d. 1504), one of the notorious Wolf brothers, which contained *On the Misery of the Human Condition* by the Bolognese humanist Giovanni Garzoni, a teacher of Peter Schott's, who managed to discuss the human condition at length with only one Christian allusion. Jacob Sturm's contribution, a Latin couplet, is the only thing he ever published.

THE SHADOW OF ERASMUS

Into this milieu in the mid-1510s, the great Erasmus of Rotterdam (1466/69–1536) shot like a meteor. His program made Wimpheling's obsolete, for he taught the reform of learning through a return to the classics, the reform of piety through a return to the original meaning of Scripture, and the moral amelioration of society through the general reform of education. The first sign of his influence on the young humanists at Strasbourg was their plunge into the direct study of pagan antiquity, classical Latinity, and Greek, which carried them toward a great new world, the international republic of letters, and drew them a further step away from the everyday, local world, where an ignorantly superstitious laity, in the Erasmian view, clung to its rituals, blind to the edifying wonders of ancient philosophy.

A dramatic moment in the Erasmian conquest of Wimpheling's circle came in August 1514, when the great man himself stopped on his way upstream to Basel. The Strasbourgeois laid on a splendid dinner—Wimpheling and Brant presiding—in the house of the Knights Hospitaler, called St. John's on the Green Island, which the Netherlander repaid in his best coin, effusive and elegantly framed praise. At Strasbourg, he wrote, he had discovered "the virtues of all the most celebrated city-states: Roman severity, Athenian wisdom, and Spartan self-restraint."[22] One man in particular caught his eye, the twenty-five-year-old Jacob Sturm, whom Erasmus called "that incomparable young man, Jacob Sturm, who adds luster to his distinguished family by his own high character, who crowns his youth with a seriousness worthy of riper years, and whose incredible modesty lends great charm to his uncommon learning."[23] Fifteen years later, his opinion had not changed: "First . . . among the nobles now for doctrine, sincerity, candor, and prudence is the most noble Jacob Sturm, to whose counsels not only the illustrious city of Strasbourg is indebted, but nearly all of Germany as well."[24] Erasmus's praise, in turn, evoked lifelong devotion from Jacob Sturm, whose defense of Erasmus's New Testament against a local Dominican reached Erasmus's ear and won Sturm further praise as "a young man of excellent wit and good judgment, unusually learned and a very great supporter of mine."[25]

The value of Erasmianism to Jacob Sturm and his friends is difficult to overestimate, for it led them from Wimpheling's cluttered and provincial eclecticism into a broader, even international fellowship of the friends of good letters. By 1515 they were busy learning Greek, a passport to this fellowship, and making contacts with other important men. Jacob Sturm, for example, cultivated the Sélestat humanist Beatus Rhenanus (1485–1547), who gave him a copy of his edition of Hungary's leading Latin poet, János Csezmiczei (1434–72), bishop of Pécs.

Jacob Sturm's reputation gradually spread through such contacts and became fixed by the literary battles of the 1510s. Polemic is the typical weapon of the ambitious against the established, and ritualized combats in print helped to make the German-speaking humanists into a self-conscious group with a heightened sense of common interests and solidarity. By means of the literary battles of the 1510s, the Wimpheling circle merged into the larger party of good letters. Chief among them was the Reuchlin affair, the most important monument of which, the *Letters of Obscure Men* (1515–17), defended Reuchlin against the Dominicans of Cologne by means of ridicule, hyperbole, and mockery and extolled the ranks of Reuchlin's real and alleged partisans, including "Jacob Sturm, a nobleman, who is said to be a good Latinist."[26]

JACOB STURM AS HUMANIST

Although he had published nothing to warrant this reputation, other evidence confirms Jacob Sturm's commitment to the program of good letters in the Erasmian sense. In 1522 Florenz von Venningen, chancellor of the Palatinate, solicited his advice on the reform of studies at the University of Heidelberg. Sturm's reply opens with a critique of the education he had obtained at Heidelberg. "Eighteen years ago, at the age of twelve," he wrote, "I learned grammar and logic there, which have partly been wiped from my memory and partly improved in the interim." The method of instruction then, he complained, "was most pedestrian, traditional, and poor, and contrived assignments were intentionally given to squander talents and misuse the precious hours." Aristotle's books were read, though "by a most unfortunate teacher, who was nearly ignorant of both Greek and Latin, so that neither he who read nor any of his hearers understood it—a great waste of money, time, and ability, and devoid of benefit to the students."[27] Logic and rhetoric, Sturm thought, should be learned not from the old writers but from George of Trebizond or Rudolph Agricola ("whose ashes rest here in Heidelberg at the Franciscans' house"), and Aristotle from the new, humanist translations or from the paraphrases by the French humanist, Jacques Lefèvre d'Étaples. Sturm also thought that a professor of classics should be hired, who "should know both Latin and Greek and be able to teach his students the rudiments of the Greek language."

Sturm also had some ideas about theological studies, "albeit I never heard theology at Heidelberg, I fear that things there are much as in other German universities." "In my experience [at Freiburg]," he wrote, "nothing was taught but those scholastics, called 'doctors,' who wrote after the Gothic and Vandalic invasions had destroyed all good letters." Their writings, Sturm complained, "neglect the New and Old Testaments, esteem none but one Master of Sentences [Peter Lombard], and contain many curious things which are not conducive to Christian piety." The faculty should leave to the mendicants "their Thomas and Scotus" and appoint two theologians to hold daily lectures on the Bible, one on each testament, "taking also as seems good from the older Greek and Latin theologians—Origen, Basil, Gregory Nazianzen, Chrysostom, Jerome, Hilary, and Augustine."

A comparison of Sturm's proposal with his mentor's parallel one shows how far the Erasmian movement had carried him beyond Wimpheling's influence. Although Wimpheling admitted that much modern (i.e., scholastic) theology was conducive neither "to the honor of God, to the salvation of souls, nor to the progress of Christian states," and though he lamented the backwardness of Latin speech and style and condemned "neglect of the Bible and the Fathers," he balked at banishing scholastic textbooks for humanist ones.[28] Sturm had crossed the line, which Wimpheling never did, to the party that scorned most of what had been thought and written between the Germanic invasions and the fourteenth century.

A PRELATE'S SECRETARY

In 1517, after a decade of *dolce far niente*, the twenty-eight-year-old Jacob Sturm embarked on a career. By July of that year he became secretary to Count Palatine Henry (1487–1552), sixth son of the late Elector Palatine Philip and brother of the current elector. Only two years Sturm's elder, Henry already held benefices as provost of two cathedral chapters, Aachen and Strasbourg, the beginnings of his brilliant career as one of the great pluralist prelates of the age. When he became Henry's secretary, probably on Wimpheling's recommendation, Sturm began to style himself "clergyman," a sign of his embarkation on a career. Indeed, he had hitched his wagon to a mighty horse, for as provost of Strasbourg, Count Henry administered the wealth of the cathedral chapter, a body so aristocratic, Erasmus once joked, that Jesus Christ could not have joined it. For more than six years, from July 1517 to November 1523, Sturm served as secretary and looked after the prince's far-flung properties, incomes, and interests. He traveled a good deal in Henry's service, and when the prince moved to be prince-provost of Ellwangen in 1521 or 1522, Sturm acted as his agent at Strasbourg.

Sturm's new career began in hardening times. Following two bad harvests in Alsace, vines froze during the winter of 1516–17. Around Obernai, Joss Fritz tried to breathe new life into the *Bundschuh*, a conspiratorial network which penetrated many Alsatian villages, including Martin Sturm's Düppigheim. Wimpheling, who in 1517 took up residence in his parish at Sulz in Lower Alsace, expressed the somber mood of the later 1510s in a remarkable "Prayer of the Common Man to God," which voiced the just complaints of the peasants, "who nourish the whole of society and in return have only their poverty."[29]

Meanwhile, Jacob Sturm's new post introduced him to the world of high politics, in which the great German dynasties strove to hold and increase what they had. It was a sign of the times that his political initiation occurred in this world, not in the communal-federal world his great-grandfather had known. Sturm's most important task was to support Count Henry's struggle to gain the prince-provostship of Ellwangen in the Jagst Valley of Lower Swabia. Henry played on the Lutheran danger to gain backing in Rome and on local sentiment to win over the burghers of Ellwangen, and his victory, aided by "the power of his brothers, kinsmen, and friends," made a powerful impression on his young Alsatian secretary.[30]

Grateful patrons reward faithful servants, and Count Henry, as befitted such a powerful young prince, tried to reward Sturm with a good benefice. A rich store of clerical benefices flowed from the rights an emperor acquired at his election, and Count Henry got control of some of the appointments that were bargained away during the Imperial electoral negotiations for Charles V. Henry intended one of them, the next vacant canonry at St. Stephan's, Strasbourg, for his secretary. Alas, Sturm's old friend Othmar Nachtigall, then living at Augsburg, had been promised the same benefice, and the ensuing quarrel between two benefice-hunting disciples of Wimpheling went all the way to Rome and dragged on until 1523. It became so bitter that Nachtigall spread the charge that Sturm would be an absentee and intended, in any case, to leave the clergy. This may well have been so, for Sturm had earlier been frustrated in his efforts to secure a good benefice at Mainz through Wolfgang Capito, the Hagenauer whom he had known at Freiburg. Now a councilor of the elector of Mainz, Capito had stood for the provostship of St. Thomas, Strasbourg, and in June 1520 Sturm sought his aid in getting a canon at Mainz to resign in Sturm's favor. When Capito in 1521 claimed the provostship at St. Thomas in absentia, "Master Jacob Sturm, clergyman of the diocese of Strasbourg," was one of his procurators. Very possibly, Capito would help Jacob Sturm secure at last the benefice he had so long been pursuing. And pursue it he continued to do, right into the tumult of the early Reformation years at Strasbourg, where by the early 1520s the Evangelical movement had taken root, fed by sermons, pamphlets, and tales of Martin Luther's defiance of pope and emperor and of his miraculous escape from the Diet of Worms. Jacob Sturm, until now an undistinguished gentleman-clergyman in the Wimpheling mold, pricked up his ears to the reformer's message.

NOTES

1. "Allodial" means "nonfeudal," that is, owned rather than held in feudal tenure from a lord.
2. The meaning of "in Undis" is obscure, but it probably derives from the Latin word for "wave."
3. Razed after the Protestant Reformation, this church occupied part of the modern Place Gutenberg.
4. Jakob Wimpheling, *De integritate libellus* (Strasbourg: Johannes Knobloch, 1506), chap. 24.
5. *JWOS* 1, *Jakob Wimpfelings Adolescentia*, ed. Otto Herding (Munich, 1965), 31–32. Later, perhaps after he settled at Strasbourg, Wimpheling added a dedication "to Jacob Sturm and his brothers."
6. *JWOS* 3, *Briefwechsel*, ed. Otto Herding and Dieter Mertens (Munich, 1990), 372–73, no. 119; and there, too, the following quote.
7. Wimpheling, *De integritate*, chap. 1.

8. Ibid., chap. 29. In this second edition (1506), Wimpheling made the reference specific by adding "quoad Jacob Sturm."

9. Recent research has dispelled the traditional view that the clergy of this era were badly educated. The contrary view, expressed here, rests on Francis Rapp's very precise study of the diocese of Strasbourg (cited in note 17).

10. Some authors believe that the differences between the schools were substantial, while others tend to minimize them. The matter lies under discussion.

11. Joseph Anton Riegger, *Amoenitates literariae friburgenses*, 3 pts. (Ulm, 1775–76), 210.

12. Ibid., 424 (1513).

13. Specklin, no. 2190.

14. *JWOS* 1:364. The boys grandly styled themselves "Sturm von Sturmeck," an appellative used by other Sturms, though never by the adult Jacob Sturm. It referred to a mill they owned on the Ill River.

15. Specklin, no. 2163, with the wrong year of death.

16. Schott, *Works* 1:143, no. 36.

17. The phrase "mediocre program" comes from Francis Rapp, *Réformes et reformation à Strasbourg: Eglise et société dans le diocèse de Strasbourg (1450–1525)*, Collection de l'Institut des Hautes Études Alsaciennes, vol. 23 (Paris, 1974), 162–65.

18. *Adolescentia*, in *JWOS* 1:365–67.

19. Geiler, *Die Emeis*, fols. 8ᵛ–9ᵛ; and there, too, the following quote.

20. Heinrich Koller, ed., *Reformation Kaiser Siegmunds*, Monumenta Germaniae Historica, Staatschriften des späteren Mittelalters, vol. 6 (Stuttgart, 1964), 100, line 8.

21. Riegger, *Amoenitates*, 427; Charles Guillaume Adolphe Schmidt, *Répertoire bibliographique strasbourgeois jusque vers 1530*, 9 vols. (Strasbourg, 1893–96), 7:45, no. 148. The comment by Nachtigall (Luscinius) is quoted from Hermann Gumbel, "Humanitas Alsatica: Straßburger Humanismus von Jakob Wimpfeling zu Johann und Jakob Sturm," *ELJb* 17 (1938): 8.

22. P. S. Allen and H. S. Allen, eds., *Opus epistolarum Des. Erasmi Roterodami denuo recognitum et auctum*, 12 vols. (Oxford, 1906–46), 2:19, lines 85–87, no. 305; *JWOS* 3:773–77, no. 314.

23. Allen and Allen, *Opus epistolarum Des. Erasmi*, 2:20, no. 305, lines 124–30.

24. Ibid. 9:19, no. 2088, lines 87–90.

25. Ibid. 3:888, no. 948.

26. *Epistolae obscurorum virorum* 2:63, ed. Francis Griffin Stokes (London, 1909), 266, 269.

27. This and the two following quotes are from Eduard Winckelmann, ed., *Urkundenbuch der Universität Heidelberg*, 2 vols. (Heidelberg, 1886) 1:214–16, no. 162 (22 July 1522).

28. Ibid., 216–17, no. 163.

29. Joseph Knepper, *Jakob Wimpfeling (1450–1528): Sein Leben und seine Werke*, Freiburg i. Br., 1902), 247 n. 1, 303–4; *JWOS* 3:112.

30. J. A. Giefel, "Streit um die gefürstete Propstei Ellwangen im Zeitalter der Reformation," *Württembergische Vierteljahrshefte für Landesgeschichte* 7 (1884): 171 n. 2.

4

Reformation and Revolution

O God! that one might read the book of fate
And see the revolution of the times.
                    —Shakespeare, *Henry IV, Part 2* 3.1.45

Revolutions, alas, often reveal themselves clearly only in retrospect. Many a person has thought to live in revolutionary times and awakened to find the world much as it used to be. Others find that the world has indeed changed—"changéd utterly," in Yeats's lovely phrase—and broken contact between a before and an after, forcing them to accept that life, if it is to continue, must be in some sense a new life. On the lives of many people—though by no means of all—the early Reformation movement and its culminating event, the Peasants' War of 1525, had precisely this effect. For those who experienced them at first hand, the events constituted a genuine revolution.

A NEW LIFE

During the early 1520s, the religious movement of the Protestant Reformation aroused Strasbourg and the Upper Rhine from provincial torpor. Its message, initially spread by word of mouth, letters, and print, found its earliest listeners in Strasbourg and in other southern free cities among the secular clergy, the monks, and the well-to-do laity. Then, Luther's dramatic appearance in 1521 at Worms, where he defied the emperor and the Diet, transformed him into a public figure who spoke by means of a powerful flood of print. By 1523–24 the annual production of books and pamphlets in the German-speaking world had increased a thousandfold over 1517, and the number of German titles skyrocketed from about 40 per year in 1500 to 498 in 1523. Most of these titles—411 of them—concerned religion, and a large majority came from Luther's own pen.

STURM'S CONVERSION

Already a leading center of the relatively new art of printing, Strasbourg became, along with Wittenberg, Nuremberg, and Zurich, one of the new movement's most important centers. As the discussions came out of the monasteries, studies, and parlors and into the shops, taverns, and streets, burghers of all classes felt compelled to choose one side or the other. Not everyone was favorably impressed. At Strasbourg the prominent gardener Augustin Drenss doubted that the new preachers were much different from the old ones, and when Dr. Caspar Hedio (1494–1552), Geiler's successor but one in the cathedral's pulpit, married Drenss's sister with the connivance of both their mother and Ammeister Claus Kniebis, Drenss complained that "the doctor is a clergymen, and they are forbidden to marry not only by local law and custom, but also by the laws according to which Christendom has lived for a thousand years and more."[1] Meanwhile, the new gospel was capturing the hearts of many Strasbourgeois, including some who were close to Jacob Sturm. One of them was Hans Bock von Gerstheim (d. 1542), a university-educated nobleman, familiar of Wimpheling's, senior stettmeister, and Sturm's future father-in-law. At Worms in 1521, Bock had chided Luther for refusing to submit, but within a couple of years he changed his mind. The Evangelical party also brought over three ammeisters: Sturm's cousin Daniel Mieg (1484–1541), the ruling ammeister for 1524; fiery Martin Herlin (1471–1547) from the Furriers' Guild; and Claus Kniebis (1479–52), a tough, university-educated lawyer from the Smiths' Guild. To these laymen came several of Sturm's friends among the local clergy. One of them, Mathis Zell, his fellow from Freiburg days who had become pastor of the cathedral parish, emerged in 1522 as the movement's most effective local voice. More prominent yet was another old Freiburg friend, Wolfgang Capito, provost of St. Thomas, who, though sympathetic to the Evangelicals, refrained from joining them until 1523, when a series of highly public marriages by local clergymen screwed the pressure beyond what he could bear.

These changes pressed in on Jacob Sturm at a time when much of his familiar world had already slipped away. Since the mid-1510s death had taken Uncle Ludwig and Aunt Anna von Endingen in 1516, his own mother and maternal grandmother in 1519, his father in October 1521, Uncle Ott in 1518, and his younger brother Stephan shortly thereafter. These deaths left Jacob only his cousins and his five surviving siblings: Anna, Clara, and Veronica; and Friedrich and Peter. At thirty-three, Jacob had already outlived Young Peter Schott, and the coming of the religious Reformation had made it impossible for him to imitate any longer Schott's way of life as a gentleman-clergyman.

There is no evidence that Jacob Sturm experienced any kind of conversion of a classical type. In the autumn of 1523, probably in November, Sturm nonetheless decided to give up the clerical status he had enjoyed for nearly twenty years. According to a remark he made nearly twenty years later at Worms to Dr. Johann Eck, fellow Wimpheling protégé and another old Freiburg acquaintance, Sturm declared that in those days "I read the writings of both sides and was persuaded by those of our side."[2] This suggests a slow process of persuasion ending in a decision, which agrees with a report by Jacob Wimpheling, Sturm's old mentor, nearly contemporary with Sturm's decision. The seventy-year-old priest, then living in retirement at his native Sélestat, held the Evangelical movement to be a revival of the dread "Wycliffite," that is, Hussite, heresy of a century ago—neither an unreasonable nor an uncommon opinion during the first half of the 1520s. "O, how horrible," he exclaimed at the news that at Strasbourg Wolfgang Capito was preaching that one might as well "pray to a dog" as to the Mother of God, the city's patroness, and he begged Capito not to abandon traditional wisdom for the teachings of "the foul-mouthed Wycliffites."[3] In early November came worse news yet, for a friend at Strasbourg wrote that Wimpheling's favorite lamb, Jacob Sturm, "is patently infected with the Wycliffite poison." When Wimpheling asked Sturm whether the rumor were true, Sturm's reply went straight to the old man's heart: "If I am a heretic, you made me one."[4]

How is Sturm's retort to be understood? Did Luther—to adapt a famous saying—hatch the egg that Wimpheling had laid and Erasmus had incubated? Perhaps so, for up to a point Sturm had followed a fairly typical trajectory for urban clergymen of his generation and region, moving from Wimpheling's "mediocre program" through Erasmianism to Luther's reformation. The critical element that Sturm attributed to Wimpheling's pedagogy may well have been the ideal of a life devoted to self-improvement through self-discipline and devotion to learning. Erasmus's influence did not so much alter this ideal as provide it with a set of sharper critical tools. The shift is already evident in Sturm's 1522 critique of the Heidelberg curriculum, which shows typical moves away from scholastic learning and toward patristic and biblical studies. As a Wimphelingite Sturm began, as an Erasmian he developed, and as a humanist and biblicist, though more by reputation than by accomplishment, he took sides with the Evangelical movement.

Although Jacob Sturm's passage from protohumanism through humanism to Reformation presents in some respects a familiar story, his response to Luther's movement differed in one crucial feature from those of hundreds of other priests and monks who became the earliest Evangelical preachers. Many of them may have shared Sturm's disappointed eagerness for preferment in the church, but whereas most other clergymen sought to remain clerical as Evangelicals, Sturm abandoned the clergy for a career of magisterial service. Within months of his decision for the new religious movement, we find him taking his seat as a noble senator in Strasbourg's old city hall, where his brother Friedrich already sat, and where so many of their kinsmen had preceded them. His turn to the Protestant Reformation, therefore, brought Jacob Sturm initially not into a new life but into a way of life perfectly in tune with his heritage, into the service not of the church but of the city.

THE YOUNG MAGISTRATE

Sturm entered the magistracy of his native city on 7 January 1524. Around the same time he decided to marry, and his choice fell on a daughter (her name is unknown) of Hans Bock von Gerstheim and Ursula von Fleckenstein. His new parents-in-law were as eminent and well connected as any citizens of Strasbourg could be, for Hans Bock was a senior stettmeister and head of an important patrician lineage, while his wife belonged to the most powerful family of the Lower Alsatian nobility. The marriage, alas, was childless and brief, and by 1529 at the latest, the daughter who married Jacob Sturm died. In that year Jacob and Peter Sturm bought a mansion together in Fire Street (*Brandgasse*) in a quarter favored by Strasbourg's great families. The next parallel street southward was Jews' Street, where 180 years earlier their ancestor, Gosse Sturm, had tried unsuccessfully to prevent the massacre of Strasbourg's Jews. In Fire Street, Jacob and Peter lived for the rest of their lives with their bachelor elder brother, Friedrich, and their spinster sister, Veronica.

Next to hunting, the drive to preserve the lineage was perhaps the most powerful motive of aristocratic life, and the failure of these Sturm siblings to marry and have children puzzled contemporaries as much as it does the modern historian. Sister Anna did marry an ultrarespectable Zorn von Plobsheim, but Jacob never remarried, and Peter, Friedrich, and Veronica never married at all. Thus, while in their father's generation four Sturm brothers had produced at least eight male heirs, in their own only one man, Cousin Stephan, produced male heirs. Several generations later, the entire lineage came to an end with the death of the last male Sturm in 1640, four centuries after they had come across the Rhine from Offenburg. This outcome was not at all what Wimpheling had predicted when he urged Jacob Sturm into the priesthood with the words, "you have brothers, who *deo volente* can continue your lineage."

The lack of a family of his own helps to explain why Jacob Sturm could devote the last three decades of his life almost entirely to his native city's service. At Strasbourg, as in other South German and Swiss cities, the inner magistracies were full-time, unpaid offices for life, which only the well-to-do could afford to hold. For the respectable artisan master—who at Strasbourg, unlike Nuremberg, could aspire to a magistracy—a few two-year terms in the Senate was probably the most he could afford to serve. For the Sturm brothers, however, their substantial wealth left them free to choose a life in civic office. Rents in kind—wheat, rye, barley, beans, peas, chickens, and wine—from their holdings around Breuschwickersheim supplied their larder, while a long roll of peasant rents and debts from the same district filled their purses. The siblings had inherited many properties, rentes, and fiefs, the allodial portions of which passed to Cousin Stephan and via their sister Anna to the Bocks von Gerstheim, while the feudal tenures passed in 1559 from Friedrich, who held them for himself and his childless brothers, to Cousin Stephan, Uncle Ott's son. These fiefs, it may be noted, were simply property of a special kind. Their possession involved no obligations of service to a lord and no political ties of any kind, the one fixed feature of this form of property being that their formal holder was always the eldest male of the current generation. In the Sturm family, Friedrich held the fiefs for them all, and the management of their other properties seems to have fallen to Jacob's younger brother, Peter. The brothers held both property in common and individual properties, and we find Jacob's name in a 1533–34 register of civic creditors. His brother Friedrich's will contains a number of personal items, including a large debt of 1,500 rhfl. owed him by Duke Christoph of Württemberg and a considerable wealth in plate, gold chains, and cash. This will plus that of their cousin and heir, Stephan Sturm, bolsters the general impression of the Sturm's secure wealth and comfortable style of life.

Unhindered by the need to earn a living and equipped with an education unique among Strasbourg's magistrates, Jacob Sturm moved quickly upward through the hierarchy of civic offices. In the next three years he went from the Senate into the privy council of XV (domestic affairs) and then into that of the XIII (foreign affairs), in which he first took his seat in October 1526. On the following 21 December, Sturm was selected to the stettmeistership, the highest civic office a noble could hold.

From his seat in the privy council of the XIII, Sturm came to exercise a powerful influence on Strasbourg's diplomacy and foreign relations all through the Reformation era. The "old lords," as the XIIIers were called, served for life as the regime's innermost political circle, the most powerful and prestigious magistates from the noble societies and from the guilds. In this council Sturm joined some men of his own sort, such as his father-in-law, Hans Bock von Gerstheim, and others of a very different sort, whose families and money came from God alone knew where. One of them, Ammeister Claus Kniebis, who had become the Evangelical movement's principal politician, speculated in land and enriched himself from the wealth of Strasbourg's mendicant houses. Others came from merchant families high—the silk merchant Conrad Joham (d. 1551)— and low—the cloth merchants Mathis Pfarrer (1489–1568) and Martin Herlin. Such men had the skills—finance, administration, foreign languages—to rule a city, but most of them had little advanced education. Among the 102 privy councillors of the Reformation era were but a handful of university men and only one—Jacob Sturm himself—who had studied theology. Most of the leading magistrates simply hadn't the experience or the skills to deal successfully with princes, bishops, and Imperial councilors, some of whom spoke no German, or with politicians from places, such as the Hanseatic towns, whose languages and customs were more poorly comprehended at Strasbourg than were those of Venice, Milan, Lyon, or Antwerp.

In this company of able, practical, but not learned magistrates, Jacob Sturm's light shone forth. Not only did he speak Latin—though not French—and have aristocratic manners, he also possessed a fund of learning that was both deep and broad. Once, at Augsburg in 1548, Sturm astonished Bartholomäus Sastrow (1520–1603), the mayor of Stralsund on the Baltic coast, with his knowledge of the histories of Pomerania and the bishopric of Cammin—a region about as remote from Strasbourg as one could get and still be in the Empire. "In short," Sastrow recorded in his memoirs, "it was as lucid, complete and accurate a summary of the subject as if he had just finished studying it." The Stralsunders "greatly admired his wonderful memory. Verily, he was a superior, experienced, eloquent, and prudent man, who had had his share in many memorable days from an Imperial as well as from a provincial view. . . . Without him, [Johannes] Sleidan could never have written his history."[5] Sturm's abilities and skills, which evoked such admiration from his contemporaries, help to explain both his swift rise through the magisterial hierarchy's ranks, meteoric by local standards, and the influence he gained among the Empire's leading urban politicians.

For all of his learning and promise, Sturm undertook from the start the same backbreaking regimen that the other privy councillors followed: six mornings a week, except when he was on mission, which was often, he made the ten-minute walk from his mansion in Fire Street to the city hall for sessions of the Senate & XXI or one of the privy councils. Between sessions he and his fellows did their heavy committee work. The dozens of permanent commissions were supervisory bodies through which the councils' ears, eyes, and hands reached out into the city's shops, taverns, guildhalls, and homes. Sturm's first permanent assignment was the Welfare Commission, charged with supervising the city's new poor law, which he joined in 1524. Further, there were many ad hoc committees, groups of from three to five magistrates named to deal with a particular item of new business. They drafted diplomatic correspondence, dealt with petitions, handled complaints, and investigated rumors. Finally, there was the kind of informal newsgathering that made it so necessary to fill the privy councils with active men of affairs. Sturm, to take one example, reported on 13 July 1524 a conversation with Nicolaus Wurmser (d. 1536), dean of St. Thomas and also Sturm's cousin, who announced that he was no longer willing to play "the bishop's squire."[6] This was a useful tidbit at a time when the regime was trying to break the bishop's hold on the city's clergy.

In this setting Jacob Sturm soon found his true metier in foreign affairs and diplomacy. He entered the regime at a critical time, when the magistrates, pressed from below by the commune, were beginning to make changes in religious practice that were clearly illegal, at the same time hoping that someone—the emperor, the Imperial Diet, or a General Council of the church—would soon relieve them from the mounting pressure for even greater changes. This hope rose especially high during Jacob Sturm's first months in office, for in 1523 the South German free cities had sent envoys—one was Cousin Bernhard

Wurmser von Vendenheim (d. 1540)—to Emperor Charles V in Spain to seek his protection from the princes in return for their financial support. Parallel to this policy of urban solidarity and loyalty to the Crown ran the demand, pressed by Hans Bock, that the entire religious issue be laid before a General Council. Both hopes were dashed in 1524, when the emperor ordered an enforcement of the Edict of Worms against Luther's teachings and forbade the calling of a council. By the end of Sturm's first year in office, therefore, the magistrates confronted mounting popular pressure for change, from which no relief was in sight. At this moment, as all signs pointed toward a new foreign policy, the storm of revolution broke over Strasbourg, Alsace, the Upper Rhine, and South Germany.

IN THE STORM OF REVOLUTION

Behind the pressure on Strasbourg's magistrates, which reached its greatest force during 1524, Sturm's first year in office, stood an Evangelical party led by local clergymen who preferred their new designation as "preachers" to their old one as "priests." To a certain extent, these clergymen both fed and drew strength from the widespread feelings of expectation and struggle that flowed toward the great upheaval of the coming winter and spring. To lend force to their demands for protection of married priests, official approval of vernacular worship, and the suppression of the Mass, the cults of the saints, and other rituals, they were mobilizing a party from their parish pulpits, an effort in which they were clearly flirting with sedition. Catalyzed by Luther's charismatic persona and deeds, they struggled to legitimize their program, which contravened both canon and civil law, by means of appeals, on the one hand, to the idea of the Bible as the norm of action and belief and, on the other hand, to a deep tradition of sacral communalism, that is, the burghers' belief in their collective responsibility to uphold God's honor and promote the common good.

Biblicism was a watchword of the Evangelical movement, communalism was a commonplace of the age. "What else is the city," Erasmus wrote in 1518, "but a great monastery?"[7] His Swiss disciple, the Zurich preacher Huldrych Zwingli (1484–1531), echoed this idea: "The Kingdom of Christ is also external," and "a Christian city is nothing more than a Christian commune."[8] In the southwestern parts of the Empire, the Evangelical preachers revitalized and sharpened this communal ideal, providing its partisans with the perfect weapon against their bishops, but also, at least potentially, against the local magistrates. The two swords, spiritual and temporal, were going to be merged in someone's hands, but in whose—the people's, the preachers', or the magistrates'?—was still undecided. A decision could nonetheless not be far ahead, for by late 1524 the landscape was seething with signs of unrest, even insurrection. There was rising a movement inspired by a deep sense of grievance and a demand for justice founded on an assertion that the Gospel and the Christian common good were one and the same thing.

THE PEASANTS' WAR

The great German Peasants' War, which erupted in the southern Black Forest seigneuries during the autumn of 1524 and spread in the late winter and spring across the Empire's southern and central tiers, fed from such ideas about the godly law and the common good. As it spread, it cashed in the legacies of a long series of failed or planned rural revolts, including the Upper Rhenish tradition of conspiracy called the *Bundschuh*, which since 1493 had rekindled again and again. One of its recent flare-ups had involved the subjects of the Sturms and related families.

Far behind this gathering storm lay the economic upswing that had begun around 1450. As the price of agricultural commodities began to rise after a century's depression, the farmers felt a need, on the one hand, for larger, stronger, and more rationally organized states and resented, on the other, seigneurial efforts to take advantage of the rise by reimposing various types of servile dues. These motives, positive and negative, merged into the prehistory of the Peasants' War of 1525, the greatest rural insurrection in European history.

By late winter 1525, the revolt was eating its way across the Empire's southern tier and into its central zones. Although everywhere colored by local conditions, the movement aimed its demands at common grievances, such as burdensome taxes, lost fishing and timbering rights, and alienated tithes, and favored general reforms, such as the abolition of serfdom and the supression of usury by the Jews and the clergy. Its programmatic statements also demanded the reformation of territorial governments in a popular sense through the representation of the common people and an end to (noble and clerical) political privilege based on property rights in land and human labor. Further, in the regions of badly fragmented sovereignty—Upper Swabia, Franconia, and Jacob Sturm's native Upper Rhine—rebels demanded the creation of larger, more responsive states conformable to regional needs.

THE INSURRECTION IN SWABIA

The German Peasants' War of 1525 gave Jacob Sturm his political baptism by fire. The revolution was already well ablaze in early 1525, when Sturm set off on his very first mission. He was going to take Strasbourg's seat in the Imperial Governing Council, a committee of Estates—or, rather, of envoys of Estates—founded in 1521 to govern the Empire during the emperor's absence. Arriving at the council's seat at the free city of Esslingen in the Neckar Valley, Sturm found the insurrection more advanced in Swabia than on the Upper Rhine. Soon, the Governing Council sent him and another delegate, the Saxon jurist Simon Pistoris (1489–1562), to Upper Swabia (the Upper Danube Valley) to investigate the situation and to mediate between the Upper Swabian rebels and the Swabian League. The ride over the ancient, eroded ridge of the Swabian Jura, Sturm's first excursion beyond the Rhine basin, brought them to the large free city of Ulm on the Danube, where the league's assembly was trying to decide what to do. Between 30 March and about 14 April, Sturm and Pistoris rode back and forth between that city and the Upper Swabian rebels' capital at the free city of Memmingen. Their mission was to broker a truce, a policy which the Swabian League's free cities strongly supported, and though the league's war hawks had to tolerate negotations, since its army was away guarding the duchy of Württemberg, Sturm and his companion were told that "the league intends to punish the rebels and will not tolerate a truce."[9] This was true. Its general, Jörg Truchsess von Waldburg (1488–1531), brought the army back over the Rhine-Danube divide into Upper Swabia, and when Sturm left Memmingen on Sunday, 2 April, one of the rebel armies, the Baltringers, was marching out to meet Waldburg and its doom at Leipheim, two days later:

> The peasants tried to learn
> An evil lesson from the Swiss
> And become their own lords;
> But we baptized them in a different faith
> At a little place near Ulm,
> And whoever didn't get away,
> He lost his life on that day.[10]

The Baltringers' defeat spurred Sturm and Pistoris to new efforts, back and forth between the rebels' camp and the Swabian League's assembly at Ulm, to which they bore the rebels' message that if "we can't get assurance that we, as poor folk, may hold to what is good and just . . . we must rely on divine justice through self-help. Our miserable condition and the whole land's people drive us to this."[11] Rebels' appeal, envoys' proposals, all in vain, as on Good Friday (14 April) Waldburg's tough mercenaries crushed another Upper Swabian army at Wurzach. When the remaining army accepted terms in the Treaty of Weingarten on 24 April, the Upper Swabian revolution was over.

By this time Jacob Sturm was en route to another theater of the revolution, the free city of Heilbronn, which lay below Stuttgart in the Neckar Valley. He discovered there, as he reported, "all sorts of strange and incredible things."[12] When two rebel armies appeared before Heilbronn, the city's magistrates, under pressure from the burghers and "especially the women," had to open the gates to the rebels on Easter Tuesday (18 April). On the twenty-second came their commander, Jörg Metzler of Ballenberg, who with his captains set up headquarters in the city hall. "They hold their deliberations there," Sturm wrote, "having posted their own men at the gates, and do what they please. They've occupied all the convents and clerical establishments and plundered them. . . .

The Heilbronners have to put up with all this." Sturm observed that many burghers made common cause with the rebels, as they had at Memmingen. "Just as I write this here at Heilbronn," he wrote home, "a placard has been posted ordering all citizens and journeymen who want to join the army to assemble at one of the gates. The senate has to let depart anyone who will. The talk here is that Würzburg has surrendered to the peasants, but I know nothing certain about it." Then, as Heilbronn's helpless mayor stood weeping at the city's gate, his burghers streamed out to join the rebels.

The lesson of Heilbronn confirmed the lesson of Memmingen, that the world had turned upside down, had gone topsy-turvy. The burghers knew topsy-turvy, for every year in the weeks before Ash Wednesday, the rites of carnival made the world go topsy-turvy, mocking what in everyday life must be respected, praising what was normally scorned. This, however, was real topsy-turvy. Among the rebels who entered Heilbronn were the hard boys of Jäcklein Rohrbach, fresh from their massacre of nobles at Castle Weinsberg. And Metzler's reign at city hall was not mockery but deadly serious, for Sturm reported how the count of Helfenstein's widow "was brought here in a wagon and robbed of everything she had. . . . Each day many noblemen and captains come to seek terms from the army, and they are given safe-conducts. The counts of Leonstein have made peace, also the city of Wimpfen and everyone else in the neighborhood."

A topsy-turvy world, in which countesses were treated like commoners and lords sued their subjects for peace. Where was the place for mediation in such a world? It was another case for the army and its hangmen, and as Sturm rode back upriver to Esslingen, Waldburg was preparing his troops for the invasion of Franconia.

INSURRECTION ON THE UPPER RHINE

Back at Esslingen, Sturm's term on the Governing Council had expired, so he saddled up for the ride over the Black Forest, down the steep Kinzig Valley, and over the Rhine Bridge to Strasbourg, where he arrived shortly after 4 May. All around the city he found the revolution in full swing, encouraged by a long insurrectionary tradition and fueled by inflammatory preaching in the villages. By 13 May, when a Lower Alsatian army led by Erasmus Gerber (d. 1525) attacked the bishop's residential town of Saverne, Strasbourg was resonating to the shocks on the land. The whole countryside was out, including the tenants of the Sturms and the Bocks, while a flood of refugees—priests, lords, ladies, and others—streamed into the city for protection. The burghers, however, did not rise, and the guilds' Schöffen stood by the magistrates in two votes taken on 11 and 14 May. Their loyalty gave the magistrates the courage "to aid in everything that will be conducive to peace and to the dispersal of the [peasants'] army," and they sent envoys in this sense to the two princes,

Duke Antoine (1489–1544) of Lorraine and Elector Palatine Louis (1478–1544), whose armies were converging on Lower Alsace. Bishop William's absence at Mainz and the Baden margraves' paralysis left no internal force capable of pacifying the region. Into this vacuum rolled Duke Antoine's army, which streamed over the Vosges and crushed Gerber's men, who lay twelve to fifteen thousand strong at Saverne, in a tremendous mêlée on 17 May, and smashed another rebel army at Schwerwiller on the twentieth. "What a terrible price to pay," someone sang, "thirteen thousand on a single day."[13] Frantically, Strasbourg's envoys rode hither and yon, but to no avail, neither with Duke Antoine nor further northward, where Jacob Sturm and Mathis Pfarrer pleaded with Elector Louis to show mercy to the tiny free city of Wissembourg.

Eastward, on the Rhine's right bank, Strasbourg's policy of truce and peace through negotiations met with much better success, perhaps because here no princely armies lay within striking distance of the rebels. But success did not come easily or all at once. While Strasbourg's envoys persuaded the eight-thousand-man Oberkirch army—drawn from the Ortenau and the Acher and Rench Valleys—to sign a truce, farther south the Ortenauers were plundering the monasteries and moving southward to join with the Breisgauers before Freiburg, which after an eight-day siege opened its gates to the redoubtable Hans Müller of Bulgenbach. It was to deal with this victorious commander that Jacob Sturm and Conrad Joham, his fellow magistrate, came upriver on 21 May, four days after the Saverne massacre, to mediate a truce. Farther northward, Sturm's cousin, Bernhard Wurmser, was helping to negotiate the Treaty of Renchen, which became the model for all the settlements on the Rhine's east bank. Now the Baselers added their weight to Strasbourg's negotiations at Offenburg. When some Breisgau commanders moved troops northward to Lahr, eighteen kilometers south of Offenburg, an obvious attempt to influence the negotiations, Sturm, Joham, and the Baselers rode out to their camp, where fifteen thousand men lay in arms, to persuade them to move back southward. Most of them did so. This was Sturm's fourth visit to a rebel camp or a rebel-held city. The Treaty of Offenburg, which Margrave Ernest (r. 1515–53) of Baden and his subjects signed on 13 June, fixed a truce until the peace conference at Basel on July 18, which extended the Treaty of Renchen's provisions to the margrave's subjects, restored the status quo ante, and forbade the further use of force by either side. At a final meeting on 27 August at Basel, Sturm and the Basel delegates secured general assent to forty articles, plus a fine of 5 rhfl. per peasant household. The Treaty of Basel capped the most successful effort to end the great German Peasants' War by means of documents and oaths rather than pikes and guns.

Tumultuous and bloody was Jacob Sturm's introduction to Imperial politics. He spent five months in four major theaters of the revolution of 1525—Upper Swabia, the Swabian-Franconian borderlands in the Neckar Valley, Lower

Alsace, and central and southern Baden—where he gained a more intensive and extensive firsthand experience of the rebels than any other politician of his era possessed. Burdened by his multiple identities—nobleman, seigneur, burgher, magistrate, and Imperial official—Sturm rode into cities brimming with revolutionary exultation and fear, through rural landscapes dotted by plundered monasteries and smoking country houses, and into rebel camps and rebel-held towns. He saw men and women just like his own family's tenants at Breuschwickersheim and Düppigheim, who, bearing their sacred banners and pikes and flails in hand, swore to stand together to secure their rights for all time. He observed burghers, too, just like the hardworking guildsfolk he saw and greeted everyday at Strasbourg, who had joined the peasants in revolt. And he spoke with vengeful princes, or with their councilors, who swore with grimmest determination that such things should never be allowed to happen again.

These three experiences in fires of revolution in 1525 infused three corresponding lessons into the budding politician's mind and soul. First, given the right conditions, the common people would look up—the farmers from their ploughs and the burghers from their workbenches—take up arms and fight "to become their own lords." Second, the Imperial monarchy and its representatives were too feeble to govern, much less to control the course of events. Third, in the hands of the territorial princes, who commanded credit from the bankers, support from their princely kinsmen, and purchased loyalty from their mercenary troops, lay the power of decision, which the rebels could in the long run neither defeat, appropriate, nor neutralize. These were the lessons of 1525: the Common Man's courage, the Empire's weakness, and the princes' might. Jacob Sturm never forgot them.

The eerie quality of Jacob Sturm's Peasants' War came from his experience of these unprecedented events in the familiar settings of his own world—Alsace and the Upper Rhine, expanded by Swabia and a bit of Franconia—essentially the world of Old Peter Schott. Long basking in the cozy, oblique light of triumphant particularism, this world now stood on the brink of radical change. As chief agent of this change, the Reformation movement was about to burst this world's old boundedness and implode it and the Empire's other parts together in a permanent crisis which would last for the next thirty years. The vulnerability to this radical change, however, arose not from particularism itself, but from the age's least-bounded, most nearly universal system of symbols, ideas, values, and practices—the Christian religion.

JACOB STURM'S RELIGION

Jacob Sturm's experiences in 1525 cried out for reflection about how the Christian gospel was connected, or ought to connect, to everyday life. How Sturm saw this question must be pieced together from occasional statements and comments, most of which were made in connection with policy and must therefore be handled with caution. The earliest comes from the midst of the revolution, August 1525, when Strasbourg's Evangelical preachers were intensifying their campaign to abolish the Catholic Mass, the old faith's central rite, which they held to be "nothing but worthless human inventions and fantasies."[14]

STURM AND THE CATHOLIC MASS

Jacob Sturm opposed the demand that the Catholic Mass be abolished.[15] The rite was not unbiblical, he wrote in August 1525, because "it is certain and proven by Scripture that God may be praised in every tongue, so Latin singing cannot be considered improper or blasphemous, providing that the abuses which have crept in are eliminated."[16] Sturm passed over the preachers' main theological point—the Mass as sacrifice is a worthless blasphemy—in silence. His concern was policy, and he thought that to change or abolish the Mass "would awaken a great deal of ill will both inside and outside the city," so that "for the time being the collegiate churches should be allowed to sing High Mass," while the magistrates studied the matter.[17] Even more revealing are Sturm's harsh words for the preachers themselves, who ought to be admonished, he wrote, "to teach the people what Christ's purpose was in instituting the Sacrament, namely, that we should be reminded that He saves us and that through Him we have a common Father in heaven, if only we will believe in and trust Him." Further, that "we, who eat one bread and drink from one cup, are members of one body, and that we should therefore display love for one another." At the present time, by contrast, "each condemns the other, as if his Mass, his way, were better than the other's." In the spirit of faction, "some Christians call themselves 'Evangelicals' and the others 'papists' and 'hypocrites,' while the others consider themselves the true, old Christians and the others 'Hussites' and the like. Both sides are Christians, however, may God have mercy!"[18]

Alluding to the fresh experience of revolution, Sturm recommended that "because such misunderstanding exists between rulers and subjects now, many things should be tolerated and overlooked for the time being, until the Lord God grants better wisdom." The preachers, he thought, throw caution to the winds and "think that they can abolish in one year the consequences of a hundred years' decline."[19]

The preachers' chief argument against the Mass—that it was a blasphemy which endangered the commune's standing before God and, therefore, the common good—made no impression on Sturm, and it is therefore no surprise to find him not among the militantly Evangelical magistrates but among the moderates. His group won the day for the time being, as in 1526 the Senate & XXI decided "that the Mass should be preserved until the envoys to His Majesty return and we hear what His Majesty thinks." Rumor whispered that Jacob Sturm "had cast the deciding vote for the Mass."[20]

Was Sturm's antipathy for religious militancy a policy shaped by the postrevolutionary moment, or did it flow from a deeper conviction? The spotty evidence suggests that it was both. Sturm disliked all open dispute about religion. He once confessed himself—despite his own training—"not sufficiently competent" to treat "points concerning religion" in a public setting.[21] He came to despise the Protestants' own dispute about the Eucharist so deeply that for years he would not attend the sacrament of the Lord's Supper. Like most of those touched by Erasmianism, he held that practice must lead principle. "If all the evil abuses of the clergy were first abolished and reformed," he wrote in 1530, "doctrine would later follow of itself."[22]

STURM'S THEOLOGY

Sturm nonetheless did hold positive religious opinions, though they are not easy to reconstruct. They are best understood, perhaps, in terms of the two major streams of German-speaking Evangelical theology, the South German-Swiss type called Zwinglianism and the dominant type called Lutheranism. By the mid-1520s the Evangelical clergy were beginning to take sides in the theological dispute between Martin Luther and Huldrych Zwingli, the chief reformer of Zurich. On the sacrament of the Eucharist, or Lord's Supper, which eventually became the main test of orthodoxy, Sturm held the Zwinglian or "spiritualist" position that Christ's presence in the sacrament depends on the recipient's faith. This view, which the Strasbourg preachers shared, was enshrined in the doctrinal statement called the Tetrapolitan Confession, which Bucer and Capito prepared under Sturm's supervision for the Diet of Augsburg in 1530. The same view appears in Sturm's glosses on the Schwabach Articles, which the Lutherans presented in the summer of 1529 as a condition for the Protestant alliance.[23] Sturm commented that "biblical truth cannot be translated into articles of faith," and that "faith and the Spirit are given, and must be had, before the sacrament and not first through the sacrament, for the sacrament is but a witness to faith and a confirmation and sign of faith." This is mainline Zwinglianism or Sacramentarianism, and Sturm at this point made no bones about the lack of agreement between his party and the Lutherans. "As can readily be seen from the writings," wrote this former theological student, "the issue is whether the presence [of Christ] is corporeal or exists only through faith. They [the Lutherans] hold the former, the others the latter." These comments and others document Sturm's religious opinions as thoroughly Evangelical of the Zwinglian type: an Erasmian objection to using unbiblical language, a very strong animus against the papacy, a defense of infant baptism, and an insistence on the individual's inner disposition as a precondition of the sacrament's effectiveness. Jacob Sturm was a genuine Sacramentarian, who, like the other Zwinglians, as these South German Evangelicals were called, felt that the others, the Lutherans, remained captive to the Catholic error of making the divine presence in the world imminent, objective, and concrete.

Sturm was no Zwinglian, however, in his view of the church. He sharply and consistently rejected the linkage of earthly justice to divine righteousness and of communal liberty to Christian freedom, connections which characterized the Zwinglian position. To judge by his rare statements, Sturm's notion of the church insisted on the gulf between the true church and the world, which sounds more Lutheran than Zwinglian. He abhorred active politicking by the clergy. A 1526 political indiscretion by Wolfgang Capito provoked a rare outburst by Sturm against the preachers. "It seems to me," he wrote, "that one who undertakes to preach the gospel of Christ should freely cast body, life, honor, and property to the winds. For it is certain that the world, which never tolerated Christ while He was here on earth, will also not tolerate Him to the very end of time and will consider all who sincerely and openly confess Him, to be knaves and rascals and will persecute them."[24] Anyone who "preaches the true, genuine Christ," Sturm thought, "should be resigned to never pleasing the world and to being rejected by the world, except for a little band of the elect." For this reason, "the preachers ... shouldn't rely much on [the power of] large, strong cities, ... as though they trusted more to the power of this world than to Christ alone." After all, God "has promised us Christians no temporal happiness here, as He did the Jews in the Old Testament, but only suffering and persecution." This talk, of "a tiny band" enduring "suffering and persecution," echoed Luther far more than it did Zwingli.

Sturm's outburst in 1526 expressed more than just a momentary anger, for he said much the same thing twenty years later, on the eve of the Smalkaldic War.[25] "Just as in the time of Jesus, the apostles, and the martyrs," he wrote to Landgrave Philip of Hesse, "religion spread against the will and consent of the Jewish and pagan authorities, so today one household, tomorrow another, then a village, and finally a whole land receives the faith, which gradually comes to prevail despite all persecution." As it did of old, the faith will grow through persecution, until "the civil authority accepts it out of desire for peace and from necessity." Sturm saw the Reformation as a renewal of the early church, when the apostles and martyrs went out to preach the Gospel without protection and without fear. The true faith has always been the possession "of the little band of the elect ... in whose hearts the true Christ rules and is confessed." He altogether disbelieved that God intended to transform the world through His Spirit in the sense of personal emancipation, communal freedom, and social progress. Huldrych Zwingli, by contrast, held that "a Christian man is nothing more than a good and loyal citizen," and "a Christian city is nothing more than the Christian Church."[26] Sturm did not believe that, for he held with Luther that there is a necessary separation between the true church as an unobtrusive minority and the visible church as part of the necessary structure of authority in this world.

Nor did Sturm believe that the magistrates could Christianize society by enforcing moral laws—"laws," he wrote, "make hypocrites"[27]—but that they ought to foster religious unity as the best guarantee of civic unity and harmony in everyday life. "You know from experience," he once wrote, "that in our times scarcely anything else so unites people's minds or drives them apart as unity or disunity in religion does."[28] Very likely, the wild scenes he witnessed in 1525 lay behind his fear that "variety [in preaching] will lead astray the popular mind, which is not used to such matters, and through some preachers' loud cries the people might be divided into unwholesome factions."[29] This typically aristocratic, also Erasmian, opinion of the common people's understanding helps to explain why, despite his belief that true religion reflected the Spirit's promptings in the human heart, Sturm came to advocate an exclusive, established church under magisterial control. He promoted censorship of books, advocated uniformity in preaching, and masterminded the expulsion of the Anabaptists and other dissenters from Strasbourg. In all such matters, he felt repressive action was justified by the threat of "unwholesome factions" and the "great danger to our city."[30]

The fear of "faction" or disunity also informed Sturm's 1525 view of the Mass. In the following year, when the Senate & XXI decided "that the Mass should be preserved until the envoys to His Majesty return and we hear what His Majesty thinks," rumor held that Jacob Sturm "had cast the deciding vote for the Mass."[31] The Evangelical clergy nonetheless continued to attack the Mass, proclaiming, as Dr. Caspar Hedio announced in 1527 from Geiler's cathedral pulpit, "the nursemaid who washes the diapers and wipes the baby's butt does more good than a thousand priests reading three Masses each."[32] Powerful men stood on their side, including Sturm's cousin, Ammeister Daniel Mieg, and in January 1529 the Senate & XXI decided that "the Schöffen should be assembled to hear and asked their opinion as to whether the Mass should continue to be said or not."[33] Of the 300 Schöffen, 184 voted to abolish the Mass until it were proved biblical, 94 to permit it until after the Imperial Diet of Speyer, and one lone person to permit the Mass to be said forever. The decision was much closer in the Senate & XXI, where Sturm's opponents held the day by a one-vote margin, and on Saturday, 20 February 1529, the last licit Masses were sung in the city's collegiate churches.

In its marriage of Zwinglian theology with Lutheran ecclesiology, Jacob Sturm's religion illustrates how complex the Reformation movement could in practice become. From one point of view, Sturm was just one more of those younger Erasmians who made the passage into the Evangelical movement, and who maintained a spiritual-biblicist faith against the hardening of the Lutheran line. All of his statements about religion follow this pattern, which seems to make Sturm a "Zwinglian" rather than a "Lutheran." From another point of view, however, Sturm was one of those aristocrats who sided with Luther, who separated spiritual freedom from mundane liberty, rather than with Zwingli, who united them.

Sturm's views, for which the Peasants' War likely played a catalytic role, suggest the unwisdom of trying to understand "the Reformation" as a fixed idea which gathered the converted to itself as it unfolded its essence over time. Looking at Sturm in the context of his contemporaries, the movement appears rather to have developed as a bundle of attitudes and beliefs, the configurations of which differed from group to group, and which only under the press of events produced clearly differentiated streams of belief. Only for a brief moment in the years 1522–25 did all the streams flow in one bed, united behind the one belief they all shared: they rejected the idea of the church as a universal body of grace centered at Rome, which God had sustained and preserved since the time of Christ, and they asserted the supremacy of the Bible, conceived as "the Gospel," over Christian belief and practice. The glory days of the early Reformation movement were one of those uncommon moments when all society—in a representational rather than a literal sense of "all"—is able to load its grievances on one group, the priests, in whom is seen the common source of all that is wrong. "If the revolution of a people and the emancipation of a particular class of bourgeois society are to coincide," Karl Marx wrote,

> so that one group stands for all social groups, then the contrary is also true: a particular group must be despised by all others, it must embody that which blocks the desires of the others. In this case, one particular social sphere must be the locus for the notorious crimes of the entire society, so that the liberation of this sphere may appear to be a general self-emancipation.[34]

The Reformation moment was something like this. The possibility of local reform without revolution depended on the possibility of shifting civic society's melded sense of grievance and blame from the local clergy to a distant servant of Satan, the Antichrist at Rome. Had the blame instead flowed horizontally, it might have revitalized the fifteenth-century dream of "a new state and order . . . appropriate to the Christian faith."[35]

NOTES

1. Katherine G. Brady and Thomas A. Brady, Jr., eds., "Documents on Anticlericalism and the Control of Women at Strasbourg in the Age of the Reformation," in *Anticlericalism in the Late Middle Ages and Reformation*, ed. Peter Dykema and Heiko A. Oberman (Leiden, 1993), 214.
2. Johannes Timannus to the Preachers at Bremen, 18 November 1540, in N. Spiegel, "Johannes Timannus Amsterodamus und die Colloquien zu Worms und Regensburg 1540, 1541," *Zeitschrift für historische Theologie* 42 (1872): 42–44.

3. *JWOS* 3, *Briefwechsel*, ed. Otto Herding and Dieter Mertens (Munich, 1990), 3:871–72, no. 353.

4. Johannes Ficker and Otto Winckelmann, eds., *Handschriftenproben des sechszehnten Jahrhunderts nach Strassburger Originalen*, 2 vols. (Strasbourg, 1902–5), 2:48.

5. This quote and the following one are from Bartholomäus Sastrow, *Lauf meines Lebens: Ein deutscher Bürger im 16. Jahrhundert*, ed. Christfried Coler (Berlin, 1956), 218.

6. *PC* 1:93 n. 2.

7. Allen and Allen, *Opus epistolarum Des. Erasmi* 3:376, no. 858, line 561.

8. *ZW* 9:454, line 14; 14:424, line 17.

9. Wilhelm Vogt, ed., "Die Correspondenz des schwäbischen Bundeshauptmanns Ulrich Artzt von Augsburg a. d. J. 1524 und 1525," *Zeitschrift des Historischen Vereins für Schwaben und Neuburg* 6 (1879): 300, no. 22; 10 (1883): 122–23, no. 170.

10. Karl Steiff and Gebhard Mehring, eds., *Geschichtliche Lieder und Sprüche Württembergs* (Stuttgart, 1912), 221, no. 54, stanza 6.

11. Julius Volk, "Zur Frage der Reichspolitik gegenüber dem Bauernkrieg," in *Staat und Persönlichkeit: Erich Brandenburg zum 60. Geburtstag dargebracht*, ed. Alfred Doren et al. (Leipzig, 1928), 79 n. 26, 82.

12. *PC* 1:196, no. 344.

13. Alphonse Wollbrett, "Scherwiller-Châtenois et le Valle de Villé," in *La Guerre des Paysans 1525* (Saverne, 1975), 90.

14. Andreas Keller, ca. 1523–24, quoted in Heiko A. Oberman, *Masters of the Reformation: The Emergence of a New Intellectual Climate in Europe*, trans. Dennis Martin (Cambridge, 1981), 293 n. 10.

15. *BDS* 2:462–65, here at 462, lines 8–9; and the Senate's action in ibid., 466–67.

16. Sturm's memorial is published in Thomas A. Brady, Jr., "'Sind also zu beiden theilen Christen, des Gott erbarm': Le mémoire de Jacques Sturm sur le culte publique à Strasbourg (août 1525)," in *Horizons européens de la Réforme en Alsace: Mélanges offerts à Jean Rott pour son 65e anniversaire*, ed. Marijn de Kroon and Marc Lienhard (Strasbourg, 1980), 69–79, whence the quotes in this paragraph.

17. Ibid., 75, lines 68–73.

18. Ibid., 75–76 lines 76–99.

19. Ibid., 76 lines 109–19.

20. "Ann. Brant," no. 4701 (24 September 1526).

21. *PC* 4:857, no. 729.

22. Specklin, no. 2316.

23. Sturm's comments, recorded at Smalkalden in December 1529 by Chancellor Georg Vogler of Brandenburg-Ansbach, are printed by Hans von Schubert, *Bekenntnisbildung und Religionspolitik 1529/30 (1524 bis 1534). Untersuchungen und Texte* (Gotha, 1910), 167–82, from which the remaining quotes in this paragraph are taken.

24. *PC* 1:263–64, no. 464; and there, too, the remaining quotes in this paragraph.

25. Lenz 2:450 n. 2.

26. *ZW* 14:424, lines 19–22.

27. *TAE* 2:354 n. 2, line 41.

28. *PC* 2:237, no. 259.

29. Wolfgang Capito to Jacob Sturm, Strasbourg, 4 March 1526, in *In Habakuk prophetam V. Capitonis enarrationes* (Strasbourg: Wolf Köpfel, 1526), A.ii^r. The following quote is from the same source.

30. *PC* 1:264, no. 464.

31. "Ann. Brant," no. 4701.
32. Jacob von Gottesheim, "Les éphemerides de Jacques de Gottesheim, docteur en droit, prébendier du Grand-Choeur de la Cathédrale (1524–1543)," ed. Rodolphe Reuss, in *BSCMHA*, 2d ser., 19 (1898): 272.
33. "Ann. Brant," nos. 4735, 4741.
34. Karl Marx, "Kritik der Hegelschen Rechtsphilosophie. Einleitung," in Karl Marx, *Werke*, ed. Hans-Joachim Lieber, 6 vols., 2d ed. (Darmstadt, 1962), 1:501.
35. "Reformation of the Emperor Sigismund," in Strauss, *Manifestations of Discontent*, 30.

5

A NEW POLITICS

In politics the middle way is none at all.

—John Adams

Revolutionary times have a way of making traditional policies obsolete. For a time, politicians will try to steer a middle way between a discredited old policy and an indicated new one, but, sooner or later, someone will have to blaze the trail to a new policy. In precisely this uncertain situation the South German free cities, Strasbourg, and Jacob Sturm stood just after the Peasants' War.

AFTER THE REVOLUTION

The internal harmony of states is closely related to their external security, and a disruption of one will generally, at very least, unsettle the other. Hence, the local forces, which the Reformation movement set in motion, often sent magistrates and princes scurrying for new, more compatible allies. At Strasbourg, for example, the magistrates' initial reaction was to revive the old foreign policy, solidarity with the Swiss cities, and by August 1523 rumor was spreading that "the Strasbourgeois are intriguing with the Swiss."[1] The rumor was true. The twin pressures of reformation—the popular movement from below and the emperor's anti-Lutheran stance from above—worked most intensely on the southern urban regimes. It undermined their traditional policy of urban solidarity and Imperial loyalty against the princes in and outside the Imperial Diet. The deepening crisis over religion, which the Peasants' War immeasurably intensified, eroded this traditional policy's basis by sharpening the blades—an aroused commons and an intransigent monarch—of a new political scissors. The free cities' magistrates feared, as Sturm learned from the urban diet at Speyer in September 1525, the "danger to the soul's salvation, apostasy, and destruction of authority and social discipline, which have arisen from the preachers' proclamation and explanation of the holy Gospel to the common people in the cities in contradictory ways."[2]

94

The free cities' regimes wanted both relief from the anti-Lutheran Edict of Worms and a referral of the schism to a General Council of the church—precisely what they got from the Imperial Diet of Speyer in 1526. Jacob Sturm, who in the previous year had been asked to help Augsburg's Conrad Peutinger (1465–1547) to carry the cities' case to Archduke Ferdinand,[3] was named to head Strasbourg's delegation to the Diet, his first. When he and Ammeister Martin Herlin of the Furriers' Guild left for Speyer in the spring of 1526, their instruction called for a permanent religious settlement through a General Council of the church, because "no one, no matter to what party he belongs, should have to fear attack because of his faith, which in any case is, and should be, a matter of free choice."[4] Free choice by rulers, of course, not by their subjects. At Speyer reigned an atmosphere of stunned reasonableness, a fruit both of the previous year's insurrection and of terrible news of the Ottoman sultan's imminent invasion of Hungary. Desperate to aid his Hungarian brother-in-law, King Louis II (r. 1516–26), Archduke Ferdinand referred the religious question to a twenty-person committee of the Diet. Sturm, as ranking envoy of Strasbourg, sat as one of the free cities' two representatives in the committee.

Speyer was Sturm's first chance to shine in an Imperial setting, and he seized it, warning the committee that to enforce the Edict of Worms "would affect many Estates, and especially the cities, by weakening and even destroying peace, order, and unity." Instead, he urged, a General Council or an Imperial council—whatever that might be—of the church ought to be called.[5] The committee's majority agreed, and so did the Diet, and when Ferdinand promised a General Council within eighteen months, the Diet proclaimed that in the interim each regime would act "in such a way as he will be responsible for to God and the emperor."[6] This deceptively bland formula represented, as the Estates confessed, their fear of "a new and larger revolt."[7]

One sign of the tension at Strasbourg is the hero's welcome that Jacob Sturm received on his return from Speyer. To honor their new political star, the Senate & XXI ordered a medal struck, an act of recognition without precedent or parallel in this era. It bears Sturm's portrait, name, and age (IACOBUS STURM. ANNO AETA[TIS] SUE XXXVI).[8] The portrait, though not fine, is the only likeness of him from this stage of his life. It shows a young man of strong facial features, including a prominent nose, and less stout than he would later become. The hair is curly and close-cropped and the beard short but full. The medal's obverse bears trophies, the Sturm arms, and an inscription: "Patience conquers fortune. 1526" (VICTRIX FORTUNE PATIENTIA. MDXXVI). Fortune, that subject of an incessant Renaissance curiosity, yields neither to arms nor to learning—two favorite Renaissance methods—but to patience alone. It was a perfect motto in the hushed, postrevolutionary spirit of 1526, for it corresponded perfectly to the urban magistrates' quests for internal harmony and external security. So far as Sturm's career was concerned, the motto was truly prophetic.

THE EVANGELICAL PRINCES

While the postrevolutionary political surface calmed with the promise of restoration and a relief of tensions, at greater depths the tide was running toward a new Imperial politics of religious parties that cut right across social boundaries. The first signs of this turn came already at Speyer, where Sturm and some other urban envoys listened to overtures of solidarity from the Empire's two ranking Evangelical princes, Landgrave Philip of Hesse and Elector John of Saxony. The two princes, who jointly proposed an alliance based on common religion, were as different as could be imagined.

Young Philip of Hesse (b. 1504, r. 1509–67) was as handsome and as ambitious as a young German prince could be. For years, during his boyhood, his redoubtable mother had struggled to defend his succession to the Hessian lands, and now the twenty-two-year-old was emerging onto the stage of Imperial politics, headstrong, intelligent but poorly educated, and already hot for the Evangelical cause. Landgrave Philip, called "the Magnanimous," was to become the pile-driver of German Protestantism. His lands sat astride the central highlands east of the Rhine, facing both northward and southward, though in these years his gaze turned mostly southward to the tempting string of prince-bishoprics along the Main River's "priests' alley" and beyond to the duchy of Württemberg. Since the dispossession of its prince, Duke Ulrich, by the Swabian League in 1519, Württemberg as part of Austria had become an important center of Catholic resistance to the Reformation. Philip was determined to restore Ulrich, who was both his cousin and his long-term guest, to his rights and his lands, and the Reformation, by revitalizing the princely opposition to the monarchy, seemed to be making that goal thinkable, if not yet possible.

On Hesse's eastern flank lay the domains of Philip's partner, the Saxon elector, John (b. 1468, r. 1525–32), whose stolid character is suggested by his epithet, "the Steadfast" or "the Constant." John was thoughtful and cautious, as befitted one who had waited so long to succeed. Now fifty-eight years old, he had for decades stood in the shadow of his brother, Elector Frederick (b. 1463, r. 1485–1525), called "the Wise," one of the great Imperial figures of his generation. In some ways John was nevertheless a better head of the Protestant party than Frederick might have been, had he lived. Frederick had kept his religious convictions as hidden—he defended his Professor Luther while he continue to add to his great collection of relics in Wittenberg's Castle Church—as he had the reasons why, against every dynastic interest, he had refused to marry. Frederick's death in the year of the Peasants' War made John head of the Wettin dynasty's Ernestine, or senior, line, whose lands stretched from Coburg in present-day Bavaria to the environs of Berlin, and whose mines in the bowels of the Erzgebirge along the Bohemian border gorged his treasury with silver. John's freedom of action, like his brother's, was checked by a dynastic mortgage, the Ernestines' bitter rivalry with their Albertine cousins at Dresden. John was pious, loyal, and brave, though not especially intelligent and certainly no match for his Albertine cousin, Duke George, "the Bearded" (b. 1471, r. 1500–39).

In 1526, before the Diet of Speyer opened, Elector John and Landgrave Philip formed the League of Torgau-Gotha to defend what Duke George condemned as "the Lutheran sect." It was the first Evangelical alliance, the ancestor of all others. Unlike in temperament and thirty-six years apart in age, these two founders of Protestant politics also possessed two quite different ruling styles, which made them in some respects an ill-matched team. Philip, his own prime minister, recruited councilors from his own burghers and nobles and ruled the Hessian clergy with an iron hand. At Elector John's court, by contrast, the upper hand swayed back and forth between the Evangelical activists at court, who were led by Count Albert of Mansfeld, and the devout faction around Chancellor Gregor Brück.

The notion of expanding their political influence southward by military means surely came from Landgrave Philip, whose dynastic history provided him with, among other things, a high appreciation for the financial power of the great Rhenish and Swabian free cities. His first move came too early, however, for in 1526 the southerners were not yet ready to speak of the "broad alliance" he recommended to their envoys at Speyer, even though Jacob Sturm was so impressed that he asked his colleagues at home for permission to explore the princes' offer. Both sides agreed to discuss the matter again at Frankfurt during the Spring Fair, and there the matter rested. The Hessian prince had need of the cities, but they, for the moment, had no need of him. And so, when the princes' draft treaty was brought to Strasbourg, the regime told Sturm and Herlin, their envoys to the Imperial Diet of Regensburg in May 1527, to give the princes "a friendly refusal." With the emperor at war with the pope, such a move was not "useful or beneficial."[9] Later in the same year, Sturm was told that "if you are approached again concerning an alliance with Saxony and Hesse, simply repeat what we told them last time."[10]

The southern cities' standoffish tone expressed the outlook of the big folk—magistrates of Strasbourg, Nuremberg, Ulm, Frankfurt, and Augsburg—after the Peasants' War. During the next few years, they groped for an alternative, preferably an urban alternative, to the Swabian League and to the Evangelical league the two princes offered. By mid-1528 Jacob Sturm had turned skeptical about the future of a purely urban league, "because the cities are divided over the matter from which all the present troubles arise [i.e., religion], and they do not trust one another very much."[11] A better way, he thought, would be a consultation among the "neighbors and friends . . . who are favorably inclined to the cause." A league based on religion, therefore, and not of cities only. In a new instruction, in late July, he took the next logical step and opined that "the Swabian League must be blocked." By 1528, therefore, Sturm was beginning to grasp the logic of a new politics based on the religious schism, its splitting of the Imperial estates into religious parties, and its power to form new solidarities across old regional and social boundaries. He responded with his own new politics, an Evangelical politics of cities and princes allied to defend their common religion against the Swabian League and the House of Austria.

STURM'S NEW POLITICS

In these years after 1525, Sturm learned to modify his three lessons from the Peasants' War—the Common Man's courage, the Empire's weakness, and the princes' might—through the addition of a fourth lesson: the free cities' inability to defend themselves. He drew from the combination of these lessons the decison for a new politics, a search for new alliances more suited to the times. The change was not altogether lost on his colleagues at Strasbourg. For one thing, seeing his point about the Swabian League, now a Catholic bulwark, they told the Ulmers that they would enter no alliance that excepted the league from its potential enemies.[12] For another, they honored Sturm once again, this time in the context of his brand new connection to the Hessian landgrave. At the end of 1528, Sturm returned from his first tête-à-tête negotiations with Philip, bringing a fine stallion as the prince's gift to the Senate & XXI. The magistrates promptly bestowed the handsome beast on their young star. The gift marked an important moment, for, unbeknownst perhaps even to themselves, Jacob Sturm and Landgrave Philip had formed a partnership which would in time make them the architects of the Smalkaldic League.

Why did Jacob Sturm make this fateful, unprecedented turn toward the Lutheran princes of central Germany, a region to which Strasbourg had few traditional ties and in which its citizens had few interests? Why not recapture the old "new" politics of turning to those old friends and neighbors, the Swiss cities, whose communal traditions paralleled Strasbourg's, whose preachers stayed in close touch with their Strasbourg colleagues, and whose politicians spoke good Alemannic? In many ways, the Reformation movement's advance strengthened the reasons for Strasbourg's "turning Swiss" as much as the Burgundian threat had done, more than fifty years before. Strasbourg's religious reformation, after all, was sailing more or less in Zurich's wake, and its preachers boldly took Zwingli's side against Luther in the quarrel about Evangelical doctrine. Southward was the natural direction, too, in which to look for political allies, as Sturm's colleagues began to do in mid-1527, when the Schöffen gave them permission "to look for an alliance." By April 1528 the XIII, prodded "to take the matter in hand," began sending secret missions to Zurich, which led on 5 January 1530 to the formation of a Christian Federation among Strasbourg, Zurich, Basel, and Bern.[13]

STURM'S SWISS LESSONS

Jacob Sturm nonetheless preferred his own new politics of Evangelical solidarity to the Christian Federation, and his personal experiences of the Swiss reformation amply confirmed this preference. In three different contexts between November 1528 and June 1529, Sturm witnessed Swiss struggles over religion. The first occasion was his mission in mid-November 1528 to Bern, where he mediated between the regime and some of its upland subjects, who had ejected the Evangelical preachers, reinstalled their priests, restored the Mass, refused tithes, and declared their will "not to be driven from the old faith and their liberties."[14] The mediators, Sturm reported, "handled the matter as best they could, so that the subjects might be forgiven," but in the event the uplanders were ordered to "uproot the Mass, burn and destroy the images, break up and destroy the altars, and drive out the priests immediately, [or we will] do it with might and main and acts of force."[15] Two months later, Sturm—puzzled, perhaps, by his experience of common people who struggled *for* the Mass and *for* their priests—advised his colleagues at Strasbourg not to suppress the Mass with force.

Troubling, too, was Sturm's mission of mediation at Basel toward the end of 1528. He came "to see if they [he and other mediators] couldn't help plant a goodly peace and unity among us [Baselers], so that we should come to an agreement about God's Word."[16] He found the city on the brink of insurrection, he told Landgrave Philip, as "the two parties had assembled in arms on Christmas Eve" but were persuaded to go home and to address petitions to the senate. When two thousand Baselers sided with the Evangelical preachers and four to five hundred with the priests and the Mass, the magistrates and mediators got the two parties to agree that "from now on nothing but the pure Word of God should be preached, grounded in Holy Scripture, both Old Testament and New. Whoever preaches otherwise will be sacked."[17] The whole matter was to be put to a public disputation on Sunday after Trinity (30 May), whereupon the burghers "will be asked to judge by their consciences whether the Mass should remain or be abolished, and what the majority decides, the city will stick to."[18] The impatient Evangelicals, however, took direct action in January, whereupon the magistrates drew the obvious lesson and abolished the Mass. At Basel the Reformation was decided by the burghers, in whose judgment about religion Sturm had so little trust.

Sturm's third experience of Swiss conflict over religion found the confederacy at the very brink of war. In June 1529 he went to mediate between the Evangelical city-states and the Catholic "Five Members" of the interior (Uri, Schwyz, Unterwalden, Zug, and Lucerne), who took up arms against Zurich's efforts to push Zwingli's doctrines into the jointly ruled lands called "common lordships." Sturm and Conrad Joham passed through Basel on 14 June on their way to the front at Kappel, which lay in Zurich territory west of Lake Zurich. At Kappel, Bernese diffidence and rain, which delayed the Austrians' arrival, cooled the two sides' ardor for battle. Tradition says that Sturm rode between the battle lines at Kappel, and Basel reports gave the Strasbourgeois the lion's share of credit for the peace signed on 25 June. According to a story reported by Heinrich Bullinger, Sturm expressed his wonder at how quickly the parties' mood turned from war to peace. "You confederates," he said, "are wondrous folk. When you are at loggerheads, you are really united, for even then you don't forget the old friendship."[19] After a tremendous feast at Zurich, where 726 guildsmen feted them as heroes, Sturm and Joham rode off to Basel and then home. The confederacy had averted "this time," as Sturm said, a confessional war.

Jacob Sturm's three missions among the Swiss in 1528–29 dramatized for him the volatile possibilities posed by disunity over religion in general and the Reformation's collision with particularist populism—native to the confederacy, but also to the Upper Rhine—in particular. All the late medieval political struggles in these regions had drawn strength from the spirit of party, intensified by social enmities, as small corporations and communes strove to protect themselves from the dominion of larger, wealthier, or more prestigious powers. This was as true of Strasbourg's own guild revolts as it had been of the great alliance against the Burgundian power. The positive valence of this tradition came into a new light, however, with the Peasants' War of 1525. The addition of religion to the grounds of party—"faction," he called it—turned Sturm against the entire tradition. It was his own tradition, for, once upon a time, his great-grandfather had journeyed to Bern to preach red war against the Burgundians. At the end of the 1520s, Sturm came among the Swiss as a messenger of religious peace—between subjects and rulers, between guilds and magistrates, and between the Swiss powers themselves. New times, new politics.

Among the new times' important features was the renaissance of heavy infantry, which at last allowed the military potential of the common people to make its weight felt on the battlefields of Europe. If such folk wielded pike and gun in the service of emperors, kings, princes, and urban regimes, why not in their own? Why not, indeed, especially if inspired by the spirit of religious party and the ideal of justice in the form of "godly law"? Men of authority all across the German-speaking world knew what that meant, for less than a century had passed since the end of the Hussite Wars. The disunity and uncertainty about religion, which was spreading through the Empire at this time, threatened to unhinge the entire political order based on small, relatively weakly defined, nonsovereign governments and to split their political bodies into irreconcilable religious parties. Jacob Sturm was fully aware of this danger—his responses to the Peasants' War show this—which supplied the strongest possible reason for him to see in the central German Evangelical princes more adequate allies than the Swiss cities.

PROTESTANTS: SPEYER 1529

Jacob Sturm's influence alone helps to explain his regime's decision in the summer of 1529 to pursue not only "a neighborly alliance with the Swiss" but also "at the same time . . . the Christian alliance" with the Lutheran princes.[20] It seemed like the right time to hedge all bets, for in April the Evangelical cities and princes had come together during the Imperial Diet of Speyer. They united behind a protest against the Diet's decision on religion—hence the name, Protestants. This Diet, presided over by King Ferdinand, who now wore the crowns of Hungary and Bohemia, disspelled the post-1525 uncertainty and for the first time lent dramatic scope and palpable form to the confessional parties.

The Strasbourgeois' initial experience of the new confessional politics was not pleasant. "Christ is handed over to Caiphas and Pilate," Ammeister Mathis Pfarrer wrote home when the Diet's committee recommended enforcement of the Edict of Worms. In reply, Strasbourg's XIII gave Sturm and Pfarrer a relatively free hand to negotiate with "electors and princes, also lords and cities," especially those "who adhere to the Gospel," though not to strike an alliance.[21] If they needed a sure sign of the new situation, it came when Sturm's cousin, Ammeister Daniel Mieg, arrived at Speyer to take Strasbourg's seat in the Governing Council—it had moved there from Esslingen—and was ejected because his regime had abolished the Mass. "If Strasbourg is to be deprived of its rights for having worked for the greater glory of God and dethroning idolatry," Sturm angrily scolded the Diet, "then the city can no longer take any regard for the Empire in its affairs." Instead, the Strasbourgeois would turn to the king of France, who "has wanted to treat with us and has offered us an annual subsidy of several thousand crowns," and to "our Swiss neighbors, who will be equally willing to admit us to their Confederacy, just as they took in Basel twenty-nine years ago. We certainly do not lack friends."[22] Brave words, yet France and the Swiss were far away. Much nearer were the Evangelical princes, and on 12 April Sturm went over to their policy of refusing taxes. Ten days later, Sturm, contrary to his instructions from home, signed a six-year mutual defense pact with the Saxon elector, the Hessian landgrave, and the cities of Nuremberg and Ulm.

THE EUCHARISTIC DISPUTE

The new alliance, called Protestant after its protest against the Diet's decision on religion, was crippled from birth, for it was founded on the assumption of a common faith at a time when the very content of that faith stood at issue between parties headed respectively by Martin Luther and Huldrych Zwingli. The roots of this quarrel reached back about five years, when the first disagreements had begun to surface between the followers of the Wittenberg professor and those of the Zurich preacher. Although it gradually crystallized around the issue of Christ's real presence in the Eucharist, the Zwinglians holding that He was present only "by faith" and the Lutherans that He was "really" present, that is, regardless of the communicant's belief, the Evangelical split involved many other issues as well. Modern opinion tends to hold that the breach was inevitable, whether because of differences of intellectual heritage, Luther coming from Augustinian scholasticism, Zwingli from Erasmian biblicism, or of social milieu—Luther and the princes, Zwingli and the burghers. What is certain is that most of the South German urban preachers tended to take the Zwinglian side of the quarrel, but the political consolidation of German Protestantism eventually pulled most of them, or at least their cities, back into the Lutheran camp. The Swiss Zwinglians, meanwhile, maintained their aloofness from the Lutheranism and contributed to the later rise of German-speaking Calvinism. Here, in the heart of the German-speaking world during the Reformation's first decade, therefore, formed the fissure that would one day divide Protestant Christianity into two great, relatively antagonistic wings, Lutheran and Reformed. This outcome was nonetheless very remote in 1529, when the quarrel's chief import was to disrupt the first Protestant union.

In the beginning, Jacob Sturm badly misjudged the danger this quarrel posed to the new Protestant party, whose members had at Speyer defined themselves simply as those who adhered to "the divine Word." Was this sufficiently clear? Apparently not, for Sturm had also handed to the Saxons a brief statement of what the Strasbourgeois preached on the main issue, the sacrament of the Eucharist, or Lord's Supper. This document—"error clothed in such finely ornamented and chosen words," Nuremberg's preachers later called it—denied the real presence of Christ in the sacrament and insisted that each side be permitted to hold its own opinion, so long as it confessed belief in God through Jesus Christ.[23] Sturm thought the statement adequate, and so did the Hessian landgrave, who reported that the Evangelicals found themselves "in agreement on the chief doctrine, though differing in their understandings of it."[24] All too soon, however, Lutheran theologians in Saxony, at Nuremberg, and elsewhere were claiming that "Sacramentarians"—their name for those who held Zwingli's representational doctrine of the Eucharist—opened the door to religious and political rebellion à la Müntzer and 1525. "They teach," Philip Melanchthon complained, "that the Holy Spirit is not given through the Word or the Sacrament but is given without the Word and the Sacrament." Thomas Müntzer, the arch-rebel of 1525, he sniffed, had "taught the same thing."[25] This Lutheran charge, howled Martin Bucer at Strasbourg, was "the most intolerable and terrible that can be imagined."[26]

Sturm apparently felt, or hoped, that the theological storm would blow over, for he and his colleagues steamed ahead on their chosen course. They pledged the landgrave their aid in case of attack and asked their Swiss friends to make room for the Hessian prince in their own Christian Federation. This suited Landgrave Philip just fine, for he was working to bring Luther and Zwingli together at Castle Marburg in the fall. Alas, at this moment, in early summer 1529, the Lutheran storm began to break over the southern Sacramentarians. The first signal came to Strasbourg in early June, when Mathis Pfarrer brought home from Rodach in Franconia a new set of Saxon conditions for making good on the promise to form an alliance. The second came in August, when Sturm and Pfarrer arrived for a meeting at Schwabach, also in Franconia, only to learn that the elector had canceled it without notice.

THE MARBURG COLLOQUY

Preparations nonetheless rolled ahead for the Luther-Zwingli meeting in September at Marburg in Hesse, where, Sturm hinted to the Baselers, "perhaps there would be discussion not only about the [doctrinal] concord but also about highly important matters concerning the welfare of the German nation."[27] Landgrave Philip told Sturm that "for pressing reasons, we want you especially to be present" and to bring "two judicious, unquarrelsome [preachers], who are inclined to peace and unity."[28] The whole purpose of the Marburg discussion, called a "colloquy," was to reopen the way to a consolidation of the Evangelicals into a broadly based military alliance.

The Marburg-bound Swiss, including Zwingli, Johannes Oecolampadius (1482–1531) of Basel, and magistrates from Zurich and Basel, assembled in mid-September at Strasbourg, whence Sturm conducted them via friendly stations to Marburg in Hesse. At Marburg, alas, reigned rancor instead of the expected concord, and, fearing the worst, on 3 October Sturm moved to head off a disaster. "Gracious lord," he said to Landgrave Philip, "you have arranged this meeting in order to achieve, with God's help, unity about the disputed article on the Sacrament." Here at Marburg, however, "Doctor Martin Luther charged that the doctrine taught at Strasbourg contains errors not only about the Sacrament, but about other points as well. I find it intolerable, having been sent to reach concord on a single point, to have to go home and report disunity on four or five different points." Sturm asked the landgrave "to allow one of our preachers, Martin Bucer, to be heard on behalf of my masters concerning the doctrine in question, and that, if we are in error, it be explained to us just where we err."[29] To no avail, for Bucer's intervention achieved nothing, and Luther and Zwingli parted on the worst possible terms.

The undaunted Hessian prince nonetheless moved ahead on the political front. Flanked by Sturm and Duke Ulrich, at Marburg Philip suggested to the Swiss politicians that the Habsburg menace could be countered by a union of "all or the majority of the governments that have, up to this time, encouraged the proclamation of God's Word in their lands," and he promised that in case of war he would ride to their aid with two thousand horse, artillery, and provisions.[30] The politicians took his words home, and ten months later a short-lived Hessian-Strasbourg-Swiss alliance came into being.

The colloquy at Marburg went down in history as the sole face-to-face meeting of Luther and Zwingli, whose quarrel sealed a split that permanently divided the Protestant churches. If Marburg signaled the end of Protestant unity, it also marked the beginnings of the potent collaboration between Jacob Sturm and Martin Bucer, who for the next fifteen years formed the most effective political team in the Protestant camp. The most remarkable part of this story concerns not Sturm, who in a certain sense was born to power, but Bucer, an artisan's son, whose ascent from obscurity and social marginality began in May 1523, when as a penniless refugee he arrived at Strasbourg. Although his father had once been a local citizen, Bucer's early association with the notorious Franz von Sickingen had caused the magistrates initially to treat him with "a good deal of reserve."[31] Gradually, though, his militancy, tireless advocacy, and fertile pen made him the colleague, then the rival, and finally the superior of the better educated, better connected, but languid and mercurial Wolfgang Capito. Not only did Capito's poor political judgment win him Jacob Sturm's ire, he also had a fatal hankering for Anabaptist company.

Meanwhile, Bucer's star was in ascent. Very likely it was Sturm who first brought him to the attention of Landgrave Philip, who asked Sturm to bring to Marburg "two judicious, unquarrelsome [preachers], who are inclined to peace and unity" and suggested that Bucer be one of them.[32] At Marburg Bucer and Sturm worked in the same harness for the first time, and Bucer's performance there made him Sturm's theologian of choice for political affairs. This interesting collaboration between Sturm, who had been born somebody, and Bucer, a nobody who had worked hard to become somebody, proved the strongest weapon for Protestant unity, and it also made them good friends. All the more bitter, therefore, would be their parting in the late 1540s, when they quarreled irreconcilably over what was owed respectively to God and to Mammon.

PROTESTANTISM DIVIDED

At the moment, the Lutheran storm was breaking over Sacramentarian heads. One month after Marburg, Strasbourg's regime learned that the Saxon elector would consummate the alliance only if all parties signed a decidedly Lutheran statement of doctrine called the Schwabach Articles. The landgrave fumed,

reckoning that the elector would be a fool to throw away the cities' might—
fifty to sixty thousand infantry, he reckoned—for one point of doctrine. To
Jacob Sturm he opened his heart as never before: "Dear Jacob Sturm, it is
time. If we sleep and let the lamps burn out, the Bridegroom will not let us
in." Perhaps Philip knew the magnificent portrayal of the wise and foolish
virgins on the central west portal of Strasbourg's cathedral. In any case, he
thought that the crisis posed three choices: submission to the emperor and
revocation of the reforms, passive resistance and resignation to persecution, or
active defense. "In the latter choice lie fortune and hope, in the others absolutely nothing."[33]

The XIII of Strasbourg agreed, and they instructed Sturm to say at the next
meeting, called for Smalkalden in Thuringia at the end of November 1529,
that "we are agreed on the chief points of our true Christian faith, [namely,]
that Almighty God, out of love for the human race, sent His only-begotten
Son into this world, Who in His true, assumed human nature, died for us and
for our justification arose from the dead."[34] Arriving at Smalkalden on 28
November in the company of Mathis Pfarrer, Sturm told the princes' envoys
that "the [Schwabach] articles are somewhat excessive and argumentative," and
that "it is to be feared that if the preachers have or develop divergent opinions
about them, it will help our enemies and lead to divisions." On 2 December,
flanked by Ulm's Bernhard Besserer (1471–1542), Sturm declared that "our
masters will also agree to no league in any form, except one which protects
and guards their faith, such as they have held it for some time and, with the
Almighty's help, intend to hold in the future."[35] Then the Strasbourgeois rode
right across the Empire toward home, where Sturm laid the situation before
the Senate & XXI on 15 December. He quoted the landgrave's words: "The
matter rests on three alternatives: we await God's pleasure; we try to placate
the emperor; or we prepare to expect his wrath."[36] Three days later, the regime
sent envoys "up to the [Swiss] Confederacy to treat of all manner of business,
about which you [Landgrave Philip] know from us, finally to agree upon it,
and if possible to conclude it."[37] The treaty's text was ready by 20 December,
and Strasbourg's Schöffen voted on it on the twenty-ninth: 184 for the treaty,
30 for delay, and only 4 against. On 9 January 1530, the Senate & XXI approved the treaty—38 votes to 11—and eight days later the ammeister announced to the guilds that "it is done and approved."[38] The very first fruit of
the Reformation in the area of foreign policy, therefore, was to restore the old
network of political particularism. Strasbourg had turned Swiss, and who was
to gainsay those who predicted that, like its sister Alsatian city, Basel, it might
so remain?

NOTES

1. Hermann Baumgarten, *Geschichte Karls V.*, 3 vols. (Stuttgart, 1885–92), 2:313 n.
2. Georg Schmidt, *Der Städtetag in der Reichsverfassung: Eine Untersuchung zur korporativen Politik der Freien und Reichsstädte in der ersten Hälfte des 16. Jahrhunderts* (Wiesbaden, 1984), 490; and the following quote is at 491.
3. This mission was later canceled.
4. "Ann. Brant," no. 4682; *PC* 1:255–56, no. 450, and the following quote is at 255.
5. *PC* 1:259, no. 453.
6. Johann Jakob Schmauss, ed., *Neue und vollständigere Sammlung der Reichs-Abschiede*, 4 vols. (Frankfurt am Main, 1747; reprint, Osnabrück, 1967), 2:274.
7. Walter Friedensburg, *Der Reichstag zu Speier 1526 im Zusammenhang der politischen und kirchlichen Entwicklung Deutschlands im Reformationszeitalter* (Berlin, 1887; reprint, 1970), 560.
8. Reproduced by Johannes Ficker, ed., *Bildnisse der Straßburger Reformation* (Strasbourg, 1914), table 1.
9. *PC* 1:280–83, nos. 491–92.
10. Ibid., no. 501.
11. Ibid. 1:296–98, no. 525. There, too, are the other quotes in this paragraph.
12. In the German tradition of forming leagues, it was the practice to name those against whom the alliance would have no binding force. This normally included the emperor and the Empire and, in the southern regions, the Swabian League, which had quasi-official status as a peace-keeping alliance.
13. "Ann. Brant," no. 4734.
14. Rudolf Dellsperger, "Zehn Jahre bernischer Reformationsgeschichte (1522–1532): Eine Einführung," in *450 Jahre Berner Reformation: Beiträge zur Geschichte der Berner Reformation und zu Niklaus Manuel*, ed. by the Historischer Verein des Kantons Bern (Bern, 1980), 47.
15. *AGBR* 3:185, no. 263; Dellsperger, "Zehn Jahre," 45.
16. Fridolin Ryff, *Die Chronik des Fridolin Ryff 1514–1541 mit der Fortsetzung des Peter Ryff 1543–85*, ed. Wilhelm Vischer and Alfred Stern (Leipzig, 1872), 73.
17. *AGBR* 3:238–39, no. 348; and there, too, the remaining quotes in this paragraph.
18. Hans R. Guggisberg, *Basel in the Sixteenth Century: Aspects of the City Republic Before, During, and After the Reformation* (St. Louis, 1982), 29.
19. Heinrich Bullinger, *Reformationsgeschichte nach dem Autographon herausgegeben*, ed. Johann Jakob Hottinger and H. H. Vögeli, 3 vols. (Frauenfeld, 1838–40; reprint, 1985), 2:183.
20. "Ann. Brant," no. 4794.
21. *PC* 1:321, no. 559; "Ann. Brant," 4779; *PC* 1:326.
22. Specklin, no. 2302; Jakob Trausch, "Straßburgische Chronik," in Jakob Trausch and Johann Wencker, "Les chroniques strasbourgeoises," ed. Léon Dacheux, *BSCMHA*, 2d ser., 15 (1892): no. 2682.
23. Johann Baptist Riederer, *Nachrichten zur Kirchen-, Gelehrten- und Bücher-Geschichte*, 4 vols. (Nuremberg, 1764–68), 2:218.
24. *RTA, jR* 7, ed. Johannes Kühn (Gotha, 1935; reprint, 1963), 820–21.
25. *CR* 1:1101, no. 637.
26. *BDS* 3:355.
27. *ZW* 10: no. 910.
28. *PC* 1:382, no. 632; Lenz 1:8.

29. Walter Köhler, ed. *Das Marburger Religionsgespräch: Versuch einer Rekonstruktion* (Leipzig, 1929), 127–28.
30. *EA* 4, pt. 1b, 484, no. 196 zu "b."
31. *BDS* 1:346–47.
32. *PC* 1:382, no. 632; Lenz, 1:8.
33. *PC* 1:408, no. 675.
34. *PC* 1:412–18, no. 682; also in *RTA, jR* 8:389–94, no. 1214.
35. *PC* 1:419; Walther Köhler, *Zwingli und Luther: Ihr Streit um das Abendmahl nach seinen politischen und religiösen Beziehungen*, 2 vols. (Leipzig, 1924; reprint, Gütersloh, 1953), 2:170.
36. "Ann. Brant," no. 4828.
37. *PC* 1:425, no. 689; *RTA, jR* 8:521.
38. Strasbourg, Archives du Chapître de St.-Thomas, 47/I, no. 18; "Ann. Brant," nos. 4836, 4843.

6

THE CONSTRUCTION OF PROTESTANTISM

All Protestantism, even the most cold and passive, is a sort of dissent.
—Edmund Burke

Born amidst high hopes in April 1529, by year's end the Protestant alliance lay in shambles. As the clerical war of words heated up and began to split the Evangelicals into parties, the Protestant powers' thoughts turned to Italy, where their monarch, now a crowned Holy Roman emperor, was making ready to return after nearly a decade's absence. During the past five years, Charles's army had made him master of Italy. In 1525 it smashed the French army at Pavia and made the king a prisoner, and in 1527 it broke the anti-Imperial League of Cognac and looted Clement VII's Rome, after Jerusalem the holiest city in Christendom. Then Charles made peace with the pope (29 June 1529) and with Francis I (3 August 1529), and after Clement crowned him Holy Roman emperor at Bologna on 23 February 1530, he made ready to come over the Alps to settle the German schism.

What would Charles V do in the Empire's heartlands, where his face had not been seen since 1521? The emperor was now thirty years old, no longer the untried youth who had come to Worms a decade ago, but a mature monarch and a lord of battles. His call for the Imperial Estates to meet him at Augsburg announced that he intended to settle the dispute over religion. Some thought, correctly, that he was prepared to deal with the Evangelicals reasonably, even generously, though some Protestant powers preferred not to wait and see. So, in the winter of 1529–30, envoys streamed southward to force fortune's hand, if they could. Among them were Ulmers and also agents from Elector John of Saxony, who wanted Habsburg backing against his Wettin cousin at Dresden. To that end, most probably, he would sacrifice his Sacramentarian friends, including Jacob Sturm's Strasbourg, if he must. The elector's interest converged with that of Ferdinand, Bohemia's king and his feudal overlord, for Ferdinand wanted John's vote to make him King of the

Romans and emperor-elect. Charles, similarly, wanted the German question settled, so he could counterattack the Ottomans. Everyone, it seemed, wanted the schism settled in order to get on with some greater venture.

THE RIGHT OF RESISTANCE

Sound reasons of policy thus persuaded Elector John of Saxony and his advisors to repudiate their Sacramentarian allies on the grounds that the Zwinglians erred not only in their Eucharistic doctrine but also in their advocacy of the right actively to resist the emperor. Contrary to legend, Martin Luther did not formulate the opposing, Lutheran doctrine of passive resistance. It was rather the work of South German urban Lutherans as part of their attack on the Swiss errors of Sacramentarianism and rebellion.

A chief teacher of non-resistance was Nuremberg's town clerk, Lazarus Spengler (1479–1534), who wrote in November 1529 that although a Christian *can* "resist with all his power anyone who wants to drive him with force away from Christ's kingdom and into the realm of the Antichrist, it is not a question of what a person, but of what a Christian, should do, and not according to natural or human law but properly in obedience to God's command, law, and order."[1] What, after all, "has the darkness in common with the light, or what reason or natural, carnal wisdom with the Spirit of God?" Johannes Brenz (1499–1570), a Lutheran theologian from Schwäbisch Hall, took up the theme and focused it against the Swiss, whom he condemned in late November 1529 as "a people without a head, which they lack both in heaven and on earth, [who have] left the unity of the Christian church and lost the head, Jesus Christ, and [have] exterminated their own lords."[2] Finally, Philip Melanchthon (1497–1560), Luther's colleague but by origin also a southern burgher, recoined the message into a formula, Sacramentarians rebels, and declared that even if the Swiss Evangelicals were orthodox, the Protestant alliance would be unchristian because of the damage it would cause to the church and to all authority.

What might happen, such writers must have speculated, if Landgrave Philip of Hesse were to ally with the Sacramentarians and invade Württemberg? Well might the landgrave exclaim in disgust, "Oh, dear God, we have such a narrow conscience concerning damage to our subjects and to the truth, but when our property is at stake, we take a much broader view. One could well say to us, as Christ said to those pompous scholars: 'you swallow a camel and gag at a gnat [Matt. 23:24].'" One could indeed well say that, but in early March 1530, when the emperor was moving northward toward Augsburg to convene the Imperial Diet, the Wittenberg theologians swallowed the camel, gagged at the gnat, and went over to nonresistance. "The lawyers are right," they declared, "that a Christian may resist, though not as a Christian but as a citizen or member of the political body."[3] The theologians therefore consented, "though it does not behoove us, and is even dangerous to our consciences, to counsel the formation of an alliance."

The Wittenberg theologians' fears were fully justified, for in the winter of 1529–30 Landgrave Philip and Zwingli were plotting not to resist the emperor but to attack him. They outlined a campaign in the Southwest, with French backing, to split the western from the eastern Austrian lands. Jacob Sturm, who learned of this design from Zwingli at the end of February 1530 and again at Basel in mid-March, saw in it a threat to the policy of Protestant solidarity, which he aimed to revive during the coming session of the Imperial Diet. He hoped to persuade the Lutheran powers that the Sacramentarian dispute was largely verbal, and that "no one should be forced to surrender his opinion on this point, and that each should be permitted his view, so long as he believes in God through Christ and in the love of neighbor through faith."[4] The time for this tack was growing near, and on 22 May Sturm and Ammeister Mathis Pfarrer crossed the Rhine Bridge, rode up over the Black Forest and eastward to Ulm, and went thence by boat to Augsburg.

THE DIET OF AUGSBURG 1530

ASSEMBLING THE DIET

Strasbourg's envoys found the great city on the Lech a cauldron, heated by inflammatory preaching and aboil with anticipation of the emperor's approach. Charles was still en route, and his enormous cavalcade, already across the Brenner Pass, was preparing itself at Innsbruck for the passage over the Fernpass and down the Lech River to Augsburg. Charles and Ferdinand reached the city's outskirts on 15 June. With them came their sister, Queen Mary of Hungary (d. 1558), whose husband had fallen four years ago on the field of Mohács, plus the papal legate, courtiers, and clergy—Spaniards, Italians, Netherlanders, Germans, Hungarians, and Bohemians—guarded by the three-hundred-man Imperial bodyguard and one thousand mercenary infantry, and trailed by the Imperial cooks, apothecaries, falconers, horse-handlers, teamsters, and two hundred Spanish hunting dogs.

Forth from the city to greet the monarchs came the Holy Roman Empire personified: electors, princes, bishops, burghers, and the magistrates and militia of Augsburg. Electors John of Saxony and Joachim of Brandenburg (1484–1535) rode with 200 and 150 horse, respectively. Behind them came Landgrave Philip of Hesse in the midst of 120 crossbowmen dressed in gray, on whose sleeves could be read the motto V.D.M.I.E. It stood for "God's Word endures forever," though naughty Catholics joked that it really meant, "Get the hell out of town!"[5] When the two processions met in a meadow on the Lech's west bank, Conrad Peutinger, Augsburg's town clerk, welcomed the emperor in fine Latin, all the guns and cannon were fired in greeting, and the grand entry began. Across the riverside meadows and into the city the monarchs came, escorted by the electors and other princes and their entourages, the envoys of sixty-one free cities, and the mayor of Augsburg at the head of 1,000 armed guild militia and 200 armored horse. In the van came Charles's bodyguard of infantry, then the emperor, flanked by his brother and the cardinal-legate, riding under Augsburg's official red-white-green canopy carried by six magistrates. Straight into the city's heart they rode, to the Perlach tower by the old town hall, where the bishop and clergy took Charles in their midst and led him to the cathedral. After the Te Deum in the cathedral, to which "none of the common folk was admitted,"[6] Charles went to the episcopal palace on foot, accompanied by his royal brother, the cardinal-legate, "and all the princes and lords."[7] There he resided for about four months, his presence both enriching the burghers and reminding them of their dependence on him and the world he represented.

The Diet of Augsburg in 1530 was the most glittering, most splendid Imperial assembly of the Reformation era, a theatrical dramatization of the Empire itself. Here, in the city on the Lech, the contest among the emperor, the king, the papal legate, and the religious parties truly began; here, thirty-five years later, it would find its provisional end in the Religious Peace of Augsburg of 1555. Nothing, however, ever rivaled the pomp and splendor of the entry and the Diet of 1530, a gigantic and complex act of propaganda which dramatized, on the one hand, the might and splendor of the House of Austria and, on the other, the power of the Empire's great lords, from whose ranks, if from anywhere, effective opposition to the Habsburgs had to come. The burghers, by contrast, played no very significant role, either in the negotiations that formed the Diet's main business or in the whirl of entertainments—parties, balls, dinners, and hunts—that kept the nobles amused while the burghers cooled their heels.

Jacob Sturm had his first glimpse of his monarch at Augsburg on 15 June 1530, the day of Charles's entry. He would have his last at Cologne in September 1548, when he made rebel Strasbourg's submission to its sovereign. Charles was a slim man of middle height, bearing the long nose and thrusting lower jaw that marked members of the House of Austria. A lonely man, whose portraits—after 1532 he allowed no one but Titian to paint him—show him unaccompanied by family members or courtiers, at most by hunting dogs, as if to say that he truly trusted no other human being. He was a quiet man who kept his own counsel, of whom Luther, who admired him to the end, said that "he talks as much in one year as I do on one day."[8] A devout man in his way, too, though in this, as in his dress and habits, and perhaps in his conception of empire, quite unlike his medieval predecessors. A French-speaking Netherlander by upbringing, Charles had inherited from his paternal grandfather the Austrian lands and an expectation on the Imperial crown, plus the great Burgundian dream of restoring Christendom to unity. To this legacy came others: the Iberian heritage of his maternal grandparents, the revived Ottoman challenge under Sultan Suleÿman I, and the nagging German schism.

Charles V came to Augsburg determined to settle the schism not by compromise or force but through negotiation and arbitration. On the way hither he took a terrible blow, the death of Grand Chancellor Mercurino Arborio di Gattinara (d. 1530), the Piedmontese nobleman who, more than any other person, had drilled into the young emperor his duty to bring universal peace to Christendom. At Charles's accession in 1519, Gattinara had boasted that "what was begun by Charles the Great will be completed by Charles the Greatest."[9] His death left the way open to Nicholas Perrenot de Granvelle (1486–1550), a Burgundian who took Gattinara's place, though not his title. The new chancellor would soon play a major role in Charles's German affairs, though at Augsburg he was still untested.

NEGOTIATIONS ON DOCTRINE

Once Charles, Ferdinand, and the legate had arrived, the Diet could begin. The emperor's organization of religious negotiations with the Protestants posed a great menace to Jacob Sturm and his policy, mainly because of the danger that the Lutherans, led by John of Saxony, would reach agreement with the emperor and his theologians, leaving the Zwinglian Sacramentarians out on a limb. Sturm's suspicions were aroused by his discovery that the Saxon clergy were preaching "in a very unfriendly manner against our theologians' opinions," as though the Zwinglians "were hatching marvelous plots to ally with foreign nations, to divide up the bishoprics among ourselves, and all in all to arouse tremendous rebellion and war."[10] Worse yet, when the elector's theologians prepared a doctrinal statement, to be called the Confession of Augsburg, he would not let Sturm and his friends sign, for "since they do not agree with our theologians on the doctrine of the Lord's Supper, they will not permit us to join them in this matter."[11]

What to do? Well, Sturm had foresightedly sent home for his own theologians, and, hidden away in his lodgings, Bucer and Capito were working up a statement, later called the Four Cities' Confession. The name spoke for itself: only Constance, Memmingen, and Lindau would sign it, and even the loyal Constancers found it "excessive or disputatious."[12] This pitiful showing got the respect it merited. While the Lutheran princes and cities had their Confession of Augsburg solemnly read to the monarchs and two hundred notables on 25 June, Sturm delivered the Tetrapolitan Confession to the Imperial chancellery without ceremony on 9 July. And while the Lutheran confession received a reply in four weeks, Sturm and his little band had to wait more than fourteen. Then, on 25 October, they stood for three hours before Charles, Ferdinand, and all the Catholic princes, prelates, and envoys while a secretary read a refutation in which "we are so much and so often called heretics, worse than the people of Capharnum, worse than the Jews, and it is said that we are more unbelieving than the Devil."[13] Sturm rose to respond. The refutation, he declared, "is filled with the sharpest and most provocative words, such as 'heretical,' 'blasphemous,' 'impious,' 'wanton,' and the like," and it "contains all sorts of matters and tales quite unknown to us, especially concerning the most worthy Sacrament of the body and blood of Christ, which are not preached in our cities. Even if they were, our governments would punish those who preached them."[14] "It was a tough, difficult thing," Hans Ehinger (1487–1545) proudly wrote home to Memmingen, "for five good men and burghers to speak up and give reply to the Roman emperor, electors, princes, and so many Estates as supported them."[15] A brave but futile act.

And yet, all was not lost, for the Strasbourg confession's true audience was not the emperor and the Catholic bishops, but the Lutherans. The cunning Sturm had decided to induce Huldrych Zwingli himself to demonstrate how little Zwinglian Strasbourg's position was. To this end, he sent the Zuricher a copy of the Lutheran Schwabach Articles and suggested that "if *you and your people* meanwhile compose apologies to the emperor and the princes, in which you give an account of *your* faith, I do not believe *your* effort will be fruitless."[16] Zwingli took the bait and sent to Augsburg his defiant statement of faith (*Fidei ratio*), which just happened to fall into the Lutherans' hands and made their theologians howl with rage—at Zwingli.

Sturm's maneuver was a gamble, based on the possibility that the emperor's negotiations with the Saxon elector and his clients might fail. His gamble began to pay off on 24 August with the news that Bucer and Melanchthon had talked, and that the landgrave was trying to get Sturm "a secret interview" with the elector's men. As the Lutherans' talks with the emperor's theologians soured, Melanchthon discovered that Bucer's opinions were "not so bad as they were made out to be and were comparable to Luther's view," and by mid-September Sturm, seeing light at the end of the tunnel, dispatched Bucer to Luther and Capito to Switzerland.

JOHN OF SAXONY'S RETRENCHMENT

Everything now hung on the elector, who, a few days before he departed Augsburg for home, said to Sturm, "God grant His grace that all of us Protestant princes and Imperial cities will shortly come together again in a united alliance."[17] Sturm nodded solemnly and replied that Strasbourg had "been forced to yield a bit only on account of the Common Man, who had taken up the new opinion, so that there would be no tumult."[18] With everything clicking into place for a Protestant alliance, on 12–13 October Sturm and Pfarrer talked with Count Albert of Mansfeld, among the electoral councilors the leading advocate of a forward policy. Speaking as though nothing now stood between them and an alliance, Sturm told Count Albert to ask the elector "not to separate from or reject the city of Strasbourg, but rather to unite with it, since in faith, so far as concerns the Holy Sacrament, there is no difference between His Electoral Grace and his allies and Strasbourg." Although there had indeed existed a certain verbal dispute between their preachers," Sturm acknowledged, yet "there is no real dispute about the presence of the true body and blood." If, therefore, "this union and alliance is established between His Electoral Grace and Strasbourg, it will be useful and encouraging to both parties for resistance and other purposes."[19] Count Albert, who was no fool, asked bluntly whether Strasbourg would sign the Confession of Augsburg. Sturm stalled. He said that Albert could be confident that "there would be no problem there," because Bucer had said of the confession "that he saw nothing wanting in it nor anything that needed changing."[20] Next day Sturm and Albert made plans to canvass the Evangelical powers for bilateral talks "to agree upon a common defense and mutual aid. And since the matter cannot be long delayed, as firm a commitment as possible should be made at that meeting."[21] At Augsburg on these two days in mid-October 1530, the Protestant alliance arose from the dead.

Elector John of Saxony also knew how to save appearances, and in early November he informed Strasbourg that "the councilors we left at Augsburg have reported the statement your envoys made to them concerning the most worthy Sacrament of the body and blood of Christ. Now that there is no disagreement between us, we receive that report with special favor and enthusiasm."[22] A fragile moment, this aftermath of the Diet of Augsburg, and Sturm fully appreciated its fragility. On his way home he stopped at Ulm, where he told the leading magistrates that "everything depends on whether we have the proper love for one another. If we are allied, and this love is not present, then the alliance will have been made in vain. At the first sign of trouble, members will offer trivial excuses and begin to withdraw from the league."[23] With this phrase, "the proper love for one another," Sturm meant the inclination and sense of trust, which in the burghers' political culture could alone transform common interests into lasting federations. The "proper sort of love for one another" was what his great-grandfather had preached to the Bernese against Burgundy, more than fifty years ago. "If we attend yet another meeting," Sturm told the Ulmers, "only to learn that the elector will ally with none but those who share his beliefs, then all this effort will be for nothing. He cannot expect that my government and others will permit him to dictate the norms of faith." Not so, for in the end this was precisely what the Strasbourgeois did permit.

BIRTH OF THE SMALKALDIC LEAGUE

The time had come to drive the nail home. When he rode in the evening of 22 December 1530 into Smalkalden, the scene of his humiliation one year before, Sturm's saddlebags contained full powers to represent Constance, Lindau, and Memmingen, more limited powers for Zurich and Bern, and instructions from Strasbourg to bring the treaty home, for "we must confer and decide with the commune and not as an individual person."[24] The negotiations ran for nine days until, on the old year's final day, the allies formed "a Christian association for defense and protection against violent assault" and agreed to send the emperor an appeal "for the amelioration of the intolerable recess" of Augsburg.[25] Sweeping aside all delicate formulations about resistance, the allies proclaimed solidarity against "the Imperial Fiscal [the Imperial Chamber Court's enforcement office], the Swabian League, the emperor's commissioners, or any other agency."[26]

Momentarily, the renewed sense of fellowship embraced even the Swiss Sacramentarians, for Count Albert told Sturm on 31 December that "it would be good if the league could be expanded, and the elector and the princes desire that we treat with Zurich, Bern, and Basel to the extent that they will also subscribe to our [Tetrapolitan] confession."[27] Though he was reluctant to drop the Swiss, Sturm feared, as he told the landgrave, "that there are those who would like to disrupt our concord for the sole purpose of putting an end to the Christian alliance founded at Smalkalden."[28] "If one has the desire, will, and love for unity," he continued, "such a concord can begin with the confession that the body and blood of Christ are truly present in the Eucharist, truly offered, eaten, and drunk." The finer points, "whether He is actually eaten and drunk through the physical mouth and by the unbelievers and the godless, will work themselves out in time and perhaps to degree better than we can now conceive." "The desire, will, and love for unity"—this typically Sturmian language touched the Smalkaldic League's central nerve, juxtaposing the burghers' definition of solidarity as friendship to the theologians' definition of it as common doctrine. Only with a solid moral basis in mutual commitment, Sturm believed, could the alliance endure.

The price for this alliance soon became clear to Sturm, for though he was able to lead Ulm and other South German cities into the Smalkaldic League, the Evangelical Swiss cities would not follow. It was a cruel price for Sturm, whose ancestors had fought alongside Swiss comrades, but to pay it must have seemed right to him during those heady days just after Smalkalden. As if to confirm its rightness, Elector John of Saxony wrote to commend Sturm, "whom we now recognize as one who knows best how to further the cause and who understands, better than others do, the grace of the Almighty. We graciously ask that you exert every possible effort to see that your preachers . . . adhere to the articles upon which we agree."[29] There the line was drawn, and the Swiss would not cross it. As Zwingli pithily retorted to Bucer, if the Lutherans believed in Christ "in one place, in the bread, and in the wine, then they are simply papists."[30]

The Protestant alliance introduced an entirely new element into Strasbourg's policy, a commitment which, however motivated, was inconceivable apart from the ties created by the Reformation. Although at first the Reformation had rekindled the city's old particularist solidarity with the Swiss, now it animated a new and unprecedented alliance between southern free cities and central German princes. No political tradition, no economic interest, and no social affinities help to explain the formation of the Smalkaldic League, this first and most impressive creation of the Empire's Protestant politics.

THE HALCYON DAYS

The Smalkaldic League's birth fell during very hard times on the Upper Rhine. In 1529 a terrible famine had begun, filling the cities with the desperate and the destitute, 23,548 of whom—more than the city's resident population—were fed at Strasbourg alone between June 1530 and June 1531.[31] On the road to Eckbolsheim were found the corpses of a woman and two children, dead of hunger, and when the civic granary opened to sell cheap flour, the crowd surged forward and crushed a young girl to death. Taxes had to be raised, of course, and when the magistrates added two pence to the property rates, "the citizens were astonished, for in this year there was a great famine."[32] A terrible year, a year of portents, and on Pentecost Sunday, at nine o'clock in the morning, a new star appeared in the heavens.

THE PEACE OF NUREMBERG, 1532

Such portents hardly touched the new Protestant alliance, which quickly became a major force in Imperial politics and ushered in the German Reformation's halcyon days. The era of hardly mixed success ran from the Peace of Nuremberg in 1532, which gave the Protestants relief from legal suits for the restoration of ecclesiastical properties, to the mid-1530s, when the league acquired its constitution (1535) and the Evangelical theologians settled their quarrels in the Wittenberg Concord (1536), and then on down nearly to the decade's end.

This string of successes depended very much on the creation of barriers to the domination of Imperial politics by the confessional parties. For one thing, Charles V wanted conciliation and peace in the Empire, because he needed the Protestants' support for his brother's royal election and for the wars against the Ottomans and France. For another, his policy of conciliation gained strength from the formation after the Diet of Augsburg of a Catholic party of mediation, electors and princes who, whatever their views on religion, stayed neutral between the confessional blocs. Charles depended on the neutrals, for after the Diet of Augsburg he sat, in Luther's German phrase, "in the midst of many snakes" and could hardly refuse to meet the Protestant princes, in Ferdinand's Spanish phrase, "beard to beard."[33] On 8 July 1531, he suspended the restitution suits until the next Diet and instructed two Catholic electors, Louis of the Palatinate and Albert of Mainz, to negotiate with "the duke of Saxony, his son

[Prince John Frederick], the landgrave of Hesse, and their supporters concerning the articles of faith."[34] The mediators and the allies met at Schweinfurt in April 1532, while Charles was hurrying from the Netherlands to convene the Imperial Diet at Regensburg.

Jacob Sturm did not go to Regensburg. He did agree, despite his ailments, to ride to Schweinfurt in Franconia for the Protestants' meeting with the mediating electors. This meant that Ammeister Claus Kniebis, no very experienced diplomat, undertook the even longer journey to Regensburg. Because the emperor had stipulated that the peace would cover only those who accepted "the opinion and assertion of said duke, landgrave, and allies as presented in the said Confession of Augsburg," Sturm persuaded Strasbourg's preachers to affirm that this Lutheran confession "is in agreement with our faith and understanding of the Bible, and it all agrees with our own [Tetrapolitan] confession."[35] Their affirmation did not suffice, for at Schweinfurt in early April 1532, the hard Lutheran party attacked the Strasbourgeois as heretics. Sturm rejoined that if they would only stick to the Bible's language, "namely, that one receives in the Eucharist the true body and true blood of Christ," and leave out all the irritating words—"symbolic," "figurative," "bodily," "essentially," "spiritually," and the like—there would be neither a quarrel nor grounds for one.[36]

The bitter moment was made no sweeter by Cardinal Albert of Mainz, who taunted Sturm: "How will your preachers explain it [at home] that you now subscribe to the Saxon confession, though they used to teach quite differently?" "If our preachers were here," Sturm responded, "they would be able to answer you. To the extent that they were in error and now reject what they formerly taught—mind you, they were accused of teaching much they never taught—they should be praised rather than blamed." "I imagine," Sturm turned the barb back on the cardinal, "that if we abandoned our faith for Your Grace's, Your Grace would lay that to our credit."[37] "Let's speak of it no more," the prelate replied.

As the Schweinfurt negotiations moved forward, the Imperial Diet sat at Regensburg awaiting their outcome. The news from Hungary grew more terrible each week, so bad that at Strasbourg the XIII decided that the city should "offer its share of the tax with good will" so as not to endanger the peace.[38] Finally, on 2 August 1532 Charles suspended the suits for restitution until a General Council met, thereby conceding de facto toleration to the Lutheran powers, who agreed to keep the public peace and support the defense of Hungary.

Although both parties regarded the peace as temporary, it in fact represented the first step toward the peaces of Augsburg in 1555 and Westphalia in 1648, which made the Empire one country with two, legally equal religions. The peace, which was renewed in 1534 and again in 1539, also provided the Protestant powers with the time and the security to bring their churches under

control and to deal with religious radicalism in the form of Anabaptism. It was
a deal, and Sturm and the XIII kept their side of it. On 29 July 1532, 388
infantry marched out of Strasbourg—the cavalry followed on 12 August—under
the command of Bernhard Wurmser von Vendenheim, with his cousin Friedrich
Sturm, Jacob's older brother, as paymaster. They were bound for Vienna and
the Ottoman front, living proof of their masters' good faith and belief "that
such aid [should] be given willingly and without compulsion."[39]

THE RESTORATION IN WÜRTTEMBERG, 1534

Given breathing space by the Peace of Nuremberg, Landgrave Philip's gaze
turned once more to Württemberg, and in the summer of 1534, fortified by
good luck, daring, Jacob Sturm's support, Bavarian backing, and French gold,
he invaded Württemberg and restored Duke Ulrich at Stuttgart. It was one of
the very few times that the German Protestants seized and made full use of an
opportunity, and they thereby guaranteed their religion's survival in the German Southwest.

Württemberg fell at the slightest of strokes. Time and religious change had
transformed Ulrich, its exiled duke, from a tyrannical and murderous spend-
thrift—a "prince of thieves," Johannes Reuchlin once called him—into a wronged
Evangelical hero.[40] With King Ferdinand's attention fixed away in the East, his
Austrian regime at Stuttgart hardly resisted when Landgrave Philip, backed by
Jacob Sturm, plucked the duchy of Württemberg, "practically the heart of
Germany," from the Austrian grasp.[41] They had help, of course, but not from
the other Protestants. The Bavarian dukes, solid Catholics, backed the landgrave,
and so did the king of France, while the other Smalkaldic chief, Elector John
Frederick (r. 1532–47) of Saxony, sat tight. The young Saxon elector, as the
landgrave told Chancellor Eck of Bavaria, "is no warrior and is not inclined to
war. He will gladly help the young Württemberger [Duke Christoph] as best
he can with words, but he cannot be brought to follow them with deeds." The
elector would "remain hard for the alliance against the [Ferdinand's] election,
but he cannot be moved to make war for that cause."[42] In the event, though
restoration in Württemberg materially advanced the Reformation in southern
Germany, it owed much less to the new, Protestant alliance than to the Reformation's revivification of princely opposition to the House of Austria, backed,
as of old, by France. While all the other Smalkaldic allies watched disapprov-
ingly from the sidelines, Strasbourg alone supported the landgrave's bold stroke.

Jacob Sturm knew Württemberg and appreciated what its strategic position
and its size—eighty thousand square kilometers and 250,000 people—would
mean to the league's military position in South Germany. In case of a general
war, he later told Duke Ulrich, "the landgrave would supply the cavalry, you
the infantry, and the southern cities the artillery."[43] The coarse, unbridled duke
himself was another story, and the landgrave had to remind Sturm that "you

know perfectly well what Duke Ulrich's religion is, and that he has a special feeling for the city of Strasbourg. If he regains his land, he would act tolerably toward Ulm and all the other Protestant cities in the south."[44] That took some believing, and was perfectly untrue besides, but Sturm decided his regime should back the landgrave, and in April 1534 they allowed his agents to borrow 46,000 rhfl. to recruit infantry in the district, to buy pikes from the civic arsenal, and to hire local gunners. With their aid, the landgrave routed the Austrian governor's troops near Lauffen on 12–13 May and entered Stuttgart three days later.

The fall of Württemberg presented Strasbourg's preachers with a golden opportunity, a whole duchy to reform right on their doorstep, where they would not bow to the Saxons as they had at Schweinfurt. Asked by the landgrave to supply two "impartial" men, they nominated two hard-core Zwinglians, one of whom was Ambrosius Blarer (1492–1564) of Constance. But whereas the preachers viewed Württemberg as a test of their own independence, Jacob Sturm dreaded a renewal of the struggle with the Lutherans. He therefore objected strongly to the Treaty of Kaaden, which Elector John Frederick mediated between King Ferdinand and Duke Ulrich, because it excluded from the peace "the Sacramentarians, Anabaptist sects, and also other new, unchristian sects."[45] The landgrave tried to soothe his anger, but Sturm shot back that "the king and the mediators mean us with this word—please God, no one else will say the same—and will seize the opportunity to drag us under this name, whether we wish it or no."[46] This was no idle fear, not in the summer of 1534, when the Anabaptist kingdom at Münster in far Westphalia was the scandal of the Empire, and when its spiritual father, Melchior Hofmann (d. 1543), lay rotting in Strasbourg's jail. Eventually, of course, Sturm had to yield, "though at the same time I did not refrain from pointing out the dangers to His Grace [Ulrich], if His Grace did not ratify the treaty."[47]

Once the duchy lay securely in Ulrich's hands, the old quarrel flared anew, as Landgrave Philip's Lutheran chaplain, Erhard Schnepf (1496–1558), began calling Ambrosius Blarer and his Strasbourg sponsors "fanatics." "The papists take his charge," Sturm complained, "as an indication of who the Sacramentarians are, who are excluded from the peace [of Kaaden]."[48] "By God's grace it has happened," he wrote resignedly to the landgrave in August 1534, "that peace has reigned for quite a while among the southern cities. Now we hoped that should My Gracious Lord, Duke Ulrich, get his land back, . . . things would get even better. Perhaps God wills it otherwise, so that the victories and good fortune don't make us haughty."[49] Sturm went often to Stuttgart in the summer of 1534, though he resisted the landgrave's pressure to take service in Ulrich's regime. He advised the duke to enforce the Confession of Augsburg as the norm of preaching in Württemberg, and "so long as preaching accords with the Saxon confession, no one should be pressed beyond the words of Scripture into other words."[50] In his zeal to keep the peace, therefore, Jacob

Sturm became a promoter of the Lutherans' Confession of Augsburg.

The plans for a Zwinglian reformation in Württemberg had little chance for success, as the smug Lutheran clergy knew, and eventually Duke Ulrich took the prudent path via the Confession of Augsburg into the Smalkaldic League, to which he was admitted in 1536. For the league, which had contributed nothing to make it possible, Württemberg's reformation was that rarest of political prizes, a gain without risks. Or so it seemed, though in fact this easy victory reawakened an old problem by whetting Landgrave Philip's enthusiasm for the plan he had formed with Zwingli, a general war against the House of Austria. The very idea made Jacob Sturm's blood run cold, to the landgrave's great disgust. "I wish that Jacob Sturm and the cities," the Hessian later wrote to Ulrich, "had given the needed money and had argued as strongly *for* an attack on the king as they in fact argued *against* it—then would have been the right time. But they gave Your Grace nothing free."[51]

TOWARD THE WITTENBERG CONCORD, 1536

The burghers, indeed, had every right to be wary, for the adventure in Württemberg had also rekindled the old passions among the theologians. When Elector John Frederick proposed in late 1534 that the league members send their theologians to a meeting "to reach agreement on this dispute," Sturm told the landgrave "confidentially" about his misgivings. "I fear," he wrote, "that some who proposed this assembly of scholars to the elector" did so "not because they seek agreement but because they expect, knowing how some of the scholars think, there will be no agreement. Then they can wrest the elector away from us."[52] Such preachers should not be invited to a meeting, Sturm advised, "but only some few from both side's scholars—ones who are not stubborn and self-centered but reasonable and pacific—should be called together."[53]

If Sturm truly believed that the "quarrel of words" could be settled by words alone, he was building castles in Spain, for from Wittenberg the largest calibers in the Protestant world were taking southern cities, one after another, under fire. "At Augsburg," Luther had raged in August 1531, "Satan himself reigns through the enemies of the Sacrament . . . , and the same is true at Ulm."[54] Luther blasted the Zwinglians at Kempten, at Augsburg, and at Frankfurt am Main, always sensing behind them "the double-tongued gang" at Strasbourg, who clung to the old error "that the Sacrament is mere wine and bread" and were fit only to serve a church "built in a pigsty."[55] Ulm, where the Zwinglian clergy had nearly revolted against the Schweinfurt agreement, was no better, and Augsburg's church remained in the hands of obdurate Zwinglian splitters. Still, the Protestant success in Württemberg turned Luther's mind toward concord, not least because of the nightmarish prospect of a Zwinglian rampage there.

Encouraged by Luther's words, Sturm and Bucer crisscrossed South Germany in 1534 and 1535, cajoling the regimes and preachers to subscribe to the Confession of Augsburg and to enter the league. To his friends at Ulm, Sturm purred that "so far as I know, . . . your preachers share and are in agreement with Bucer's opinion and the moderation that he represents in this mediation."[56] The two Strasbourgeois jumped at the landgrave's offer to host a meeting between Bucer and Melanchthon at the end of 1534 in Kassel. But there was to be one more price for concord. When the Augsburg magistrates, coached by Bucer, agreed to request a Lutheran preacher, only the stalwartly Zwinglian Constancers continued to resist. It would be better to tolerate differences in doctrine, they grumbled, "than to burden the churches with newly prescribed rules and requirements."[57]

Doctrine was clerical business, and the leading theologians gathered at Wittenberg, where on 29 May 1536 they approved the Wittenberg Concord, a document no one could stretch in a non-Lutheran direction. The Swiss would never accept it, but their military paralysis since 1531 made their absence more tolerable. When the other southern Protestant powers all signed—Strasbourg, Duke Ulrich, Frankfurt, Augsburg, Kempten, Esslingen, and, after much wrangling, Ulm—the book was closed on South German Zwinglianism. The Wittenberg Concord healed the decade-old rift in the Protestant front, though at the price of permanently splitting the German-speaking Reformation movement into German and Swiss wings. For Strasbourg it meant cutting political ties to the warmest friends of its particularist heritage in return for the Smalkaldic League's protection. This exchange followed the logic of Jacob Sturm's policy and created the unlikely partnership between Sturm and Landgrave Philip, magistrate and prince, as the political brokers of German Protestantism.

NOTES

1. *RTA, jR* 8:470, lines 5–18; and there, too, the remaining quotes in this paragraph.
2. Ibid. 8:1058, lines 7–15.
3. *WA Br* 6:56, lines 11–13; and the following quote is from 57, lines 2–4.
4. Johannes Ficker, ed., "Jakob Sturms Entwurf zur Straßburger reformatorischer Verantwortung," *ELJb* 19 (1941): 152.
5. The Protestant version interprets the letters "Verbum dei manet in aeternum," while the Catholic one renders them "Vnd du musst ins Elend."
6. Clemens Sender, "Die Chronik von Clemens Sender von den ältesten Zeiten der Stadt bis zum Jahre 1536," in *Chroniken der deutschen Städte*, vol. 23 (Leipzig, 1894; reprint, Göttingen, 1966), 276, lines 20–21.
7. Ibid., 278, lines 8–9.
8. Quoted by Ferdinand Seibt, *Karl V. Der Kaiser und die Reformation* (Berlin, 1990), 114, from Luther's *Tischreden* at 9 June and 12 July 1532.
9. Quoted by John M. Headley, "The Habsburg World Empire and the Revival of Ghibellinism," *Medieval and Renaissance Studies* 7 (1978): 97–102.
10. *PC* 1:455–56, no. 741.

11. Ibid., 459, no. 746.
12. Hans Ehinger, in Friedrich Dobel, *Memmingen im Reformationszeitalter*, 5 vols. (Augsburg, 1877–78) 4:37–39.
13. Ibid. 4:88–89.
14. From two versions in *PC* 1:529–30.
15. Dobel, *Memmingen* 4:96–97.
16. *ZW* 10:599–604, no. 1035; emphases added.
17. *PC* 1:499–500, no. 794; Specklin, no. 2318.
18. Franz Bernhard von Bucholtz, *Geschichte der Regierung Ferdinands des Ersten*, 9 vols. (Vienna, 1831–38; reprint, 1971), 9:23–24.
19. Carl Eduard Förstemann, ed., *Urkundenbuch zu der Geschichte des Reichstages zu Augsburg im Jahre 1530*, 2 vols. (Halle, 1833–35; reprint, 1966) 2:727.
20. Ibid. 2:728.
21. *PC* 1:517–18.
22. Ibid., 535–36, no. 830.
23. *BOSS* 1:57; and there, too, is the following quote.
24. *PC* 1:525, 541.
25. *SBA* 1:12.
26. Ibid., 14.
27. *PC* 1:569.
28. *PC* 2:7–8, no. 10; and there, too, are the two following quotes.
29. Ibid. 2:16, no. 19.
30. *ZW* 11: no. 1168.
31. Winckelmann, *Das Fürsorgewesen der Stadt Straßburg*, 2:168, no. 118.
32. "Straßburgische Archiv-Chronik," in *Code historique et diplomatique de la Ville de Strasbourg*, ed. Louis Schnéegans (Strasbourg, 1845–47) 2:218–19, for this and the rest of the paragraph.
33. Karl Brandi, *Kaiser Karl V.: Werden und Schicksal einer Persönlichkeit und eines Weltreiches*, 2d ed. (Munich, 1967), 2: 225 (Luther); Paula Sutter Fichtner, *Ferdinand I of Austria: The Politics of Dynasticism in the Age of the Reformation* (Boulder, Colo., 1982), 89 (Ferdinand).
34. Bucholtz, *Geschichte* 9:28–29.
35. Ibid., 29; *PC* 2:108, no. 136.
36. *PC* 2:113, no. 139; Traugott Schiess, ed., *Briefwechsel der Brüder Ambrosius und Thomas Blarer 1509–1548*, 3 vols. (Freiburg i. Br., 1908–12) 1:337, no. 27.
37. *PC* 2:117–18, no. 140; and from the same source come the remaining quotes in this paragraph.
38. *PC* 2:150–53, 158–59.
39. Ibid., 159, no. 155.
40. Johann Reuchlin to Willibald Pirckheimer, Stuttgart, 8 November 1519, in Johannes Reuchlin, *Reuchlins Briefwechsel*, ed. Ludwig Geiger (Stuttgart, 1875; reprint, 1962), 319, no. 285.
41. Hans-Erich Feine, "Die Territorialbildung der Habsburger im deutschen Südwesten, vornehmlich im Mittelalter," *Zeitschrift der Savigny-Stiftung für Rechtsgeschichte, Germanistische Abteilung* 67 (1950): 294.
42. Jakob Wille, *Philipp der Großmüthige von Hessen und die Restitution Ulrichs von Wirtemberg 1526–1535* (Tübingen, 1882), 101 n. 5.
43. Thomas A. Brady, Jr., "Princes' Reformation vs. Urban Liberty: Strasbourg and the Restoration of Duke Ulrich in Württemberg, 1534," in *Städtische Gesellschaft und Reformation*, ed. Ingrid Bátori (Stuttgart, 1980), 262–63 n. 287.

44. *PC* 2:199–200, no. 204.
45. Eugen Schneider, ed., *Ausgewählte Urkunden zur württembergischen Geschichte* (Stuttgart, 1911), 97, line 35 to 98, line 4, no. 27 (29 June 1534).
46. *PC* 2:219, no. 237.
47. Ibid.
48. Ibid., 221, no. 239.
49. Ibid.
50. Ibid. 222.
51. Wille, *Philipp der Großmüthige*, 225.
52. *PC* 2:244, no. 265.
53. Ibid., 245.
54. Martin Brecht, "Luthers Beziehung zu den Oberdeutschen und Schweizern von 1530/1531 bis 1546," in *Leben und Werk Martin Luthers von 1526 bis 1546: Festgabe zu seinem 500. Geburtstag*, 2 vols., ed. Helmar Junghans (Berlin, 1983), 1:500.
55. Sigrid Jahns, *Frankfurt, Reformation und Schmalkaldischer Bund: Die Reformations- Reichs- und Bündnispolitik der Reichsstadt Frankfurt am Main 1525–1536* (Frankfurt am Main, 1976), 223.
56. *PC* 2:234, no. 254.
57. Ibid., 679.

7

THE SMALKALDIC LEAGUE

Wherefore take unto you the whole armour of God, that ye may be able to withstand in the evil day, and having done all, to stand. . . . Above all, taking the shield of faith, wherewith ye shall be able to quench all the fiery darts of the wicked.

—Ephesians 6:13, 16

The Protestant alliance known as the Smalkaldic League married a traditional political form with a novel religious purpose and an unprecedented geographical scope. Its form was the late medieval German type of federation of Imperial Estates, its purpose was the defense of the new religion, and its scope was Empire-wide. The league's parliamentary assembly or Diet, its commanderships, its division into districts, and its forms of taxation all came from the Empire's late medieval federal tradition. Its purpose, however, was new, for the Protestants aimed "to give praise and due honor to Almighty God, to foster and spread His holy Word and the Gospel, and, while remaining obedient members of the Holy Empire, to guide and keep our subjects in a Christian manner to all that is good, Christian, honorable, just, and conducive to their salvation, and to prevent by God's grace unjust, illegal violence and damages."[1] New, as well, was the league's geographical extent, for, unlike the Swabian and other regionally bounded leagues of the past, the Smalkaldic League ran up and down the Empire, from Strasbourg to Pomerania and from Augsburg to Bremen.

GOVERNANCE OF THE LEAGUE

Ever since Ranke's day, historians have recognized the Smalkaldic League's potential as a statelike alternative to the Catholic monarchy. The Protestants' creation was indeed a form of governance, though not a state in any modern sense. They fashioned a fairly effective goverment, constructed a European network of diplomacy, disrupted the Imperial judicial system, and protected their own members until the new faith was too well established to be uprooted. The league failed, however, to break through or refashion traditional forms. It would not confront fairly or effectively the central issue of ecclesiastical property; it

124

did not fashion a common church structure and order of worship to complement its common doctrine; and it failed to breach the boundary between rulers
and subjects or to create a durable political community of Evangelical Christians—as distinct from an association of Christian rulers—in the Empire. In
its role as the form and shield of early German Protestantism, the Smalkaldic
League displayed both the strengths and the weaknesses of the political context
from which it sprang, the world of late medieval German particularism.

THE LEAGUE'S CONSTITUTION

The Smalkaldic League's assembly approved its constitution at Smalkalden on
23 December 1535. The member Estates were grouped into two geographical
divisions, a northern or "Saxon" district under the Saxon elector and a southern district under the Hessian landgrave. The league's assembly originally contained nine votes—two for Saxony, two for Hesse, one for the other northern
princes and nobles, and two each for the southern and the northern free cities.
To these were added in 1536 one new vote each for Duke Ulrich of Württemberg,
the Pomeranian dukes, and the southern and the northern cities, bringing the
total to thirteen. The northern members outnumbered the southerners by seven
to six, and the princes the free cities by seven to six. The assembly met twenty-
six times during the league's fifteen-year history at places, the distribution of
which reflected the league's geographical structure: seven times at Smalkalden,
six at Frankfurt am Main, three at Worms, twice each at Schweinfurt, Brunswick, and Nuremberg, and once each at Naumburg, Arnstadt, Eisenach, and
Ulm. A glance at a map of the Empire reveals that, compared to the Imperial
Diet, the Smalkaldic League's center lay considerably further northward, roughly
along the Hessian-Saxon axis.

Unlike the Swabian League, the Smalkaldic League had no permanent administration, except for several lawyers retained at the Chamber Court and a
couple of secretaries hired around 1540, and its business was routinely handled
through the Hessian and electoral Saxon chancelleries. It also had no court, so
that quarrels between members could be handled only through arbitration. The
league did have a separate war council, organized at Veste Coburg in 1537 and
approved at Brunswick in 1538. This agreement placed the league's armies
under the command of the Saxon elector in North Germany, Landgrave Philip
in South Germany, and a troika of these two plus Duke Ernest of Brunswick-
Lüneburg in case of a general war.

The league taxed its members according to a time-honored Imperial practice
of distinguishing between an "emergency aid" of cash for a threatened member
and a "long-term aid" of troops and guns for a more general campaign. The
basic unit, called a "month," comprised two thousand horse and ten thousand
foot, or their financial equivalent, divided nearly equally between the northern
and southern districts.[2] In 1535 the main levy, figured in "double-months,"

was reckoned at 70,000 rhfl. per month; two years later it had climbed to around 105,000 rhfl.; and by the eve of the Smalkaldic War in 1546 it stood at nearly 200,000 rhfl.—55 percent from the southern and 45 percent from the northern district.

The free cities ought to have played a very powerful role in the league, given that they paid slightly over half the taxes, much more than in either the Swabian League or the Empire as a whole. The cities' ability to act together, however, was frustrated both by the great distances and by the northern cities' lack of a common Imperial political culture comparable to that of the southern free cities. The "Saxon cities," a Strasbourg document of 1538 charged, "enjoy the peace and the protection of Christendom and of the German nation, though they pay nothing toward the Imperial assessments."[3]

DIPLOMACY

The league's failure to develop a denser internal structure did not prevent it from conducting a lively if fitful diplomacy on a European scale. Denmark aside—the Danish king was also an Imperial prince—the only two powers with which the Smalkaldeners became seriously involved were England and France. Their relations with the two kings ran very similar courses. The first stage in 1531–35 witnessed a growing hope for alliance based on religious affinity, followed in 1535–36 by disillusionment; then came a decade of sporadic and fruitless contacts; and finally, in 1545–46 the league sought the kings' military aid against Charles V.

These similarities aside, Smalkaldic relations with France and England differed markedly: France was the more valuable ally, England the more sympathetic one. Although the proximity of France and its king's wealth made his favor far weightier to the German Protestants—witness his backing for the restoration in Württemberg—his persecution of the French Evangelicals after the Affair of the Placards in October 1534 made the attainment of a real understanding improbable. The English king's flirtation with Evangelical religion, on the other hand, made an English alliance more welcome and, for a time, more probable. These differences are illustrated by the addresses made by the French and English ambassadors to the league's Diet at Smalkalden in December 1535. On 19 December Guillaume du Bellay (1491–1543), sieur de Langey, asserted that the French king was persecuting only rebels disguised as religious dissenters; on 24 December Edward Fox (ca. 1496–1538), bishop of Hereford, proclaimed the English king's zeal for truly reformed religion and his opposition to Rome. There the situation lay—the French king was an effective ally but a religious foe, the Englishman a religious friend but an ineffective ally—and it stymied the Smalkaldeners.

There was a moment, in 1536, when German Protestant hopes for the more attractive, if less useful, English alliance seemed quite realistic. The Protestants' duty, Jacob Sturm wrote, "obliges us to promote and spread the true, correct, godly, and Christian religion, . . . and . . . since the English king's request concerns chiefly this matter, . . . in what way could God's Word and Christ's gospel be better promoted and encouraged in England, God's honor be increased, and His name be praised?"[4] Alas, it was not to be, for serious negotiations never began, and by 1539 changes in English religious policy drove Sturm to lament that "the king of England has become a papist once more."[5] From this point forward, Sturm believed that although "England stands somewhat closer to our religion than France does, . . . we should not put much trust in either, for we have always found that they support not our interests but only their own, and they are as changeable as the weather."[6]

RELATIONS WITH FRANCE

At Strasbourg, of course, French affairs evoked the greatest possible interest, the more so as the city's trade with France was growing during the 1530s and 1540s. Sturm and his colleagues thus faced the third Franco-Imperial war (1536–38) with trepidation.[7] They declined in August 1537 to participate in a regional defense plan, "by means of which the city of Strasbourg would become party to this feud and war, which would be inadvisable for Strasbourg in view of the French king's power." Moreover, "in view of the citizens' extensive trade and business, which is still safe and secure in France, participation would be against the city's interest."[8] In the province of Alsace, too, they noted, "the inhabitants and merchants have constant business over there and have until now been safe."[9]

The same reasoning came into play during the fourth Franco-Imperial war (1542–44), when Jacob Sturm warned that if Strasbourg refused the war taxes, "you can imagine how it would fuel the charges of those who are already crying that we are good Frenchmen."[10] The new war, he believed, "would be most burdensome and damaging to Strasbourg and to Alsace; for because they lie so close to France, on which they nearly border, they not only trade in France but gain a good part of their livelihood from Lorraine."[11]

Sturm's well-justified fears sprang from his awareness of new circumstances. With the movement of the Habsburg-Valois conflict northward out of Italy after 1530, Alsace became a border zone and Strasbourg a frontier fortress in an entirely new sense. At the same time, the growth of the city's and the region's trade with France willy-nilly raised their stake in any new Franco-Imperial war. These changed conditions and new interests robbed of their sense the old politics of particularism and regional federations.

The new situation also lent plausibility to repeated charges that Jacob Sturm was a French agent. Early on, Sturm himself had planted this suspicion, notably at Speyer in 1529, when he replied to Cousin Daniel Mieg's exclusion from the Imperial Governing Council with the boast that "for some time the king of France has wanted to treat with us and has offered us an annual subsidy of several thousand crowns."[12] A dangerous and fruitless boast, whatever the provocation. He may also have said, as Duke Henry of Brunswick-Wolfenbüttel charged in 1543, that "the French king is a good lord and chief to me."[13] But probably he did not, for Sturm protested his reputation for francophilia and claimed that its sole basis lay in the widespread confusion, based on the common surname, of himself with Jean Sturm, the highly gallicized rector of the Latin school. "Yes," Jacob Sturm once sighed, "I, too, am suspected by many, because of my name, as though I were the other Sturm. Even Lord Granvelle [the Imperial chancellor] said to me privately that the emperor himself suspected me until he was informed that there are two Sturms at Strasbourg."[14] Eventually, Charles V acknowledged his error and praised Jacob Sturm for his "obstinacy against the French."[15]

And yet, the matter was never so simple. Jacob Sturm had no personal ties to France; he neither spoke nor read French, nor had he any sympathy for the French king or French culture. Under his leadership, however, Strasbourg became the nexus of communications between the French court and the Protestant powers in the Empire. The city served as both the Smalkaldeners' vital window on the West and a major French port of access to Imperial politics. The broker of these relations was Jean Sturm (1509–81), since his student days at Paris an agent of Jean Cardinal du Bellay (ca. 1492–1560), who was head of the anti-Habsburg party at the French court.[16] Long after he became rector of Strasbourg's Latin school in 1538, Jean Sturm remained a salaried informant of the French king. He became mentor to the French-speaking religious refugees who flocked to Strasbourg, and from whose ranks the Smalkaldeners recruited their French-speaking diplomats, interpreters, scholars, and spies.

Behind this entire network stood Jacob Sturm, who had begun to build it during the mid-1530s, when prospects for a French alliance had been at their rosiest. At times he became very thick with the French agents. On 4 June 1536, for example, Guillaume du Bellay wrote to his brother, the cardinal, that he could be contacted either at Metz or "at Strasbourg at Sturm's house."[17] Since Jean Sturm did not come to Strasbourg until two years later, du Bellay can only have meant Jacob Sturm's mansion in Fire Street. It was Jacob Sturm, too, who brought two of the cardinal's German agents, Jean Sturm and Johann Sleidan (1506–56), to Strasbourg, where, with the help of Dr. Ulrich Geiger (called "Chelius," d. 1561), they handled the league's French business.

Later on, when relations with France soured, Jacob Sturm regretted his encouragement of the French network's operations. "Both Jean Sturm and Dr. Ulrich Geiger are learned and loyal men, and both are dear to me," he complained in 1544, "but I really think that they are doing things which I not only cannot praise, but which I think may damage themselves and our city."[18] Feeling the heat from "the great hue and cry at the Imperial court" about how

Sturm and Geiger were always writing to France, "and that every Frenchman [who comes] goes to their houses, especially Jean Sturm's, and even lodges there," Jacob Sturm exasperatedly concluded that "they are simply notorious and will have to pay for it." He had warned them "enough times . . . that they must stop doing this—to little effect, I see," though he feared that too strong a scolding might drive away Jean Sturm, "who has done our schools a lot of good and made them famous." Besides, by these times in the 1540s, not only had relations with the French king deteriorated, but the presence of so many French-speaking refugees at Strasbourg was inflaming the burghers' prejudices against the "Latins."

None of these diplomatic labors yielded much edible fruit. When it came to war in 1546, both monarchs, the French and the English, left the Smalkaldeners to face the emperor alone.

CAMPAIGN AGAINST THE IMPERIAL COURTS

The league's paltry diplomatic achievements contrast sharply with its successful operations against the Imperial government, especially the courts. From the beginning, one of the chief reasons why free cities and princes joined the alliance was to secure its protection against suits for restitution of clerical properties and rights before the Imperial Chamber Court at Speyer. This struggle began with the first such judgment against the cities of Constance and Ulm in 1531 and ended only with the court's suspension by Charles V in 1543. The campaign against the Chamber Court was long, bitter, and disruptive, turning as it did on a question to which there was no single, compelling answer: if "religious matters" should be excluded from the court's jurisdiction, on what basis should they be distinguished from other grounds for suits? In 1532 the Peace of Nuremberg promised to suspend all suits "concerning the faith."[19] What did that mean? Charles V left its definition to the Chamber Court, whose judges declined to accept the task, holding it to be impossible.

The Smalkaldeners thus enjoyed a guarantee from the emperor, which neither they nor he could enforce. By the mid-1530s, therefore, they began to discuss a policy of recusing—declaring incompetent because of religious bias—some or all of the court's judges. The landgrave wanted to go further and recuse the court "in all matters and not just in religious ones," since it was impossible for court and league to agree on a definition of a "religious matter."[20] That was surely correct, and the Strasbourgeois agreed. They sought the league's sanction against all judgments, notably one spoken in 1537 in favor of Count Philip of Hanau-Lichtenberg, who had brought a purely civil suit against Strasbourg to the Chamber Court.

The critical stage of this policy came at the end of the 1530s, when the Chamber Court began to issue decrees of outlawry against members of the league—Minden in 1539 and Goslar in 1540. Then, the league's invasion of

Brunswick-Wolfenbüttel in September 1542 gave the final impulse for a general recusation in 1543 of the Chamber Court's jurisdiction in *all* matters, until the court should be "reformed," that is, its Catholic complexion altered through replacement of judges. Charles V suspended the court in 1543, and it was not restored until 1548, following the emperor's victory over the Protestants. In many respects, the disruption of Imperial justice was the Smalkaldic League's most important purely political achievement.

THE PROBLEM OF ECCLESIASTICAL PROPERTY

At the root of the leaguers' attack on the Imperial courts lay the extremely explosive issue of ecclesiastical property. The Protestant Reformation had strongly accelerated the advance of lay hegemony over the church's substance and effected a radical redistribution of benefices and other properties, sometimes to pastoral, educational, and caritative purposes, often to princely treasuries and noble pockets. Most of this process violated existing law, but no agency—Imperial or territorial—had the clear authority to deal cleanly with the issue. Ecclesiastical property became the Smalkaldic League's albatross, for not only did the issue drive the Smalkaldeners to disrupt the Imperial courts, it also blocked all efforts to complement the Protestants' common confession of faith with a common Evangelical church order—a question the Protestants early on broached but never acted upon—and created deep divisions in the Protestant ranks.

When the league turned its attention to ecclesiastical property during the years from 1537 to 1540, the issue tended to split the cities from the princes. The Protestant cities mostly turned ecclesiastical properties to pastoral, caritative, and educational purposes, while the Protestant princes handled the properties, especially the monastic ones, pretty much as they pleased. Duke Ulrich's behavior in Württemberg was notorious, but the Saxon and Hessian princes were not much better. This difference reflected a gulf between the burghers' communal and the princes' patrimonial conception of property. The former was expressed in a memorial which Jacob Sturm submitted to the league's assembly at Eisenach in the summer of 1538, in which it was stated that "no emperor, king, bishop, pope, or any human can transfer them or alienate them from the church, except to give them to other churches, to monasteries, or to civil uses."[21] The contrary view is illustrated by a Saxon official's advice to the Magdeburgers in 1546: "Don't ask, for it is better to act than to ask. Indisputably, the priests are all our enemies, so just grab. If you get something, you have it and can keep it."[22] In vain Sturm stormed against greedy rulers, avowing that his own government "took nothing for its own treasury but solely to support the ministers and the schools, all with the consent of the convents' inmates."[23] Although he demanded a formal investigation of "the distribution of church properties," all the league did in 1540 was to issue a bland declaration that once the churches and schools were provided for, the rulers as "patrons" might turn the surplus to their own needs. It was a total victory for particularism, much as in 1526, when the Imperial Diet had relegated decisions on religion to the consciences of lay rulers and magistrates.

THE ISSUE OF MEMBERSHIP

The decision on property confirmed that the Smalkaldic League, like the Empire, was a federation of regimes and rulers, not a state composed of individual subjects, nor yet a political community of Evangelical Christians. If the German Reformation is seen in the light of subsequent developments in the Calvinist reformations of France, the Netherlands, Scotland, and England, it becomes clear how the German Protestants refused to make "godliness," that is, conformity not only of belief but also of behavior to the Gospel, a test of political legitimacy. This refusal clearly weakened the internal discipline of the Smalkaldeners, and it probably dampened their collective religious aggressiveness as well.

It has been common to see the source of this conservative position in Luther's attack on everyone—Andreas Bodenstein von Karlstadt, Huldrych Zwingli, the revolutionaries of 1525, and the Anabaptists—who saw in the Gospel a form of a law which governs Christian behavior. The Smalkaldeners, however, never blindly followed Luther in political matters, and it is far more probable that their refusal to make "godliness" a political norm arose from the very nature of the league—and the Empire—as a federation of rulers. Rulers, moreover, whose experience of "godliness" in 1525 had been quite sufficient. One case arose, nevertheless, which tested the members' convictions about how the Gospel bore, if at all, on the boundaries between rulers and subjects. The test came in 1543, when the embattled Evangelical minority at Metz applied for admission to the league.

THE LEAGUE AND THE REFORMATION AT METZ

At Metz, a francophone free city in northern Lorraine, an Evangelical mayor, Gaspard de Heu (1507–58), decided in the summer of 1542 to force his regime to guarantee religious toleration to his own minority party of Evangelicals. To this end he sent envoys to Strasbourg to ask that the Smalkaldeners admit his party to the league. The XIII and Landgrave Philip were for it, and on 24 September 1542 a league embassy led by Jacob Sturm set out for Metz. They found the plague-ravaged city seething with religious factionalism, and after sparring a bit with the magistrates, they returned to Strasbourg. Meanwhile, Mayor Heu led his party out of the city for a demonstration, hoping that the Smalkaldeners would rush to their aid.

Heu's party already had the support of Strasbourg's XIII, who, while they admitted the request's problematical nature, "because it comes not from the whole council or the whole commune, but perhaps only from a minority," nonetheless argued with more force than justice that the Evangelical party included "important, prestigious, honorable, and honest persons from the nobility and the commons," who were equal to their foes "in substance if not in numbers."[24] The magistrates knew quite well that the proposal involved federation with another ruler's subjects, something they would never have tolerated at Strasbourg, and the real reason behind their advocacy was the belief in Heu's promise that the league's backing would turn Metz into an Evangelical city "within a month or two."[25] Once this happened, "a large part of France, Brabant, Flanders, Luxembourg, and also Lorraine and Burgundy could be brought over by means of the common [French] language." Metz as the Reformation's springboard into French-speaking Europe! To the imagination a grand vision, in reality a pipe dream.

When this proposal reached the authorities in Saxony, who were quite familiar with the argument that Christian fellowship dissolved the bonds between rulers and subjects, Martin Luther found the proposal most "peculiar."[26] So did Elector John Frederick and others. When Gaspard de Heu came in January 1543 to Nuremberg, where the league and the Imperial Diet were sitting, he bore a letter of recommendation and advocacy from Strasbourg's regime to Jacob Sturm, who headed the committee that considered the Messins' plea for admission to the league. Sturm sided with the Saxons and against his own regime, and his report recommended against the Messins' request and doomed their cause. Thereafter, the Evangelicals of Metz drifted in to settle as refugees at Strasbourg, while the Smalkaldeners dealt with problems elsewhere in the Empire. The Metz affair nevertheless marks the Protestants' definitive rejection of Christian fellowship as a political principle, on the basis of which they might have redefined the Empire, or part of the Empire, as the community of Evangelical faith. Why did they reject it? One answer is that in German Protestantism the religious principle of community was too weak to disrupt the nature of the Empire as a federation of rulers. Another is that the larger issue—whether the Gospel as godly law breaks human law[27]—had in the Empire been so thoroughly mortgaged by the Peasants' War that it could no longer be asserted without seeming to advocate revolution.

JACOB STURM AND GOVERNANCE OF THE LEAGUE

The Metz affair illustrates almost perfectly the marriage between particularist politics and Evangelical religion. Despite his role in this affair, Jacob Sturm still harbored a dream of forging the league into a new political community, but on a particularist, not a centralist basis. His proposal of 1545 for the Smalkaldic League's reform illustrates how daunting this task was, for it reveals a deep conflict within the particularist political culture between, on the one hand, the burghers' corporate notion of a political community governed by responsible magistrates and, on the other, the princes' particularist conception of politics based on personal loyalty and inherited rights.

By the mid-1540s Jacob Sturm came to believe that the league needed more regular and more centralized governance, and when the league in 1545–46 debated on what terms it would be renewed, Sturm brought forward his concept of what the league should become, because, as he said on the eve of the debate, "on the issues which will be treated now depend our city's prosperity or ruin."[28] He wanted to enhance the league's statelike qualities and to ensure greater fairness in its conduct of business. Members, he thought, ought to settle their conflicts not "with the deed" but through arbitration, even though, since the league was founded on religion, this raised the disruptive issue of what constituted "religious matters." The neuralgic point remained ecclesiastical property, and Sturm proposed that any ruler who employed such properties for any but sanctioned ends be denied the league's protection. "Many believe," he confessed, "that the church properties have been handled selfishly and against what biblical principles ordain or allow, which could incur God's wrath and easily cause much dissent and grievances among the allies, and dissuade others from joining us on grounds of conscience."[29] It was a simple, impossible solution to the league's most bedeviling issue.

STURM'S PROPOSALS

Sturm next turned an eye to the league's government. He wanted to establish a permanent executive commission, as in the old Swabian League, or at least to have the assembly meet regularly at Frankfurt, with its plentiful inns, doctors, and druggists, rather than in dreary little Thuringian backwaters such as Arnstadt and Naumburg. He also wanted to redistribute the assembly's votes equally between cities and princes, with ties to be decided by lot, instead of the seven-to-six advantage the princes currently held, and to transfer decisions about peace and war to the assembly from the war council, whose members were "such folk as think more of war than of peace, and who know least of all about the league's affairs."[30]

Pecunia nervus belli (money is the nerve of war) went a favorite sixteenth-century saying, and finance lay at the heart of the power of the league, as of every other political body in that era. Sturm's proposal on finance reflected the burghers' view that good government is chiefly a matter of managing money well, and he felt that the princes regarded the cities as cows to be milked. Strasbourg's fare share, he thought, would be about a quarter, not the current 36 percent, of what the Saxon elector paid, or about as much as the larger northern cities "whose wealth is greater than Strasbourg's."[31] His main aim, however, was to replace the matricular levies with "a common tax and contribution" in the form of a property tax "from which kind of levy other nations finance their wars and other large expenses."[32] The Imperial Diet had reintroduced such a tax, the Common Penny, in 1544, a year before Sturm proposed it to the league. The Protestants, he urged, should regard their lands as "one body" and levy a tax of 0.5 percent. If no more equitable mode of taxation were found, Sturm sighed, "nothing can prevent the dissolution of this alliance."[33] Even a barely rational person, Sturm chided, might judge which alternative is preferable, "to pay this tax or levy of 0.5-1.0 percent on wealth and to keep one's own property, the true religion, life, limb, and ancient liberty, or to lose all and suffer the penalties I have mentioned." If the taxpayers, "rich or poor, are well informed of the reasons, they will pay willingly and without complaint." This, of course, expressed the mentality of burghers, who were quite accustomed to paying property taxes. Sturm also believed that a fairer system of taxation would draw new members into the league and become the key to "a thoroughgoing, complete, and Christian reform of all Christendom."

These arguments reveal the Reformation's profound impact on the particularist political heritage to which Jacob Sturm was heir. The conflict over religion not only revitalized, as has often been noted, the burghers' sense of communal responsibility to God and to one another, it also awakened—at least in Sturm— a new sense of wider political community based on a common faith. In the mid-1540s, shoving aside his misgivings over the princes' behavior in Brunswick-Wolfenbüttel and the northern cities' blithe disregard of their financial obligations, Sturm worked to transform the Smalkaldic League from a late medieval federation into a statelike political body. He conceived it not as a narrowly defined league to defend its members alone, but as the political body of all Protestant powers in the Empire.

Sturm was preparing the future, for as the Evangelical faith spread across the land, as Sturm believed it would, the league, becoming coterminous with the Empire itself, would serve as the cradle of a new, reformed Empire to house the reformed Christian church. Only their common religion opened the way to this future, for, as Sturm very pointedly told the Smalkaldeners at Worms in April 1546, "if his masters look only to themselves, they could well dispense with this league. But when they regard the common cause and the dangerous state of current affairs, they believe that this league can best be preserved through loyal cooperation."[34] Sturm was well aware that the absence of common temporal interests jeopardized the league's future, and, as he had argued at the Frankfurt assembly during the previous winter, this made a fair and equitable system of taxation all the more urgent. "On this account," he told the allies, "rather than indulging so much mistrust in the league and its business, it should be enough that we are dealing with honorable and Christian persons, who rest the matter on trust and faith, . . . for then God will make the cause flourish."[35] Equity, fairness, and brotherly love should make the league a model, against which the Empire, with its chronically unjust taxation and inability to protect its members from violence, could be measured with an eye to reform.

Further Sturm would not go. He may have come to regret his prominent role in the league's rebuff of the Evangelical Messins in 1543, but he agreed with its rationale, that the fellowship of the Gospel did not obliterate the distinctions between rulers and subjects. Precisely here lay the boundary of "the proper sort of love for one another."

THE LEAGUE AND THE CULTURE OF IMPERIAL POLITICS

Jacob Sturm's reform proposals betray deep roots in the political culture of the German-speaking burghers: good government means good financial management; equitable taxation fosters a sense of the common good; and common ideals and friendship, not contracts or property, should underpin political association. One cannot be sure how far Sturm would have defended this "bourgeois" vision of the league, had its interests and those of his native city become irreconcilable. It is nonetheless clear that his political vision both heartened the princes, in that his notion of religious fellowship did not disturb the obligation of subject to ruler, and challenged them, in that his principles of good government clashed with the princes' sense of political propriety and aristocratic right. The Smalkaldic chiefs, by contrast, believed that their welfare and their security embodied the interests of the Smalkaldic League and, by extension, the true Gospel's future in the Empire. They were accustomed to consultation, to be sure, but not to true debate or, worse yet, to votes on policy. They also tended, at least in the burghers' view, to favor military solutions to legal ones and to pose false expectations of deference and obedience. One wonders what Landgrave Philip thought of Bucer's comment that "equity is the basis of all communities, and inequity is like the very quicksilver, which destroys everything, especially religious community."[36]

The deeper conflict of political cultures in the Smalkaldic League, as in the Imperial Diet, rested on the princes' inability to recognize urban regimes as "rulers," in all essentials just like themselves. Nor could they accept that the regimes' envoys were merely representatives of civic magistrates, who in turn had—or said they had—to consult their own communes. This distinction between the ruler as a person and the ruler as corporate person expressed one of the deepest tensions in European political development, and the German princes of the sixteenth century may be forgiven for their inability to grasp it or, grasping, to accept it.

A bedrock understanding of authority as a collective enterprise underlay the differences between burghers' and aristocrats' political culture. The Holy Roman Empire had no "state" except for this vast, far-flung congery of princes, prelates, nobles, and magistrates, who, possessing only faint legitimacy of a traditional kind, nonetheless ruled the Empire under the emperor's name. Their power was not just local, and their incentive for cooperation, for collective police of the boundaries between rulers and subjects, lent Imperial governance both a resilience and resistance to disruption, on the one hand, and, on the other, a local effectiveness which no more centralized regime could achieve. In the league, as in the Empire, this common enterprise dulled the differences between the political subcultures of the aristocracy and the burghers.

Its incorporation into this political culture via the Smalkaldic League and the Empire both gave the German Reformation a future and constrained it from ever supplying religious legitimacy to revolutionary action. The political culture of particularism, far more than Lutheran doctrine, as is often alleged, lay at the root of the political passivity for which German Protestantism, especially Lutheranism, was to become notorious. For when Luther bragged that "since the time of the apostles, no doctor or writer, no theologian or lawyer, has confirmed, instructed, and comforted secular authority more gloriously and clearly than I was able to do through special divine grace,"[37] he was boasting about his service to this kind of particularist rule, not to "the State" or even to centralized monarchy of the western European type.

THE LEAGUE AND PARTICULARISM

The Smalkaldic League conformed in every respect to the political culture of particularism. The league's most clearly untraditional feature, its dedication to the defense of a common faith, did not disrupt its character as an alliance of rulers in the traditional mold. For it to burst these bounds and strive to transform the Empire into a community of Evangelical Christians, a godly kingdom, would have shattered the boundaries between rulers and subjects. Instead, with the Reformation the rulers' representation of their subjects assumed a religious aspect. The Smalkaldic League's members easily absorbed their subjects' consciences into their own, even though no religious basis, Lutheran or other, existed for asserting that rulers qua rulers, as distinct from rulers as sinful men in need of salvation, possessed consciences at all.

Far from separating "religion" from "politics," therefore, the German Reformation intensified their fusion and thereby dampened their power to transform one another. The crucial step in this process was the fusion of religion and power on the local, particular level, which left no space for a separately constituted ecclesiastical order. John Calvin, whose sharp eye saw very clearly what had happened in the Empire, struggled mightily to prevent the same outcome at Geneva, with considerable success. In the Netherlands his movement helped to undermine the traditional political culture of submission to the prince and encouraged the formation of a new state. In other countries, too, notably France and Scotland, Calvinism allied with aristocratic challenges to royal authority.

Nothing similar happened, could happen, in the Empire. Here, the local authorities—princes, nobles, and magistrates—absorbed religious authority to stabilize their power, and they captured the Evangelical movements' explosive potential in the local cells of the vast collective structure of particularist rule. They did so not just to contain revolution, but also because they needed the sacral authority the movement could extract from the old church. They also took this step with enthusiastic support from the Evangelical reformers, who traded this authority for the security they required. Later, far too late, the preachers might have regrets, as Martin Bucer did during his bitter exile in England. Once the revolutionary movement was past, however, their regrets weighed as nothing against the immense density of particularist rule, and the old dream of a reform of both Empire and church—pressed by reformers for a hundred years before Luther's reformation—faded into history.

In his own combination of communal politics and spiritual religion, Jacob Sturm represents perfectly the fusion of particularism and reformation. His plans for this Smalkaldic League in 1545–46 reveal very clearly the limits this fusion implied. Sturm wished to reform the league in a sense which, though informed by the burghers' conception of good government, respected the limits set by the particularist structure in its magisterial, that is, burghers', version. His respect dictated his role in the league's rebuff in 1543 of the Evangelical Messins, whose fate he deeply pitied. Haunted by the memory of 1525, Sturm, along with his whole generation of rulers, faced the era's religious struggles in the knowledge that, whatever the outcome, in their time the world must remain what it has always been, the realm of mammon under the eye of God. One day, perhaps, "the proper sort of love for one another" might so suffuse the world as to transform mammon's kingdom into that of Christ. That time, however, was not yet. The bare hope of this transformation nonetheless distinguished Jacob Sturm from his more famous Florentine contemporary, Niccolò Machiavelli.

JOHANN SLEIDAN, HISTORIAN OF THE SMALKALDIC LEAGUE

Like Machiavelli, Sturm appreciated the importance of the world's opinion. From his wish to memorialize the Smalkaldic League in the minds of the living and the memories of generations to come arose a plan for the first history of the German Reformation, Johann Sleidan's *Commentaries on the Condition of Religion and Politics under the Emperor Charles V.* Sleidan, who came from Schleiden in the county of Manderscheid in the Eifel region, had studied at Liège and Paris, and like Jean Sturm, who hailed from the same town, he became an agent of Cardinal du Bellay. Jacob Sturm first met Sleidan during the colloquys at Hagenau in 1540 and at Worms in 1541. In 1544, after much negotiation with the cardinal, Sleidan came to settle at Strasbourg, where he remained both a French agent and a German Evangelical, a situation which,

as he admitted, caused him much difficulty. "Although I am the king's servant," he once told Christopher Mundt, Henry VIII's German agent, "I do
not forget where my fatherland is."[38]

The idea for a history of the Reformation and the league was conceived,
Martin Bucer relates, by himself and Sturm during the summer of 1544, and
in Sleidan they thought to have found the man for the task. On 2 May 1545
Jacob Sturm reported that the Smalkaldic leaders had agreed to appoint Sleidan
as historiographer to the league, at an annual salary of 250 rhfl., to compile a
"history of the renewal of religion . . . and likewise of other things done in the
affairs of the league."[39] Almost immediately, this tall, handsome, highly gallicized
German, who was blind in his left eye, set out, in the words of one modern
historian, "to be the Polybius of the Reformation."[40] From the outset, however, the princes interrupted his labors with translating and diplomatic tasks,
including a fruitless mission to England on the eve of the Smalkaldic War.
Returning to Strasbourg in late January 1546, the historian settled down in a
double sense. He married Iola, daughter to the exiled Dr. Johann von Niedpruck
of Metz and a French-speaker, and began to write the league's history. What
with the war of 1546–47 and several missions on behalf of the league and the
city, most of the work was not composed until the first half of the 1550s.

Through Jacob Sturm's sponsorship, therefore, Johann Sleidan became the
first historian of the German Reformation. In its original Latin version, which
appeared in 1555, two years after Sturm's death and one year before his own,
and in the translations into German (twice), English, Italian, French, and Spanish,
his *Commentaries* became the most widely read history by a German-speaking
author during the entire early modern era. Employing the highest Renaissance
methods and style, the work preserves Jacob Sturm's vision of the course of
the Reformation and the founding, growth, and fate of the league. Indeed, to
a far greater degree than is commonly realized, Sleidan's history reflects Sturm's
viewpoint and Strasbourg's records, for despite his brave intention of scouring
the league members' archives, Sleidan received next to nothing from abroad.

Jacob Sturm's role in the progress of the history was very large, for Sleidan
relied heavily on Sturm's memory and Strasbourg's archive. When the project
was finished, the Strasbourg secretary Heinrich Walther described how Sleidan
had worked. "There is a very learned man here, Johann Sleidan," he related,
"who proposed to write a history of the origins of our religion and what happened as a consequence, and after it was described by the late Jacob Sturm and
other allies at a meeting of the league, he was asked to continue the work."
After the league's defeat, Sleidan was asked "in the names of all of them to
continue the history down to the present day," to which purpose "my lords
[the magistrates] gave him to read the documents concerning all of the meetings, so that the matters would be portrayed, so far as possible, as they in fact
happened at the time."[41] Sleidan himself confirmed that "my lords here [at

Strasbourg] gave me the documents."[42] One such document was a [now lost] letter sent by Strasbourg's regime to the Imperial Governing Council on 13 February 1525, in the winter of the Peasants' War, which contained the regime's earliest apology for religious changes: "[The magistrates] have done nothing they had no power to do, and in order to prevent greater disorder in the city, they had to allow the people access to the teaching of the Gospel, which has been spreading day by day."[43]

Sleidan also incorporated information he got from Jacob Sturm, who read and corrected the manuscripts of the first sixteen (of twenty) books. "I began this work more than ten years ago at the behest and command of great, important persons," Sleidan wrote in 1555, "and I informed myself diligently not from hearsay but from authentic extant documents. And I also consulted whenever necessary the late Sir Jacob Sturm for his memories and his explanations, as his two brothers can attest. Before his illness he read sixteen books and, where necessary, corrected them."[44]

Some passages in the *Commentaries* clearly reflect Sturm's own memories. Much of the account of the Peasants' War of 1525, for example, follows Sturm's travels as a mediator in Upper Swabia:

> But the Governing Council, seeing the Common Man in rebellion and what a grave danger that posed, sent an embassy of mediation to the Swabian League's delegates assembled at Ulm. It was composed of Simon Pistoris, who represented Duke George of Saxony, and Jacob Sturm, a nobleman and magistrate of Strasbourg, who at that time represented the city in the Governing Council.[45]

Sleidan's reliance on Jacob Sturm's reportage is particularly noteworthy in his portrayal of the Imperial Diet of 1547–48, the nickname of which, "the armored Diet," was apparently his coinage.[46] The eyewitness's special authority shines through Sleidan's account, which is not known from another source, of how the free cities, with Sturm at their head, escaped the emperor's pressure to accept the Council of Trent's decisions. "Now the cities alone held out," he begins,

> and they saw clearly that it would be dangerous to submit themselves unreservedly to the council's final decisions. Chancellor Granvelle and Heinrich Hass negotiated with them for a long time, and meantime a rumor spread through the city that the cities were being recalcitrant, and that they rejected the measures already agreed to by the electors and princes. Threats also were heard that they would be punished more severely than heretofore.[47]

Sleidan's relation now turns this tense situation into a humorous one, for he tells that "a means was found to satisfy the emperor." They stipulated (through Sturm, who is not named) the conditions under which they would accept the council, and Charles, who clearly did not quite understand the situation, replied that "he was quite pleased that they would deal with the matter as the other

Estates had done and unite with them." "He understood more from them," the historian editorializes, "than they had said or were willing to say, for they had not followed the other Estates."[48]

Another scene from the same Imperial Diet completes this picture of Sleidan's reliance on Sturm's experiences. The passage portrays the interview between Chancellor Granvelle and Jacob Sturm on 25 February 1548, in which the chancellor tried to force Sturm to accept the emperor's religious settlement, called the Interim. At the end, Sleidan has Granvelle threaten Sturm and his allies with a heretic's fate: "For those who have once accepted the faith and later deny it, can be forced by means of fire." Sturm replies, "One can execute them by fire, but no one can be forced to believe something other than what he believes."[49] Sleidan's text reproduces almost verbatim Sturm's own account of the interview.

Johann Sleidan's history of the German Reformation thus re-created much of the story from Strasbourg's experience, drawing both from the documents in the city's archive and from Jacob Sturm's living memories. Out of them and other materials, the historian was raising a monument and fixing an interpretation of what had happened, as no one realized better than did his patron. It was Sturm who decided that a German version of Sleidan's history must await a truly gifted translator, for "a German translation must be done by an able person who has a special talent for it. Such a man must be as well informed as Sleidan is."[50] Meanwhile, the fine Latin, which Sleidan had polished in France, would make the text accessible to all of Latin-reading Europe. Sleidan's knowledge of the ancient and medieval historians, some of whose works he had edited, also suited his history for this international audience and determined the coolly detached voice in which he tells it. Here, he and Jacob Sturm stood on common ground, Renaissance ground, where his neoclassical sense of proper historical discourse blended with Jacob Sturm's calm fortitude—"patience conquers fortune." This mood suited the state of affairs around 1550, when Sleidan was writing, that moment when the German Reformation had proved itself a religious success and a political failure.

NOTES

1. Ekkehart Fabian, *Die Entstehung des Schmalkaldischen Bundes und seiner Verfassung 1524/29–1531/35: Brück, Philipp von Hessen und Jakob Sturm*, 2d ed. (Tübingen, 1962), 358, line 17 to 359, line 6.
2. This, like most of the Smalkaldic League's other institutions, was modeled on the Empire and the Swabian League.
3. *PC* 2:509, no. 536.
4. Ibid., 371, no. 381.
5. Ibid., 627, no. 635.

6. Ibid. 4:71–72, no. 53.
7. Numbering only the Franco-Imperial wars under Charles V.
8. *PC* 2:442, no. 464.
9. Ibid., 443, no. 464.
10. Ibid. 3:467–68, no. 443.
11. Ibid., 471–72, no. 445.
12. Jakob Trausch, "Straßburgische Chronik," in Jakob Trausch and Johann Wencker, "Les chroniques strasbourgeoises," ed. Léon Dacheux, *BSCMHA*, 2d ser. 15 (1892): no. 2682, which rests on tradition.
13. Friedrich Hortleder, ed., *Der Röm. key.- u. königlichen Maiesten, auch des Heil. Röm. Reichs geistl. und weltl. Stände, Churfürsten, Fürsten Handlungen und Ausschreiben, Sendbrieff, Klag und Supplikationsschriften von den Ursachen des Teutschen Krieges keyser Carls des Fünften wider die schmalkaldischen Bundesoberste Chur- und Fürsten, Sachsen und Hessen und Mitverwandte anno 1546 u. 47*, 2 vols. (Frankfurt am Main, 1645), 1:1813 (= bk. 4, chap. 47).
14. *PC* 3:474, no. 448.
15. Charles Weiss, ed., *Papiers d'état du Cardinal de Granvelle d'après les manuscrits de la bibliothèque de Besançon*, 9 vols. (Paris, 1841–52), 3:365.
16. This man is called in the literature variously "Johann," "Johannes," and "Jean." I employ the French form as providing maximum protection against confusion of the two Sturms.
17. Victor-Louis Bourrilly, "Jean Sleidan et le Cardinal du Bellay: Premier séjour de Jean Sleidan en France (1533–1540)," *Bulletin de la Société pour l'Histoire du Protestantisme Français* 50 (1901): 227 n. 2.
18. *PC* 3:474–75, no. 448, from which the following quotes also come.
19. Gabriele Schlütter-Schindler, *Der Schmalkaldische Bund und das Problem der causa religionis* (Frankfurt am Main, 1986), 31.
20. Ekkehart Fabian, ed., *Urkunden und Akten der Reformationsprozesse am Reichskammergericht, am kaiserlichen Hofgericht zu Rottweil und an anderen Gerichten*, pt. 1 (Tübingen, 1961), 211, no. 76, of which an excerpt is in *PC* 2:202, no. 209.
21. Lenz 1:48 n. 1.
22. Kurt Körber, *Kirchengüterfrage und schmalkaldischer Bund* (Leipzig, 1913), 182.
23. *PC* 3:35–38.
24. This is the medieval notion of the better (*melior*), weightier (*valeor*), or sounder (*sanior*) part.
25. *PC* 3:370, no. 349.
26. *WA Br* 10:191.
27. This phrase echoes the common expression in medieval German law about the hierachy of laws, such as "city law breaks territorial law."
28. *PC* 3:675 n. 5.
29. Ibid., 676.
30. Ibid., 677.
31. Ibid.
32. Ibid. 4:7–8, no. 9; and there, too, the following quotes.
33. Ibid., 22–23, no. 23, is the basis of the remainder of this paragraph.
34. Ibid., 82, no. 62.
35. Ibid., no. 23.
36. Lenz 2:96, no. 145.
37. Martin Luther, "Verantwortung der aufgelegten Aufruhr von Herzog Georg (1533)," in *WA* 38:102, lines 31ff.

38. Quoted by Friedrich Prüser, *England und die Schmalkaldener 1535–1540* (Marburg, 1928), 305.
39. Hermann Baumgarten, ed., *Sleidans Briefwechsel* (Strasbourg, 1881), 47, no. 23.
40. Peter Burke, *The Renaissance Sense of the Past* (London, 1969), 124.
41. Baumgarten, ed., *Sleidans Briefwechsel*, 309, no. 162.
42. Johann Sleidan to Duke John Frederick of Saxony, Strasbourg, 24 June 1553, in ibid., 262, no. 127.
43. Johann Sleidan and Michael Beuther, *Ordenliche Beschreibung und verzeychniss allerley fürnemer händel, so sich in glaubens und anderen weltlichen sachen bei regierung der grossmächtigen keyser Carls' dises namen des Fünfften, Ferdinandi des Ersten, maximiliani und rudolphi der Anderen, inn und ausserhalb des Heyligen römischen reichs teutscher nation biss auff das tausent fünff hundert vier und achtzigste jar, zugetragen und verlauffen haben, durch Johannem Sleidanum und Michaelem Beutherum* (Strasbourg: Theodosius Rihel, 1597), 85 (book 4). This letter seems to be lost. It would belong in *PC* 1:97.
44. Baumgarten, ed., *Sleidans Briefwechsel*, 275–76, no. 275.
45. Johann Sleidan, *De statu religionis et reipublicae Carolo V Caesare commentarii* (Strasbourg: Wendelin Rihel, 1555), bk. 4.
46. Ibid., bk. 19.
47. Ibid.
48. Ibid.
49. Sleidan, *Commentarii*, bk. 20. Sturm's own account, in *PC* 4:1017, no. 791, is excerpted in chapter 13.
50. Baumgarten, ed., *Sleidans Briefwechsel*, 309, no. 162.

8

REFORMATION CHURCH
AND RENAISSANCE SCHOOL

He cannot have God for his father who has not the church for his mother.
—St. Cyprian

The Reformation passed from liberation to reconstruction decisively, swiftly, and early. Popular involvement in sometimes violent movements for change supplied new and daunting urgency to the magistrates' need to establish their own authority over the practice of religion. It was axiomatic, of course, that religion ought to nourish peace and harmony, and most Christians could have agreed with the fourteenth-century Muslim philosopher Ibn Khaldûn (1332–1406), who wrote that "only by God's help in establishing His religion do individual desires come together in agreement to press their claims, and hearts become united."[1] If mismanaged or neglected, however, religion could spark discord and become the chief nemesis of the magistrates who claimed custody of the civic commonweal. Jacob Sturm had to confess in 1534 that "in our times scarcely anything else so unites people's minds or drives them apart as unity or disunity in religion does."[2] He may have been thinking about his own Strasbourg during the early 1520s, when the Evangelicals' cries had sounded in the churches of Strasbourg; or of the grim days of 1525, when topsy-turvy had ruled the land and threatened the cities.

THE RISE AND FALL OF THE SECTS

In the wake of the terrible days of 1525, a new threat had arisen in the South. The hydra of rebellion sprouted new heads, dissenters whose foes called them Anabaptists or Baptists. At Strasbourg, their growth in numbers and activity between 1528 and 1533 disrupted the Evangelical preachers' efforts to manage the local church and sharpened the Lutheran allies' suspicions about Strasbourg's orthodoxy. Something had to be done, and Jacob Sturm, who in 1525 had pleaded for tolerance, became mastermind of the suppression of religious dissent in the city. In the struggle against the sects during the first half of the

143

1530s, Sturm also became architect of the new church order, the magisterial constitution under which the city's church would live for the remainder of the sixteenth century.

THE ANABAPTISTS COME TO STRASBOURG

The Anabaptists, "rebaptizers," so-called because of their practice of adult or "believers'" baptism only, sprouted just after the Peasants' War in the Empire's southern tier, most vigorously in Franconia, Thuringia, Swabia, the Tyrol, and eastern Switzerland. Everywhere they gathered, these folk demanded a voluntary but more radical, less worldly, more communal reformation against what seemed to them the Evangelical reformers' half-hearted and compromising ways. Some were millenarians, some not; some were pacifists, some not; and some were communists, some not. All, however, eschewed infant baptism, swearing oaths, military service, and the subordination of religious life to governments. The authorities and the clergy, in turn, considered the Anabaptists to be subversive of the social order, which they were—not by their doctrines but by their behavior—for their radical separation of church from world struck at the very heart of a culture in which religion was supposed to bind man to wife, parents to children, neighbor to neighbor, burghers to magistrates, and subjects to lords.

By the end of the 1520s, a full decade after its inception, the Evangelical reformation had indeed become vulnerable to just such a charge of compromise. By siding with the rulers in 1525, the preachers had rescued the possibility for the reform of whole local churches, though at the price of vulnerability to Anabaptist poaching and sniping in the sullen postrevolutionary atmosphere. It had proved easier, after all, to rouse popular fury and magisterial action against the Catholic clergy and practice than, once victorious, to reconstruct the church and foster a godly atmosphere in the cities. Strasbourg's preachers, for example, had to admit that their own mediocre success had opened burghers' ears to other religious messages. Preaching from Geiler's splendid pulpit to the magistrates on *Schwörtag* 1534, Caspar Hedio painted a grim picture of the city. "Many have thrown off the papacy," he said, "and slipped out from under its heavy human yoke. But they do not now want to take up the Gospel and place themselves under the light yoke of Christ. . . . One no longer hears Mass, but then one also does not hear the Gospel." Alas, he lamented, whereas formerly "the priests, monks, and nuns used to devour the income and goods of the church, . . . now it is the workers and youth who run wild, and many have no respect for God, worship, good works, or any honorable thing. The same is true of the peasantry on the land."[3]

His audience knew that Hedio spoke the truth, for over the past five years they had labored to construct, step by step, a new system of religious and moral discipline, from new laws against immorality (1529) and a new marriage court (1529) to the appointment of parish churchwardens (1531). Last year they had held a municipal synod, the first in history, and now they faced the task of preparing and enacting a new ordinance on religious doctrine and discipline.

The chief spur to this escalation of religious surveillance and discipline were the Anabaptists, who during the late 1520s began streaming into their "New Jerusalem" on the Rhine from Switzerland, Swabia, and Franconia. In their ranks were Swiss Brethren, whose biblicism and pacifism attracted local admirers, notably Wolfgang Capito; Hans Hut's (d. 1527) followers from Augsburg, bearing the chiliastic and communistic heritage of Thomas Müntzer's revolution; and harmless followers of Hans Denck (1500?–27), the Bavarian spiritualist. Two more figures arrived in May and June 1529 to spice this bubbling sectarian stew: Caspar Schwenckfeld (1489–1561), an elegant Silesian nobleman, and Melchior Hoffman (d. 1543), a Swabian furrier and chiliast. Schwenckfeld posed no real threat, for he traveled mostly in respectable circles, where his mockery of the idea of "Christian government" won him admirers among those whom the preachers called "epicureans," men and women who branded the new police of religion and morals "a new papacy." He possessed an entire network of such admirers across southwestern Germany, including Jacob Sturm's distant cousin, Hans Konrad Thumb von Neuburg, the hereditary marshal of Württemberg.

Melchior Hofmann was an altogether different story. A veteran of religious agitation all through the Geman-speaking Northeast, he was now teaching that Strasbourg was the New Jerusalem—just as Rome was the new Babylon—from which 144,000 saints would pour forth to spread the true Gospel. True or not, his message only aggravated the city's reputation abroad for heterodoxy in general and Sacramentarianism in particular.

RECONSTRUCTION OF THE CHURCH

It is ironical that the Anabaptists and other sectarians met their downfall at the hands of Jacob Sturm, an Erasmian Protestant who in principle disliked compulsion in religion. He had often scolded the Evangelical preachers for relying more on government than on the Gospel. "God promised us Christians," he once wrote, "not happiness in this life (as He did to the Jews in the Old Testament) but only suffering and persecution."[4] Sturm did not propose to make Strasbourg more godly by suppressing dissent, for, as he once put it, "laws make hypocrites."[5]

If not more godly, then more united and more secure, and to this end Sturm did not reject the use of compulsion. The Senate & XXI raided the sects' conventicles and arrested and banished their leaders in order to cow the followers, but when force and intimidation failed, they resorted to reason. In early winter 1531 the magistrates staged a remarkable debate between their own clergy and Pilgram Marpeck (ca. 1495–1556), a Tyrolean engineer who declared that "between the papists and the Lutherans the dispute is largely a temporal quarrel." Martin Bucer and his like, Marpeck charged, preached "either in the absence of the Common Man or in the presence of princes and urban magistrates, instead of preaching freely before the cross of Christ."[6] Sturm himself had said much the same about Capito in 1526, but as the crisis deepened—Claus Kniebis reported that on *Schwörtag* 1532 some burghers had refused to raise their hands and swear the oath—he yielded to the preachers' logic that all Christian rulers "are obliged to help us all they can" to fight this blasphemy, to the end "that Strasbourg, too, will at last have one doctrine and religion."[7] The magistrates expelled Marpeck, arrested Hofmann, warned the Spanish antitrinitarian Michael Servetus (1511–53) "to stay out of Strasbourg, or he will be punished," and began to crack down on clandestine printing.[8] Heresy or sedition, it was all one to them.

Still, the preachers were not satisfied, for in their eyes the sectarian problem merely intensified the real issue, which was the need for stricter religious discipline. "Every authority," they thought, "should oblige its subjects to refrain from blaspheming the true faith, to hear the truth, and to encourage their dependents to do the same," for otherwise, God "will cast the ruler down entirely and hand the entire people over to the Devil."[9] Would the burghers stand for such a religious regimen? Sturm thought not. Nor did his colleagues, for when, in late November 1532, the magistrates decided to sponsor a municipal synod, they went out of their way to declare that its goal was "not at all, as some allege, to compel anyone to belief, but to suppress public offenses, which is the obligation of every ruler according to divine and Imperial law."[10] Sturm agreed, feeling that the time had come "to combat the sects, hold a disputation, and hold to one [i.e., infant] baptism."[11] Strasbourg's youth might be compelled to go to church, but Sturm drew the line at forcing the adults. "How can they be ordered to do it?" he asked himself, and "who should and would determine this? . . . It is good that they be gathered in to listen, but I don't know how. And how should transgressors be found out and punished? Yet, if they are not punished and warned, gradually order will be greeted with contempt."[12] There it was. The puzzling contradiction between a freely preached Gospel and the perceived need for public morality—one of the great conundrums of Christian history—had come home to rest, as Sturm the Erasmian wrestled with Sturm the magistrate.

STRASBOURG'S FIRST SYNOD, 1533

On 3 June 1533, Sturm as senior president in the chair, a municipal synod, an assembly of the clergy under lay supervision, convened behind closed doors. The reason for the synod, Sturm announced, was that "since much disagreement over the faith and doctrine has arisen, the Senate's presidents are to deliberate with the churchwardens, preachers, pastors, and curates about how we can achieve unity in doctrine."[13] He warned them of the consequences of failure, for if the clergy could not agree to accept a formula—Bucer's work—called the Sixteen Articles, then "the presidents and the churchwardens will deliberate on the majority and minority views and bring them before the Senate and XXI, who will determine what may be pleasing to God."[14] In this assembly, "everyone should speak his mind freely, and it will be listened to in a friendly spirit, for otherwise, if there is a dispute later, it will serve the church little and God even less."[15]

Sturm might as well have tried to harness the wind, as around him howled a gale of grumbling, recriminations, accusations, and dissent. Putting a warning edge to his voice, he admonished the clergymen that "this assembly was arranged solely to further the honor of God and the welfare of this city," and to "ask them to have regard for this end and stick to it, and to lay aside whatever one may have against another."[16] The preachers, after all—Sturm bared his teeth—"have opponents on all sides among the Catholics and the sects, who might say that their disunity is proof of their false teachings. They ought to reflect on this." After he reported to the Senate & XXI on 4 June that "the matter is more serious and bigger than my lords had realized,"[17] the magistrates decided to bring official representatives of the guilds into the meeting hall, "so that during the synod no disorder arises from the press of the common folk, and so that some from the people can nonetheless be present."[18] That should calm, as it was meant to, the quarrelsome clergymen. In this atmosphere the dissenters were heard, both the big fish and the little fellows, such as Claus Frey, a furrier from Rottenburg on the Neckar, who paid with his life for the folly of forgetting to divorce his wife before marrying a baron's sister.

As the synod dragged on, Sturm had to acknowledge that the quarrels about religion centrally concerned authority and, therefore, government. At the opening of the final session on 23 October 1533, he declared that "the Senate does not intend to force anyone in matters of faith, but only to suppress conspiracies that might lead to division of the commonweal."[19] The central article and sticking point, clearly, was the article "concerning government," on which, Sturm declared, "the entire matter must rest." The magistrates alone had to decide "which of the doctrines we have heard is to be held as God's Word, for it would be fruitless to take up the other points before we have decided which one we hold to be God's Word."[20] Religious truth was to be defined, as it always had been, by authority, only now by local gentlemen, merchants, and artisans rather than by popes, bishops, and university professors. Knowing well how unsuited were his fellow magistrates to this task, Sturm distributed to them printed copies of the Tetrapolitan Confession, because many magistrates would not sit still long enough for it to be read aloud. They nonetheless did as he ordered, and on 4 March 1534 they voted "unanimously . . . to remain with the oft-mentioned [Tetrapolitan] confession and the [Sixteen] articles read to the synod, and to have them preached here as the correct Christian doctrine and enforced as such."[21] In this vote the Senate & XXI of Strasbourg acted as General Councils, popes, and Christian Roman emperors had acted, "to determine what may be pleasing to God."[22] These words, Jacob Sturm's words, sealed the sects' doom at Strasbourg.

THE CHURCH ORDINANCE OF 1534

To condemn the sects was one thing, to reconstruct religious discipline quite another. The most ticklish issue Sturm faced, as he drafted the new church ordinance for the city, was how to instill godly discipline in the burghers, many of whom looked on the official clergy "as scoundrels and asskissers, who had never preached God's Word," for they "are hated by many people, and many nasty things are said of them."[23] "It would be a good thing," he wrote, "if we could find a way to get the people to come to church and hear the Word of God." This could hardly be achieved through laws, however, "for in matters of faith, which is a voluntary act and gift of God, little can be gained through laws. Then, too, the hearing of sermons is an external thing, not an act of faith itself." He feared the scandal that might arise "if the law were not obeyed and the violators were not punished, it would only diminish the government's authority . . . and prompt people to say that 'a new papacy has been established.'"[24] Sturm's was the perennial dilemma of those who desire to promote both spiritual religion and social order. The best remedy he could imagine was a lame one, namely, that the magistrates should set a good example for their fellow burghers, and "on Sunday every member of the government should hear at least one sermon and, since the common people look up to them, they shouldn't go strolling about the city during the sermon."[25] Further he would not go, for he both disbelieved in the *religious* value of compulsion and feared to stir up the burghers' resistance to a stricter ecclesiastical discipline. Martin Bucer, now Strasbourg's leading churchman, disagreed, and on this point—compulsive religious discipline—he and Sturm would one day come to, and remain at, loggerheads. For the moment, however, the two leaders agreed on the need for doctrinal unity against the sects. "Since we have already decided," Sturm announced, "to hold to the [Tetrapolitan] confession submitted at Augsburg and the synod's [Sixteen] articles, it follows that all other sects, who oppose this doctrine, are not to be tolerated, and their supporters should be dealt with."[26] Just as in the Smalkaldic League, at Strasbourg there was to be unity of doctrine, but no strict regime of compulsion in religious practice.

This principle informed Sturm's draft of the ordinance that was to govern Strasbourg's church for the next half-century. The speech, with which the ammeister presented this ordinance to the guilds' Schöffen on 7 February 1535, was also Sturm's work. In it he took occasion to review the course of Strasbourg's reformation. "Years ago," he wrote, "it was asserted and decided by the stettmeister and Senate & XXI and also by the Schöffen and ammeister, that in this city of Strasbourg the holy Gospel was to be preached purely and clearly, and also that all sorts of anti-Scriptural abuses should be abolished." Later, when these actions seemed to provoke a threat to the city, "our lords, with the knowledge and approval of Schöffen and ammeister, entered into a Christian alliance with some electors, princes, counts, and cities who agree with us on faith. This happened so that we might more peacefully hold to the confessed truth and the biblical doctrine." Now, however, there have arisen "all sorts of heretical sects, unnecessary argument, and contentious opinions about the faith in this city, which caused many to fall away from the confessed truth and to have contempt for the doctrine and preaching of the holy Gospel and its preachers alike." From this contention had come "many harmful splits and divisions to considerable scandal and provocation of many Christians and to the destruction of civic peace and unity." The magistrates, therefore, faced with this situation, were compelled to act against "the seducers, most of whom first came here from foreign parts." The new church ordinance, which the Schöffen were asked to approve, would "forestall such evils, prevent divisions, and avert the ruin, physical and spiritual, of the whole city and its citizens."

This speech, Jacob Sturm's most detailed statement on the reformation at Strasbourg, offered at once an account of and an apology for the reforms and for his own alliance policy. He dissembled, of course, about the tensions, even conflicts, that had arisen between the restored Gospel and the civic common good, blaming all the trouble on those who came from "foreign parts." Sturm had once pleaded for tolerance on the grounds that "both sides are Christians, may God have mercy!" Now, he was determined never to give the sectarians the chance to serve the Evangelicals as he and his fellows had earlier served the Catholics.

The issue had been framed in precisely these terms by a soapmaker named Leupold Scharnschlager (d. 1563), when he scolded the magistrates in his harsh Tyrolean accent. "You accept and press us," this brave dissenter began, "to abandon our faith and accept yours. That is just the same as when the emperor said to you, you should abandon your faith and accept his. Now I speak to your consciences: do you think it right to obey the emperor in such things? Ah, well, then you might also say that we ought to obey you in such things." In that case, he mocked them, "you would be obliged to reinstate all the idolatry and the papist convents, also the Mass and other things." Since, however, the magistrates refused to obey the emperor in such matters, "so I, a poor Christian, ask and admonish you for the love of God and the salvation of your own souls, that you leave our consciences alone in the matter and have mercy on and protect us poor folk."[27] This was the central issue, and no one ever stated it more precisely or more frankly than Scharnschlager did, as he stood before the glowering magistrates in Strasbourg's city hall and hoisted them neatly with their own petard. On the magistrates' benches sat one man, Hans Bock von Gerstheim, who had heard Martin Luther speak the terrible words at Worms in 1521: "I send not peace, but the sword."

The dissenting soapmaker's brave reproach did nothing to soften the hearts of Strasbourg's magistrates, who, like their colleagues in other cities, could hardly doubt the deep inner correspondence between the Gospel of Christ and the common good—the existing order of things—of their own communities. Huldrych Zwingli provided this belief with a theoretical formulation in his doctrine of two coordinated authorities, civil and religious, which experience in the Protestant cities contradicted and Scharnschlager's bold words condemned. If it were to remain free, the Gospel had to work through an agency that was differently constituted and differently shaped—either larger or smaller—than the commune. In some sense, therefore, the Anabaptists' struggle for a voluntary community of believers continued, with different weapons, the medieval struggle for the "liberty of the Church" against the emperors and kings. The magistrates' world view, on the other hand, required a coordination of common good and Gospel in one community—the commune united at work and at prayer—under one authority, magisterial authority. Otherwise, the clergy, whether charismatic prophets or Evangelical preachers, would become "new popes," to forestall which event the magistrates had to become "new Caesars." Since the movements of the 1520s, an inexorable logic toward this position had developed out of the preachers' appeals for magisterial protection from and action against the old church. It required a shrewd outsider to recognize where this logic would lead, and such a man appeared at Strasbourg in 1538. Based on his observations at Strasbourg, this French-speaking refugee formulated a new and daring solution to this Reformation dilemma. The man's name, of course, was John Calvin.

THE ANABAPTIST KINGDOM AT MÜNSTER

It was not only a desire for internal peace which led Jacob Sturm and his colleagues down the path of persecution, for the external situation presented another face of menace. The climax of the struggle against the sects at Strasbourg coincided with the restoration of Duke Ulrich in Württemberg, followed by the Treaty of Kaaden, which contained an explicit condemnation of all Sacramentarians and associated them with heretics and rebels.

REACTIONS TO MÜNSTER

Far more important, the crushing of dissent at Strasbourg coincided with the crisis in the Empire over the radical Anabaptist kingdom at Münster. The Netherlandish leader at Münster, Jan Beukelszoon (d. 1535), was known to be a follower of Melchior Hoffman, who languished in the Hangman's Tower at

Strasbourg. The connection gave rise in November 1533 to a rumor in north-western Germany, as Sturm reported, that "Melchior Hoffman has won out here, and the whole city [of Strasbourg] holds his opinion."[28] Melchiorite lore did indeed link Strasbourg with Münster, where the leaders "told the common folk that they had a vision of three cities in the night.... One was the city of Münster, the second Strasbourg, and the third was Deventer. These same cities ... God has chosen as the places where he will raise up a holy people."[29]

The danger posed to Strasbourg by reactions to Münster are only explicable in the light of two facts. First, the Anabapist kingdom became a scandal of Imperial proportions when news from Münster, spiced by reports of commu-nism and polygamy, spread over the Empire. Second, many, and not just the Münsterites themselves, held Strasbourg to be a font of radical heresy and dissent. Heinrich Bullinger, Zwingli's successor at Zurich, blamed the whole thing on Caspar Schwenckfeld and sighed, "O poor polluted Strasbourg, from which such unwanted birds take wing."[30] If this is how the leading Zwinglian thought, the Lutheran reactions may well be imagined.

The events at Münster thus posed a palpable danger to Sturm's alliance policy. Initially, the connections were not clear, and the magistrates, perhaps thinking wishfully, failed to see the danger and refused to pay for Imperial countermeasures against Münster on the grounds of the affair's "remoteness." Later on, they saw the light and punctually paid their share of the tax to besiege and take Münster, which fell on 25 June 1535. By this time official interest in the case had intensified at Strasbourg and in other southern Protestant cities. In November 1535 Bernhard Wurmser, Jacob Sturm's cousin, and Eitelhans Besserer of Ulm were dispatched to Westphalia to investigate the matter, but with particular attention to the alleged connections between the Anabaptist kingdom and Melchior Hoffman. Wurmser reported their interviews with Jan van Leiden, who "says that he had never met Melchior Hoffman nor had any correspondence with him, though he had looked at Hoffman's writings."[31]

The shock waves from the Anabaptist kingdom rumbled through the entire northwestern sector of the Empire, touching off, among other things, new reform initiatives in the leading Rhenish principalities. But they resonated in the far South, too, where the episode reawakened memories of 1525—community of goods, attacks on authority, and the coming kingdom of righteousness—and threatened to disrupt Jacob Sturm's incomplete concord with his Lutheran allies.

THE SECOND SYNOD

At Strasbourg the Münster affair intensified the magistrates' movement to as-sume willy-nilly a new degree of command over the city's religious life, a de-gree which would have been unthinkable as recently as Sturm's boyhood days. To this purpose they needed an organ to supervise day-to-day church affairs, which emerged in the form of the Church Assembly (*Kirchenkonvent*). This largely clerical body—it officially included the churchwardens—had developed informally during the 1520s and received official recognition in 1531. By now a purely clerical body, it met weekly to discuss the assignment of duties, lay discipline, education, and additional reforms of the church. In this spirit a second municipal synod gathered on 26–28 May 1539 to address, in an altogether calmer atmosphere than in 1533, the problem of "uniformity" in preaching and in the administration of the sacraments. The Senate & XXI, well satisfied with existing arrangements, took nearly five years to publish the second synod's recommendations. Frustrated by the magistrates' Fabian tactics, the preachers even turned to the new Catholic bishop, Erasmus of Limburg (b. 1507, r. 1541–68), about a general reform of religion in the diocese. A novel idea, but one with no future.

Meanwhile, since the fall of the sects the church at Strasbourg came gradually under the norms and practices of a Lutheran religious pedagogy. This shift, which neatly dovetailed with Jacob Sturm's alliance policy, had to begin with the recruitment and formation of clergymen. More and more, the city hired pastors who were prepared at the local Latin school and trained in theology at Wittenberg or Tübingen, both Lutheran universities. Richard Hillis, an English cloth merchant resident at Strasbourg since 1540, wrote in 1546 that "[Johann] Marbach is altogether a Lutheran: but this is nothing among us, because almost all the preachers here are chiefly imbibing and inculcating Lutheranism."[32]

THE CHURCH SETTLEMENT AT STRASBOURG

The church settlement of the 1530s at Strasbourg flowed easily from both the Protestants' decision to make Lutheran doctrine their normative faith and Jacob Sturm's alliance policy. It meant the crushing of the sects, but also the doom of the "Zwinglian" character of the native reformation. The Lutheran displacement of Zwinglianism at Strasbourg thus occurred not after Bucer's banishment in 1549—as local legend would have it—but under the very eyes of Bucer and Jacob Sturm. It was not a dramatic shift, particularly not for the common people, for to Evangelical Christians everything associated with Luther took authority from his undiminished reputation as a God-sent restorer of Christian religion. Then, too, the Lutheran-Zwinglian split was chiefly a clerical matter, and the differences on the sacrament of the Lord's Supper—its representative issue—became a normative boundary between distinct churches, called "confessions," only after the rise of Calvinism during the next generation. This is not to say the shift was unimportant, merely that its impact on the laity was probably more liturgical than doctrinal. It is visible, for example, in the new hymnal of 1541, which replaced most of the familiar hymns of Strasbourg and Constance provenance with Luther's compositions. And yet, this was not a truly "confessional" act, for no local productions ever rivaled the power of Luther's hymns, his catechism, or his "German Mass," which assured that all German Evangelicals would be, in some sense, Lutherans.

Strasbourg's shift toward the Lutherans nonetheless set the stage for protoconfessional conflict in later years. In the 1560s, well after Jacob Sturm's death, strife erupted over the correct forms of belief and practice, this time between Lutherans and admirers of Calvin, and in this context the legacy of Strasbourg's original reform and the evolution of its church became material for controversy.

And so they remained, for a hoary tradition holds that the coming of Lutheran orthodoxy to Strasbourg subverted Martin Bucer's liberal, humanist, and tolerant reformation after his death. Nothing could be further from the truth. The roots of what is called "Lutheran orthodoxy" at Strasbourg went far back beyond the Wittenberg Concord of 1536, beyond Strasbourg's church ordinance of 1534, beyond Strasbourg's signature to the Confession of Augsburg at Schweinfurt in 1532, beyond the founding of the Smalkaldic League in 1531, and even beyond the original Protestant agreement at Speyer in 1529. It went back ultimately to Jacob Sturm's new politics of 1528, the chief goal of which was an alliance with the Evangelical princes of central Germany. According to the logic of Protestant politics and the centrality of Lutheran Saxony, from that point onward the success of Sturm's policy meant both the failure of the Christian Federation with the Swiss Evangelicals and the doom of what is called Zwinglianism at Strasbourg and in other southern free cities. It came to this breach not because Strasbourg's preachers were more Lutheran and less Zwinglian than the Swiss, nor because Strasbourg's reformation movement differed fundamentally from Zurich's. No, the difference lay in the logic of political structures, for Zurich found its security, and maintained it—despite Zwingli and beyond all religious strife—within the Swiss Confederacy, the purest guardian of pure particularism, while Strasbourg remained within the Imperial system. Strasbourg's politics, therefore, developed as an Imperial Protestant politics, and since the beginning of the 1530s this meant Saxon leadership and Lutheran identity.

Sturm's leadership on this path thus represented a qualification of the politics of pure particularism. Otherwise, he would have accepted the path favored by some of his Evangelical colleagues, merger with the Swiss. His politics, however, qualified pure particularism in order to gain and protect religious particularism in the form of the fusion of spiritual with temporal authority in the hands of the local magistracy. This intensely local purpose seems inappropriate to Sturm's own background as an Erasmian, but the appearance is deceiving. For if the church had become, had to become, a locally bounded world of order and discipline—though not too strict—there remained another world, unbounded and universal, in which the desire for freedom and the sense of a larger belonging could find freer play. This world was the Renaissance republic of letters, as broad as Christendom itself, into which Sturm labored to build a noteworthy and durable port of entry in the schools of Strasbourg.

THE SCHOOL BOARD AND THE SCHOOLS

"Void of learning is Mother Strasbourg," wrote a knowledgeable fellow around 1520.[33] He merely echoed Jakob Wimpheling's fervent but fruitless plea in 1501 for a civic Latin school. By the end of the 1530s, Wimpheling's prize pupil had remedied the lack and more, for under Jacob Sturm's hand the schools of Strasbourg developed into a model for Evangelical pedagogy in the Empire and a vibrant window on the Erasmian "republic of letters."

FOUNDING THE SCHOOL BOARD

The original impulse for improvement of the schools came not from Sturm but from the preachers, who in the year of the great Peasants' War petitioned the magistrates for a series of reforms, including civic schools. On 9 February 1526 the Senate & XXI appointed the first School Board, or "scholarchs," whose three members were privy councilors chosen for life according to the usual Strasbourg formula, one noble and two commoners. Jacob Sturm became the first noble member of the School Board, a post he held until his death. His two colleagues were the Ammeister Claus Kniebis, who had studied at Freiburg, and Jacob Meyer (d. 1562), president of the Masons' Guild, who, though a man of substance, probably had no Latin. Sturm, the best educated magistrate of his, or any previous, generation, immediately became and remained until his death the School Board's dominant figure.

During the following twelve years, under Sturm's guidance the School Board dramatically transformed Strasbourg, long "devoid of learning," into one of the Empire's most important fonts of curricular innovation. They built step by step, assuming supervision of the existing schools, establishing a library, creating a school treasury out of the properties and incomes of the dissolved mendicant houses, and deploying benefices at St. Thomas, the city's second most important collegiate church, to pay teachers. "So that none of the priests will lack for better instruction," the scholarchs declared in 1530, "we have on our own provided for the two schools, where boys are taught Latin and Greek, that experienced and learned scholars shall give instruction in the Dominican convent in Hebrew, Greek, rhetoric, poetry, mathematics, and civil laws; the Holy Bible is taught at St. Thomas."[34]

The establishment of a civic school monopoly fitted perfectly the magistrates' conception of the common good as both local and centralized. Jacob Sturm's ordinance for the grammar schools, issued on 19 November 1531, consolidated magisterial control over all schooling in the city: "First, that no one should hold school or teach publicly here at Strasbourg, unless he has first come before the scholarchs and gained their permission."[35] Two and a half years later, in March 1534, Sturm drafted a comprehensive ordinance for the city's grammar schools—the most centralized for any German-speaking city of the time.

THE NEW SCHOOLS

Yet Sturm's alliance policy created another kind of community among the southern Evangelical free cities, and soon there arose a desire for a common higher school to prepare qualified clergy for their civic churches. In early 1534 Martin Bucer and the Constance reformer Ambrosius Blarer discussed the need for a college—"a nursery for sacred studies," in Bucer's words—to train clergymen for the cities of Strasbourg, Constance, Lindau, Biberach, and Isny.[36] Two wealthy patricians of Isny, the Bufflers, endowed the school, and on 10 June 1534 Joachim Maler, Constance's city attorney, brought the first eight Swabian schoolboys to Strasbourg. First housed in the old Dominican convent, the college later moved to the former house of the Williamite monks, Jakob Wimpheling's first residence at Strasbourg.

The speed, with which the new preachers' college came into being, whetted Bucer's appetite, and when news arrived of Landgrave Philip's triumphant invasion of Württemberg, he began to think in much grander terms, nothing less than a full university at Strasbourg. "Outside of Wittenberg and Marburg," he noted, "there is no university to which the youth can be sent with benefit both to their learning and to their holiness." He therefore recommended the organization of instruction in languages, dialectic, philosophy, rhetoric, mathematics, and civil law, "so that the foundations may be laid for all faculties."[37] The plan suited the scope of Jacob Sturm's alliance policy, to be sure, but it did not sit well with another scholarch, Claus Kniebis. The ammeister thought Bucer's plan grandiose, for "we [i.e., the School Board] are not charged with providing instruction in all faculties and disciplines, nor is the schools' income large enough to make it feasible." Instead, instruction should be provided only in the disciplines "which foster our common good," such as grammar, theology, moral philosophy, natural philosophy, and the Bible. As for Roman law, Kniebis, who held a licentiate in civil law, thought that "civil law is needed for dealings with other peoples, and we must accept it to the degree that it is not expressly against God. Otherwise, God's own law provides a sufficient standard of justice." A university, he estimated, "would cost about 3,000 gulden per year, which we don't have."[38] Kniebis, who had been an early and strong Evangelical, held fast to the old particularist tradition.

The care of the schools captured Jacob Sturm's heart as no other task ever did. Unlike diplomacy, in which the terms were ever-changing and uncontrollable, the schools' problems yielded to determination, a meticulous attention to details, and patience, the victor over fortune. Sturm scrutinized every detail of the college's everyday life—instruction, teaching staff, and living conditions.

Each year he presided over the audit of the college accounts, and nothing, not even a report that the cook was accused of stealing wine and preserved meat from the college stores, was too trivial for his attention. The preachers' college housed an average of thirty students of theology from Strasbourg and other cities, and its reputation for nonpartisanship drew pupils from Zwinglian Bern as well as from Lutheran Esslingen.

Building the preachers' college prepared Sturm for his finest creation, the great Latin school, which brought Strasbourg international fame for pedagogy. The idea grew from a plan formulated by Sturm, Bucer, and others in January 1538. To supervise the school as rector he brought from Paris his unrelated namesake, Jean Sturm, who drafted the plan of studies with which the school opened at Easter 1539 in the Dominican convent. The Latin school became the city's central educational institution, as all of the previously established lectureships were incorporated into it, and its ten teachers and eleven or twelve professors were combined into the corps of "school employees."

Centralization and control to serve local needs through the redeployment of the church's resources—in its main theme the story of Strasbourg's schools mirrors that of its church. Indeed, with the founding of the Latin school the School Board itself took on the final, fixed form toward which it had been moving for a dozen years. Since 1535 its manager kept a record of the board's decisions, while the presiding scholarch kept minutes of their frequent but irregularly scheduled meetings. Four times a year they held a scrutiny of the schools, at which time every teacher in the German elementary schools and in the Latin school had to appear before the board to report problems and receive criticism. The routine work of supervision and criticism was performed by two, since 1538 three, visitors, who made regular reports to the School Board. By 1538, the scholarchs boasted, this system worked so well "that the schools, thank God, improve from day to day, and it has come to pass that many honorable folk in other towns send their children to our schools."[39] This was true, for under Jean Sturm's rectorship the Latin school drew pupils from far beyond the Upper Rhine, or even the South German region, and its neoclassical curriculum radiated its ideal of "learned piety" into many corners of the German-speaking world.

SUPERVISION OF THE SCHOOLS

In the schools, as in the church, preachers and teachers worked under a magisterial authority which, in Jacob Sturm's time, was never challenged. Only one of the top six school officials, Caspar Hedio, who was one of the three "visitors," was a clergyman, and he had nothing to do with the schools' finances or the hiring of staff, which lay exclusively in the hands of the School Board as a permanent commission of the Senate & XXI. Managing money was a task well suited to abilities of the average privy councilor, but personnel matters, especially as the Latin school rose to international reputation, posed burdens on the scholarchs to which Jacob Sturm alone was equal. He set standards his successors simply could not maintain, not even his brother Peter, who succeeded him. Within a month of Jacob's death the School Board for the first time decided to refer the hiring of a schoolteacher to the full Senate & XXI. It was a fateful hiring, for the nominee was the Florentine theologian Peter Martyr Vermigli (1500–62), whose orthodoxy already lay in doubt. Peter Sturm's successor as noble scholarch, his cousin Heinrich von Mülnheim (1507–78), accepted the office only under protest and exercised it unwillingly and desultorily, so that by the early 1570s, the Senate & XXI regularly had to deal with matters which had formerly been managed by the scholarchs alone.

The deterioration of direct lay control of the schools contributed in an important way to the struggles between preachers and teachers that rocked Strasbourg in the decades after Jacob Sturm's death. As the reins slipped from his hands, Jean Sturm tightened his grip on the Latin school, whose corps of teachers, together with the French parish, formed the major center of resistance to Lutheran orthodoxy at Strasbourg. The struggles between the teachers and the parish clergy, who were almost all Lutherans, culminated in the dismissal of Jean Sturm in 1580 and in the end of Jacob Sturm's system of church and school as two separate, parallel structures under direct lay control.

THE LATIN SCHOOL AND THE LEGACY OF HUMANISM

The rise of the Latin school, some of whose teachers were men of wide scholarly reputation, renewed Jacob Sturm's access to the international world of humanism, which was a realm of relative spiritual freedom beyond the local constraints posed by regime and church, that is, beyond the civil and religious fruits of particularism. Dealing with the schools also gave him respite from the grinding pace of official business and brought him back to the liberal studies he had first savored as a budding gentleman-clergyman under Jakob Wimpheling's wing. Only one book survives from the large library he left to the schools. It is a Clement of Alexandria, printed in Greek at Florence in 1550, which he purchased as a gift to the school sometime in the last three years of his life. Beyond that, all but the memory of Sturm's library perished during the siege of Strasbourg in 1870. It was his last gift to his native city, though not his greatest gift, for that honor belongs to the Latin school itself.

THE LEGACY OF WIMPHELING

The founding of the Latin school realized the vision that Wimpheling had pressed on the magistrates in 1501. At least in part, for in the meantime the aims of humanist pedagogy had profoundly changed. Whereas Wimpheling had aspired to spread good burgher values of moral virtue, practicality, the common good, and sound piety in Italianate dress to the local elite and would-be elite, Jean Sturm's aristocratic pedagogy offered eloquence as a kind of professional course for political elites of a much wider variety. His school drew noble students—academic orations customarily began by addressing the "counts and barons"—especially from Hungary, Bohemia, Poland, and Prussia, though also from parts of west-central Germany, such as the Wetterau and the Kraichgau. In both tone and substance, his pedagogy was far more classical, more international, and less Italianate than Wimpheling's had been, for since Jacob Sturm's youth humanism had grown from an exotic Italian import into an international wave that was flowing into the Empire from centers in Italy, the Netherlands, and France.

THE WIDER WORLD

Some effects of the Latin school's obtrusion into Strasbourg's bounded world can be read from how it changed the character of the most highly educated classes. The Evangelical clergy in Jacob Sturm's time were all South Germans: twelve from the lands west of the Rhine (Alsace, Lorraine, the Palatinate), three from the right-bank lands (Breisgau, Baden), five from Swabia, and one each from Franconia and Tyrol. The Protestant schoolmasters at Strasbourg before the founding of the Latin school were also South Germans, but after Jean Sturm's arrival the scholarchs began to hire non-German-speakers, such as Paolo Lazise (d. 1544) of Verona, the aforementioned Dr. Vermigli and Emanuele Tremellio (1510–80) of Florence, and Francisco de Enzinas (called "Dryander") of Burgos in Castile. When Bucer sponsored Justus Velsius (ca. 1510–81) of The Hague for a teaching post in 1545, the mathematician Christmann Herlin (d. 1562)—an ammeister's nephew—blamed Bucer for recruiting North Germans and Netherlanders, beginning with Jean Sturm, instead of South Germans. Though Jacob Sturm and the other scholarchs hesitated at first, they appointed the arrogant Hollander to the Latin school, and Bucer secured him a prebend at St. Thomas. It was a decision they all lived to regret, for in 1549 Velsius had to be dismissed for his defense of Charles V's religious policy.

Jean Sturm's influence on appointments strengthened after Jacob Sturm's death in 1553. The rector liked to promote and protect scholars whose talents he admired, even when their behavior left something or even much to be desired. One was Michael Toxites (ca. 1515–81), a South Tyrolean whose drinking and indiscipline repeatedly got him into hot water. Later on, Jean Sturm urged the hiring of scholars whose refusal to conform to Lutheran doctrine provided easy targets to the guardians of orthodoxy. The split for and against Lutheranism ran along both institutional and cultural lines. Whereas the Lutheran parish clergy were mostly pastors of South German origin, as their predecessors had been—Johann Marbach and his successor, Johann Pappus, were both Lindauers—the Latin school's staff numbered many "foreigners," such as

Peter Martyr Vermigli, Girolamo Zanchi (1516–90) from near Bergamo, François Baudoin (1520–73) of Arras, François Hotman (1524–90) of Paris, and Hubert Giphanius (1534–1604) of Buren in Gelderland. Vermigli and Zanchi became special targets of the Lutheran clergy during the great doctrinal quarrels that rocked Strasbourg's church and school after Jacob Sturm's death.

The immediate local effects of this divergent development of church and school can be illustrated by means of the lists of the clergy and teachers who signed the Strasbourg Concord of 18 March 1563, the year of Peter Sturm's death. The twenty parish clergyman came from the regions covered by Jacob Sturm's alliance policy: seven from the Upper Rhine (of whom, four Strasbourgeois and two other Alsatians), four Swabians, three Franconians, and six from Thuringia and Saxony. At least eight had studied at Strasbourg and at least nine at the University of Wittenberg. The fourteen schoolteachers who signed the local formula of concord came from quite different parts of Europe: ten from German-speaking lands west of the Rhine (of whom, six Strasbourgeois and one [Jean Sturm] educated in the Netherlands and France), two Italians, one from the Graubünden, and one unknown. Nine of the teachers had studied at Strasbourg, but none at Wittenberg. The recruitment of clergy, therefore, had continued to reflect Jacob Sturm's foreign policy, while that of teachers continued to reflect his appreciation for the international world of humanism centered in Italy, France, and the Netherlands—the lands where Calvinism was just then coming onto the scene.

Jacob Sturm hitched Strasbourg's church to the Lutheran party in the Empire; he also linked the Latin school to the international humanist culture and willy-nilly to the intellectual milieu that nourished international Calvinism. Accordingly, when the intra-Evangelical doctrinal quarrels came to a head in the 1570s, the local leaders of both sides, Johann Marbach for the church and orthodox Lutheranism, Jean Sturm for the school and Calvinism, could with equal justice claim Jacob Sturm's mantle and the heritage of Strasbourg's reformation.

NOTES

1. Ibn Kahldûn, *The Muqaddimah: An Introduction to History*, trans. Franz Rosenthal and ed. N. J. Dawood (Princeton, 1967), 125.
2. *PC* 2:237, no. 259.
3. Caspar Hedio, *Radts predig: Wie die oberkeit für sich selbs und die vnderthonen für ire oberkeiten in disser geuerlichen sorglichen zeit zu bitten haben* (Strasbourg, 1534), unpaginated. These passages are not in the excerpts in *TAE* 2:262–64, no. 492.
4. *PC* 1:263–64, no. 464.
5. *TAE* 1:354, line 41.

6. Ibid. 1:356, lines 33–36, no. 283.
7. Ibid. 1:358, lines 6–7.
8. Ibid. 1:355, no. 280; 358–59, no. 286.
9. Ibid. 1:549, lines 3–9.
10. Ibid. 2:575, no. 348, lines 20–23.
11. Ibid. 1:577 n. 1, line 40.
12. Ibid., lines 30–34.
13. Ibid. 2:36, lines 7–10.
14. Ibid., lines 13–15.
15. Ibid. 2:36, lines 15–20.
16. Ibid. 1:43, line 34 to 44, line 10; and there, too, the following quote.
17. Ibid. 1:63, lines 17–18.
18. Ibid. 1:65, no. 376, lines 15–20.
19. Ibid. 1:178, lines 26–31.
20. Ibid. 1:205, lines 8–34; 272, lines 14–15, 23–26.
21. Ibid. 1:294, no. 523.
22. Ibid. 2:36, lines 13–15.
23. Ibid. 2:354, lines 2–3.
24. Ibid. 1:354, lines 10–23.
25. Ibid. 1:354, lines 25–31.
26. Ibid. 1:355, lines 19–24.
27. Ibid. 2:348, line 2 to 349, line 11.
28. Ibid. 2:204, lines 8–9.
29. Heinrich Gresbeck, "Bericht von der Wiedertaufe in Münster," in *Berichte der Augenzeugen über das münsterische Wiedertäuferreich*, ed. C. A. Cornelius (Münster, 1853; reprint, 1965), 22–23.
30. *TAE* 2:255, no. 483.
31. Ibid. 2:482, lines 17–19.
32. Hastings Robinson, ed., *Original Letters Relating to the English Reformation*, 2 vols. (Cambridge, 1846–47; reprint, 1968), vol. 1, no. 115.
33. Ernst-Wilhelm Kohls, *Die Schule bei Martin Bucer in ihrem Verhältnis zu Kirche und Obrigkeit* (Heidelberg, 1963), 40.
34. *BDS* 3:354–55.
35. Kohls, *Die Schule*, 216 n. 17.
36. Schiess, ed., *Briefwechsel der Brüder Ambrosius und Thomas Blarer* 1:424, no. 363.
37. *BDS* 7:525.
38. Ibid. 7:533–35.
39. Carl Engel, *Das Schulwesen in Straßburg vor der Gründung des Protestantischen Gymnasiums, 1538* (Strasbourg, 1886), 72.

9

THE EMPIRE RESTORED

Finality is not the language of politics.

—Benjamin Disraeli

Nothing tempts the historian more than to master the seething stew of the past by pouring it an iron mold of inevitability. Historians of the German Reformation long believed that because the main issue, religion, could hardly be compromised, Catholic rulers inevitably took up arms to force their subjects back to the old faith and Protestant subjects just as inevitably resisted them. In the Empire, therefore, religious war was the inevitable outcome of the Protestant challenge, and accounts of the years between the Diet of Augsburg in 1530 and the outbreak of the Smalkaldic War in 1546 often tremble with impatience at the delay between Protestant provocation and Catholic attack. In fact, the Imperial system of governance recovered fairly swiftly from the crisis posed by the formation of confessional parties in 1529–30.

THE CRISIS OF 1539

The 1530s were the halcyon days of Protestant politics in the Empire. Ruler after ruler came over to the new faith, and most of them entered the Smalkaldic League. By the end of the decade, Catholic resistance nonetheless began to stiffen, and the Imperial Chamber Court began to issue new judgments for restitution of rights and properties to the Catholics. First to be hit was Minden, a smallish town just north of where the Weser River debouches from the central highlands into the North German plain. On 9 October 1538 Minden was outlawed by the Chamber Court on account of the religious changes its regime had made. When the news reached Strasbourg, six days later, the Smalkaldic chiefs were already preparing for war. The heads of the Catholic party of action followed suit, and by early winter the Empire probably stood nearer civil war than at any time since 1504. On both sides, however, strong voices spoke for peace. One of them belonged to Jacob Sturm, who told Landgrave Philip of Hesse that "we have seen all sorts of examples of how badly things went, when the sword was taken in hand," and though he admitted the danger of

161

waiting for the other side to strike first, he thought the prospects for victory poorer than they earlier had been.[1] Sturm believed that although the Minden affair was surely a "religious matter" in the league's understanding of that category, the Smalkaldeners must not strike first.

The crisis of 1539 did not plunge the Empire into a religious war, and the Peace of Frankfurt confirmed Sturm's judgment about the possibility for a peaceful management of the German schism. There followed a series of meetings, colloquys, about the schism and a resumption of the Imperial Diet's sessions. By 1542 the forces of Imperial politics began to run once more in the old channels, and, on the surface at least, the Reformation's disruption of the Empire appeared to have run its course.

Powerful forces promoted this restoration. For one thing, Charles V's general preference for conciliation over coercion was reinforced by his preoccupation with Mediterranean affairs and his differences with King Ferdinand about whether Hungary or North Africa should have priority in the war against the Ottomans. For another, the Catholic powers were badly split, and the Catholic party of action, headed by the Bavarian dukes and Duke Henry of Brunswick-Wolfenbüttel, was much less influential than was the meditating party of neutrals, headed by the electors of Mainz, Brandenburg, and the Palatinate. Third, the Protestants were divided. Not only did Nuremberg stay loyal to the emperor, but the Smalkaldic League split over whether they should strike first.

THE PEACE OF FRANKFURT, 1539

When the league's assembly sat at Frankfurt from 14 to 18 February 1539 to debate the Minden crisis, the war hawks were in full cry. Fortified by the Wittenberg theologians' declaration that "a preventive war is a defensive war," Landgrave Philip of Hesse announced that "Saxony and Hesse are open, unfortified lands, and if the foe strikes first and invades them, he will take all the money, artillery, horses, etc., while if we strike first, we will occupy their lands." If the Smalkaldeners could not quickly get a tolerable peace, he thought, "then we should not await their first strike."[2] On the other side, Strasbourg's Jacob Sturm spoke for peace. The news of war preparations was not conclusive, he said, "and in such doubtful situations, one should pursue the course that is in principle the best. Peace is better than war." Next day (17 February) Sturm delivered the meeting's major address. "We should seek peace now," he urged, "for the [mediating] electors' attitude will tell us what the other side intends to do." Whoever strikes first, he warned, "the damage to the German nation will be so great that it will last for a hundred years." If the league struck first, Sturm believed, "then the emperor would exert all his might against us, also the pope, Portugal, and perhaps even France. The bishops in the [Catholic] League of Nuremberg would also act, for they would fear attacks from us." Therefore, he concluded, "we should not start a war, but we should pursue every means, embassies and others, to see if these negotiations can't bring peace. In this cause we should deal with the emperor, the mediators, the other side, or anyone else."

Sturm's arguments carried the majority for peace against the Saxon elector and against Martin Bucer, who trumpeted to the landgrave that "we know from experience that if we strive to advance Christ's kingdom in the right way, it goes forward. Just think of the aid you received from God and men in the Württemberg affair!"[3] "Too many cooks," the landgrave replied, "seldom make a good soup."

THE COLLOQUYS

The Peace of Frankfurt of 1539 renewed the Peace of Nuremberg's suspension of all suits for restitution. At a price, for the Smalkaldic powers agreed to pay taxes for the Ottoman war and to participate in negotiations aimed at healing the religious schism. The first, unofficial talks at Leipzig in January 1539 produced surprising progress, and the Peace of Frankfurt provided that they should continue at Nuremberg on 1 August 1539, though another ten months passed before the participants actually assembled at Hagenau in Alsace under King Ferdinand's eye. Disrupted by an epidemic, the Hagenau Colloquy nonetheless reached an agreement on procedure before it adjourned until 28 October 1540. The next stage at Worms produced a provisional text on one disputed point—justification—before the colloquy was again translated, this time to Regensburg, where the Imperial Diet convened in January 1541. The colloquy's concluding phase at Regensburg proved, despite the remarkably irenic Regensburg Book, that no union was possible on essential points, such as the Eucharist. The colloquys nonetheless yielded just enough progress to secure from Charles V what the Smalkaldeners really wanted, an extension and updating of the Peace of Nuremberg. Although they did not heal the schism, therefore, the colloquys did make possible a remarkable restoration of Imperial political life during the early 1540s.

JACOB STURM ON COLLOQUYS

Jacob Sturm did not believe that the colloquys would lead to reunion. It often happens, he wrote, "that people agree in substance but not in words," and he thought the Leipzig Colloquy in January 1539 "more a political matter than a theological one."[4] An official colloquy under the emperor's sponsorship, however, was another kettle of fish, and Sturm thought that "when we come together face-to-face, and if our princes are there, perhaps through God's grace the cause will be helped."[5] Sturm promoted the colloquy, because he saw behind it the figure of the Imperial chancellor Nicolas Perrenot de Granvelle (1486–1550), the suave, learned, able, and ambitious Franche-Comtois who had risen at court to become one of Europe's leading figures. Granvelle, Sturm wrote, "enjoys great prestige, is favorably disposed, and knows about the matter;

if the emperor had displayed a tyrannical attitude against us, Granvelle would hardly have acted in such a friendly manner." The friendship, however, was feigned, for "Granvelle has adopted this manner deliberately and given us fine words, so that we will think in the future that he is responsible for whatever [concessions] we receive."[6] Accordingly, the Smalkaldeners should repay him "in words just as fine, with elaborate thanks and other gestures," even though "we can infer that Granvelle lacks a [true] knowledge of God." They should increase the pressure on Granvelle by pointing out to him that since he is a Burgundian "and by heritage a German who wishes the German nation well, he should be all the more active in this cause."[7]

The colloquy nonetheless also posed a risk. "If we fail to show him [Granvelle] what we really want and what it will require to satisfy our demands about religion," Sturm told the Hessian agents at Smalkalden in March 1540, "our willingness to negotiate and our appearance of softness will lead them to think us much more pacific than we are." If, "as seems likely, they understand nothing of the true needs of the church, purity of religion, duty, or the constraints of a believing conscience, but seek religious conciliation solely for worldly reasons, they will hope for concessions from us in matters in which we can make none."[8] The Protestants had nonetheless to disguise their true aims, for "if we tell this man [Granvelle] and others like him, what our cause is truly about, I worry that he will be too frightened to permit us to have this hearing and these negotiations." Sturm's skepticism about reunion represented the reverse of his firm confidence in the ultimate triumph of the Gospel in an Evangelical sense. The main point was to win time. Time worked *for* the Gospel—this and this alone justified participation in the colloquy—and might bring important princes over to their side.

COLLOQUY OF WORMS, 1540

Temporizing and soft words, of course, were a game at which two could play, and in early November 1540 an Imperial vice-chancellor, the Luxembourgeois Jean de Naves (d. 1547), stopped at Strasbourg, where he spoke with Dr. Caspar Hedio, an old acquaintance.[9] "I found this Naves a good man," Hedio wrote to Jacob Sturm and Mathis Pfarrer, "who sees the matter rightly, and who speaks best to the Protestant cause. He is a frank man and a good Strasbourgeois, and he thinks our theologians are by themselves a match for the Spanish theologians and sophists." Naves's impression was reinforced by Granvelle himself, who on 18 November 1540 stopped at Strasbourg on his way to Worms, lodged in Conrad Joham's great mansion in Jews' Street, and after gifts and a greeting from the town clerk Johann Meyer (1501–53), whose Latinity was doubtless below Burgundian standards, rode off toward Worms.

Jacob Sturm was already at Worms, where he expected that "the antichristians will flee the light of truth, if they can."[10] He and Mathis Pfarrer had brought an imposing group of experts, including Bucer, Capito, John Calvin, "who is learned in the Church Fathers," and Jean Sturm, "because of his Greek."[11] They were parceled out among delegations that lacked adequate talent, Jean Sturm and John Calvin to Brunswick-Lüneburg and Bucer to the landgrave. "You should in all things act only after consultation with Sir Jacob Sturm and Dr. Martin Bucer, about how the colloquy should be begun," the landgrave instructed his own men, and although "you should also hear what the other allies' envoys say, especially those of the Saxon elector, always listen to Sturm's and Bucer's opinions more than to anyone else's."[12]

Granvelle sensed the Strasbourgeois' leading position on the Protestant side, and when the colloquy reached a procedural impasse, he turned to them for help. Bucer, blooming with confidence that the "neutrals"—the electors of Brandenburg and the Palatinate and the duke of Cleves-Jülich—were about to turn Protestant, was clearly flattered when Granvelle's secretary asked on 14 December that he and Capito talk with Johann Gropper (1503–59) of Cologne, "who is not unfavorable to reform," about the disputed articles.[13] They did so, though against Sturm's advice, and reported that Granvelle had revealed "how anxious he is for peace and reform," how highly he regarded the landgrave, and how impossibly the Catholic theologians were behaving. Charmed by these words, Bucer and Capito agreed to meet secretly with Gropper and the secretary, Gerard Veltwyk (ca. 1505–55), and, to their amazement, they nearly reached agreement on original sin and justification. Bucer, of course, was officially acting not for Strasbourg but for the landgrave, who asked him, "what harm can come from trying it?"[14] The chancellor's charm had made another conquest, and Bucer mused that "although he does not follow our religion, he is also no papist or defender of abuses, but he truly wants to help bring a reformation and sees how useful and honorable this would be for the emperor."[15] Granvelle wanted him to ride to the landgrave with the union formula, but Sturm would not allow it, for Bucer had already violated the Protestant party's stricture against private negotiations, and Sturm's orders forbade a departure from the agreed-upon procedures. Sturm felt torn between these orders and his desire to respond to Granvelle's overture, "so that the other side cannot say, as they are doing, that we fear the light."[16] The other Protestants, however, threw cold water on both Sturm and Bucer, and soon the colloquy was adjourned to Regensburg, its sole positive accomplishment a formula on original sin, which subsequently became the basis of the Regensburg Book.

Why did Sturm, in violatation of his instructions and against the Protestant majority's will, permit Bucer and Capito to participate in the unauthorized talks that salvaged the Colloquy of Worms? Possibly, he, too, succumbed to Granvelle's charm, even though he had fresh evidence that the split between the parties remained as deep as ever. One evening at Worms, as he strolled near the cathedral, he met Dr. Johann Eck, an old acquaintance and fellow

Wimpheling-protégé.[17] "Oh, Sir Jacob," Eck sighed, "we are no longer good comrades, as we used to be," a point Sturm then acknowledged. "Whose fault is that," Eck replied, "if not yours? You abandoned the church and left us, because you were not one of us, while I remained in the fold." "It's a damned sorry fold," responded Sturm, "and since you abandoned true doctrine and the apostolic church, the true departure was made by you, not by us, who desire only to hold to the apostolic church and evangelical truth." Eck charged that Sturm had been misled by wicked men, to which Sturm replied that "I read the writings of both sides and was persuaded by those of our side." "No," jibed Eck, recalling the young Sturm's fruitless pursuit of preferment, "in those days you expected preferment to a benefice," failing which, "you turned against the clergy." When asked whether he knew Eck's reputation as a writer, Sturm responded with irony, "Yes, I know you to be a man of great fame." The talk then moved on to the Protestant theologians, whom Eck called "apostates and whoremongers, not husbands," and he cursed Bucer in particular. Finally, Eck lapsed into Swabian, which Sturm, an Alemannic-speaker, easily understood: "If you don't die in my faith, you can go to the Devil!"

Despite this encounter the wind at Worms smelled of peace and conciliation, at least with the Catholics. Between Sturm and Bucer, however, partners since the Marburg Colloquy in 1529, a gap was opening. Bucer had recently drawn much closer to Landgrave Philip of Hesse, who was just at this time pulling away from his Smalkaldic allies to lessen the risks of his own conduct. The landgrave was in deep trouble, for he had recently become a bigamist.

THE HESSIAN BIGAMY

Sometime in the summer or early fall of 1539, Philip of Hesse decided to marry his noble mistress, Margarethe von der Sale. In early November Bucer went to Hesse to counsel the prince—bigamy was a capital crime—though he didn't dare tell Jacob Sturm what was afoot. Sturm first learned of it at Smalkalden in March or early April 1540—the landgrave's betrothal occurred on 4 March—when Gregor Brück (1482–1557) of Saxony took him for a walk in the churchyard, revealed the bigamy, and spoke of his fear that if the elector and the allies did not support the landgrave, "he will leave the Christian alliance."[18] Jacob Sturm, who knew the penalty for bigamy—in 1533 he had interrogated the bigamist Claus Frey, who paid with his life—heard Brück's news "with a heavy heart. The news itself did not please me; its consequences will please me even less. Every day I have thought about what great trouble and how many losses it will cause, even among those who are most closely attached to or are favorable to our religion."[19] Sturm thought the landgrave should not admit his bigamy openly, for few would believe he acted out of necessity, and, therefore, "the longer it can be kept quiet, the better. If not, then it were better to void the [marriage] contract, for all pious and good-hearted people will regard it with horror, while our foes will use it to divide us and to suppress the Word of God as best they can." Sturm confessed that "I have no idea how to handle it with my own colleagues, and if it cannot be defended by the scholars, especially Dr. Martin Luther, from the Bible, I cannot imagine what the consequences might be. May God grant His grace and free the weak, feeble, reviving church from this terrible burden."

The bigamy could not be kept secret, of course, and news of it delighted the Catholics and enraged the allies, whose reactions so embittered the Hessian prince that he began to think of reconciling himself to the emperor and abandoning the league altogether. In fact, secret negotiations to that end were already under way. Although Sturm never defended the bigamy publicly, as Bucer did, nor even believed that it was defensible, the landgrave judged correctly that he, "if he looks into his own conscience, cannot turn his back on us."[20] There was far too much at stake to abandon this willful prince now.

The Hessian bigamy nonetheless drove the first wedge between Jacob Sturm and Landgrave Philip of Hesse. Moreover, Bucer's defense of it encouraged his own enemies at Strasbourg to come out of the woodwork. He discovered that "a few Schwenckfelders have turned the entire magistracy and many pious, good-hearted burghers against me in the most terrible way," and that their leader was Michel Han, a city attorney and son-in-law of an ammeister.[21] The landgrave noted Bucer's estrangement at Strasbourg and suggested that he come to run the Hessian church, for the very handsome salary of 500 rhfl. per year, or perhaps work for Duke Moritz of Saxony.

With the revelation of the Hessian bigamy, active leadership of the Smalkaldic League shifted permanently from the landgrave to the Saxon elector. Even before the alarm bells rang over Minden, John Frederick of Saxony had begun to make some belligerent noises, which distinguished him from his stolid father, and to revive Protestant courtship of the English and French kings. When a Saxon chancellor referred favorably to the Swiss as defenders of liberty, as Brück did to John Frederick, the atmosphere at the electoral court had certainly changed. By early 1539 John Frederick was certain that war was not far off, and he meant to strike first. The whole thing hinged on a French alliance, of course, and Martin Bucer, ever the activist, worked to win the landgrave for this policy. The revelation of the landgrave's bigamy torpedoed the entire scheme and encouraged Sturm's temporizing policy. One reason for waiting was that the emperor was returning to his German-speaking lands.

THE REGENSBURG COLLOQUY, 1541

When Charles V entered Regensburg on 23 February 1541, Granvelle at his side, he wanted to end the schism and get his hands free to strike at Algiers.

Meanwhile, Ferdinand's army in Hungary was trying to take Ofen before Ottoman forces arrived to relieve it. En route from the Netherlands, Charles advertised his intention by suspending the decrees of outlawry against Minden and Goslar and all the suits of restitution against Protestant powers. To the Catholic side of the colloquy he named exclusively men who supported his policy of conciliation, while on the Protestant side were ranged as theologians Melanchthon, Bucer, and Johann Pistoris, and as lay auditors the two commanders' chancellors, Franz Burkhardt and Johann Feige, and Jacob Sturm. The colloquents added some statements on relatively unproblematical topics to the partial agreements achieved at Worms, but no amount of goodwill could produce consensus on transsubstantiation and the authority of the hierarchy, the Mass, penance, and the veneration of the saints. These very partial results pleased no one but those who had framed them. Faced with the colloquy's failure, the emperor issued on 29 July a secret declaration of toleration, in which he conceded to the Protestants the right of "Christian reformation" in return for their acceptance of the Diet's recess, which confirmed both the Peace of Nuremberg and the recess of Augsburg of 1530. With the situation thoroughly confused, Charles slipped away southward to begin his Mediterranean campaign, leaving Ferdinand and his Hungarian army to face the oncoming Ottomans.

At Regensburg Jacob Sturm crowned his role as the principal leader of the Protestant peace party. When the emperor appointed him one of the three Protestant lay auditors of the colloquy, Sturm was not especially hopeful, for "without God's special help, the prospect looks bleak. With Him, however, all things are possible."[22] With Sturm for peace stood Chancellor Johann Feige of Hesse, of course, and Martin Bucer, who at a critical point proclaimed that "Germany is moving toward the Gospel, and for that reason I am driven by zeal to enlighten those in error."[23] To the side stood the elector of Saxony's men, and Melanchthon and Bucer soon found themselves at loggerheads. Sturm was hopeful and thought the Protestants should hold to "the substance of the confession [of Augsburg]," because "in the colloquy it has happened that often they are agreed in substance, but not in words."[24] John Frederick would have none of such talk, finding the Protestants' formulations on episcopal power and the clergy "much too soft."[25] In the end, Sturm helped to make the Regensburg accord, secured by what his ally, the Hessian Feige, called "a good, suitable declaration, which contains many good points never before conceded."[26] The two of them actually drafted the declaration of toleration, which Charles would not incorporate into the Diet's recess. "So," Feige reported to his prince, "Sir Jacob and I took on the task, and he took in hand the proposed recess and the draft of a declaration, and I took up my pen, and we drafted the declaration." "It was simply so," he proudly attested, "that Sir Jacob and I would not budge: either we got the declaration or we would refer the recess to our masters [instead of signing it]."[27] Otherwise, "had we not received the declaration, we would also not have approved the recess. We did all we could under these conditions."[28]

The theologians' tally of full and partial agreements, collected in the Regensburg Book, has often been seen as a step toward religious reunion. In fact, the formula fostered divisions in both confessional parties. Sturm and Bucer had conceded too much, thought many Evangelicals—for example, at Augsburg, where, "to speak confidentially, Martin Bucer and Jacob Sturm are suspected of being the chief culprits."[29] The convergence of Sturm's policy with Chancellor Granvelle's nonetheless lent new strength to the cause of peace, helped to ease the consequences of the Hessian scandal, and put off a reckoning on the schism into the indefinite future. The greatest advance, however, consisted in the revival of the old patterns of Imperial politics.

The events of 1539–41—the Peace of Frankfurt and the colloquys—opened the way to the restoration of Imperial politics in its pre-Reformation patterns. Three important changes of this era underlay this shift. First, from 1542 on, the Habsburg brothers faced a two-front war against the Ottomans and against France, and their need for taxes converged with the Catholic neutrals' promotion of "moderation and order," as a Palatine document put it, and with the Protestants' longing for protection from suits of restitution. Second, the menace posed to the Netherlands by the French war was so great—"since the days of our grandfather, Emperor Maximilian, the Netherlands never stood in such danger," Queen Mary wrote—that Charles could no longer neglect the German question.[30] Third, Charles and Ferdinand were beginning to rebuild the old Habsburg clientele in the Empire, especially among the free cities and the free knights, by means of a new system of peace-keeping leagues. This policy aimed less to make the Empire a monarchy *à la française* than to establish Charles as, in Granvelle's words, "lord of Germany."[31] For all of these reasons, Imperial political life began to flow back into its pre-Reformation pattern of bargaining over taxes between monarch and Imperial Estates. Restoration also meant a revival of the old strife between princes and free cities, and Jacob Sturm, long a major spokesman for the Protestant alliance, became during these years the chief voice for urban rights and tax reform.

THE RESTORATION OF IMPERIAL POLITICS

The free cities, long split by the confessionalization of Imperial politics—their own, separate assembly met but once between 1529 and 1538—were coming back together. At the Diet of Regensburg in 1541, the leading Catholic cities—Cologne, Worms, Speyer, and Metz—joined with the Protestant cities to protest the Diet's recess, because the two upper houses refused to recognize the free cities' rights. "Ancient custom dictates," the electors and princes declared, "that they must not only agree with us, but must accept and obey whatever is decided by the majority among us, just as in our houses the weaker party must yield to the stronger."[32] To struggle against this position, the cities rebuilt their old solidarity, meeting eight times between 1541 and 1545, and put their trust in the leadership of Jacob Sturm, on whom, as Elector John Frederick remarked in 1541, "the southerners all depend."[33] The success of this role brought Sturm during the years 1541 to 1544 to the pinnacle of his career as an Imperial politician.

THE DEBATE OVER TAXATION

The free cities' old solidarity revived in the context of the restored Imperial Diet, the sessions of which became frequent (Regensburg, 1541; Speyer, 1542; Nuremberg, 1542 and 1543; Speyer, 1544; Worms, 1545) and long—the Diet was sitting approximately half the time between April 1541 and August 1545. The Diet's restoration brought taxation right back into the center of politics, and with it the issue of who should pay what, and how? Since Emperor Maximilian's day, the Empire had known two ways of assessing taxes: the matricular levy, based on an army of standard size (twenty thousand foot and four thousand horse), granted in multiples called "Roman months," and assessed on the Estates according to registers; and the Common Penny, a direct property tax on all Imperial subjects, both immediate and mediate, granted as a rate on property and graduated by tax classes. Although the Diet had experimented with the Common Penny in 1495, under Charles V military taxes were granted (except for 1542 and 1544) according to the matricular system. The latter was based on the registers drawn up at Worms in 1521, the accuracy and fairness of which were bitterly contested by almost everyone. Between 1521 and 1550, this method yielded a total about 2 million rhfl., or about 60 percent of the cost of one year's campaign against the Ottomans.

The debates over Imperial taxation during the early 1540s focused on two issues: the relative fairness of the two methods and the fairness of the Worms registers. Fairness is often a matter of perspective, and Sturm, ever a partisan of direct taxes, commented in 1542 that the wealthier, more centralized powers preferred the matricular levy, while the mass of small Estates, the weaker large ones, and the free cities favored the Common Penny. The electors and princes condemned the Common Penny as having a "curiously Swiss appearance" and alleged that the cities intended through it to "make all things in common."[34] The issue split the Protestant party, placing its two commanders and Augsburg on one side and the other Smalkaldic cities—along with most of the bishops, prelates, and counts—on the other.

The second issue, the matricular system's unfairness, was a perennial source of grievance. Some years before, at Eisenach in 1538, Sturm had raised the issue of unfair assessments, arguing that "the electors and princes, who have wide lands and many subjects, should pay more than the cities."[35] Strasbourg

complained about the assessments—echoed by other cities—justly, to judge by
the register of 1521, which assessed Strasbourg 225 foot and 40 horse and the
electors 277 foot and 60 horse each. The unfairness was magnified by sharply
rising military taxes, which prompted Sturm to declare in 1542 that the princes'
proposal on taxes would squeeze from Strasbourg the sum of 120,000 rhfl.,
more than from Duke Moritz of Saxony with his vast lands and rich mines,
and more than from the bishop of Würzburg, "who is just about the richest
bishop in Germany."[36] He prudently did not mention the Hessian assessment,
which was only slightly higher than Strasbourg's.

The cities' best defense was to refuse consent to taxes so long as they were
not consulted about granting them. At the Diet of Speyer in 1542, for example, they told the two upper houses that "the procedure followed by this Diet,
and in particular the presentation of this decision, violates ancient custom; and
they ask that their opinions be heard in open session, and then the matter
could be decided."[37] Religion made no difference, for, as Bucer wrote, "at this
Diet the Protestant princes as well as the others have recommended and voted
for the suppression of the cities; and many papists mock the cities for having
put so much trust in the Protestant princes."[38] This time the shadow passed, as
the Diet of Speyer levied the Common Penny, which most cities favored, for
the first time in Charles's reign, and the urban delegates signed the recess with
some enthusiasm. Sturm noted that if the direct property tax failed, the princes
and electors would fall back on the matricular system, which would be doubly
dangerous. "Although the cities were always unfairly assessed," he wrote, "the
unfairness was small then compared to what it now is. This can be easily proved
from the old recesses." Nowadays, "the levies—doubled, tripled, and quadru-
pled—have grown so burdensome to us that while a prince must send every
hundredth man to the front, a city must send every fourth, third, or even
every other man." Then, too, "the old Imperial levies were employed only for
emergency purposes, not for long campaigns. It was bearable then, but now
the higher levies are being proposed for longer and even long-term aids, which
the cities cannot endure." The registers were out of date, for they failed to
reflect the decline in the number of free cities, and "it is to be feared that if
the burdens are not reduced to fair levels, more cities will be forced to break
away or to free themselves in other ways from this ruinous levy."[39] What would
be a fair assessement? Well, Sturm thought that his Strasbourg should pay
about one-fourth of an elector's assessment.

Jacob Sturm's worries show that he clearly understood the danger posed by
skyrocketing military costs in Hungary, the expanding mercenary system, larger
armies, new fortifications, and new weaponry. Whereas the matricular system
reckoned costs at about 125,000 rhfl. for wages and salaries alone, by 1542 it
cost nearly 3 million rhfl. to fight the Ottomans for one year. Where was such
a sum to be found? The Germans, understandably, scanned the huge Habsburg-

Trastámara inheritance, saw realms fabled for their wealth and military strength—
Milan, Tuscany, Castile, Brabant, and Flanders—and expected rivers of cash
to flow from such fonts—through Germany, naturally—toward Christendom's
common defense in Hungary. Sturm, who shared this expectation, once declared that the cities should balk at paying unless "such taxes are assessed on
all the estates of Christendom, or at least on the whole German nation."[40]
How could he or any other German politician comprehend the relationships
between taxation and wealth in the Netherlands, Castile, and Italy, when the
subject baffled Charles's own advisors?

THE STRUGGLE FOR THE CITIES' RIGHTS

Sturm and the other urban politicians sought ways to ease the massive fiscal
weight on their burghers' wealth and trade. They could protest, of course, as
Sturm did the Imperial recesses of Nuremberg in 1542 and 1543, only to find
his name among those of the signatories. When he protested, Chancellor Jacob
Jonas (ca. 1500–58) of Mainz sighed, "Who can tell me, when you are going
to obey for a change?" "When you make fair recesses and enforce them," came
Sturm's retort, "then we will accept them. But you make unfair, incorrect recesses, which contradict earlier ones, and you don't enforce them. Therefore,
we cannot accept them, though this is not disobedience on our part."[41]

The burghers' best weapons were not pikes and guns but laws and facts, and
at Nuremberg in the summer of 1542, the leading urban politicians decided to
comb their cities' chancelleries and archives for documentary evidence of the
cities' traditional corporate rights. Strasbourg was asked to oversee this process,
and once back home Sturm threw himself into the search for the practice of
the past. He looked for those "private or unofficial documents" which were
"obviously old, being composed many years ago," and of which copies were
now to be found in "the archives, chancelleries, or vaults of the cities."[42] He
hunted through Strasbourg's chancellery, which his brother Peter had helped
to put in order, and consulted the archives of at least seven other free cities,
casting his net back all the way to 1427. As he read through the local acts, he
must have nodded in agreement when he read a lament by Matern Drachenfels,
Strasbourg's envoy to the Diet of Nuremberg in 1479, that "the cities are the
sleepiest folk of all."[43] He must have marveled, too, at how Emperor Frederick
III had come in person to an urban assembly at Speyer in 1486 to beg the
cities to pay their taxes. Year by year he followed the great assemblies of the
1490s, when so much of the Diet's procedure had taken shape, and when his
own father and uncles had helped to rule Strasbourg, and everywhere he looked
for hard evidence that the free cities had taken part in Imperial Diets, sat in
their committees, and signed their recesses.

Sturm's researches contributed to a 1544 decision to establish an archive of
the free cities at Speyer. His materials also fed into the memorial that a com-

mittee of lawyers from Nuremberg, Frankfurt, and Strasbourg composed in early 1543 at the Diet of Nuremberg. Dr. Ludwig Gremp (1509–83), Strasbourg's city attorney, helped to compile this *Summary and Substance of all Documents Submitted, and the Opinions Based on Them, Concerning the Honorable Free Cities' Parliamentary Rights*. Using data uncovered by Sturm and others, the lawyers sought to prove that the free cities' claims "are well grounded in all natural law, law of nations, civil and canon law, the Golden Bull, the emperor's reform decree of 1442, the Imperial ordinances, ancient custom and tradition, and also reasonable, reliable, and weighty reasons."[44] Even as the lawyers labored, however, the Diet's two upper houses decided once more to exclude the cities from their decision on taxes.

Just as they had done during the early 1520s, the free cities turned from the Diet to the emperor. Charles V had sailed in May 1543 from Spain—he would never see those lands again as emperor—for Genoa and Germany, bent on throwing his whole system's weight against France. After a swift campaign in the Netherlands, he came to Speyer in 1544 much as his grandfather had come to Cologne in 1505, a victorious warlord in all of his gout-tortured glory. The Smalkaldic chiefs, who had failed to aid Duke William of Cleves-Jülich against Charles and, besides, had their hands full of an illegally seized Brunswick-Wolfenbüttel, were in no position to resist him. Landgrave Philip ranted against France, the Lutheran theologians bawled against the French king's alliance with the pope and the sultan, and the Diet quickly and with little rancor voted twenty-four thousand foot and four thousand horse for six months. The emperor then headed for Metz, whence he mounted a lightning campaign on the Marne. On 19 September 1544 he concluded the Treaty of Crépy with the king of France, having profited more from the Imperial Diet's generosity, perhaps, than he had ever done before or ever would again.

No one feared a war against France more than did Strasbourg's magistrates and merchants, "for because they lie so close to France, on which they nearly border, they not only trade in France but gain a good part of their livelihood from Lorraine."[45] The Protestant princes' solid support for the war isolated Strasbourg, and "if Strasbourg were to resist alone, or with a few allies," Sturm wrote home, "you can imagine how that would fuel the charges of those who are already crying that we are good Frenchmen."[46] "Strasbourg," Sturm declared, "cannot stand alone."[47]

This threat spurred Sturm to redouble his efforts at the Diet of Speyer, where on 6 March 1544 the urban delegates submitted to the emperor a petition for their rights, which alone could protect them from burdensome taxation. They prepared the memorial in German and Latin—with a French summary for Charles—based on the brief prepared the year before by Gremp and the other lawyers. The emperor's positive if weak response—the other houses did not recognize the cities' rights at all until 1548—left the issue of taxation unresolved. The Diet now tried to square the circle—the matricular levy against the French and the Common Penny against the Ottomans—and called on all the Circles to assemble and study the registers in the interests of tax reform. Jacob Sturm represented the Upper Rhenish Circle in this assembly, which, sitting at Worms from 28 October 1544 until February 1545, issued the most important tax reform under Charles V and fixed the pattern of Imperial tax assessments until 1803. The outcome surprised even Sturm, who reported early on that "hardly anything can be done, for the delegates who have assembled have no instructions to make binding decisions."[48] Gradually, however, he began to change his mind. The Upper Rhenish Circle's delegation elected him their speaker, "and even though I would gladly lay this business aside, they won't let me do it, for we are all especially engaged in this business."[49] The outcome was a "quite positive" revision of the Worms register, which lowered the cities' total assessment by about a quarter, changed relative ranks, and shifted the collective burden away from the middling cities toward the larger ones.

The restoration of Imperial politics in these years made Jacob Sturm into a politician of truly Imperial rank. As all the old patterns revived, Sturm led the free cities in their struggle for parliamentary rights and tax reform. It was as though the Reformation had been but a twenty-year episode in the Empire's history, for the Diet was functioning again, the princes once more bullied the free cities about taxes, and the Imperial Circles finally began to function as regional organs of government.

Strasbourg lay at the geographical center of the Upper Rhenish Circle, which in theory stretched from Hesse and Baden in the east to Lorraine and Savoy in the west and embraced an area much like the political world of Sturm's great-grandfather, Old Peter Schott. Here in the old heartland of Imperial particularism, the apparent return of the good, old days was symbolized by the free cities' recognition of their leader. On 31 July 1545 the cities of the Upper Rhenish Circle—Strasbourg, Metz, Frankfurt, Speyer, Worms, Hagenau, Colmar, and all the other little free cities of Alsace—sent Jacob Sturm a letter of thanks, and at year's end they presented him with an expensive (472 rhfl.) silver bowl, made by Strasbourg's Martin Kroßweiler, and a contribution to his expenses while at Worms. This greatest honor of Sturm's career came not from the Protestant powers of the Smalkaldic League but the good, old friends and neighbors, the free cities of Strasbourg's home region. In 1526 Strasbourg's magistrates had struck a medal to mark Sturm's first triumph in the world of Imperial politics; in 1545 the region's free cities honored Sturm for his leadership in the campaign for tax reform. It was a grand gesture, one which Old Peter Schott would have understood and enjoyed, a tribute to the ability of patience to conquer fortune. Patience had indeed done so, but only in a restored Imperial system centered in the South, where the Reformation movement had lost its power to change the political landscape. All this while, another story was unfolding in the North, where in 1542 Sturm and his southern allies had taken the fateful step of authorizing the Smalkaldic League's invasion of far-off Brunswick-Wolfenbüttel, a place the Strasbourgeois knew less about than they did about Venice or Milan. It was a step they would live to regret.

Notes

1. *PC* 2:519–22, no. 545; 530, no. 554.
2. Otto Meinardus, ed., "Die Verhandlungen des Schmalkaldischen Bundes vom 14.–18. Febr. 1539 in Frankfurt am Main," *Forschungen zur Deutschen Geschichte* 22 (1882): 642; and the following quotes are at 646, 651–52.
3. Lenz 1:75, no. 24; and the following quote is at 85, no. 26.
4. Ibid. 2:28; *PC* 2:532–33, no. 556.
5. *PC* 3:48–49, no. 33.
6. Lenz 1:156 n. 8; and there, too, the following quote.
7. Ibid.; and there, too, the following quote.
8. Ibid., 162–63, no. 61.
9. *PC*, vol. 3:117–20, no. 127.
10. Lenz 1:188–89, no. 73.
11. *PC* 3:108–10.
12. Günther Franz, ed., *Urkundliche Quellen zur hessischen Reformationsgeschichte*, 2 vols. (Marburg, 1952), 2:341.
13. Lenz 1:274–79, no. 101.
14. Ibid., 281–82, no. 103.
15. Ibid., 286, 287–91, nos. 104, 106.
16. *PC* 3:160–61, no. 168.
17. Johannes Timannus to the Preachers at Bremen, 18 November 1540, in N. Spiegel, "Johannes Timannus Amsterodamus und die Colloquien zu Worms und Regensburg 1540, 1541," *Zeitschrift für historische Theologie* 42 (1872): 42–44.
18. *PC* 3:716.
19. Ibid., 716–17; and there, too, the remaining quotes in this paragraph.
20. Lenz 1:266, no. 96.
21. Ibid. 2:65, no. 135, and 81, no. 140.
22. *PC* 3:181, no. 190.
23. Wilhelm H. Neuser, ed., *Die Vorbereitung der Religionsgespräche von Worms und Regensburg 1540/41* (Neukirchen-Vluyn, 1974), 219.
24. Lenz 3:28–29.
25. Elector John Frederick to his Councilors at Regensburg, Liebenwerda, 26 July 1541, in Staatsarchiv Weimar, Reg. E, 48^r–50^r, no. 99, vol. 3, fol. 236^r.
26. Lenz 3:130.
27. Ibid., 134.
28. Ibid., 129.
29. Friedrich Roth, ed., "Zur Geschichte des Reichstages in Regensburg im Jahr 1541: Die Korrespondenz der Augsburger Gesandten Wolfgang Rehlinger, Simprecht Hoser und Dr. Konrad Hel mit dem Rathe, den Geheimen und dem Bürgermeister Herwart

nebst Briefen von Dr. Gereon Sailer und Wolfgang Musculus an den letzteren," *ARG* 2 (1904/5): 276.

30. Brandi, *Kaiser Karl V.*, vol. 1, *Darstellung*, 6th ed. (Munich, 1959), 398.
31. *Nuntiaturberichte aus Deutschland nebst ergänzenden Aktenstücke*, Abt. I, 12 vols. (Gotha, 1892–1910; reprint, 1968), 8:733.
32. G. Schmidt, *Städtetag*, 278.
33. Lenz 2:43 n. 2.
34. Quoted by G. Schmidt, *Städtetag*, 401.
35. *PC* 2:509, no. 536.
36. Ibid. 3:221–22, no. 216.
37. Lenz 2:62 n. 5.
38. Ibid., 60–62, no. 134; and the remaining quotes in the paragraph are from this same letter.
39. *PC* 3:280–81, no. 269.
40. Ibid. 2:611–12, no. 616.
41. Ibid. 3:350, no. 331.
42. Eberhard Isenmann, "Reichsstadt und Reich an der Wende vom späten Mittelalter zur frühen Neuzeit," in *Mittel und Wege früher Verfassungspolitik*, ed. Josef Engel (Stuttgart, 1979), 161 n. 481.
43. Jacob Sturm, "Außzug aller gehaltener Reichs Tage und Summarie, dabey beschrieben wie und waß uff einem jeden gehandelt worden vom Jahre 1427 biß ad annum 1517 inclusive," ed. Jakob Wencker, in Philipp Knipschildt, *Tractatus politico-juridicus de juribus et privilegiis civitatum imperialium*, 3d ed. (Strasbourg, 1740), 13: "Es seyen kein grössere Schläfer denn die Fryen Richs-Stette."
44. Isenmann, "Reichsstadt und Reich," 152–53.
45. *PC* 3:472–73, no. 446.
46. Ibid., 467–68, no. 443.
47. Ibid., 476, no. 451.
48. Ibid., 536, no. 506.
49. Ibid., 543, no. 515.

10

NORTHERN STORMS

Oh, wherefore come ye forth in triumph from the north,
With your hands, and your feet, and your raiment all red?
— Thomas Babington Macaulay

The history of the German Reformation is often told as a southern story. The
movement sparks from Luther's Saxony to the southern cities—Nuremberg,
Zurich, Strasbourg—erupts in the southern Peasants' War, and reaches its political peaks in the great Reformation Diets held at Worms, Augsburg, and
Speyer. This story is partly accurate, for by the mid-1530s the Protestant cause
had reached approximately the permanent limits of its South German configu-
ration. With one important exception, the Electoral Palatinate, no important
South German state converted to Protestant religion after this point. Moreover, the restoration of the Imperial political system after 1539 took the new
alignments largely into account and functioned fairly well despite the confessional parties in the Diet. The origins of the Smalkaldic War, the Empire's
first religious war, lay not directly in this story but in the struggle for the
North, which began in earnest during the 1530s.

STRUGGLES FOR THE NORTHWEST

The Empire's vast northern stretches were known to Jacob Sturm only through
books. One can imagine seeing them from a vantage point high above the
northern edge of the central highlands. The mind's eye swings down the rainswept
plains toward the cool northern seas that wash the Empire's shores on either
side of Jutland. Westward, the Rhine breaches the central highlands to open
an ancient pathway between the Empire's two oldest cores, its Southwest and
its Northwest. Eastward, by contrast, the plains lie with their backs to the
highlands, and their lands look down the rivers, which debouch one by one
from the highlands and flow northwestward across the great plain toward the
seas. In the sixteenth century these smooth, heavily glaciated northern landscapes formed a world of their own, the contours of which were shaped by
intensive farming, by the Hansa's network of trading cities, and by a series of

177

large but poor territorial states. To Strasbourg and other southern cities, whose merchants knew the Netherlands fairly well, this plain that stretched eastward, all the way to the Oder River, presented a world more alien than either northern Italy or southern France.

For many generations, the southern and the northern tiers of the Empire had developed along different lines, and the Imperial heritage and its system of governance, which meant so much in the South, exerted far less weight on the northern plain. The Reformation did bring the regions together, intertwining their interests with the fates of the old religion and the new by forming confessional communities that would survive the Empire itself. Though Protestant Reformation came nearly a decade later to the North than to the South, once planted it spread rapidly and more evenly. Its advance was punctuated in the mid-1530s by social upheavals not unlike the southern Peasants' War, and the greatest of them, Jan van Leiden's Anabaptist kingdom at Münster and Jürgen Wullenwever's hegemony at Lübeck, set the whole northern world aboil.

Three factors favored the growth of Evangelical religion and Protestant politics in the Empire's northern tier. For one thing, the much weaker Imperial presence meant that the protection of Catholicism there fell less to the Imperial government than to the Habsburg regime in the Netherlands, the power of which was an object of suspicion at many a lesser court. Second, the Smalkaldic chiefs held a strategically interior position between the two Habsburg centers, Austria and the Netherlands, and the Protestant shift of Brandenburg and Albertine Saxony around 1540 secured their eastern flank and freed their hands for actions northward and northwestward. Third, the northern tier contained the most tempting prizes of secularization, for across the Northwest between the Protestant heartlands and the Habsburg Netherlands lay a great arc of prince-bishoprics, a weak shield to the Netherlands and a tempting string of pearls to the Protestant princes. During the era of Imperial restoration in the early 1540s, the Protestants' chief targets of opportunity lay in this sector: Duke William V, called "the Rich," of Cleves-Jülich (1516–92), who wanted the duchy of Gelderland; Elector Herman of Cologne (b. 1477, r. 1515–47) and Bishop Franz von Waldeck (r. 1532–58) of Münster and Osnabrück, who proposed to convert their lands to the new religion and continue to rule them; and Duke Henry of Brunswick-Wolfenbüttel (b. 1489, r. 1514–68), the lone remaining Catholic lay prince on the northern plain. One by one, the Smalkaldeners sniffed at these opportunities and backed away from them, until Brunswick-Wolfenbüttel. When they grabbed this duchy in 1542, they set the Empire on the road to civil war.

CLEVES-JÜLICH

Cleves-Jülich's location along both banks of the Lower Rhine and in neighboring Westphalia made this middle-sized territorial conglomerate a natural rival to the Habsburg Netherlands and a natural target of Protestant attentions. Its ruler might well become a Protestant fox in the Lower Rhenish–Westphalian henhouse, which contained many plump ecclesiastical hens: Cologne, Trier, Münster, Osnabrück, and Paderborn. Dukes John III (r. 1521–39) and William V (r. 1539–92) were Catholic neutrals, whose flirtations with the Smalkaldeners arose from their expectancy on the duchy of Gelderland, that perennial autonomous thorn in the flesh of the Netherlands. When Gelderland's estates elected Duke William in 1538 to succeed the last duke of the Egmond line, no one expected that Charles V, whose dynasty had claimed the duchy since 1473, would allow him to keep it. William, whose sister, Duchess Sybil (1512–54), was married to John Frederick of Saxony, nevertheless counted on the Smalkaldeners' aid to make good his claim.

John Frederick proposed to admit Duke William to the league, if he would allow Evangelical preaching in his lands. Jacob Sturm agreed that "we should not oppose rendering him adequate aid, because we would thereby bring these powerful lands all over to our side."[1] His colleagues at home assented, because "according to conscience and the terms of our alliance, we could not exclude him but must, on grounds of fairness, take him in, . . . for even we, the [current] members, have no bond among ourselves except the defense of religion." Besides—realism reinforced idealism—"we won't soon find another Imperial prince who has such power and such good cavalry, with which he could support and aid us when we need him." Sound religion and good cavalry made a welcome combination in the South, where men fought on foot and reliable cavalry was scarce. Moreover, to reject him might drive William into the other camp. The enthusiasm expressed by Sturm and Strasbourg nonetheless disguised the presence of an important risk in hitching the alliance for religion to the Smalkaldic chiefs' dynastic interests. Perhaps the currently stable situation in South Germany blinded them to the dangers of initiating aggressive action in the far North. They did acknowledge a connection between southern and northern security. If the emperor moved against William of Cleves-Jülich, it was thought at Strasbourg, "Saxony and Hesse as his dear kinsmen cannot easily abandon him. And if it goes badly for him and the emperor wins, these two could be drawn into the conflict and suffer losses in it, which would weaken us through damage to our two mightiest princes and leave us open to future attacks."[2] The Protestant Reformation, they were well aware, created strategic ties and communities of fortune undreamed of by their predecessors, and willy-nilly they must bend to the imperatives of their new alliance.

As the contest for Gelderland mounted toward its first crisis in 1540, Duke William and the Smalkaldic chiefs coordinated their plans for war: twelve thousand foot and a large cavalry force would seek out Charles's army, crush it, and raise the Netherlandish towns and provincial estates against Queen Mary's regime at Brussels.[3] This grandiose scheme aimed at nothing less than seizure of the Empire's entire northwestern sector. Its execution, however, depended on the Smalkaldeners' resources and their will to fight for Cleves-Jülich as the key to the northwestern bishoprics, a point on which Landgrave Philip sounded out Jacob Sturm in early January 1540. If the emperor seized Gelderland and Cleves-Jülich, the landgrave predicted, he would "control Münster, Osnabrück, and the lands all the way to Paderborn, also the neighboring territories of Cologne and Trier. Then, when bishops are elected, [the chapters] will have to accept and elect bishops approved by the emperor and the House of Burgundy."[4] Control of these lands would also place in Charles's grip the sources of the best cavalry. Would Sturm and his government support the landgrave, the Saxon elector, Württemberg, and, perhaps, the king of Denmark in backing Duke William against the emperor? Sturm, whose ardor for a strike in the Northwest had meanwhile cooled a bit, replied that the XIII were "not disinclined" to back a war to prevent even greater harm, but they dared not bring the proposal before the Senate & XXI or the Schöffen. The landgrave "ought to proceed cautiously and carefully in this affair," Sturm advised, "so that Your Grace, out of loyalty and a desire to preserve German liberty, does not get himself, alone or with a few allies, into a position from which he cannot easily get out."[5] Sturm was no war hawk, and the other southern allies proved "even more off the mark," with the consequence, the landgrave grumbled, that "Jülich won't join the Protestant league, he won't come over to our religion or faith, . . . and everything is so confused that we don't know what to do."[6]

Sensing the peril of entering a war with such allies, Duke William courted the French king, the traditional friend of all foes of Burgundy in general and of Gelderland's dukes in particular, and married his niece. When his trial by combat came in 1543, William's territorial army nevertheless faced Charles V's forty thousand troops alone, and after two weeks of hopeless resistance, the duke made his submission to Charles at Venlo on 7 September. The Smalkaldeners left him to his fate, the landgrave—for the moment an Imperial loyalist because of his bigamy—with a hypocritical sneer that "he has now got his reward" for intriguing with the French.

These events forced Jacob Sturm to revise his views about backing in North Germany the combination—the Gospel and German (i.e., aristocratic) liberty—that had proven so successful in the South, notably in 1534. The biggest difference between the two situations lay in the fact that whereas in 1534 King Ferdinand's failure to act had lost Württemberg, in 1543 Charles's prompt, resolute action secured Gelderland, once and for all, for the Netherlands. The victorious emperor now stood approximately where his grandfather had stood in 1505. "The black eagle is a powerful bird," Sturm mused, "and he does not tolerate contempt—just as the Palatine elector discovered years ago [in 1504]."[7] Outside of Heidelberg, no one had better reason to remember that discovery than did the Strasbourgeois.

COLOGNE

In contrast to Cleves-Jülich, where the Protestants had to deal with the ruling duke as an equal partner, in the neighboring prince-archbishopric of Cologne they hoped to gain commanding influence over the ruling elector and trade their protection for a Lutheran reformation in his lands. Herman, count of Wied and prince-archbishop and elector of Cologne since 1515, was one of those pre-Reformation prelates who tried to move with the times, migrating in easy stages through the party of Catholic neutrals toward the Protestants. Following the colloquy at Regensburg in 1541, Herman called on the Smalkaldeners for help in reforming his principality.

The situation at Cologne was complicated. The lay estates of his territorial parliament supported Elector Herman, while against him stood the cathedral chapter and the magistrates and most of the burghers of the city of Cologne, who, a Hessian councilor groused in 1543, "understand plenty about business, pleasure, and prosperity, but little about God."[8] A Protestant reformation in the principality of Cologne—the archdiocese, much of it ruled by other princes, was a different story—could therefore be effected only from above, and the involvement of the Protestants, including Strasbourgeois, rested entirely on their influence with the elector. Herman, though no warrior, was in one respect a greater catch than Duke William of Cleves-Jülich, for all of his cavalry, might have been, for Herman was an elector of the Holy Roman Empire. The very thought of his vote—added to those of Saxony, and, perhaps, Brandenburg and the Palatine elector—quickened in Protestant hearts that most thrilling of their secret hopes, a Protestant on the Imperial throne. Then, too, with Herman and Bishop Franz of Münster and Osnabrück in the Protestant fold, the old church would be doomed in the Empire's northwestern reaches.

When the elector called for help, therefore, all the Protestant powers took heed, and soon Martin Bucer came downriver to guide the reformation process in Herman's lands. The situation, he trumpeted after a first look in Bonn, "is entirely ours."[9] When he returned with Caspar Hedio in December 1542 for an eight-month stay, Bucer drafted the main plan of reform, called the "Simple Opinion," which Elector Herman might have introduced into his state, as the territorial parliament empowered him to do in July 1543.

The fall of Cleves-Jülich to the emperor in 1543, however, quickly cooled Elector Herman's ardor for reform and in the longer run doomed Bucer's work there to an impressive but fruitless effort. The Smalkaldeners failed Elector Herman as they had failed Duke William. When the league's assembly voted in the winter of 1545–46 to aid Herman if he were attacked, John Frederick of Saxony wrote to the landgrave that "it would in our view have been better, had the estates [of the league] not promised to help him [Elector Herman], for you know how these things go." Landgrave Philip did indeed know, for "it would have been wiser to investigate the matter more thoroughly or to have been more prudent in assuring the archbishop of our support."[10] Strasbourg's magistrates also entertained second thoughts and declared their preference for the old sort of alliance, "when neighbor allies with neighbor."[11] In the end, it was probably just as well, for by 1545 the Smalkaldic League's freedom of action and its internal cohesion had been badly damaged by its embroilment since 1542 in the duchy of Brunswick-Wolfenbüttel.

THE CONQUEST OF BRUNSWICK-WOLFENBÜTTEL

The roots of the Brunswick affair went back to 1540, when the death of Duke Eric "the Elder" (r. 1495–1540) of Brunswick-Calenberg left his cousin, Duke Henry, called "the Younger," of Brunswick-Wolfenbüttel as the last firmly Catholic temporal prince on the North German plain. Vigorous, able, ambitious, and vain, Henry, who was just Jacob Sturm's age, became a stalwart in the Catholic party of action and a commander of the Catholic League of Nuremberg. By the early 1540s, depending on one's party, Henry was either Catholicism's last, best hope in the Empire's northern reaches or the last, toughest barrier to the triumph of the Evangelical cause there. His downfall began with political feuds against the cities of Goslar and Brunswick and personal quarrels with the Smalkaldic chiefs. Even though the quarrels' roots were purely mundane, at Regensburg in July 1541 the league recognized Goslar's case as a "religious matter" and therefore eligible for military aid. When the Chamber Court handed down decrees of outlawry against Duke Henry's foes, therefore, the league's obligation to defend the cities of Brunswick and Goslar came into play. It was both a cause of, and a pretext for, the Brunswick affair.

Henry's situation was complicated by his bitter personal feud with Philip of Hesse and his only slightly less nasty one with John Frederick of Saxony. A series of insults led in 1539 to a flood of printed invective from both sides— more than sixty titles in 1542 alone—which entertained, infuriated, and frightened partisans on both sides. Henry jibed at the landgrave's bigamy, Philip retailed gossip about Henry's mistress, and soon the language became violent and coarse. Typical of its tone was Martin Luther's scurrilous *Against Hanswurst*: "You should not write a book, until you have heard an old sow fart. Then you should gape in wonder and say, 'Thank you, beautiful nightingale, there I hear a text for me!'"[12] The war of printed words so heightened confessional tensions that the Smalkaldic declaration of war on 13 July 1542 and the taking of the duchy came as a catharsis, best expressed by Luther's triumphant cry: "This is a truly divine victory, for God has done it all. He is the *fac totum*, and we may now hope that the last days are at hand!"[13]

THE BRUNSWICK CAMPAIGN

The Brunswick campaign began, like the Württemberg campaign in 1534, not as a defensive operation in the interest of religion but as a dynastic war among rival princes. On 26 October 1541, three Protestant princes, the two Smalkaldic chiefs and Duke Moritz of Saxony (r. 1547–53), met in person at Naumburg and decided for war. Next, with the league's backing they invaded Brunswick-Wolfenbüttel, installed their own governor, and began a Lutheran reformation of the land. Once in control, however, the princes could not let go, because they could not decide whether to partition the lands or to hold them in trust for the legitimate heirs, Henry's sons. For three years they kept the duchy in hand, enjoyed its revenues, and bullied their allies into paying the costs of its occupation. The Smalkaldic chiefs' seizure of Brunswick-Wolfenbüttel was an act of pure aggression to settle scores between princes, lacking even the shadow of legality that hung over the restoration in Württemberg eight years before. Their strike belied the Smalkaldic League's avowed defensive purpose, it deeply wounded the league by provoking dissension and strengthening suspicions between South and North and between cities and princes, and it provided Emperor Charles V with an excellent reason to settle the German question by force of arms.

The attitudes of Jacob Sturm and his Strasbourg colleagues toward this affair illustrate its debilitating effects on Protestant solidarity. The Strasbourgeois had always been the strongest southern advocates of solidarity with the northern Protestants. They had supported aid to both Goslar and Brunswick against Duke Henry, arguing that Henry's Catholicism made Goslar's cause a "religious matter."[14] On the other hand, they defended the league's constitution, which the commanders violated in 1541 by their private decision to invade Brunswick-Wolfenbüttel. This was probably why Landgrave Philip decided to take Sturm into his confidence even before the decision for war fell at Naumburg. He needed Sturm's blessing, "because, as is well known, the southerners all follow Jacob Sturm."[15] And so, when Sturm arrived at Speyer for the Imperial Diet on 1 February 1542, a Hessian agent named Rudolf Schenck von Schweinsberg (d. 1551), "on special orders and under his sworn oath of loyalty" to the landgrave, revealed the three princes' plan of campaign. Sturm, Rudolf reported, "judged the matter very positively."[16] The landgrave proposed to tell other southern politicians of the plan—"though not Augsburg"—on Jacob Sturm's advice, "so they will be mobilized ahead of time to support the levy of 7,000 foot and 3,000 horse for Goslar." Jacob Sturm thus knew since February 1542—four months before the league's assembly learned of the plan—that the three princes would invade Brunswick under the pretext of defending Goslar. Bucer, who may have learned of the plan even earlier than Sturm did, confirmed that "Sir Jacob recognizes Your Grace's proposal as the best and swiftest, . . . and he doesn't doubt that the estates will be glad to take part in it."[17] When the time came, Strasbourg supported the strike against Duke Henry, though its war councilor, Ulman Böcklin von Böcklinsau (d. ca. 1565), who was also Sturm's cousin, was instructed to protest the unconstitutional way in which the decision had fallen.[18]

As the summer wore on, however, opinion at Strasbourg began to shift against the Brunswick enterprise. Even Martin Bucer, a perennial war hawk, fell victim to the spreading suspicion that the princes were using the affair to bilk the southerners. "Our alliance is a Protestant alliance," Bucer lectured Landgrave Philip, "in which no one should make money or seek to become richer than he is, but in which everyone should maintain the highest standards of loyalty and equity." "Equity," he thought, expressing a typical burghers' idea, "is the basis of all communities, inequity is like the very quicksilver, which destroys everything, especially religious community."[19] Bucer might just as well have flung words into the wind, for soon came distressing reports of the conquered duchy's plundering. Meanwhile, the occupation sucked up large sums from the allies, and the issue of the war's constitutionality would not die. By year's end the loyal Strasbourgeois were grumbling about how the princes "remain in the field with large forces and at great expense."[20]

Once they had properly plundered their prize, the Smalkaldic chiefs found themselves in the position of the dog who habitually chases automobiles and finally catches one. What to do with Brunswick-Wolfenbüttel? By March 1543, when he began to face this issue, Jacob Sturm thought "it would be much better, and do more for our reputation, to sign a treaty with Duke Henry's children, to restore the land to them, and with the duke himself. That is our first choice, and so we have advised."[21] Failing this, the Smalkaldeners should grit their teeth and deal with Duke Henry himself, "so that the affair may be put to rest." If the allies could raze Henry's fortresses, require his territorial estates to go surety for his conduct, and bind him through a treaty confirmed by the emperor, "we can trim his claws, so that he cannot start anything, or, if he does, he must lose." The religious argument, Sturm confessed, was a phony one, for though Henry would probably restore Catholicism, "this is not sufficient reason to deprive him of his lands. This is not the reason they were taken." Once Goslar and Brunswick were secure and the Smalkaldeners had recovered their costs, "we will have no claims on the land or his subjects, which are his hereditary fief and the property of His Majesty and the Empire. It is none of our affair, what religion is established in such a land." So much for the Brunswick war as a "religious matter." At heart a conservative legalist, Sturm recognized that Henry must be restored, whatever the religious consequences, "for otherwise we could take other papist princes' lands from them, bring the people over to our religion, and then refuse to restore the lands." As for Henry's undoubted crimes, "we are not his lord or judge, but only His Imperial Majesty has such jurisdiction. If he will not punish the duke, we may not."

The irony of the Brunswick affair as the northern counterpart of the Württemberg affair was not lost on Jacob Sturm. In 1534 he and his government had backed restoration in Württemberg on the legal grounds that Duke Ulrich had been unjustly dispossessed; nine years later, he advanced a similar argument in favor of Duke Henry against the Smalkaldic chiefs. That Ulrich had turned a Catholic land to Lutheranism and Henry would restore a Lutheranized land to Catholicism, if he could, did not change the matter's legality in Sturm's eyes. This legalism fitted perfectly Sturm's spiritual idea of religion, for in his view the Gospel was the Holy Spirit's promptings in the individual heart, not a godly law which broke the laws of this world. This lesson, learned under Wimpheling and Erasmus and fixed by the Peasants' War, Sturm never forgot.

THE DEBATE ON BRUNSWICK

When the allies met at Smalkalden in July 1543 to decide the fate of Brunswick-Wolfenbüttel, bitter words flew about the Saxon-Hessian domination of the occupation government, which the princes refused to allow to be sworn to the league rather than themselves. Their refusal to raze the duchy's castles seemed a clear sign that they intended to retain the conquered lands. Sturm confessed that although the fortifications' fate was "not very important, because the land is far away, . . . the occupation's costs are unbearable."[22] The conflict worsened at the league's next assembly in the autumn at Frankfurt. Landgrave Philip, who was trying to turn the southerners toward his point of view, complained "how ramshackle our alliance's affairs have become," a state of affairs for which he blamed Jacob Sturm's "timid" position on the Brunswick affair.[23]

Echoing his princely patron, Martin Bucer blamed the educated lawyers and their "tyrannical" Roman law, but also those who, like Sturm, "don't just look at the matters as they are, but listen to the lawyers about what will and won't be approved by the Chamber Court, which makes them either happy or timid."[24] It all came from a false respect for Roman law, for "Sir Jacob [Sturm] knows as well as anyone does, that by means of the Franks, God broke the Roman law of tyranny in the German lands." Instead, "He gave us the free, Frankish law, which should now be the German law, according to which the free princes and estates may drive out such an unbearable tyrant [i.e., Duke Henry], even without the sovereign's permission." Since the rise of the Chamber Court, however, its lawyers had "reined in and suppressed the free, Frankish law and brought in and replaced it with the tyrannical Roman law." The court's obduracy was growing with the emperor's power, so that "now Sir Jacob will see what coin has value, and what sort of law will be enforced. There is a proverb: a willing audience is more important than a good singer. The point is this: what counts is not how many rights you have, but how much you give the judge." Bucer's cynicism about the law played to deep contemporary prejudices against the courts, the lawyers, and the "common written law," but it did not convince Jacob Sturm.

At Speyer in 1544, Jacob Sturm and Philip of Hesse finally stood face to face on the Brunswick affair. Three times the landgrave sent for Sturm and lectured him about Brunswick. On the first occasion, he berated Sturm for worrying about the local merchants and money, sneering that he would rather the business were in the hands of the XIII or the Senate than in Sturm's.[25] Sturm gravely assumed a diplomat's defense: he followed his instructions, and, if he received different ones, he would follow those. In a subsequent interview the landgrave poured out his resentment on Sturm.[26] "We are truly astonished," he hectored, that "Henry's violent acts against Goslar and his intentions against Saxony and ourselves don't persuade you, but that you recommend that we make a treaty with him and let him come back into his lands." In fact, "you were ever of such a mind," the landgrave charged, "since the day when Rudolf Schenck told you in confidence what the elector, Duke Moritz, and we were planning to do. Even then you concluded that we wanted to make war and were using defense merely as an excuse." Sturm ought to search his own conscience, however, and see "that we had this revealed to you because we trusted you; for you know that we have never kept anything from you, about war or anything else. We expect, therefore, since we have so trusted you, that you should not criticize but praise us."

This was not the worst Sturm had to hear from Landgrave Philip, for the prince now recounted his own motives in this affair, the decision to support the cities of Brunswick and Goslar, the princes' rejection of offensive war, and the league's apparent authorization of action by its commanders. "These were the origins of the entire affair," he said, "and this is its true history." The prince pointed out that Sturm had told a Hessian agent that he would prefer that the princes attack Duke Henry alone, "without expense to the other estates, and that it not be done for the sake of religion or reasons connected with our religion," so that the Catholics would not be moved to help Henry. The landgrave had concurred, but "God did not want that to happen" and brought it about in quite a different way, so that "Sir Jacob must reasonably conclude that this affair is an act of God. And he must then not look on the affair with the eyes of this world alone."

Having endured the Hessian prince's "vehement" words, Sturm inferred from them "that the two, elector and landgrave, have decided to retain the duchy and want therefore to prevent a peaceful settlement of this affair, no matter what we think of it."[27] Sturm believed, to the contrary, that if the Brunswick affair came before the emperor, "there are many reasons why Duke Henry would find [in him] on this matter a more favorable judge than we would. If the judgment goes against us, we will have to pay all the costs and restore the lands."[28] Sturm lost the play, as the league's majority backed the princes' stand against arbitration, though over Sturm's protest. "The princes," he wrote home, "lead us ever deeper into this game. . . . It would be grievous to handle the affair in such a way that no treaty is possible; it would also be grievous to part company over this affair."[29] Sturm pleaded that to defer a settlement would only favor Duke Henry and endanger the league, since the emperor was more likely to have a free hand later than he did at the moment, "but this argument has no effect on our princes, because they are too hot and emotional against Duke Henry."[30]

By late winter 1544, Jacob Sturm had comprehended how deeply irrational the Smalkaldic chiefs' engagement against Duke Henry had become, how recklessly they were dragging the league into conflict with the emperor, and how pitifully feeble were the league's defenses against exploitation by its own chiefs. Their aggression threatened to strip the Smalkaldic League of the respect of those who, whatever their motives—neutralism, reform-mindedness, or anti-Habsburg policy—opposed the use of force against the league. The Protestant alliance might be, as Sturm thought it was, a military match for the militant Catholic powers alone, but it could not fight the emperor except in the broader fellowship of the German opposition, the friends of "German liberty." If Charles and Ferdinand could catch the Smalkaldic League isolated from the rest of this princely opposition, they would settle the German schism once and for all in their own sense.

This fear of isolation, sharpened by the financial burdens, led Jacob Sturm and other southern Protestants in 1544 to favor the "sequestration" of Brunswick-Wolfenbüttel, that is, the duchy's delivery into the hands of Charles V as receiver. The Smalkaldic chiefs favored a different solution, according to which some of the duchy would eventually go to Henry's sons, though "the choicest parts would be given to the elector and the landgrave."[31] Bucer, taking once again the landgrave's side, reported that Sturm opposed this solution. "He is hindered," Bucer wrote, "by the provision of the public peace that the lands taken from a violator of the peace must revert to the feudal lord, and that the protectors of the peace may recover only their costs. From this he concludes that according to the law, we may not retain possession of the land except by force."[32] Worse yet, Sturm held that the Protestants possessed no right of reform (*jus reformandi*) in the conquered duchy, for "if we have no right to retain possession, then we are obliged to keep hands off the religion of the land as we found it." As they had done in other lands, even in the prince-bishoprics, "which according to all the laws of their church belong not to their possessors but to the people of God. That was the case in Metz and with others, whom we turned away, as you well know." That touched a sensitive nerve, as Sturm had every reason to know.

Sturm's agony over Brunswick intensified during the Diet of Speyer of 1544, for not only did the Smalkaldic chiefs rush to support the French war, so dreaded at Strasbourg, but Duke Henry, who prowled about demanding his rights, singled out Sturm and accused him, both orally and in print, of having said publicly at Nuremberg in 1543 that "the French king is a good lord and chief to me."[33] Conflict over the French war merely widened the deep gulf that had opened between Landgrave Philip and Jacob Sturm. Bucer pleaded with the prince "not to be angry about Sir Jacob's timidity. He is loyal, and he is more afraid of illegality than of violence." Sturm "fears God's wrath, if things are not kept properly and in correct order. Then, too, he always goes further than he can promise to go, and our masters will truly stand by Your Princely Grace to the last."[34] This last, at least, was true, and it would cost Strasbourg dearly.

THE SPLIT OVER BRUNSWICK

When the allies assembled in February 1545 at Worms, where the Imperial Diet was sitting, relations between the league's two chiefs and its southern cities had reached their nadir. So deeply did the costs of the Brunswick affair depress him that, according to Bucer, Jacob Sturm considered renouncing his citizenship and leaving Strasbourg. Indeed, Sturm's reports home crackled with uncharacteristic sarcasm about the allies' bickering over money: "This is an enterprise from which the cities certainly will not become rich."[35] Sturm felt keenly his growing isolation, for his colleagues at home tended to favor the Hessian-Saxon policy of holding the duchy, and the landgrave, hearing of this disagreement (via Bucer?), tried to exploit it. In deepest resignation, Sturm wrote home that "I can only commend the matter to God. I could well tolerate that someone else were sent here, who could do better than I can." If they yielded to the princes, he insisted, "we would have . . . paid out fifty or sixty thousand gulden more, all for nothing."[36]

Sturm held the day at last. The league decided to deliver Brunswick-Wolfenbüttel into the emperor's hands within one month, providing that Duke Henry were not allowed into the land, and that for the time being no changes were made in the regime of occupation. Meanwhile, Duke Henry assembled a small army and tried to retake his lands, which led to a fresh defeat at Kalefeld on 14 October 1545.

As Duke Henry was surrendering, Jacob Sturm sat down at home—he had spent eleven of the past thirteen months in lodgings at Worms—to draft an apology of his views for the landgrave's eyes. It was the clearest statement he ever made of their different conceptions of the league's aims.[37] "Your councilors and envoys have often heard my reasons," he began, "for I believed . . . it would be best to negotiate even if both sides were already mobilized, in order to prevent terrible damage to the German nation." If the Smalkaldeners could win and keep Brunswick-Wolfenbüttel, Sturm thought, "we must either place it in His Majesty's receivership or hold it, which will involve such expense and trouble, that our allies cannot bear it in the long run." Therefore, "even if we win, we will gain greater expenses, which we cannot recover from Duke Henry or from his land or officials, but nothing more." The possession of Brunswick-Wolfenbüttel threatened the league's entire future, not only because of the land's debts, but even more because its occupation would dissuade other Protestant powers from joining the league. In sum, "the burden and expense rest only on a few, who day-by-day become fewer."

Sturm then parried the landgrave's charges against himself. It was untrue, he protested, that "I look only to the advantage of my masters or of other cities, rather than to the common cause." Neither he nor his colleagues would shirk their duties to the league. "It is hard," however, "and will be in the long run impossible for those of good will to bear the load alone, while others slip the harness. I am afraid it will ruin them all." The uncharacteristic emotion in Sturm's closing betrayed how low relations had sunk between the two men— Hessian and Strasbourgeois, prince and noble, lord and burgher. They would never recover.

In for a penny, in for a pound, and the costs of the second Brunswick campaign had to be piled on earlier debts and, one hoped, spread as widely as possible. On the day of the Battle of Kalefeld (14 October 1545), when Sturm, Martin Herlin, and Conrad Joham met to draft a recommendation to Strasbourg's XIII, they allowed the emergency to override their scruples. Since this action "is too expensive for those powers who are engaged in the defense of Brunswick," they thought, "the landgrave should circularize the other allies and tell them that the affair concerns not only those now involved but all the allies and the whole cause of true religion." Philip should "draw them into deliberations about this common religious matter, so that the affair does not end in trouble and damages for us, and thus for our religion as a whole."[38] This accorded with what had been the landgrave's view from the start—whether sincere or not, is beside the point—that the security of the Protestant powers was itself a "religious matter." The distinction, therefore, between "religious" and "worldly" was a purely tactical matter. Whatever they said now, Sturm and his colleagues had earlier employed precisely the same argument about their suits for restitution of ecclesiastical properties. Hoisted by their own petard, a committee of Strasbourg's regime admitted as much in 1546. They said the northerners should be reminded "how loyally we helped them against Brunswick, which was basically not a religious matter."[39] For years the Reformation movement had drawn energy from the inherent indefinability of the boundary between religion and the world. That the same indefinability should now come to plague the Smalkaldic League was only to be expected.

NOTES

1. *PC* 3:549, no. 571.
2. Ibid., 554–56, no. 573.
3. Lenz 1:411–12, from which come the following quotes.

4. *PC* 3:4, no. 4.
5. Ibid., 13–14, no. 11.
6. Lenz 1:150, no. 56.
7. Georg Mentz, *Johann Friedrich der Großmütige 1503–1554*, 3 vols. (Jena, 1903–8), 3:492, no. 43.
8. Conrad Varrentrapp, *Hermann von Wied und sein Reformationsversuch in Köln: Ein Beitrag zur deutschen Reformationsgeschichte* (Leipzig, 1878), 1:208.
9. Martin Bucer to Nikolaus Pruckner, 24 January 1542, in Strasbourg, Bibliothèque Nationale et Universitaire, Thesaurus Baumianus, 13:151.
10. Varrentrapp, *Hermann von Wied* 2:109–11, and the landgrave's reply quoted at 111 n. 1.
11. *PC* 3:568, no. 540.
12. Mark U. Edwards, Jr., *Luther's Last Battles: Politics and Polemics, 1531–46* (Ithaca, N.Y., 1983), 154.
13. Ibid., 158.
14. *PC* 3:135–38, no. 148; 156, no. 165.
15. Lenz 2:43 n. 2; and there, too, the following quote.
16. Ibid., 56 n. 2; and there, too, the following quote.
17. Ibid., 64, no. 134.
18. *PC* 3:275, no. 265; and there, too, the remaining quotes in this paragraph.
19. Lenz 2:96, no. 145.
20. *PC* 3:340, no. 327.
21. Ibid., 346–47; the remaining quotes in this paragraph are also from this document.
22. Ibid., 420, no. 394.
23. Lenz 2:195, 200, no. 179.
24. Ibid. 2:208, no. 181; 213–15, no. 183, from which the following quotes in the paragraph come.
25. *PC* 3:460–61, no. 437.
26. Lenz 2:252 n. 4; *PC* 3:454–55, no. 432.
27. *PC* 3:455, no. 432.
28. Ibid., 462, no. 437.
29. Ibid., 463–64, no. 439.
30. Ibid., 468–69, no. 443.
31. Friedrich Roth, ed., "Aus dem Briefwechsel Gereon Sailers mit den Augsburger Bürgermeistern Georg Herwart und Simprecht Hoser (April–Juni 1544)," *ARG* 1 (1903/4): 94.
32. Lenz 2:258–59.
33. Friedrich Hortleder, *Der Röm. key.- u. königlichen Maiesten, Handlungen und Ausschreiben . . .* , 1:1813 (= bk. 4, chap. 47).
34. Lenz 2:263, no. 194.
35. *PC* 3:559–60, no. 526.
36. Ibid., 588, no. 560.
37. Ibid., 644–45, no. 606 (27 September 1545), from which the quotes in this and the following paragraph come.
38. Ibid., 658–59, no. 620.
39. *PC* 4:446, no. 422.

11

BREAKDOWN

When he [Aristotle] was asked "What is a friend?" he said "One soul inhabiting two bodies."

—Diogenes Laertius

When the grateful Upper Rhenish free cities honored him in 1545, Jacob Sturm stood at the summit of his career. Just about this time, Hans Baldung Grien (1484/85–1545), Strasbourg's greatest Renaissance painter and Sturm's fellow magistrate, fixed his image forever in an oil portait. The original is now lost, but a copy reveals Sturm in his prime as short in stature and full of figure. He wears a squarish beard and is dressed in a beret, gentleman's mantle, hose, and sword, and he holds a glove in one hand, while with the other he closes his cloak and displays his seal ring. He resembles, as one historian charmingly wrote, "a middle-class Henry VIII."[1] His visage is grave and somewhat ascetic, as though his shoulders bear the republic's entire weight.

THE BURDENS OF DIPLOMACY

And so they nearly did, for twenty years of the Senate & XXI's and the privy councils' sessions, committee work, long travels by boat and on horseback, and endless negotiations with theologians and magistrates, lawyers and princes, bishops and electors, and a king and an emperor had exacted their toll. As long ago as 1532, Sturm had "excused himself on account of ill health and asked to be spared the ride" to Regensburg, though in the end he had vowed "to spare neither health nor wealth for the city's sake."[2] The following years brought no relief, for as older colleagues withdrew from diplomatic work, few younger ones came forward who possessed the requisite education, languages, speaking skills, and willingness to serve this commune in this way. Despite frequent appeals by the senior magistrates to "do their best," no recruits were found, and the situation got no better. When Peter Sturm reported in February 1545 that Jacob, then at Worms, had fallen ill with swelling of the ankles every evening, the alarmed magistrates dispatched a physician to treat him. In June, still at Worms, Sturm wrote that "nothing would suit me better now than to

191

get free of these difficult doings and rest up at home, so as to recover more peace and health in body and mind."[3] He nonetheless stayed on to the end, a slave to his sense of duty, though rumors were already abroad that "Sir Jacob Sturm is said to be weakening mentally and not so sharp as he used to be."[4]

Now in his mid-fifties, Sturm was keenly aware of how utterly Strasbourg's policy rested on his shoulders alone. When he agreed in 1545 to travel to the league's assembly at Frankfurt, he used the occasion to warn his colleagues of his own mortality.[5] "I have always placed, and will continue to prefer, the common good ahead of all my own affairs and even my own health." "Gradually," however, at Strasbourg "everything has come to rest on one man, which is not the case in other cities. You should reflect whether it is good to have everything in one man's head." The other magistrates, Sturm complained, had become accustomed to leaving official business in the hands of a few, and "if the affair goes well, they say, 'How could it have gone otherwise?' If it goes badly, they say, 'It is not good that the whole city's welfare lies in the hands of one man.'" "More men are needed," he concluded, "for one day soon I will no longer be able to travel, or I may even be dead, and someone else must be acquainted with these matters."

The other urban regimes mostly had similar difficulties in recruiting able diplomats from among their own unpaid magistrates. With few exceptions, the men they chose could not cope with the ever stiffer demands generated by the Imperial politics in the Reformation era, and by midcentury they were routinely turning over diplomatic chores to paid civil servants. In Sturm's generation, however, Strasbourg still relied on magistrates, most of whom turned in mediocre performances at best.

Jacob Sturm thus in no way typified the free cities' politicians, and even the most prominent of the others, such as Ulm's Bernhard Besserer or Constance's Thomas Blarer, operated mostly in his shadow. Sturm's unusual combination of qualities—personal integrity, dedication, education, eloquence, and patience—commanded respect from all sides, but especially from the great princes and their councilors. His stature had increased since the 1530s, when the quickening tempo of the league's activities had begun to strain the human resources of most southern members. The greater distances tested the burghers' sense of dedication, and the cultural differences between South and North tested both their grasp of wider affairs and their linguistic abilities. Besides, as Sturm once complained in a rare moment of candor, "food is very expensive in this land [Thuringia], and the wine is very sour, so that our servants have fallen ill, and the meals are not cooked in our fashion."[6] Perhaps Sturm had heard the Thuringian joke about the "three-man wine," which was so sour that two had to hold down the third man while he drank it.

REFORM OF THE SMALKALDIC LEAGUE

Very many of Sturm's missions—tradition numbers them at more than ninety—involved the Smalkaldic League, and the deterioration of that body during the Brunswick affair must have cost him much sleep and energy. And not only Sturm, for Elector John Frederick, whom some southerners thought "lazy," contemplated giving up his command and even leaving the league, while the landgrave complained repeatedly about having to neglect his own lands for the league's sake. The Strasbourgeois, on the other side, reminded themselves that, except for the common religion, they had no reason to continue membership in "so widely scattered an alliance."[7] The root of this gradual estrangement lay deep in the Brunswick affair, which eroded the league's religious bonds of unity and allowed the geographical and social tensions greater freedom to divide allies from one another. In July 1545, during the second campaign in Brunswick, Augsburg's leaders predicted that this erosion would jeopardize the league's future. "Because the [quarrels about] the audit and the [cities'] ingratitude have made princes, especially Saxony and Hesse, who risked life, land, and people [in Brunswick], just as diffident as the cities," they wrote in alarm, "it could easily happen that if the cities simply wait for the princes to open the question, the [league's] treaty will elapse and the two groups will become estranged from one another."[8] Just this fear, apparently, prompted the Smalkaldic chiefs to call on 20 October 1545, the day before they captured Duke Henry, the Smalkaldeners and other Protestant powers to assemble on 6 December at Frankfurt to deliberate on renewal and reform of the league.

The problem of reform, and Jacob Sturm's role in it, has to be seen in the larger context of the league's three main weaknesses, with the Brunswick affair thrown into high relief. First, the league suffered from the social division between the cities, whose trade-oriented regimes naturally favored peace over war, and the princes, who regarded war as a natural, if often risky, extension of policy. Second, the league suffered from its immense extent and inadequate density, for it literally marched with the Empire itself, from Strasbourg to Pomerania and from Constance to Hamburg. Third, the league suffered from an ideological confusion, which the Reformation had intensified but not created, about boundaries between religious and temporal affairs. In other words, the league rested on a common religion alone, unsupported by common economic interests, a common political culture, or common problems of regional security. It had no palpable interests except for religion to foster what Jacob Sturm called "the proper sort of love for one another."

STURM'S STRUGGLE FOR REFORM

All of these weaknesses came into play when the urban politicians began to think about renewal and reform. Sturm reflected on these matters in March 1544, when King Ferdinand's men were talking up a new league of southern powers under royal leadership. Such a revival of the old Swabian League, he thought, would be good for such rulers and cities as "lie near one another," but otherwise "such a league would be of little use, for the federation and system of legal arbitration, which the allies establish together, covers only the members." If such a league did not include the neighboring powers, "with whom the city might any day come into conflict, membership would have little purpose—as we saw some years ago, when Strasbourg for a while joined the Swabian League."[9] This was an apt parallel, for a nonconfessional alliance would provide security Strasbourg did not need. "We don't have so much civic and private wealth, manufactures, and trade as exist in Nuremberg, Augsburg, Ulm, and other cities," the Strasbourgeois reflected, "so that we also don't have, thank God, so many factions, feuds, and enmity as others. Most of our enemies and conflicts, so far as we know, arise because of the Christian religion and God's holy Word, and for this purpose we already have a league." Besides, "if we should join alliances for secular reasons, they would profit us little, since the public peace forbids the use of force, even if violence is used against us."[10] At Strasbourg the old sensibility lived on, despite Sturm's alliance policy, that the city lay in a region without powerful princes. Similar thoughts of reversion to more familiar, regional concepts of security stirred at Ulm, so much so that the frightened Augsburgers began to work furiously for the league's renewal.

The main leadership nonetheless remained in Jacob Sturm's hands. He attended the league's assembly at Frankfurt between 7 December 1545 and 7 February 1546 in the company of Heinrich von Mülnheim (1507–78), his kinsman, and the guildsman Michael Schwencker (d. 1556). Well aware that his entire policy lay in peril, Sturm wearily agreed to go to Frankfurt, for "on the issues which will be treated now depend our city's prosperity or ruin."[11] Strasbourg's plan for reform, almost certainly Sturm's work, aimed to promote the league's statelike qualities, to strengthen its administrative and judicial apparatus, to redistribute its votes, and to cultivate fairness in taxation through adoption of a direct tax, the Common Penny.

At Frankfurt in December 1545 a surprising consensus emerged for reform. The two commanders declared that although "the multiplication of business and affairs causes them to neglect their own lands and people," and although they "have become targets of great displeasure and resentment," nevertheless "the league must not be allowed to die."[12] Sturm asked for a point-by-point review of the constitution; the Augsburgers declared themselves "ready for anything"; and all of the cities' and most of the princes' envoys complained about taxes. Indeed, taxation roused a storm of complaints, leading the Saxons to say that "the situation was never so desperate as now." Meanwhile, Sturm emptied his satchel of arguments for the Common Penny, hammering them home with repeated appeals to the league's essence, the community of religion.[13] "If his masters look only to themselves," he said, "they could well dispense with this league. But when they regard the common cause and the dangerous state of current affairs, they believe that this league can best be preserved through loyal cooperation."[14] "On this account," he told the allies, "rather than indulging so much mistrust in the league and its business, it should be enough that we are dealing with honorable and Christian persons, who rest the matter on trust and faith, ... for then God will make the cause flourish."[15] All in vain, for the league would not accept direct taxation, deciding instead to retain the old matricular lists. It was a sad commentary on the league's condition that the Imperial Diet, which had long been plagued by similar quarrels, had nonetheless accepted the direct property tax.

THE FAILURE OF REFORM

By May 1546 the Smalkaldic League lay in shambles, so much so that its two architects, Jacob Sturm and Landgrave Philip, considered scrapping it for a new kind of alliance. The landgrave did so because he feared Sturm's centralizing reforms, while Sturm, disheartened by his failure and by the northern cities' selfishness, thought that "the honorable southern cities might ally alone with His Princely Grace [the landgrave]."[16] On the eve of the league's last peacetime assembly, he analyzed the failed cooperation between Protestant North and Protestant South. The northerners "have been so slow and dilatory with their payments," he thought, "though the Brunswick affair concerned them more than it did the southerners and was undertaken for their benefit. Possibly, since they behave so slowly and improperly in their own cause, they would act even more slowly and improperly if the action took place in the South."[17] They would indeed, as the following months were to reveal.

The last chance for reform of any kind slipped away at Worms in the spring of 1546, when the allies gathered for the largest meeting of the league's assembly. Fifty-six chancellors, councilors, mayors, and attorneys represented thirty of the league's thirty-six members and eleven other Protestant or sympathetic nonmembers. But no princes, for the princes were at home making ready for war, and within a matter of weeks after Jacob Sturm's return from Worms, the league and the emperor were at war.

OPPOSITIONS AT STRASBOURG

MARTIN BUCER'S OPPOSITION

This unraveling of the league's fabric in the wake of the Brunswick affair resonated with disruptions of Sturm's policy on other levels. At Strasbourg, relations worsened between Sturm and Martin Bucer, the artisan's son who had become a churchman of Imperial rank. During the decade after Sturm had taken him to Marburg in 1529, Bucer's hand had touched other reformations all across South Germany in both cities (Bern, Basel, Nuremberg, Ulm, Frankfurt, and

Augsburg) and territories (Württemberg and Hesse), making him the Reformation's clerical broker in the South. Then, backed by his new Hessian patron, Bucer played more or less prominent roles in attempts to reform other lands, such as Cleves-Jülich and the prince-archbishoprics of Hamburg and Cologne. As his horizons expanded, Bucer, who was more heedless of existing laws and rights, advocated more radical enterprises than Sturm could swallow. While Sturm, for example, aimed to strengthen conciliar government in the league, Bucer called for a dictatorship, for "it would be better to have only one head with full authority and to give him some councilors. The Romans did this, and so did everyone who ever accomplished great deeds. They established a dictator without charge or limits but to assure that the city came to no harm. He had power over all money, people, and everything."[18]

The split between Sturm and Bucer over the league's governance echoed their differences about stricter religious discipline at Strasbourg. Bucer's view, if not his practice, was uncompromising. "We must revive and most zealously uphold moral discipline and conduct our common prayers most faithfully," he wrote, "for otherwise the Lord will not be with us. Our contributions of money, men, and whatever else is needed must have no other purpose or goal than to secure a proper peace and general, true reformation for the whole German nation."[19] Despite occasional fits of irenic spirit, Bucer was at heart a crusader who dreamed of a godly people marshalled behind an armed and godly ruler.

The expansion of Bucer's horizons beyond Strasbourg and the Upper Rhine liberated energies which he turned back critically upon Strasbourg's own—in his eyes—stalled reformation. During the late 1530s he reflected on how to push forward toward a more godly city, and he presented his idea of a "second reformation" in a work on pastoral theology, *On the True Cure of Souls and Correct Pastoral Service* (1538). Bucer was searching for a way to break or circumvent the magistrates' grip on Strasbourg's incomplete reformation, for although he now possessed all the marks of success—the deanship of St. Thomas, a big house, a handsome salary, and a new wife—the yearning for a purer, more disciplined church gnawed at him. As it left him no peace, so he left the magistrates none. "Truly," he wrote, "if we do not acknowledge, accept, hold to, and enforce God's holy covenant better than we do now, God will break it and will no longer be our God and Savior. He will deliver us most terribly into the hands of our enemies, to our ruin, both temporal and eternal, just as he did His people of old."[20]

Trouble arose between Bucer and his masters not when he formulated his ideas—they didn't care much what he wrote—but when he and some other pastors put them into practice. Sometime in late 1544 or early 1545, he and other clergymen organized circles of the devout—later called "Christian communities"—within their parishes. The groups were clearly meant to be models for the commune, for when their existence became generally known toward the end of 1545, Bucer wrote his

On the Church's Defects and Failings, which he submitted to the Senate & XXI on Epiphany (6 January) 1546. The book was a manifesto for a second reformation at Strasbourg. Its first sentence set the work's tone:

> One of the leading causes of the current ignorance of the difference between ecclesiastical and civil government is the people's feelings of great disdain and outrage, whenever the church's power of the keys is mentioned. They have insufficient knowledge of how the two governments differ from one another and the limits of each, imagining that they are subject to the authority of the temporal ruler alone.[21]

The church as a distinct kind of government! What a contrary song to the one Bucer had sung in the 1520s and early 1530s, when he had demanded magisterial action against the Catholics and the Anabaptists. Bucer now talked like a "new pope" who wanted to resurrect the clerical authority he had then denied, including the right to excommunicate, stricter religious discipline, and parish autonomy. All of which, predictably, the baffled magistrates refused to grant.

CLAUS KNIEBIS'S OPPOSITION

As Bucer agitated against Jacob Sturm's ecclesiastical settlement, Sturm's alliance policy also came under fire. Its principal critic was Ammeister Claus Kniebis, in happier days the political chief of Strasbourg's Evangelical movement. Although he had withdrawn from diplomacy after the Diet of Regensburg in 1532, a decade later, when the Smalkaldic League invaded Brunswick-Wolfenbüttel and the cities were once again struggling for their rights in the Imperial Diet, his patience with Sturm's policy broke. This policy, he felt, had sold the cities, their liberty, and their devotion to the Gospel into the clutches of greedy, heedless, and violent princes. At heart an old-fashioned particularist, Kniebis believed it best to return to the old policy of regional security based on urban solidarity, a variation on the lost dream of "turning Swiss." The ammeister's confidant was Basel's mayor, Bernhard Meyer (d. 1558), whom Kniebis asked to warn the Swiss that "we must not wait until we have been stripped clean of our wealth . . . or until some of us have been mediatized," but they must "care for one another with true brotherly love . . . [and] take the trouble of one as the concern of all and support one another's just and equal rights." Kniebis proposed to revive "the good, old neighborliness, which Strasbourg many years ago had with your friends, the Confederates, and especially with your city of Basel" to protect it from the princes, who "want the lion's share and treat us without fairness or justice. May Almighty God help us to free ourselves from these raging wolves!" Burghers—Evangelicals and Catholics alike—ought to stand together against this raging menace. The spirit of Kniebis's program was also Zwinglian, if Zwinglianism be taken to mean a linkage between worldly liberty and Christian freedom. It also bore a certain affinity to Bucer's dream of turning Strasbourg into a godly city.

The trouble with Kniebis's idea was that for eighty years all purely urban leagues had failed, and even in the days of "the good, old neighborliness," Strasbourg had also enjoyed friendly relations with a powerful prince of the region, the Elector Palatine. After the Palatine power was crushed in 1504, no other prince filled those shoes. Duke Ulrich, the terror of the free cities, was entirely unfit for the role, and Landgrave Philip of Hesse, the most likely candidate during the 1520s and 1530s, had fish to fry in other sectors of the Empire. Still, the niche for a powerful prince in the Southwest remained, only now he must be a Protestant. In 1544, as if evoked by this empty niche, a new candidate appeared. After years of Palatine vacillation, the Reformation was knocking at Heidelberg's gates.

THE PALATINE PROJECT

Once the chief princes of the Empire's western lands and natural leaders of aristocratic opposition to the monarchy, the Wittelsbach princes of the Rhenish-Palatine line had languished in torpor since their terrible defeat at Emperor Maximilian's hands in 1504. That war had chased Jacob Sturm home from the University of Heidelberg. The Palatine niche in the Southwest's political landscape remained empty all through the first twenty years of the Reformation movement, as Elector Louis V had pursued a policy of "laissez–faire, laissez–aller" in religion at home and confessional neutrality abroad. At Louis's death in 1544, however, a change was expected from his brother and successor, Frederick (r. 1544–56), known to some as "Frederick the Wise" and to others as "Frederick the Penniless." Long in Habsburg service, this elderly playboy had wooed several of the dynasty's princesses and finally married one, Dorothy, who brought him a definite but hopeless claim to the Danish throne. Protestant hearts stirred at Frederick's succession at Heidelberg in 1544, and though he initially made few changes, by the end of 1545 he seemed to be moving toward an open declaration for Evangelical religion and the Smalkaldic League.

Or so it seemed to Jacob Sturm, who had discussed religion with Frederick at Strasbourg in October 1538. Sturm and his brothers were Palatine vassals, of course, and through his dead wife's family, the Bocks, he possessed ties to several of the most powerful figures in the late elector's government. Over such paths, perhaps, came the first feelers to Sturm from a small group of Frederick's officials during the Imperial Diet at Worms in 1545. One of them, Philipp von Helmstett, later arranged to meet with Sturm secretly at Neckarhausen, where they talked in the mayor's house on 4 or 5 December. They formed a plan that Elector Frederick should be invited to the league's parliamentary assembly at Frankfurt, where the landgrave would persuade him to initiate religious reforms in his lands and to join the league. Sturm would broach this plan in the assembly's committee, as though it were merely his own idea, and recruit the landgrave and the others for the scheme. "We must strike," Helmstett pressed, and Sturm echoed, "while the iron is hot."[22]

For a time it looked as if they would succeed. Sturm duly planted the idea of inviting Frederick to Frankfurt and volunteered to head the embassy the league sent to Heidelberg on 11 January. In response, the elector did send envoys to Frankfurt, and although no agreement was reached, the whole matter looked very promising when the assembly disbanded in February.

When the allies reassembled at Worms in April, alas, the situation had changed. At the Palatine envoys' request, the league even lowered the military levies by a third, but shortly thereafter the judicious Frederick, as lukewarm a Protestant as he had been a Catholic, veered toward the Imperial camp. Thus slipped from Sturm's grasp the Palatine possibility, for the sake of which he had dissembled to his allies in the league and his colleagues at Strasbourg.

In characteristically Sturmian language, Sturm told Helmstett how much the Palatine project meant to him. "Personally," he said, "I view [the project] as both good and useful, and I will gladly and faithfully do whatever I can to help it forward. For if it comes to be, I can well imagine what it will mean to have the Palatinate firm for the Gospel, and I hope that others will feel the same." He thought it would promote the cause, perserving "the peace of the German nation," which "I will ever support with my poor ability." "I firmly believe," he went on, "that if everyone wholeheartedly seeks and clamors [for it], we will do it. If, however, this someone looks for this advantage and the other for another, it will go on such as we now see. May the Lord change it all for the better."[23] More immediately, of course, the admission of the Elector Palatine would have strengthened the league's southern wing and supplied the princely anchor that the free cities missed both in Landgrave Philip of Hesse and in Duke Ulrich.

By this time, as spring turned to summer 1546, the storm of war was coming fast. Watching the clouds darken, Landgrave Philip wrote gloomily in mid-May to his Strasbourg friends that "it seems to me that we no longer possess the spirit and the feeling that we all used to have." In the old days, he reflected, "we were far fewer in numbers, but we formed the league, assumed large tax burdens, and with God's help we accomplished many things, both great and small." Nowadays, by contrast, "when fortune smiles on us and our cause's need is greatest and comes to its critical point, we are so small-minded and so stingy with our money, our possession of which is not secure for an hour's time." "If we are stingy in this crisis," Philip warned his best allies, "we will save it only for our enemies' use, when we and our lands come under their yoke."[24] At this moment, a quarter-century since Luther had stood before Charles V at the Diet of Worms, the time had come to determine who was going to live under whose yoke.

NOTES

1. Miriam Usher Chrisman, *Strasbourg and the Reform: A Study in the Process of Change* (New Haven, 1967), 94.
2. "Ann. Brant," no. 4963.
3. *PC* 3:601, no. 572.
4. Lenz 3:318.
5. *PC* 3:675 n. 5. The remaining quotes in this paragraph come from Thomas A. Brady, Jr., *Ruling Class, Regime, and Reformation at Strasbourg, 1520–1555* (Leiden, 1978), 254.
6. *PC* 2:655, no. 654.
7. *PC* 3:674, no. 642.
8. Friedrich Roth, *Augsburgs Reformationsgeschichte*, 4 vols. (Munich, 1901–11), 3:325–26 (7 July 1545).
9. *PC* 3:479–80, no. 454.
10. Ibid., 572.
11. Ibid., 675 n. 5.
12. Ibid., 698.
13. Ibid., 700.
14. *PC* 4:82, no. 62.
15. Ibid., 24, no. 23.
16. Ibid., 30, no. 29 n. 5.
17. Ibid., 58, no. 49.
18. Lenz 2:373, no. 220.
19. Ibid., 373, no. 220.
20. Martin Greschat, *Martin Bucer: Ein Reformator und seine Zeit 1491–1551* (Munich, 1990), 211.
21. *BDS* 17:159, line 3.
22. Adolf Hasenclever, "Kurfürst Friedrich II. von der Pfalz und der schmalkaldische Bundestag zu Frankfurt vom Dezember 1545: Ein Beitrag zur pfälzischen Reformationsgeschichte," *Zeitschrift für die Geschichte des Oberrheins* 57 (1903): 76, 80.
23. Ibid., 80–81.
24. Lenz 2:441, no. 235.

12

THE SMALKALDIC WAR

Peace shall go sleep with Turks and infidels,
And in this seat of peace tumultuous wars
Shall kin with kin and kind with kind confound;
Disorder, horror, fear and mutiny
Shall here inhabit, and this land be called
The field of Golgotha and dead men's skulls.
　　　　　　　—Shakespeare, *Richard II* 4.1. lines 139–44

The Emperor Charles V stopped in March 1546 at Speyer on his way from
the Netherlands to Regensburg, whither he had called the Imperial Diet. Among
those who came to meet him was Landgrave Philip of Hesse, hawk on arm,
with two hundred retainers. After the hunt, as emperor and prince sat over
dinner, Charles asked the Hessian prince how things stood with the Smalkaldic
League. "My Gracious Lord Emperor," Philip replied, "I lack only one man."
When Charles inquired whom he meant, Philip responded, "Why, I mean to
have Your Imperial Majesty among the pious folk." Charles chuckled, "No,
no, I will not join the party of error."[1]

All joking aside, by Eastertide 1546 Landgrave Philip and his allies found
themselves in sad disarray. A rumor was circulating, Augsburg's town clerk
told the landgrave in March, that the league's southern wing was "in a state of
great mistrust and misunderstanding, and especially Sir Jacob Sturm is said to
have become mistrusted, which greatly threatens the whole common enterprise
and especially the southern cities."[2] The Strasbourgeois were reported to be
negotiating "a privilege from the king of France, which will favor their affairs
to the disadvantage of the other cities."[3]

War was in the wind, and to all appearances the contest would be an un-
equal one. On the one side, the Catholics: with the French and Ottoman
fronts now at peace, pope, emperor, and Bavarian duke were negotiating the
financial and strategic basis of a German campaign. On the other side, the
Protestants: the Smalkaldic League dissolving into each man for himself and
the Devil take the hindmost. Martin Luther had foretold a great war between
the princes and the emperor, to which the Peasants' War of 1525 would seem

201

in retrospect but a prelude. His death on 18 February 1546 could be taken as a portent of the coming struggle.

THE COMING OF THE WAR

Regensburg, where Charles V arrived on 10 April, hummed with the reckless excitement that commonly signals an imminent catastrophe. The theologians' colloquy, which had resumed on 27 January 1546, droned on for six weeks in a spirit of meanness, acrimony, and intransigence on both sides, and when Charles arrived to open the Diet, the poisoned atmosphere and sparse attendance quashed his remaining faith in talk with the Protestants. Jacob Sturm agreed, for by May it was clear, as he wrote to the landgrave, "by means of these colloquys, national assemblies, diets, or other institutional paths, no truly Christian concord can be hoped for at this time." His mood was dark and resigned. "Just as religion in the time of Jesus, the apostles, and the martyrs spread against the will and consent of the Jewish and pagan authorities," he mused, "so today a household, tomorrow another, then a village, and finally a whole land receives the faith, which gradually comes to prevail despite all persecution."[4] Persecution, martyrdom, and ultimate triumph—grim thoughts as the Empire plunged toward the long-expected civil war.

When Charles V decided that the German schism would not yield to colloquys and learned that the Protestants refused to attend the Council of Trent, his last doubts fell away. By mid-June he was asking Queen Mary and the bishops to prepare for war. He also offered royal marriages to cement the loyalties of two leading Catholic dynasties, Cleves-Jülich and Bavaria, while treaties with Pope Paul III and with Duke Moritz of Saxony promised money and troops for the coming campaign. The emperor's mobilization orders went out on 10 June, while the Diet dragged on at Regensburg, and the papal troops started northward toward Germany at the beginning of July, just as Charles was announcing the deposition of Cologne's Elector Herman (3 July). Meanwhile, the Smalkaldic chiefs met at Ichtershausen near Erfurt, issued orders for the league's mobilization, and sent embassies to France and to England for aid.

MOBILIZATIONS

The league's southern cities responded to their commanders' call with dispatch, offering to pay even more than the three double-months initially levied for the war. Their commander, Sebastian Schertlin von Burtenbach (1486–1577), struck with eleven thousand foot and twenty-six guns toward the Upper Lech, hoping to disrupt Austrian musters and prevent the papal troops from joining Charles. This raid aside, the Danube campaign nonetheless began much as Charles's experts had planned. His Germans and Spaniards and the pope's Italians—in all about thirty-six thousand foot, six thousand horse, and seventy guns—united at Landshut in Bavaria on 13 August, only three weeks after the Diet had risen on 24 July. They faced the league's somewhat stronger army with more than one hundred guns, which had combined near Ingolstadt at the beginning of August. At the Protestants' backs, however, came a Netherlandish army, twelve thousand foot and eight thousand horse under Maximilian Egmont, count of Buren, who slipped by the league's shadowing forces, crossed the Rhine unhindered at Bingen, and marched southeastward to play anvil to the emperor's hammer.

Rarely in sixteenth-century warfare did a strategic plan so nearly succeed as the emperor's did in the Danube campaign. Time was on his side, for the league could only win by attacking and winning an early, decisive battle. Count William of Fürstenberg (1491–1549), an experienced commander, told them as much after inspecting their troops. "Dear lords and friends," he said, "you have laid your preparations very well. But Emperor Charles is a warrior not for a summer but for several years, if he must. You are lost, for Charles is a fighter and can stand a long war, which you cannot. In the end, though you don't see it now, you will not prevail against him."[5]

The moment of decision at Ingoldstadt fell after a two-day bombardment of the Imperial entrenchments on 31 August and 1 September. Despite the menace of Buren's oncoming Netherlanders at their backs, the Smalkaldic chiefs failed to order the assault, and at this moment, probably, they lost the war. Instead of attacking, they moved off upstream. Charles and his army followed, and now the campaign became a running play of feint-and-duck, the Protestants afraid to stop and give battle, Charles unwilling to risk his entire force against them. Eventually, the Smalkaldic chiefs went into camp outside of Giengen, while Charles moved off toward Ulm and also pitched camp. To the astonishment of all observers, there was no more combat, and bad weather, poor rations, lack of pay, and disease received full play to wear the two armies down.

STRASBOURG'S CONTRIBUTIONS

The city of Strasbourg contributed heavily to the Smalkaldeners' campaign on the Danube. Its regime supplied three men to help run the war: Ulman Böcklin von Böcklinsau, who accompanied the army as war councilor; his brother, Wolff, who served as delegate to the league's southern district at Ulm; and the secretary Michel Han, who served both in the southern district's assembly and in the treasury, which was created at Ulm to manage the army's finances. Strasbourg also played a major role in the financing of the campaign: more than 210,000 rhfl. in direct levies, plus the loans taken up at home, in Switzerland, and at Lyon. Finally, the city served as a supply point for troops on the march and as a communications node between the commanders and the league's agents abroad.

Considering the extent of Strasbourg's contributions to the Danube campaign, Jacob Sturm's absence from the front, until just before the end, begs for explanation. Between Easter Sunday (25 April) and the beginning of November, Sturm remained at Strasbourg, although time and again he was urged and begged to the front. Instead, he managed communications with the envoys in France and in England, a largely fruitless enterprise, because Jean Sturm's four missions to France and Johann von Niedbruck's three to England yielded only one loan that arrived too late to save the league.

Why did Sturm retreat into the shadows during the Smalkaldic War? Perhaps because he saw the war as a fruit of political failure, as God's judgment on the Protestants, and as a call to martyrdom. In July he had written to Count Palatine Otto Henry (b. 1502, r. 1556–59), that "if it must come, we on our side are determined to stick to God and His Word, and to risk all that we have for their sake. May the Lord grant us His grace, and that, if we must suffer, we bear it with Christian forbearance, so that we do not betray Our Jesus Christ for the sake of worldly advantage."[6]

Sturm realized that his inaction had disappointed others' expectations, and in November, when he finally arrived in the Smalkaldeners' camp near Giengen, he tried to justify his behavior. "Since this war began last summer between the emperor and the Christian allies," he said, "a great deal of damage has been done to both sides and to the German nation. I have observed this with deep sadness, and I would much rather, had it been God's will, that this terrible war had never been begun. In that case, I would have stayed at Strasbourg." Now, however, "I see that the war has become a long one and may become longer, on which account I decided to leave Strasbourg on behalf of the peace, order, and unity of the German nation, to place myself at the service of the elector of Saxony, the landgrave of Hesse, and the war council, and to demonstrate to them how the continuation of the war will ruin and destroy all law and order, nobility, property, and morals in the German nation."[7] Missed opportunities, impending defeat, signs of human failure, and God's displeasure—all because of a war which should never have been fought.

THE DANUBE CAMPAIGN

Sturm had plenty of reason to be depressed, for the Danube campaign unmasked the Smalkaldic League's crippled solidarity. "Money," as the saying went, "is the nerve of war," and Sturm's colleague, Ammeister Claus Kniebis, had predicted that "if we cannot raise large sums for our side, it will go badly for us."[8] Indeed it would, and the league's failure to supply enough money matched the commanders' failure to strike the emperor early and hard.

The root of the financial problem was the northern allies' simple refusal to pay their shares of the league's levies. While the southerners paid—Württemberg, Augsburg, Ulm, and Strasbourg together coughed up 72 percent of the league's war levies—the northerners sent little or nothing. No wonder Strasbourg's XIII complained so bitterly that "if all members of the league paid their eighteen double-months, we reckon, it would yield more than 3,000,000 rhfl., with which the army could be maintained for some time."[9] The northerners, who had been glad enough for southern money to rid them of Henry of Brunswick-Wolfenbüttel, looked on and kept a close grip on their pursestrings.

JACOB STURM AT THE FRONT

The allies' failure grimly realized all of Jacob Sturm's warnings during the failed negotiations on reform of the league. He had every reason to be depressed, therefore, and when he finally did come to the front in early November, he brought no words of hope. At Ulm, where the league's assembly was meeting in continuous session, Sturm announced that although his regime was willing to levy a direct tax of 1 percent on their subjects—the old Common Penny—"it would not be enough." He reminded the envoys that "if, at the beginning of the war, the southern allies had sat quietly at home, which they could have done, the war would have taken place in Saxony and Hesse."[10] "In these most important negotiations," Württemberg's war councilor wrote to Stuttgart, "I was glad to have had Sir Jacob Sturm, a partisan of the Gospel and a talented and experienced man, come here and speak devoutly, ably, moderately, and impartially," even though his words were "disheartening and without consolation, and neither I nor the other allies got counsel from him how this whole situation is to be dealt with."[11] They got no counsel, because Sturm had none left.

From Ulm to the army's camp near the little free city of Giengen was not far, and Sturm's arrival there on 10 November can only have deepened his depression. He found no psalm-singing host of fighters for the Lord but a typical sixteenth-century army of tough, hard-drinking mercenaries. "We live such a life," the Prussian envoy wrote home, "full of eating, drinking, blaspheming, and bad conduct, that it would be no wonder if God, instead of sparing His elect, would punish us." The clergy's sermons had no effect, he sighed, "and I hope that, like David, we will be punished by God and not by the enemy."[12]

In this setting Sturm made his last play. Strasbourg's government, he said, was determined not to approve a "dishonorable settlement," though as things stood, "perhaps they will have to alter their policy."[13] In desperation he pleaded for the princes to attack the foe, whose "inquisitions and edicts show that he wants to uproot our religion entirely. Besides, to sue for peace would diminish our stature and drive away potential allies." The best policy, therefore, "is to give battle, though I cannot tell whether it is feasible. I have hope, however, that if we attempt it, God will grant us good fortune." At this moment, alas, fortune would no longer yield to patience, but to God alone. And to action, for Sturm pleaded with the princes not to abandon the South without attacking the emperor, "who is tired and weak, and driving him from the field. After that, what the elector of Saxony [i.e., through Duke Moritz's invasion of his lands] has lost can easily be recouped."[14] Far better to seek a battle of decision "than to let the army sit in camp and be ruined and die from the cold and wet and other causes," for then the emperor will "easily gain new strength from the bishops and others, who until now have been dissuaded by fear, and will attack Württemberg and the southern cities with forces greater than they can withstand." Desperate for action, Sturm harangued the commanders and envoys. "If you are so little committed," he said, "that for the sake of money alone you are willing to sacrifice your people instead of accepting minor damages, then, truly, I don't know what to say. I do believe, however, it is a great foolishness to let this army withdraw from the South."[15] These hot words fell on ears of stone. No wonder, for at the army's back the troops of King Ferdinand and Duke Moritz were ravaging John Frederick's lands, and Hesse would be the next item on their menu.

Returning to Ulm, Sturm urged the same policy—action, attack—on the assembly and recapitulated the reasons for which they were fighting. "What my lords and others have done here in the South," he said on 19 November, his voice dark with emotion, "concerns both temporal and eternal life, and the matter now stands so, that we must either lay down our tools or see how we can rescue it." If legislating the Common Penny did not help the situation, "then I know no other way."[16] Nor did the other envoys, whereupon Sturm, now at the end of his tether, made one last plea: "Here is how it stands. The cities cannot pay another assessment, and there is no other solution. Either we pay the Common Penny or nothing!"[17] He might as well have shouted into the wind, for the assembly would not vote a direct property tax. In the Smalkaldic League, as in the Imperial Diet, the direct tax stood for centralization and for weakening the several powers' autonomy in favor of a common purpose and direction. The assembly's refusal, in the face of military defeat and against the pleas of its premier politician, to alter this policy demonstrates how thoroughly the political program of German Protestantism had melded with the political traditions of late medieval particularism. Sturm, who struggled against this symbiosis, struggled in vain. As the assembly rose, the league's commanders started their forces for home.

THE BREAK WITH LANDGRAVE PHILIP

This bitter failure shattered the last bonds of trust between Jacob Sturm and Landgrave Philip of Hesse. Sturm made one more plea in writing: "For otherwise, if you retreat and leave the enemy the field with the freedom to crush us one after another, and if God shows us no way to help His people and His churches, we Germans will lose our reputation among all other nations, and the just cause of the Holy Gospel will be besmirched."[18] In despair, Sturm reached for highly uncharacteristic, apocalyptic language. There could be no peace, he wrote to the landgrave, for the Protestants could never "secure, now or ever, any acceptable peace from the enemy, unless we surrender God and His word. You are dealing not only with the emperor but with the Antichrist at Rome, who instigated and organized this whole thing against us."[19] Heated words, reckless words, the language of a Martin Bucer, perhaps, but not of a politician who believed that patience could conquer fortune.

Landgrave Philip, his decision for retreat taken, remained proof against Sturm's pleas. He'd had a belly full of this kind of war, in which "the doctors and secretaries want to be soldiers, and the soldiers want to be doctors."[20] Sturm, he thought, simply didn't understand the military situation. "Whoever told you the emperor was weak," he wrote on 22 November, "was surely wrong, for we know from some of our nobles, whom the emperor had captured, and from our spies that he is very strong." Philip wrote these words on the very day that his army started for home.[21] Anticlimactic, this exchange, but it was not yet the end between Landgrave Philip and Jacob Sturm.

In November's waning days, Cousin Wolff Böcklin at his side, Sturm rode westward over the Swabian Jura and down into the Neckar Valley, bound for home in a mood of deepest dejection. Stopping at Stuttgart on 27 November, he found, to his surprise, that Landgrave Philip had just arrived on a final, wretched mission to beg more money from his former client, Duke Ulrich. They came together one last time—Landgrave Philip, Duke Ulrich, and Jacob Sturm—the winning team from the glory days of 1534. And Philip recalled those days, as well he might, when he asked Ulrich for 50,000 rhfl. When the duke refused, Philip turned to Sturm to ask "if such a sum couldn't be raised at Strasbourg." "This is surely impossible," Sturm replied, for "even if the regime were willing, they could not raise such a sum in the city; the sums they have spent on this war were raised from their own citizens."[22] There the matter stood. With the South lost and the league's heartlands in peril, the landgrave rode off to rejoin his retreating army and Jacob Sturm headed for home. The Smalkaldic League's two architects never met again.

SURRENDER OR RESISTANCE?

It was the morning of 8 December 1546, and in the chamber of Strasbourg's Senate & XXI all eyes were glued on Jacob Sturm as the aging statesman rose to report on his mission to the Danube front. After hearing his words, the magistrates appointed Sturm and three colleagues to recommend action: "Whether the war should be continued, or we should seek peace, and whether and how the Common Penny should be collected."[23] Meanwhile, the 300,000 gulden from Lyon arrived—far too late, for Duke Ulrich, Ulm, and other allies were already suing the emperor for peace.

THE DEBATE AT STRASBOURG

On the new year's fourth day, Sturm and three colleagues laid out the arguments for and against the only possible courses of action, surrender and resistance.[24] If the Strasbourgeois made peace with the emperor, they would betray their allies and, "according to the custom of the Latin nation, few or none of the terms would be honored." Eventually, the emperor would require attendance at the papal council, and "we would then have to reestablish the Mass and all papal ordinances and to restore the ecclesiastical properties." The city would also lose its ancient immunity from paying homage to the emperor, it would have to submit to the Imperial Chamber Court's Catholic judges, and it would be taxed "according to the emperor's pleasure, just as in his hereditary lands." Furthermore, the Imperial troops quartered on Strasbourg would "harm women and children, levy contributions, and do as they please, to which we are quite unaccustomed," and the bishop would recover his "old rights."

Resistance, the alternative course, would lead just as surely to ruin. A siege would bring threats from the city's own mercenaries, shortage of money and provisions, and devastation of the countryside, "on which the city mostly depends for its rents and dues." Even without a siege, Imperial cavalry would still harry the countryside, "so that the rich burghers, merchants, and also the common burghers and artisans could not do their business." If the emperor outlawed the city, which was likely, no one would pay his debts to the city or its citizens, and all payment of interest by foreigners would cease. Moreover, "if the nobles and rich burghers received no interest, rents, or other dues, they would hardly be able to maintain their standing, nor would the common artisan, who depends on the nobles and the rich and lives from them." Then, too, there was "the unreliability of the Common Man, who perhaps at first favored the cause, but, now that things have gone badly, might suddenly turn about and favor a treaty, since he has little to lose—unlike the rich." Finally, if Strasbourg resisted, it would resist alone, "for it is not to be expected that our allies will be able to raise another army."[25]

Surrender or resistance, two paths, each leading to ruin. The Senate & XXI decided to consult the Schöffen, and on 19 January five squads of magistrates polled them in their guildhalls: 180 Schöffen opposed any dealings with the emperor, because, they said, whatever he promised, he would not keep his word. To Sturm and perhaps others, who knew that the city would have to negotiate, this highly unwelcome vote signaled future trouble.

At its outbreak, the Smalkaldic War had not aroused much enthusiasm at Strasbourg. The Catholic painter Sebald Büheler reports that "I never saw anyone, in the streets or elsewhere, fall on his knees" during the moment of official prayer for victory.[26] Gradually, however, among the guildsmen sentiment for resistance and against the emperor had grown stronger, and Bucer and other preachers strove to unite their little "Christian communities" with this shift in the popular mood. They made it hot for the magistrates, who, one source reported, "are doing nothing about the situation."[27] Still others whispered that "my lords are divided, and that Sir Mathis Pfarrer two or three times tried to run out of the chamber, saying that he had to tell this to the commune, but he was pulled back by his coattails."[28]

In the midst of the furor, just as some burghers suspected, Sturm and his colleagues were planning Strasbourg's surrender to Charles V. At the end of January came the first peace feelers from Chancellor Granvelle, who proposed through Sturm's kinsman, the former Augsburger Wolfgang Rehlinger (d. 1557), that Strasbourg must "make a proper submission," abandon the league and agree not to enter another, support and obey the Chamber Court, and pay "a tolerable fine." In return, Charles would restore the city and citizens to grace, forgive them their actions as belligerents, confirm their privileges, and promise not to suppress their religion by force. These very generous terms reflected Granvelle's appreciation for Strasbourg's impregnability and for its proximity to France. And the terms were accepted, as on 31 January, Sturm and his committee—all staunch Evangelicals—recommended that Granvelle should be told "that we will enter negotiations."[29] First, however, they needed the Schöffen's approval, which they got, but barely, on 3 February with 162 votes out of 300. The opposition was loud and belligerent, and Hans Mennlich of the tailors accused Jacob Sturm of duplicity, throwing in his teeth his own words of last summer "that the emperor has never kept faith."[30]

The surrender to the Emperor Charles V in February 1547 was one of the great political coups of Jacob Sturm's career. It was unthinkable, given what was happening to other allies, that Strasbourg, a principal belligerent, should escape from the Smalkaldic War with its liberties and reformed religion entirely intact. Yet this is exactly what happened. In return, Strasbourg's leaders began to transform their rebel city into a loyal Protestant city in the Nuremberg mold. Sturm defeated the party of resistance the only way he could, by gradually rallying the guilds' notables to his policy of peace.

Great risk attended the early stages of Sturm's new course. In the initial poll of the Schöffen on 19 January 1547, the hard division for peace or resistance ran roughly along class lines: the patricians, the merchants, and the rich generally favored peace, while the militant resisters mostly came from poorer trades and poorer guilds. One bastion of resistance was the Masons' Guild, whose Georg Büheler demanded that "the whoredom so prevalent among rich and poor must be punished, and it would not hurt to purge the regime of evildoers, both nobles and commoners."[31] In the middle, however, stood a considerable group which wanted peace, if it could be had "with honor," that is, without compromising the city's liberties and religion. Sturm won out by rallying this middle to the government's side, thereby isolating the party of resistance. By the ancient rule of self-governing cities' politics, the stability of rule by the elite depended on keeping the support of middling folk. On the other side, the agitating preachers knew what they wanted—"to establish the right of excommunication in their own hands"[32]—and they saw their chance in the split over surrender or resistance. They were defeated, however, at least partly because, at the crucial moment, they came forward with no alternative policy. Two possible alternatives were to turn Swiss or to turn French. In fact, there was nothing much in either alternative. Rumors flew—all false—that Strasbourg, Augsburg, Constance, and Duke Ulrich would join the Swiss Confederacy rather than submit, while the French alliance, the natural resort of all resisters to the emperor, proved impossible, both because the militant Protestants at Strasbourg hated the French king as a persecutor, and because King Francis I died on the last day of March 1547.

THE SURRENDER

The peace negotiations crept forward in deepest secrecy, and on 10 February after dark a forester named Veltin slipped into Strasbourg to give Sturm and Conrad Joham the emperor's safe-conduct and letters from Jean de Naves and Wolfgang Rehlinger. Next day Sturm read them to the Senate & XXI and prepared his instructions, which rejected the renunciation of the league as unnecessary, since the league would expire in two weeks' time (on 27 February 1547), but conceded the prohibition of future alliances. The oath of allegiance, if absolutely required, should be taken by the ammeister and XXI alone "in the name of the whole city," and the ritual submission was also to be made. In return, the regime hoped that no troops would be stationed in Alsace, that the emperor would confirm the city's traditional liberties, and that the religious questions would be settled not through force but "through a regular, Christian, amicable way in an Imperial Diet."[33] Then, Sturm, Mathis Pfarrer, and a young patrician named Marx Hag (ca. 1510–51) crossed the Rhine and rode over the Black Forest and eastward to Ulm, where they found the emperor in the company of his court and twenty-four thousand veteran troops.

The lord of all South Germany was a man in a hurry, for King Ferdinand and Duke Moritz awaited his approach to strike John Frederick's army in Saxony. Charles needed a swift victory over the Protestant chiefs in order to stave off decisions by the Council of Trent (now sitting at Bologna) that might trump his own plan for a German settlement. When they came to occupied Ulm on 19 February, the Strasbourgeois got in touch with Granvelle's son, Bishop Antoine Perrenot (1517–86) of Arras, who thought the fine they offered to pay—30,000 gulden—puny. The final terms required Strasbourg to renounce the league and all other alliances, to swear an oath of loyalty, and to furnish Charles with several large cannon.

THE SELLING OF SURRENDER

Now came the difficult task of selling the terms to the Schöffen back home. When they assembled on 5 March for a third vote on peace or resistance, the ammeister read the long speech that Sturm had drafted for him. This masterpiece of Sturmian oratory announced the terms "on which the whole city of

Strasbourg and its people might be reconciled with the emperor," namely, a fine of 30,000 gulden—much less than others had to pay—plus six siege guns and six field pieces. To refuse these terms would condemn city and burghers "plus the whole neighboring countryside to war and total ruin and to the humiliation and crimes against women and children, which war brings with it." Coming to the oath, a sticking point, Sturm told—through the mouth of Ammeister Jacob von Duntzenheim (d. 1554)—of how his great-grandfather, Old Peter Schott, and Philips von Mülnheim had journeyed in 1473 to Metz to see Emperor Frederick III and, acceding to the emperor's demand, had sworn an oath in the commune's name. How much more willingly, this little lesson in civic history asked, should the commune swear "now, with this very powerful emperor and in these circumstances?" Any oath was preferable to resistance, for "when we are destitute and ruined, . . . we will have to surrender unconditionally." "Dear friends," Sturm's speech concluded, "you can easily understand why we are inclined more to peace than to war." Stripped of human powers to resist, the city could expect no aid from above, for "because we see . . . how little preaching of the Gospel has changed our lives, we cannot presume that the Almighty will uphold His honor and name in other ways and, because of our devotion, perform a special miracle." The emperor's terms "will be better and less costly for the city of Strasbourg and its citizens than war against such a popular emperor, who now has almost half the German nation in his grip." These words moved minds, and 243 Schöffen empowered the Senate & XXI to conclude peace on the stipulated terms. In six weeks, support for Sturm's peace policy had grown from less than a third (32.9 percent) to more than four-fifths (81 percent) of the officials of the guilds.

Jacob Sturm rode out again on 9 March, this time accompanied by Marx Hag and a wealthy merchant named Friedrich von Gottesheim, both of whom spoke French. At Pforzheim, where they stopped briefly, Sturm heard the pathetic story of Duke Ulrich's submission, how at Ulm on 4 March the gouty old sinner had to be carried in a chair into the emperor's presence and "to apologize, while seated, for his inability to make his submission on his knees."[34] Sturm and his companions found the emperor at Nördlingen on 13 March. During their audience in the afternoon of 21 March, delayed by an attack of Imperial gout, Sturm and his companions knelt before the monarch to make their city's submission in the presence of a mere thirty persons.

Strasbourg was reconciled, the envoys thought, as their sovereign climbed back in his litter to begin the painful passage of Franconia toward Nuremberg and on to Saxony to crush the remaining Protestant rebels. The treaty of 21 March 1547 "composed," as Sturm put it, the breach between emperor and free city in terms very like those Granvelle had proposed in February. Whether, even with the Schöffen's backing, the terms could be sold to the broader public at Strasbourg, remained to be seen.

Martin Bucer, sensing Sturm's imminent victory, at last turned southward for inspiration: "Look how God made and kept the Swiss free!"[35] "One needs only biblical courage and willingness to fight, for all else—money, food, supplies—God will provide!" The entire predicament, he wrote to Landgrave Philip, had arisen from the magistrates' refusal of his demand "that religion ought to be properly ordered and maintained." They "are in great fear of God and the Common Man," he sneered, and he praised Elector John Frederick's stalwart resistance, for "that is the right way, even if it leads to death, for [such a] death will place him high in esteem before God and men—which, surely, is the highest thing a pious and godfearing man can desire." "Dear God," Bucer raged against Sturm's treaty, "blessed is he who now finds death through his trust in God! God's Son will now surely show Himself and proclaim and enforce *His* treaty, which says that all lordship is His alone." Landgrave Philip, who knew a lot about lordship, commented sarcastically, "I marvel at how the wise, godfearing folk at Strasbourg could do no better, for they have never seen a foe or suffered a siege, and they have such a strong, well provisioned and populated city with the Swiss and French at their backs."[36]

It remained for Sturm to persuade the Strasbourgeois to choose good sense over martyrdom. The first thing, once he had reported on his mission, was to get after the preachers and their followers, whose conventicles had raised a howl of protest upon his return from Nördlingen.[37] By this time, Bucer and some other preachers aimed at nothing less than defeat of the treaty and overthrow of the magisterial church order of 1534. They planned to do it by the method, tested and tried during the early 1520s, of raising the common people against the magistrates by appealing from the magistrates and the Schöffen to the whole commune. "The Common Man resists," Bucer wrote to the landgrave, "he demands to be consulted both individually and as a whole and not just through the guilds. For it was the common man who was the cause of [the restoration of] religion."[38] It was indeed, and Sturm was determined that such a thing would never happen again.

The opposition, just as Bucer said, presented a demand that the treaty come before the entire commune, not just the Schöffen. This demand was unprecedented. It was also inflammatory in a city which lay, as many thought, on the verge of insurrection. Though tempted to yield the point and consult the entire commune, the Senate & XXI decided to address the Schöffen alone on 20 April. This time the case for peace was framed by the aging Claus Kniebis, long Sturm's critic but also a friend of law and order. His address emphasized the emperor's assurance "that concerning religion" everything would remain as it was until the whole matter was decided "by a General Council or through other, proper ways and means." This done, the magistrates received the Imperial commissioner, Christoph von Schauenburg, who found the unrest in the city unsettling. Sturm reassured him that "my lords are agreed about this,"[39] and he and Mathis Pfarrer escorted Schauenburg to city hall, where the magistrates swore the oath of loyalty to the emperor. The date was 25 April 1547, and no one at Strasbourg knew that on the day before, the emperor and his allies had crushed Elector John Frederick's army at Mühlberg on the River Elbe.

The oath sworn, the next task was to restore law and order. The magistrates sought out and warned those accused of "harmful talk," admonished rumormongers and grumblers against the preachers, investigated dereliction among guards of the city gates, arrested and jailed obdurate agitators, and forbade public gatherings, such as the annual parade of the bakers' apprentices on Ascension Day. Odd things were happening. One day in church a country woman called "Longnails" cried out during the service that "the emperor is coming, and the altars and the Mass will be restored."[40] She was taken and ejected from the city. The atmosphere was further troubled by the deep and pervasive prejudice against the "Latins," an old problem at Strasbourg. The natives tended to "make no distinctions among Spaniards, Italians, and Frenchmen," even "though some have been driven from their own lands because of their faith."[41] The party of opposition played on such prejudices to feed fears of the "Latin" emperor and his troops. The magistrates quashed such talk and warned offending preachers "to preach the Word of God . . . and say nothing about the news that runs about."[42] Such steps, plus denunciations, arrests, jailings, and threats did their work, and by late summer Sturm and his colleagues had the reins of law and order firmly in hand.

There remained one great point, the settlement concerning religion, and it lay in the hands of an emperor who was now truly master in his Imperial house. On 19 May at Wittenberg, John Frederick of Saxony had signed over his electorate and parts of his lands to his cousin, Duke Moritz, who for his collaboration with Charles was now reviled by other German Protestants as "the German Judas" and "the Judas of Meissen." The Hessian landgrave, too, bent his knee while his chancellor read a plea for mercy. The Holy Roman Empire was no England, Charles V was no Henry VIII, and so the Smalkaldic chiefs kept their heads—but, for the moment, little else. By early July, the two captive princes in tow, Charles was moving southward through eastern Franconia toward the Danube and Augsburg. Now at the summit of his career, an armed and armored conqueror just as Titian painted him, the forty-seven-year-old monarch was coming back to the Imperial heartlands in the South, where he meant to settle the German schism.

NOTES

1. *PC* 4:93, no. 65 n. 1.
2. Lenz 3:400.
3. Ibid., 404.

4. Lenz 2:450 n. 2.
5. I have put together two different versions of this story from the *Zimmerische Chronik*, ed. Karl August von Barack, 4 vols. (Tübingen, 1869), 3:19, line 28 to 20, line 4, and 425, lines 14–23.
6. PC 4:235, no. 208.
7. Ibid., 479–80, no. 451. My translation transposes the text into the first person.
8. Ibid., 260, no. 239.
9. Ibid., 398–99, no. 375.
10. Ibid., 475, no. 449 n. 2.
11. Ibid., 476, no. 449 n. 5.
12. Asverus von Brandt, ed., *Berichte und Briefe des Rats und Gesandten Herzog Albrechts von Preußen*, ed. Adalbert Bezzenberger, 2 vols. (Königsberg i. Pr., 1904), 2:212, no. 73.
13. PC 4:478, no. 450.
14. Ibid., 488–90, no. 458, from which come the remaining quotes in this paragraph.
15. Lenz 2:494–95, no. 252.
16. PC 4:491–92, no. 460.
17. Ibid., 492, no. 460 n. 2.
18. Ibid., 494–95, no. 462; and there, too, the following quote.
19. Ibid., 495, no. 462.
20. Walter Möllenberg, ed., "Die Verhandlungen im Schmalkaldischen Lager vor Giengen und Landgraf Philipps Rechenschaftsbericht," *Zeitschrift des Vereins für hessische Geschichte und Landeskunde* 38 (1904): 34.
21. PC 4:495–97, no. 463, from which the following quote also comes.
22. Landgrave Philip to Elector John Frederick, Stuttgart, 27 November 1547, in StA Weimar, Reg. I, pagg. 190–193, J, no. 1, fols. 57^r–60^r, here at 58^r; and the following quote is at 58^v.
23. PC 4:508, no. 474.
24. Ibid., 556–57, no. 514, from which come the quotes in this and in the following paragraph.
25. Ibid., 558, no. 515, from which come the quotes in this paragraph.
26. Sebald Büheler, "La chronique strasbourgeoise," ed. Léon Dacheux, in *BSCMHA*, 2d ser., 13 (1888): nos. 302–3.
27. AMS, XXI 1546, fols. 644^r, 648^v–49^r, 653^r.
28. Ibid., fol. 22^r.
29. PC 4:588–91, no. 545.
30. Ibid., 656, no. 586 n. 8.
31. Brady, *Ruling Class*, 271.
32. AMS, XXI 1547, fols. 41^r, 63^v, 64^r, 65^r; PC 4:656, no. 586 n. 7.
33. PC 4:605, no. 555.
34. Ibid., 659, no. 580.
35. Lenz 2:490–92, no. 250.
36. Ibid., 498, no. 253.
37. PC 4:668–69, no. 593 n. 10.
38. Lenz 2:493, no. 251.
39. PC 4:692, no. 614.
40. AMS, XXI 1547, fols. 363^v–64^r.
41. Ibid., fol. 4^v.
42. Ibid., fol. 345^{r-v}.

13

DEFEAT AND REVOLUTION

Let war yield to peace, laurels to paeans.

—Cicero

"Is it peace?" And Jehu said, "What hast thou to do with peace? Turn thee behind me."

—II Kings 9:18

Flushed with victory and wracked by gout, Charles V was moving slowly southward during the summer of 1547. From Strasbourg, Jacob Sturm watched the conquering emperor's progress in a mood of deepening anxiety. If Charles were to come as near as Ulm or Speyer, he mused on 1 July, "he will not neglect to visit this city, too, for he some time ago expressed a wish to see it. His desire to enhance his reputation abroad, especially in France, will bring him hither to display his power over this city, which abroad has a reputation for strength greater than it deserves."[1] All southwestern Germany lay open to the approaching monarch, for "there is hardly a fortified place not in his hands, except for Strasbourg, and it is to be feared that he will want to have this one as well." Strasbourg, after all, "was the principal city in the league and was more disobedient than any other."[2] What to do? If it came to a siege, Sturm thought, "in the end, as one says, the city must 'come to the stake' and surrender."

THE ARMORED DIET OF AUGSBURG, 1547–1548

In the event, Sturm mistook Charles's intentions, for the emperor aimed to establish not a centralized royal regime, what the Germans called a "monarchy," as the Protestants feared, but an Imperial peace-keeping federation of the traditional German sort, though on an immense scale. He assembled the Estates at Augsburg in late summer 1547 to discuss this proposal and to negotiate what he intended to be a settlement of the religious schism. This "armored Diet," so named by Johannes Sleidan "because of the many soldiers present,"[3] was Sturm's last and longest. It sat for ten months from 1 September 1547 until 30 June 1548, and high on its long agenda stood the one issue that Strasbourg's recent treaty with the emperor had not settled: the future of religion.

215

Now fifty-nine years old, Sturm came to Augsburg as the senior statesman and chief spokesman of the free cities. The lost war had cost him little of his influence among the urban delegates, who rallied to his policy of opposition to any religious settlement except by a "free, Christian council." Whatever this meant—it was an old Protestant gambit—it did not include the papally convoked Council of Trent, which the emperor wanted the Protestant rulers to acknowledge and attend. Most of all, Sturm aimed to separate the religious question from Charles V's postwar political settlement in the Empire. The Diet's proper business, Sturm asserted, was "how peace and quiet can meanwhile be maintained among the rulers."[4] The free cities' delegates held firm behind Sturm until mid-January 1548, when Cristoforo Cardinal Madruzzo of Trent reported that Pope Paul would neither return the General Council to Trent (which, unlike Bologna, lay in the Empire) nor permit the emperor to settle the religious question in Germany. Charles then struck the Council of Trent from his immediate plans and turned to the solution Sturm most feared, a provisional religious settlement for the Empire alone. He appointed a sixteen-member committee of the Diet, including Sturm and Ulm's Jörg Besserer (1502–69)—Bernhard's son—for the cities, to advise him on how this could be done.

STURM IN THE REFORM COMMITTEE

The three sessions of the Diet's committee on religion show Jacob Sturm at his tactical best. At the very start he deprecated the competence of laymen, including himself, in religious affairs. "I am not equal to this task," he said, "but for obedience's sake I will try to do it. Since the matter has been referred to a General Council and our task is to deal with an interim arrangement alone, I will serve and am content to let others propose ways and means."[5] These modest words were but a prelude to his declaration on 11 February to the committee's second session that the German schism ought to be settled in Germany, not in Christendom, and by an Imperial church council, not by the Imperial Diet. "There can be no lasting peace without composition of the religious schism," he asserted, but since the pope has blocked the General Council, "the German nation must make a beginning and not wait for other peoples to act." "The German nation is sick," Sturm declared, "and I cannot imagine why it should not heal itself through a national council."

Sturm did everything possible to divert discussion from the causes of the schism toward possible means for managing it, chiefly to the creative but not novel idea of a "national" council. He objected to Leonhard von Eck's statement that "robbery of the church is the cause of this schism," because "we well know how all pious churchmen have for many centuries described and complained of the church's fall and its need for reformation." But nothing was done, and "the abuses have now thoroughly penetrated doctrine and Christian life, as everyone knows, and the failure to improve them, despite the writings and preaching, has caused this schism."[6] Before proceeding to correction, however, "first we must find a way to live together." Next, the issue of doctrine had to be addressed, for "first we must agree about religion and what constitutes an abuse of it, because no restitution can precede an agreement on religion." And a reform of the church could only follow concord in doctrine. These were the three stages of Sturm's agenda—pacification, doctrinal agreement, and reform. Any other course, he warned, would have the sort of consequences they all remembered. "I don't want to speak of rebellion," his voice grew dark, "for I know my duty to obey the emperor.... Whether rebellion can be justified before God, I don't care to say, but I believe that we must speak again about reaching agreement on religion and about what is and is not an abuse." "I have never taken anyone's property," he continued, "and the city of Strasbourg has never driven anyone out; and the goods have been employed there, where they belong. For 400 years there has been no serious effort at reform."

In this committee Sturm finally forsook his longstanding tactical deprecation of doctrinal quarrels as "mere verbal disputes." During the committee's third and final session on 20 February, he admitted that the entire schism arose from a fundamental disagreement about the meaning of the Christian religion. "If it were true that we have abandoned the 1,500-year-old apostolic religion, and the other side has maintained it, not only would restitution . . . be just, but His Majesty ought to force us to recant and accept again the same old Catholic faith." The Evangelicals naturally denied this "and hope that we have the true, old, apostolic faith. Our theologians offer to explain how this can be so." This "chief dispute about religion . . . has been referred to a free, Christian council to be decided according to God's Word and the writings of holy teachers." Restitution—property, churches, episcopal jurisdictions—before reform would leave the Protestants without pastors or churches. "That is no peaceful interim arrangement."

This argument brought Sturm back to the central issue of ecclesiastical property. Although the plaintiffs claim to have been expropriated, he said, it is well known that the properties belong not to the benefice-holders

> but to the church, which is why they are variously called "the properties of the poor" and "the patrimony of Christ or of the Crucified One"—those are the true owners. A "church," however, is the community of believers in one place, so that a principality has many churches, and each city and village has one. The clergy are the administrators of these common properties as public properties, not their lords; and many laws, rules, and written confessions specify how they may use the properties. . . . All other uses are sacrilegious.

If restitution should precede a doctrinal concord and reform, he noted, "we at Strasbourg must imitate St. Ambrose, who said to the emperor: 'if you take the church's goods, we will take up collections and see how to support our poor.'"

In his closing remarks Sturm played his favorite trump, what may be called the "card of 1525." "If the common people, who want the true Christian religion, would see it suppressed," he warned the committee, "they would suffer and even die to prevent it, which would lead to insurrection and much suffering by innocent people." For himself, Sturm said, "I am not impassioned about what is done in public. I would like to see worship follow the teachings of the old Fathers, and I would not resist, except in spirit." If he could not in conscience accept a settlement, "I will obey and suffer whatever the emperor commands. But the Common Man will not do that. To live a Christian and godfearing way of life requires unity in religion, which is why it was decided to hold a General Council, or, lacking that, a national one or a Diet. . . . And even if there is no council, why should we not help to suppress the abuses and thereby quiet the Common Man?"[7] Lasting peace could be attained only by satisfying the popular desire for reform. This was the lesson of 1525, and it must have been satisfying for Sturm to use it against the Bavarian chancellor, Leonhard von Eck, who at Ulm during the terrible spring of 1525 had mocked the burghers for their timidity.

THE INTERIM

When Sturm's obstructionist tactics helped to deadlock the Diet's committee, the emperor simply issued his own provisional religious settlement, called the Interim. As his councilors negotiated the individual Estates' acceptance of this document, they finally managed to break Sturm's hold on the free cities. Isolated, Sturm remained adamant. After an audience on 23 March Chancellor Granvelle took him by the arm to ask, "How can such matters be resolved?" Sturm's reply—presumably they spoke in Latin—that "it might help if learned men came together and discussed them without quarreling," caused a rare crack in the chancellor's charm, and the Burgundian aristocrat poured out his anger on the Protestants for having brought on this terrible schism. "Think how this split has damaged our religion," he shot back at Sturm, "for the German nation was esteemed before all others for its virtue, which has all run into the sand. The princes have neither faith nor honor; the nobles are mere bandits; and the cities house only usurers. Thus the Germans have lost the virtues for which their ancestors were famed."[8]

The chancellor now let his anger run. If Jacob Sturm really wanted to know what was said of him personally, Granvelle declared, "it is said that you are one of the chief causes of this thing." Not daring to rise to this provocation, Sturm quietly replied that "I must bear whatever is said of me. It is unjustly said, however, because those who know my deeds and thoughts would speak differently of me." Now, his voice growing grim, Granvelle warned Sturm,

"You must see how the thing can be mended, for if you do not, it will redound to great personal disadvantage for you." Once more, Sturm refused the provocation: "A Christian may suffer what he cannot accept." Martin Luther, now more than a year in his grave, could not have said it better. "Suffering and the cross," Luther had written, "are the norm of Christian life."

The Interim, which Sturm continued to resist, was not a vindictive document. At first glance its terms impressed Martin Bucer, whom Sturm fetched over from Ulm to examine it, fairly favorably. Gradually, though, Bucer's reservations hardened, and on 13 April he was arrested and then released again after signing the Interim—"under duress," he later wrote—on the twentieth.[9] Seething with anger at his humiliation, Bucer left for home.

STURM AND GRANVELLE DEBATE THE REFORMATION

Meanwhile, at Augsburg the cities were tumbling under Granvelle's pressure until only Strasbourg, Frankfurt, Constance, and Lindau held out against the Interim. On 28 June 1548 Granvelle tried once again to crack Jacob Sturm, this time speaking not directly but through Heinrich Hass, an Imperial councilor and a Swabian.[10] The emperor, Hass told Sturm, "is not a little displeased" at Strasbourg's refusal to sign. Sturm replied—in Latin for Granvelle's benefit— that the Diet's referral of the matter to the emperor had been intended to cover "only external matters, which concern peace and justice, not the disputed articles on religion, which have been referred to a free, Christian council to judge after hearing both sides." This was Sturm's basic policy: temporal affairs before the Diet, spiritual ones before a council, though a "national" and not the papal one. Such a strict distinction between religious and worldly affairs was essentially tactical, for neither Sturm nor his regime recognized any such clean separation at home. Indeed, the fusion of "conscience" and "government," the respective authorities in the two realms, was characteristic of the Reformation in general and its urban representatives in particular. Sturm, for example, remarked to Granvelle that "my government . . . are convinced in their consciences, that if they accept all provisions of the Interim, they will act against God and their souls' salvation, so that His Majesty should tolerate the other side until a settlement by a free, Christian council." He used the term "conscience" in a magisterial, not an individual, sense, meaning that he and the other magistrates represented the burghers before God. And before the emperor as well, for Sturm followed these words about the "consciences" of the "government" with time-honored precepts about conscience. "It is a grievous thing for a Christian to act against his conscience," he said to Granvelle, "and even if one errs, still he wants to be heard and instructed by a free council, for St. Paul says, 'whoever acts against conscience, acts to his own condemnation.'"

The truth was, Sturm could no more see a path to reconciliation in 1548 than he had in 1525—"both sides are Christians, may God have mercy!" "We believe," he told Granvelle, "that there are godfearing people on both sides, whose consciences are entirely opposed to each other. From this sprang the religious schism, and it is difficult for any pious Christian to confess or act other than as he holds for right and Christian in his conscience." That was too much for Granvelle. "Are you so clever," he mocked Sturm and his Strasbourg colleague, Hans von Odratzheim, "that you wanted to believe and stand alone against all Christendom and thereby separate yourselves from it? You had no right to make such changes without the permission of Christendom and its heads."

Sturm now played once more his favorite trump, the threat of rebellion. To force a settlement, he warned, would provoke another mass insurrection. Since the matters at issue "concern the soul's salvation and eternal life," Sturm said, "it would be a terrible thing to force people against their consciences, especially as it would burden only the pious, who fear to displease God. For the others, who care nothing about religion, it's all the same." To force the believers, however, "would not only not contribute to peace and harmony, it would create a great 'movement.'" Granvelle had doubtless seen this card played before. "Visibly upset," he shifted his tone and warned Sturm that more was at stake than unanimity in the Diet, namely, Strasbourg's future relations with the emperor. He accused the city of harboring all sorts of "murderers, traitors, and scoundrels" and of scheming to seek French aid. "Let the French say what they will," Sturm replied, "we have nothing in common with them. He who knows the French will not much rely on them."

This ended the interview, but as Sturm and Hans von Odratzheim were leaving the building, a servant called them back. There ensued a highly revealing conversation, for when Sturm asserted that "faith cannot be forced," Granvelle replied, "Yes, one cannot force a non-Christian, but an apostate may be forced with fire." "Well," Sturm rejoindered, "one might kill him with fire, but he couldn't be made thereby to change his beliefs."[11] Perhaps Granvelle took his point, and at any rate the chancellor neglected to fix a deadline for Strasbourg's acceptance of the Interim.

This remarkable interview between Jacob Sturm and Chancellor Granvelle on 28 June at Augsburg throws revealing light on what divided and what united these aristocrats across the religious schism. Sturm made a typically Evangelical passage from conscience as an individual faculty to conscience as something in the custody, not of the church—this was Granvelle's view—but of his local government, which in effect had become the church. Of just this migration of sacral authority the Anabaptists, with a large sense of satisfaction, commonly and loudly complained. The interview also illuminates the tactical, temporizing nature of Sturm's appeal to a "free, Christian council . . . sometime in the distant future." Sturm's real policy, magisterial authority over religion, expressed perfectly the fundamental character of Strasbourg's own reformation. The exchange about heresy expressed the same point, for Sturm's colleagues could avoid killing dissenters by banishing them into someone else's lands, a solution which in Granvelle's universalist notion of the church was no solution at all. This impasse between Sturm's particularist and Granvelle's universalist view of the church dramatizes two different experiences of religious community, each quite as real as the other.

THE CAMPAIGN AGAINST THE INTERIM

When the Diet of Augsburg rose on 30 June 1548, Sturm and Odratzheim, still protesting the recess, left for home. They arrived on 4 July, relieved to be back after ten months living in an Augsburg inn. In his report to the Senate & XXI on the ninth, Sturm tried to re-create the context of his failure at Augsburg. "In sum," he told his colleagues, "the emperor was so well supplied with German and Latin troops that the electors and princes dared not resist. We burghers, however, stood fast and proclaimed our grievances, but to no effect, for the threats assured that we could accomplish nothing."[12] A gloomy admission of failure, this, just twenty-two years after the moment in 1526, when the young politician had returned in triumph from his first Imperial Diet. This time, patience had not conquered fortune. Not yet.

MARTIN BUCER MOBILIZES

On 3 July, the day before Sturm came home, Martin Bucer launched his campaign against "what the pope and his gang have done this time with their Interim."[13] Inflamed by his humiliation at Augsburg, Bucer painted the Interim as a diabolical thrust from Rome and closed with words that set the tone of his crusade against it: "[God] does not know or accept those who cry, 'Lord Lord' and reject the pope's yoke, but who won't obey the will of our only, eternal Saviour and His Father, and won't submit to His yoke. May He give us grace and help and remain with us, for evening is nigh. Amen."[14] He meant Sturm and the other magistrates, whose pretensions to command the church he still intended to break. "The true servants of Christ," he thundered, "whatever their rank in the churches, high or low, great or small, have received from the Lord the same spiritual authority and charge to establish the whole of the church's life, including doctrine, the sacraments, discipline, poor relief." This was Bucer's truest policy, that the elect, not the magistrates, are chosen by God to "feed Christ's flock in every needful way, for the sake of eternal life."[15] It is God, not the magistrates, who constitutes authority in the church. Pope Gregory VII had never said it more plainly.

Martin Bucer's moment had struck. The war of words became so hot that Ammeister Kniebis, who knew the Interim would have to go before the Schöffen, opined "that in the past hundred years things were never so dangerous as they are right now." When consulted on 23 July, however, the Schöffen held firmly to the magistrates and consented unanimously to a new embassy to the emperor. Then came catastrophe, for on 9 August arrived news that the emperor would neither make new concessions to Strasbourg nor grant its theologians a hearing. This news unleashed the opposition's fury.

The following three weeks witnessed the deepest civic crisis of Jacob Sturm's career, more dangerous by far than the crisis of the Peasants' War in 1525 had been in the city. Many, both at Strasbourg and elsewhere, believed that revolution was at hand. "There is no choice," Bucer trumpeted to John Calvin, "either we must accept the Antichrist completely and give him back all and pay him homage, or we must place everything in gravest jeopardy. . . . My fellow clergyman stand bravely, and with them many from all classes."[16] Several preachers had their congregations sing in these days a hymn which began, "Keep us, O Lord, by your Word / And kill the pope and the Turks." This was too much, and Sturm came round to warn that "if you don't practice more moderation, the emperor will force our regime to send you all away. This has happened at Augsburg, Memmingen, and Ulm and in Württemberg, where all preachers but two have been dismissed." After all, "your office is to preach the Gospel with love and gentleness, not to cause conflict and to insult others."[17] It was the old Sturmian line: preachers should tend to their preaching and let the magistrates rule.

THE CRISIS OF SUMMER 1548

The prospect of having to restore popish idolatry was grievous, surely, but perhaps even worse was in store. When the magistrates settled on their benches at city hall on 9 August, all minds were fixed on news of the daring attempt of fifteen hundred Spanish troops to take Constance in the night of 6 August, the day on which the emperor had outlawed that city. Next they listened to a torrent of reports and proposals on security, provisioning, and civic unrest, in the midst of which came the first resignation by a magistrate, Sebastian Münch, XVer from the Tanners' Guild. He had cause, for at that very moment two hundred critics of the regime were gathering for "harmful talk." A week later a committee met at Pastor Paul Fagius's (1504–49) house to plan a delegation of forty men, two from each guild, to warn the Senate & XXI "not to be so somnolent,"[18] and at New St. Peter's, Fagius's parish, the gardeners, that vanguard of every popular demonstration at Strasbourg, were plotting an illegal assembly of all the guilds.

By mid-August Strasbourg lay in crisis, as the opposition to the Interim tried to marshal the commons against the magistrates. The Walloon nobleman Valérand Poullain (d. 1558) bluntly told King Henry II of France that "the nobles, who are the minority, mostly accept the Interim and the city's subjection to the emperor, . . . while the majority of the said Schöffen are wholly opposed to the Interim."[19] This was more or less true, and the pressure on the rich to save themselves from both the commons and from the emperor's wrath through flight soon became irresistible. On 15 August Wolfgang Rehlinger, an exile from Augsburg and Sturm's cousin, declared that he no longer felt safe in Strasbourg; on the eighteenth Philips Ingold, head of a principal banking family, did the same for his clan; and on the twenty-second Caspar Hedio reported that "the rich, the nobles, and the merchants are leaving the city in great numbers."[20] The tension at city hall became excruciating. "Each day," a contemporary witness recorded, "the Senate was deep in deliberation about the Interim, while two or three thousand citizens were gathered constantly before the town hall, and nobody knew what to do." Again and again, "the regime asked the people to trust them and to go to their homes." Many magistrates, "fearing for their own skins and afraid of the emperor, wanted to flee; but Sir Jacob Sturm stood at the door and wouldn't let anyone leave until a decision had been reached." Some had Imperial sympathies and held Imperial fiefs, the reporter speculated, and "they were afraid of the people, realizing that they would be the targets of a possible rebellion. They decided to accept the book or Interim, for the rumor was true that the emperor intended to come, just as he said." Then, "for the sake of civic peace, these men renounced their citizenship and went abroad until the crisis was over. The people cursed them and charged them with cowardice, following them through the streets with insults."[21]

A tumultuous scene, the likes of which no one had seen at Strasbourg for 130 years, since the terrible days of 1419, when the bulk of Strasbourg's old nobility had departed the city forever. While Jacob Sturm stood gripping the city's reins at city hall, wagon after wagon rumbled through Strasbourg's streets, carrying Strasbourg's social cream and most of Sturm's own kinfolk—Cousin Stephan Sturm, the Böcklin boys, the Wurmser men and women, the Bocks, and the Mülnheims—into exile. Their flight from the twin wraths of emperor and fellow burghers left huge gaps on the benches at city hall, as two-thirds of the Senate & XXI resigned: two XIIIers, eight XVers, one XXIer, two stettmeisters, and five patrician and three guild senators. Saddest of all was the departure of old Conrad Joham, the rich silk merchant and banker originally from Saverne, who had served Evangelical Strasbourg since the 1520s, and who in 1525 had ridden at Sturm's side through the revolution-torn lands along the Rhine's right bank. As Joham departed city hall, at his back rang terrible words from Ammeister Jacob von Duntzenheim, Batt's brother: "I would love to stick a knife through your heart!" Leaving his great mansion in Jews' Street, where once the Jewish ritual baths had stood, Joham retired to his country seat at Mundolsheim. He never came back.

STURM'S CIVIC RHETORIC

At this moment, as his beleaguered, crippled regime sagged around him, Jacob Sturm rose to the zenith of his career as a communal politician. He wrote the

ammeister's address to the Schöffen on 27 August in words that began to turn
the situation in the regime's favor. Throwing secrecy to the winds—"among
the Schöffen there are men of papal or episcopal sympathies, who will not
keep it quiet"—the magistrates assembled all the Schöffen at seven o'clock in
the morning on 27 August and put the situation to them in Jacob Sturm's
words spoken by Ammeister Duntzenheim.[22] The emperor, he opened, had
given Strasbourg a month to decide, and while the Interim contained much
that was good, the doctrinal errors and the restoration of episcopal jurisdiction
made it unacceptable in its present form.[23] On the other hand, legality aside,
"so long as the emperor commands obedience in the Empire of the German
Nation," as he now did, "it is unthinkable that the city can hold out against
him, for in the end we must surrender and obey him, as others have done, or
seek a lord outside the Empire." The magical word—"France"—flitted through
everyone's mind but remained unspoken. Indeed, the Schöffen were warned
that if the city sought a foreign protector—France, naturally—all hands in the
Empire would be raised against it, and Alsace would become an arena of chronic
violence, just like Lombardy, Piedmont, and Hungary. Once the mercenaries
poured into the region, "you know well enough what sort of religion and fear
of God would be maintained and practiced in such a state of war." Sturm, at
least, realized how things had changed since the days, only seventy years ago,
when the region's little powers had combined to destroy three Burgundian
armies and slay their prince.

Reading from Sturm's text, the ammeister next examined the religious arguments against resistance. It was not certain, he noted, that resistance was per-
missible "without an explicit command [from God] and biblical authority, for
in the past, when He has wished to save His people, God has always shown
them the ways and means in terms which human reason can comprehend."
Now, alas, "no such path is visible, and our whole experience teaches us that
almost certainly we are not such as God will save through a miracle." Since
God evidently "intends to save and preserve His own honor in some other
way, we should meanwhile tolerate and endure arbitrary power and injustice
and in suffering and patience to await deliverance by His hand, rather than
resist them without God's command and biblical warrant." Resistance could
only throw "ourselves, our wives, and our children, plus those out on the land,
into misery, degradation, and total ruin."

In the absence of a clear sign from God, that "miracle" for which Sturm
could not hope on Strasbourg's behalf, the only path was the way of the ancient church, when it happened that "some good, stalwart Christians had to
suffer for their faith with troubled consciences and perhaps even with their
blood." "We may hope," Sturm's text offered, "that since the Christian faith
came into the world through such staunch witness and confession, not through
power and resistance, it will also be preserved and restored in the same way."

Following this long exposition of the hopelessness of resistance, Sturm's speech presented the Schöffen with the regime's proposed course of action: an embassy to the emperor to tell him "why the introduction of the Interim will burden our consciences" and to ask him to order "the bishop of Strasbourg, whom the emperor holds to be our ordinary and spiritual superior," and the canons and officials of the cathedral and some other collegial churches, "whose canons and officers mostly live here in the city," to install the Interim "in some churches, about which we are willing to negotiate in a friendly manner with His Grace and the others." In other words, the magistrates would negotiate with the bishop, not with the emperor, the terms on which Catholicism might be restored in some local churches. In return, the magistrates would promise that in the other churches the preachers would be bridled, the Sacrament administered in both kinds "in an intelligible language," the fasting holy days observed, and "external discipline and propriety" maintained. The emperor could thereby observe "that we seek nothing else than what may promote God's honor and obedience to His Majesty." If these terms were accepted, the city would retain its reformed doctrine, sacraments, and liberty—all of which resistance would surely throw into jeopardy. The future lay open, and the burghers might avert the danger of a total Catholic restoration through their devotion, just as they had merited this grievous trial through their sins.

This brilliant speech offered the Schöffen both reproach and hope. The reproach, which made the burghers themselves reponsible, through their own sins, for this terrible dilemma and for the strife and pain it was causing, drew its power from the link Sturm forged between God's providence and the individual burgher's devotion and sense of communal responsibility. The hope arose from the proposal, a brilliant backdoor to the confrontation of commune and emperor, to shift the whole matter into the bishop's hands. Not a few among the older Strasbourgeois remembered the last episcopal visit to Strasbourg, forty years ago, and how firmly and well the magistrates had handled the bishop in those days. This was a different bishop, of course, but he commanded, in any case, neither Neapolitan troopers nor hardened Spanish infantry.

Reproach and hope did not carry the day, not this time. The Schöffen voted 134 to 132 (an undervote of 34) "to bring the matter before the commune, because it concerns the faith and the soul." This seemed a victory for the opposition, and the magistrates promised to consider it, though "it is not the custom or tradition here to refer anything from the Schöffen to the commune." The moment of truth had come. While the ammeister was addressing the Schöffen in Jacob Sturm's words, Paul Fagius and others were meeting at New St. Peter's, and the rumor flew about "that before noon a stout body of folk will be together."[24]

On this day, 27 August, Jacob Sturm's world tottered all around him. On the magistrates' benches he saw the empty spaces left by the exiles; the crisis had shattered friendships born of hundreds of committee meetings and dozens of diplomatic missions; and most of Sturm's own class, including many of his kinsmen and -women, were gone into exile, some of them forever. It was the end of a world, his world, the world, too, of Old Peter Schott, Geiler, and Wimpheling. Perhaps only a miracle could save that world, but against this prospect stood Sturm's own words: "Almost certainly we are not such as God will save through a miracle."

Only one thing stood on 27 August between Sturm and utter defeat: the opposition found no leader. The party divisions of the 1520s were gone, the surviving militants from those days, men such as Claus Kniebis and Egenolf Röder, either held their tongues or backed Sturm, and the younger magistrates had produced no ambitious leader. The magistrates did not split, as they had done over the Reformation movement in the 1520s, and Sturm, buoyed by this failure, drove the regime forward toward another vote on 30 August.[25]

On the thirtieth Ammeister Duntzenheim spoke once again to the Schöffen, once again in Sturm's words. He began with a statement that the majority's demand of the twenty-seventh could not be satisfied, because "it would be an unheard-of innovation for the Schöffen to bring something before the commune, for important matters have always been decided by Schöffen and ammeister." Besides, Duntzenheim said, "you misunderstood our intention [on 27 August] and thought that we want to accept and tolerate the Interim and allow our lord, the bishop of Strasbourg, to establish it in the whole city, so that the Word of God would be entirely suppressed." This misunderstanding vitiated the demand for communal consultation, for "if you, the Schöffen, who are the principal persons of the guilds and of the commune, misunderstood our intention and proposal, how much less correctly would it be understood by the whole commune?" Such a crush of people would foster further misunderstandings, and then everyone would want to speak, and each would have his supporters "and would say that his opinion was best." From such conditions would arise "inequality and conflict, and perhaps something worse." Moreover, if the vote were taken guild by guild, the large guilds would unjustly dominate the small ones. "This is why it has been justly arranged that the smallest guild has a senator and fifteen Schöffen, just like the greatest guild, so that equity shall be maintained among guilds in all things." Strasbourg was a corporate republic, not a democracy.

Following this play on tensions between guilds, Duntzenheim (in Sturm's words) now played on those between the Schöffen and the common burghers. "It is dangerous," he said, "to reveal the city's secrets to the whole commune, in which there are all sorts of people from all sorts of places and of all sorts of opinions." Such a gathering would give voice to both the fellow who just came to town and the one who will leave tomorrow, "and no one knows what sort of loyalties such outsiders have and whether they can be trusted." This is why "our ancestors wisely established that no one can become a Schöffe unless he has been a citizen for ten years." Who, after all, "would want to put his and his friends' welfare, much less that of the whole city, into the hands of such inexperienced members of the commune?" The Schöffen should reflect on the danger of such a move, "for you see that many good burghers, who provide much work, have renounced their citizenship, just because you voted to refer the matter to the commune against all tradition and custom. Many others will doubtless leave, if things stay as they are." Sturm's words aimed to restitch the seam, crucial to communal stability, between the middling elements and the civic elite, to which end he played on the feelings of substantial men against "outsiders" and other social inferiors.

Based on such considerations, the Schöffen were told, the magistrates had decided to set aside the vote taken on the twenty-seventh "by only a two-vote majority" and to ask the Schöffen once more for consent to continue negotiations with the emperor about the Interim.

This speech and its predecessor on 27 August created a kind of moral double envelopment of the leaders of Strasbourg's guilds, who formed the vital link between the magistrates and the commune. In the earlier speech, Sturm's words had appealed to their faith, their trust in God, and their willingness to sacrifice for the common good; in this second one, he stoked their dislike of foreigners and new settlers, their concern for their livelihoods, and their sense of social superiority to the common mass of the burghers. This rhetorical Cannae won the day, for on the thirtieth the Schöffen voted 206 to 4 (an undervote of 90) to authorize a resumption of negotiations. As if to seal the victory, that afternoon a clothworker named Rudolph Probst came up to Paul Fagius in Cathedral Square and said, "You rascally priest, haven't you preached enough subversive nonsense?" A bit later, when he saw the preacher again in Franciscans' Square, Probst "struck Fagius to the ground."[26]

JACOB STURM'S VICTORY

ACCEPTANCE OF THE INTERIM

With the horse in the barn, Sturm jumped to close the door. No sooner had the Schöffen been dismissed than the depleted regime named him, Mattheus Geiger (1485–1549), and Dr. Ludwig Gremp to resume negotiations with the emperor. They left Strasbourg on 2 September and, having missed Charles V at Speyer, followed him downriver to Cologne, where on 10 September Granvelle conducted Sturm and Gremp into their monarch's presence. Sturm opened the interview with a long speech, presumably in Latin, about how the cities, though they had taken up arms to defend their liberties and their religion, had never abandoned their traditional obedience to the emperors or Imperial law. He referred to Charles's declaration in 1546, that he made war not for religion but only to punish rebel princes, and he reminded the emperor of his promise to respect Strasbourg's liberties and religion until a General Council should meet. Sturm concluded that to force religious changes without the approval of a German council would burden consciences and cause disorders. Charles's reply was two-edged. He rejected, on the one hand, the proposal to preserve the Evangelical order of worship in some of Strasbourg's churches and approved, on the other, that the bishop of Strasbourg and his clergy should install the Interim at Strasbourg. Sturm, to whom Charles was unusually gracious on this occasion, could not withdraw without a parting shot, reminding the emperor that the free cities had never approved placing this decision in Charles's hands. The Strasbourgeois then headed upriver.

Back at home, Sturm's committee seized on the emperor's "sufficient" consent to local negotiations with the bishop and recommended that the preachers be admonished to support this step.[27] Sturm may well have remembered how, many years ago, the magistrates—including his father and Uncle Ott—had dictated the conditions of Bishop William's entry into Strasbourg, and he surely expected William's successor, Bishop Erasmus, to be more flexible than the emperor would have been about the terms for a Catholic restoration.

Seizing the moment, in early November the magistrates asked Bishop Erasmus to set the date for negotiations and began actions against the network of conventicles in the city's parishes. By midwinter this two-pronged program yielded the desired results, though not without bitter costs to Sturm. Katharine Schütz (1497?–1562), Mathis Zell's widow, reported how Jacob Sturm came to her in early January 1549, and "when he tried to speak to me, he wept so that he could hardly speak. So he knows how things stand."[28] He surely did, for Sturm managed the civic side of negotiations with Bishop Erasmus about the Interim from start to finish. On 30 January the Schöffen, having been informed officially of the negotiations, voted by 262 to 30 (an undervote of only 8) to accept what could "with good conscience" be accepted and to allow the bishop to deal with the rest.

The struggle at Strasbourg was over. Bishop and magistrates agreed that the Interim would be introduced in modified form at Strasbourg on the first day of the year 1550. Though mandated by Imperial authority, this agreement bound Strasbourg's Evangelical magistrates to exercise "toleration" and to protect Catholic worship in three or four of the city's churches. This very Sturmian settlement stands forth as one of Jacob Sturm's greatest political triumphs. Patience had, at last, triumphed over fortune. Strasbourg, a citadel of the insurrection, received the Interim on terms more favorable to the city's Evangelical majority and to its Protestant government than did any other former Smalkaldic power in South Germany.

GOD AND MAMMON: MARTIN BUCER'S REPROACH

Victories have their prices, and the cost of this one proved to be heavy. The flight of the rich had placed a new question mark beside the relations between the nobles and the guilds, the very foundation of civic peace. Some old comrades, such as Conrad Joham, were gone forever, while others, such as Claus Kniebis and Mathis Pfarrer, were deeply embittered. Then there was Bucer, whose friendship with Sturm the crisis had shattered. At winter's end 1549, after Bishop Erasmus demanded that Bucer be deposed as dean of St. Thomas, the Senate & XXI agreed on 1 March that Bucer and Fagius "shall be suspended for a while." Bucer had come to Strasbourg in 1522 as a nobody, a homeless former-friar hot for the Gospel; he had risen under Capito's tutelage to become the equivalent of a civic bishop; he had held back nothing in his loyal, unflagging support of Sturm's grand policy of union with the Lutheran princes; and he had devoted his entire life to reformation at home and abroad as dean, pastor, teacher, consultant, and theologian. All that counted for little now, and on 6 April 1549 he and Fagius slipped out of Strasbourg, never to return.

Jacob Sturm and Martin Bucer, the native noble politician and the upstart commoner churchman, had together made Strasbourg a hub of the German Reformation. Now their partnership ended in utter estrangement, Bucer to die amidst England's eternal fogs, Sturm in his mansion in Strasbourg's Fire Street. The breaking of their partnership, Bucer believed, came from Sturm's too great respect for the world—"Oh, cursed mammon."[29] In his only known letter to Sturm from England, Bucer meditated on the broken state of Christ's church at Strasbourg: "And I think of you because of what was introduced [i.e., the Interim], because of you personally, and mostly because of what I heard you say [at that time]."[30] Reviewing the sources of their disagreement, Bucer lectured Sturm that "the earth is the Lord's and our homeland as well," and that God alone is the source of law and liberty. It is the duty of rulers and leaders, he wrote, to observe and maintain the kingdom of Christ despite the people's weaknesses and "mammon's covetousness." The whole world, Bucer thought, must become a single godly order, in which Christ founds His kingdom on those "in whom Christ is most alive." At this point the letter's tone broke, and as the memories of other, happier days flooded in on him, the churchman shifted from censorious complaint to gentle and affectionate remembrance. "I beg you to accept my admonition as I intend it," he wrote, "for I truly love you, . . . and I am terribly concerned for your welfare."

Thus ended the German Reformation's most fruitful partnership between church and state, between churchman and politician. The Interim, which to Bucer, a man of the church, was the work of the Antichrist, was to Sturm, a man of the city, the regrettable restoration of a religious practice which, though in itself Christian, no longer suited civic needs. The crisis of 1548 exposed a deep contradiction between their respective visions of how the church related to the world. God still ruled the world of Martin Bucer, the former friar, as he affirmed in his final letter to Sturm: "The earth is the Lord's, and our homeland as well." For Jacob Sturm, the magistrate, by contrast, God worked mysteriously in individual human hearts, but the world itself was an arena in which human patience must struggle to conquer fortune. God might speak to individuals, but not to the commune as a body, for, as Sturm wrote in his address to the Schöffen, "we are not such as God will save through a miracle." Jacob Sturm was not much younger than Niccolò Machiavelli, and a lifetime in politics had taught him that the earth is not the Lord's, but the lords'.

Notes

1. *PC* 4:731, no. 650; and here, too, at 731–32 the following quote.
2. Ibid., 732; and there, too, the remaining quotes in this paragraph.
3. Harry Gerber, "Jakob Sturms Anteil an den Religionsverhandlungen des Augsburger 'geharnischten' Reichstags von 1547/48," *ELJb* 8 (1929): 169 n. 4; *PC* 4:777, no. 680.
4. Gerber, "Jakob Sturms Anteil," 175.
5. *PC* 4:857, no. 729; *ARC* 5:210, lines 34–42.
6. *PC* 4:862–63; *ARC* 5:220, lines 19–39.
7. *PC* 4:865–68; *ARC* 5:226–27.
8. *PC* 4:897, no. 743.
9. Ibid., 918–19, no. 751 n. 7; *BDS* 17:347.
10. *PC* 4:1014, no. 791; and there, too, the quotes in the following three paragraphs.
11. Johannes Sleidan incorporated these words almost verbatim into his account in the *Commentarii*, bk. 20, for which see Chapter 7.
12. *PC* 4:1025, no. 795.
13. *BDS* 17:443, lines 13–14.
14. Ibid. 17:467, lines 24–28.
15. *TAE* 4:250, nos. 1603–5; *BDS* 17:132, line 23 to 133, line 2.
16. *CR* 41:5.
17. This story is told by Johann Friese, *Neue vaterländische Geschichte der Stadt Straßburg bis 1791*, 2d ed., 6 vols. (Strasbourg, 1792–1801), 2:275–76, based on a document now lost.
18. AMS, XXI 1548, fols. 411^v–12^r; and the following report is from the same source.
19. *PC* 4:1042–44, no. 804.
20. Brady, *Ruling Class*, 280.
21. Specklin, no. 2387.
22. *PC* 4:1059, no. 816 n. 1.
23. The quotes come from ibid., 1059–63, no. 816.
24. AMS, XXI 1548, fols. 413^v–32^r.
25. *PC* 4:1065–68, no. 818.
26. AMS, XXI 1548, fols. 440^v, 441^v–42^r.
27. *PC* 4:1085–86, no. 829.
28. Roland H. Bainton, "Katherine Zell," *Medievalia et Humanistica*, n.s., 1 (1970): 25–26 n. 40.

29. J. V. Pollet, ed., *Martin Bucer: Études sur la correspondance avec de nombreux textes inédits*, 2 vols. (Paris, 1958–62), 1:256, line 1, no. 38.

30. Jean Rott, "Un recueil de correspondances strasbourgeoises du XVIe siècle à la Bibliothèque de Copenhague (Ms. Thott 497,2°)," in Jean Rott, *Investigationes historicae: Eglises et société au XVIe siècle. Gesammelte Aufsätze*, 2 vols., ed. Marijn de Kroon and Marc Lienhard (Strasbourg, 1986), 1:303, no. 10.

14

THE LAST YEARS

Ah, what is more blessed than to put cares away, when the mind lays by its burden, and tired with labour of far travel we have come to our own home and rest on the couch we have longed for? This it is which alone is worth all these toils.

—Catullus

The signature of Jacob Sturm's last years is his concentration on local affairs in a local setting. Whether this happened by choice or by necessity is beside the point, for his withdrawal from active participation in Imperial politics signaled both the decline of his own energies and the provincialization of his native city in the new Europe of the great powers.

THE LESSON OF THE WAR

Jacob Sturm and Emperor Charles drew approximately the same lesson from the Smalkaldic War and its aftermath: the influence of ordinary burghers on civic governance ought to be reduced. Sturm embodied his conclusion in a proposal, probably composed sometime in late 1548, to revise Strasbourg's constitution in favor of the rich. His unrealized plan would have created a new category of "citizens" or "notables" from the rich merchants and rentiers of the guilds and redistributed—as shown in table 1—the magistracies equally among the nobles, these "citizens," and the guilds. In effect, this would allot two-thirds of the magistracies to a well-integrated group of noble and merchant families, who together counted perhaps fifty adult males eligible for office, and the remaining guildsmen, numbering some three thousand or more, would have to be content with the remaining third. The point, so obvious it hardly requires comment, was to secure governance to those who alone, in Sturm's view, possessed the experience, education, and wisdom to protect the civic interest at home and abroad.

TABLE 1   Sturm's Proposal for Constitutional Reform at Strasbourg, ca. 1548

ESTATE	EXISTING	PROPOSED
Patricians		
(*nobiles/Adel*)		
Stettmeisters	4	4
Senators	6	6
SUBTOTAL	10	10
Notables		
(*optimates/Bürger*)		
Senators		10
SUBTOTAL		10
Guilds		
(*tribus/Handwerker*)		
Senators	20	10
SUBTOTAL	20	10
TOTAL	30	30

The councilors around Charles V drew exactly the same lesson from the events of 1546–48, though they, of course, added heresy to the reasons for the upheavals. Beginning in 1548, the councilors introduced by fiat constitutional reforms that favored the nobles and the rich and disadvantaged the guilds at Augsburg, Ulm, and the other Swabian free cities. These "rabbit regimes" (*Hasenräte*)"—so called after the Imperial councilor Heinrich Hass (*Hase*, "hare" or "rabbit")—aimed to ensure both the magistrates' loyalty and the toleration of Catholicism. Their model, ironically enough, was loyal, Lutheran Nuremberg, which had no guilds.

The Imperial scheme and Sturm's proposal shared the assumption that secure oligarchies would give the cities more responsible, less provocative regimes. The commons were too volatile to be trusted. In the past, Sturm had often played on the fear of another Peasants' War, as when he warned Chancellor Granvelle in 1548 that forcing a religious settlement on the commons "would create a great movement" à la 1525.[1] His scheme for revising Strasbourg's constitution demonstrates that this warning, far from a mere tactic, reflected his own diagnosis of what had brought the religious schism to this violent and disruptive impasse. The Imperial constitutional reforms in the free cities rested on the same analysis, for Charles's men forced them not only on cities that had never rebelled, but also on others—Leutkirch, Wangen, and Überlingen— which had remained loyal both to the emperor and to the old faith!

At Strasbourg, where the last constitutional reform had occurred under the leadership of Old Peter Schott sixty-six years earlier, Jacob Sturm's proposal acknowledged that the collapse of the Protestant cause had nearly destroyed the old order at Strasbourg as well. Catastrophe had been averted, to be sure, by means of a two-front negotiation, as Jacob Sturm, supported by a wavering oligarchy or its remnants, bargained with the emperor with one hand and soothed his own commons with the other. Realizing nonetheless how close 1548 had come to a reprise of 1525, Sturm wanted to give his regime future security from the power of a volatile, ignorant commons, which had mortgaged his and his colleagues' freedom of action.

Sturm's constitutional proposal thus aimed to curb the empowerment of ordinary burghers, which the Reformation movement had temporarily revitalized in the free cities. The Reformation, to be sure, had conferred on the magistrates a new level of legitimacy by means of the total localization of sacral authority, but this new fusion also imported religion's disruptive power into the direct magisterial sphere. One unstable relationship between local governance and local religion had been exchanged for another.

That Strasbourg came away from the crisis almost scot free, suffering less than some loyal Catholic regimes did, stemmed in part from Sturm's inspired diplomacy, his strategic sense, and his political nerve, all of which helped patience to conquer fortune. And yet, Strasbourg might have been cowed like Augsburg and Ulm, both of which submitted tamely to imposed constitutional changes. The outcome at Strasbourg, Sturm's success, depended very much on the new European situation, that is, on the emperor's appreciation for Strasbourg's strength and strategic position in the unending struggle against the king of France. In the sign of this struggle between Habsburg and Valois, harbinger of the new Europe of the great powers, Jacob Sturm lived his last years.

A RETURN TO LOCAL POLITICS

A little more than two decades after his spectacular ascent from a provincial heritage onto the stage of Imperial politics, Sturm settled during his last years back into the role of a local and provincial politician. His postcrisis policy developed on the basis of local and provincial interests framed by Imperial loyalty. It was a policy not unlike that of his great-grandfather.

The new order of things is visible in Sturm's own life, in Strasbourg's diplomacy, and in the regime's policies. His career as a politician of Imperial rank was over, for his journey to Cologne in the autumn of 1548 marked Sturm's final appearance on the stage of Imperial politics. Thereafter, during his last five years, he traveled infrequently, and then very briefly, beyond his native city's environs. Although his age—he was fifty-nine in 1548—and health partly account for this change, the patterns of civic diplomacy were also changing, as the city's representation on the Imperial and other levels passed from the hands of magistrates into those of civil servants, chiefly the city's attorneys. In 1550, for the first time ever, Strasbourg sent civil servants rather than magistrates to an Imperial Diet. Meanwhile, Sturm himself rarely left home, though he continued to hold the strings of foreign policy.

THE COUNCIL OF TRENT

One major issue remained from the postwar settlement, the Protestant role in the Council of Trent. When, after the Smalkaldic War, the Protestant leaders agreed to attend the council only under certain conditions, Charles V seized on their "yes" and ignored their "only if." The new pope, Julius III, accordingly called on the council to reconvene at Trent on 14 November 1550. When the Diet of Augsburg drew to its close in March 1551, it was time for the Protestants to comply.

Protestant participation in the Council of Trent was in the main a political charade. Few Protestant leaders had ever placed serious hopes on a church council of any kind, fewer yet on a council convened, as Trent was, by a reigning pope. Indeed, at Strasbourg the appeal to a future council had long been regarded simply as a useful tactic. Of the Council of Trent in particular, Jacob Sturm had declared before the war that "the allies cannot entrust their cause to this council," at which "our teachings will surely be condemned."[2] The contradiction, he told Chancellor Granvelle during the Diet of Worms in 1545, was fundamental.[3] Whereas "other nations and rulers consider the pope to be head of the church and vicar of Christ, from whom they expect decisions in controversies about the faith, so that this is a true and legitimate council," the Protestants "consider the pope and his adherents to be enemies of Christ, who, contrary to His teaching, introduced the abuses, so that we cannot refer our case to this council, which is neither free nor Christian." How, then, could anyone "find a middle way which is acceptable to both sides?" Sturm thought there was "only one way," a council or assembly, "in which pious, godfearing, learned men from both sides come together and organize themselves, free of all oaths and other loyalties." They should be obliged that "apart from all human passion and without fear or favor, they should consider what would conform to the Bible and usages of the early, undefiled churches; they should then bring their views before the assembly."

In the past, when Sturm had appealed to a church council, he had meant an Imperial assembly—for which there was not a scrap of precedent—in which the Protestants could protect their interests as they did in the Imperial Diet. Now, perhaps, the victorious emperor might be able to wrest control of Trent from the pope. Charles, the majority of the princes, and the electors of Mainz and Trier, Sturm thought, should refer the whole matter to the Council of Trent, "including all the affairs of the colloquy," and the emperor could then dominate the council by ordering the bishops of Austria and the Netherlands to attend. More tactics.

The same idea had doubtless crossed Charles V's mind, though, sorely as he was tempted, he did not adopt it. Instead, he pressed the German Protestant powers to send envoys to Trent, which by 1551 they agreed to do, thinking thereby to display their obedience to the emperor and, not incidentally, to defend their religious doctrine.

Attendance at Trent became more palatable to Sturm and his colleagues because of their new relationship to an important, friendly Lutheran prince. Duke Christoph of Württemberg succeeded on the death of his father, Duke Ulrich, at Tübingen on 6 November 1550. A staunch Lutheran but a stranger in his new duchy, the thirty-five-year-old prince fit easily into the role of Strasbourg's friendly neighboring prince, which in the deeper past had belonged to the Elector Palatine and more recently to Landgrave Philip of Hesse. The long association between these two Lutheran states of the Southwest, Strasbourg and Württemberg, dates from their common preparations for the Council of Trent.

It all began with Sturm's overture to the princes "of our religion" about a common policy vis-à-vis the Council of Trent.[4] Duke Christoph's positive response, that it would be good "if the theologians met beforehand," led to Strasbourg's acceptance of a new Württemberg confession at Dornstetten, on Württemberg's western border, on 4 May 1551.[5] Sturm's hope, however, that all the southern Protestants would come "to stand as one person with others of this religion," was doomed to frustration, and so great was the current fear of conspiracies that Duke Christoph decided to send his embassy to Trent alone.[6]

The duke's decision created difficulties at Strasbourg, where, as Sturm noted, "the lack of persons qualified for this task is such that we have no one to send. If Martin Bucer, Dr. Peter Martyr, or Calvin were still here, we would not consider them unqualified to be sent with the other theologians."[7] Rather than choose Johann Marbach, a young Lindauer with good Saxon connections, in the autumn of 1551 Sturm and his colleagues unexpectedly selected a layman, Johannes Sleidan, the Paris-educated historian of the Smalkaldic League. They made a virtue of necessity. "We think," they reasoned, "that at first one or two persons, no theologians, should go in the names and at the common expense of the cities who agree with us in this matter; they should have instructions to follow the lead of the Saxons and Württembergers and take counsel and make common cause with them." Later on, "should it become necessary to send learned men [i.e., theologians], we'll send someone from among the theologians."[8] The choice clearly lay with Jacob Sturm, who not only was Sleidan's chief patron at Strasbourg, but also received separate, personal reports from him during this mission.

Just after Sleidan set off for Trent on 3 November 1551, Jacob Sturm and the preachers prepared a document which sheds much light on their view of the Council of Trent.[9] Most of the Protestant powers had agreed to attend the council, they thought, "because Almighty God has justly delivered the churches of the German nation into the emperor's captivity." Strasbourg's regime decided to attend, "not because we hoped to pluck berries from among the thorns at Trent, or figs from among the thistles, but in order to proclaim, both orally and in writing, the Confession of Augsburg . . . , which is the true doctrine of Our Lord Jesus Christ, before the Council of Trent, that piece of whoremongery, and to do so stalwartly but with proper Christian modesty." To this end, in February 1552 the Senate & XXI decided to send to Trent two of its own clergymen, Johann Marbach and Christoph Söll. They arrived on 18 March and stayed just under three weeks. Marbach reported that although "no negotiations were conducted, yet we accomplished what was originally conceived, namely, to show that we don't avoid the light, and we maintain the doctrine we have held until now and have given a good account of it."[10] The Strasbourg embassy was, in fact, a pure formality, and it would never have happened had God not driven the Strasbourgeois "into the emperor's captivity."

THE COMING OF THE FRENCH, 1552

While Sleidan and the preachers were away in Trent, the last great event of Jacob Sturm's career began to unfold right on his own doorstep. King Henry II of France was coming to the Rhine at the head of an enormous army, and German princes were marching under the standard of revolt to meet him near the Rhine Bridge at Strasbourg. This classic scenario—German princes in league with France against the emperor—posed to Sturm and his colleagues a pressing question: having been delivered "into the captivity of the emperor," should they seek a foreign, French lord, as Sturm's enemies had so often accused him of doing? This was indeed the central issue, for the aims of the rebel princes, led by Elector Moritz of Saxony, the "Judas of Meissen," hardly interested Sturm and the Strasbourgeois, who knew that the "German liberty," which Henry promised in the Treaty of Chambord (15 January 1552) to restore, once he became emperor, was not liberty as they knew and loved it.

The idea of King Henry of France as liberator of the Germans never crossed Jacob Sturm's mind. In his entire career there is no trace of French sympathies, and he once remarked that the Smalkaldic League's experience had shown that "whoever knows the French, will not rely on them much."[11]

Rumors of war preceded the French king's eastward movement at the head of forty thousand foot and ten thousand horse. Breaking camp at Joinville in mid-March 1552, he traversed Lorraine toward Metz, which his generals entered on Palm Sunday (10 April) 1552. By then the Strasbourgeois had defensive preparations well under way. In late March, as the French army began to move, a defense committee headed by Sturm fashioned a new policy of "Fortress

Strasbourg." They reasoned that because "the land cannot resist a large force, we must consider how we can hold this place . . . for the protection of everyone, both laymen and clergy."[12] If the French king took the city, "he will strengthen, provision, and garrison it and use it to hold the entire land," and the emperor's attempts to retake it would turn the entire province into a battleground. If Strasbourg were to serve as the citadel of Alsace against the French, however, the costs had to be shared by the other Alsatian powers, all of whom had to be consulted—the city of Basel, the bishop and cathedral chapter of Strasbourg, the counts of Hanau-Lichtenberg and Bitsch, the other free cities, and the free knights—about regional self-defense. The French invasion of 1552 thus thrust Strasbourg neatly back into its old role of provincial metropolis and Sturm into his great-grandfather's role of its leader. His talks with envoys of the bishop and the free knights in late March and early April yielded no tangible support for his policy of "Fortress Strasbourg." Yet they show Sturm, who had once spoken for an entire house of the Imperial Diet, enjoyed the confidence of princes, and traded sharp barbs with the Imperial Chancellor, sitting among countrified squires and small-town politicians to talk of purely regional affairs. To this new work of regional solidarity he nonetheless brought the same calm voice of harmony he had spoken in the old Smalkaldic League: "We should try to compose the quarrels among us and dispel all ill will, for otherwise . . . there will come not good will but much misfortune."[13]

By early April Strasbourg lay between the fronts, as the rebel princes pushed southward out of Franconia to try to snare the fleeing emperor at Augsburg, while at Metz the French king poised to invade Alsace via Saarbrücken with thirty thousand men. "We are caught between two armies," Sleidan wrote on 16 April. "The princes threaten us from Swabia, the Frenchman from Metz, where today, it is said, he will enter the city. . . . We have only 2,000 troops. Oh, poor Germany!"[14] Two days later, a French herald came to announce the king's approach and his desire for provisions, and next day the magistrates consulted the Schöffen, who "unanimously gave my lords, the senators, powers and said they would stick by them through thick and thin."[15] Off went an embassy headed by Peter Sturm, Jacob's brother, who returned from the French camp to report that the main danger to Strasbourg lay in the French agents and sympathizers among the resident French at Strasbourg. "Rascals," Jacob Sturm had once called such men, "who act against God and their country for the sake of money."[16] And yet the French-speakers had their uses, for when Peter Sturm, Sleidan, and Friedrich von Gottesheim came to Saverne on 2 May, it needed Michel Berman, a Catholic merchant from Saint-Nicolas-de-Port in Lorraine, to identify them to the French as "men from the regime at Strasbourg."[17] The approach of the French army nevertheless inflamed anti-Latin prejudices among the native Strasbourgeois, so much so that when the Schöffen were called on 2 May, it was decided "to gather all the Latins in the inn, eat with them, and ask them to stay put, because the people are somewhat upset."[18]

Well they might be upset, for the king's generals wanted two hundred thousand loaves of bread, one hundred casks of wine, and other provisions from Strasbourg, and when Peter Sturm and the others returned to Saverne to offer a fraction of that, Constable Anne de Montmorency cried, "We are no cows who can live on fruit! We need bread!"[19] Next day the constable and the army broke camp for the Rhine, and on the seventh the king camped at Brumath, from which he could see the spires of Strasbourg. Against the city's walls, however, he could do little, and when, a week later, he moved his army off northward, the storm was past.

1552, the year of the French, had one more surprise in store for Jacob Sturm. On 7 September an Imperial official delivered a request for provisions for the Imperial army, which then lay near Bretten—Philip Melanchthon's home town— not far away, and two days later came news that Charles himself would arrive with his army on the fifteenth.

THE COMING OF CHARLES V

Following his narrow escape from the rebel princes at Innsbruck, Charles had had to tolerate a humiliating Treaty of Passau negotiated by King Ferdinand. But he could not accept it, and now, goaded by wounded honor, thirst for revenge, and hatred of France, the failing monarch aimed to cross the Rhine with seventy thousand men and retake the free city of Metz. On 13 September, the Schöffen informed, the magistrates sent out their embassy to greet their monarch. It was Jacob Sturm's last journey. Finding Charles V near Rastatt in Baden, he delivered a plea to spare the city and region and send at least some of his troops by other routes. The magistrates promised to receive him in person in a fitting manner, though they begged him to bring only a small bodyguard and to respect their liberties. Charles praised the city for its stand against the French, excused his quick passage by the lateness of the season, and promised to lead his army around the city. Strasbourg's new role as an Imperial frontier fortress had its advantages.

The embassy's return touched off a frenzy of preparations: burghers in armor and weapons, gunners on the walls, towers, and bastions, strengthened guards at the gates, and three hundred extra guards at night in the suburbs. Next day Imperial troops appeared on the Rhine Bridge, Spaniards and Italians in the van, followed by the German foot and the artillery. They camped in the nearby villages, with the usual consequences for the inhabitants' life, limb, and property. The citizens, warned via the Schöffen and the guilds to keep peace and not provoke the "Latin" troops, climbed the city's walls to view this wild and colorful array of warriors. For nearly four days the army camped, as their emperor rested in headquarters near Auenheim, and on the nineteenth they began to march off westward.

On the nineteenth, just at midday, the emperor appeared at Butchers' Gate, entered the city, and was received by the magistrates "in a most affectionate and respectful manner," as Sleidan put it.[20] With him came the great lords, among them the Duke of Alba, Margrave Hans of Brandenburg-Küstrin, Duke Emmanuel Philibert of Savoy, and Chancellor Granvelle, plus Bishop Erasmus of Strasbourg and eight hundred troopers. They moved between lines of armed burghers, stiffened with mercenaries, much as Bishop William had done in 1507, for the magistrates of Strasbourg were still masters in their own house. After meeting the city's clergy at the cathedral, Charles took his lunch in the mansion of Conrad Meyer, the rich XVer, in Cathedral Street. Around five o'clock the emperor mounted his "little brown" and rode away through the rain, the magistrates accompanying him as far as the lepers' house. He bedded down that night in the mayor's house at Bischheim, which belonged to Sturm's Böcklin cousins, and the next day he was gone. "I departed Strasbourg," he later wrote Prince Philip, "where I received the very finest demonstrations of love and good will."[21] Charles headed westward—Strasbourg was the last German-speaking city he ever saw—toward the ruin of his army and the rest of his reputation before the walls of Metz.

The emperor's reception at Strasbourg, forty-eight years after his grandfather had entered the city during the Bavarian War, symbolized Strasbourg's return to the good, old, policy: respectful loyalty to the emperor, strong regional ties, and a great measure of self-reliance. If Jacob Sturm and the other magistrates needed the wisdom of this policy confirmed, Charles did so on that wet September day in 1552, for all the while, as he toured the city, saw its sights, and ate his lunch, the emperor never once mentioned religion.

STURM'S DEATH

When Charles V departed Strasbourg, Jacob Sturm had just over one year to live. His only missions during this last year were three meetings of the Lower Alsatian association for regional defense, all held at Strasbourg. This institution framed the end of his career, as the far-flung meetings of the Smalkaldic League had framed its prime. He moved now in the small world of Austrian councilors from Ensisheim, episcopal vassals, cathedral canons, town clerks, and free knights. Some of the latter, such as Wolff Zorn von Plobsheim and Ludwig Bock von Gerstheim, Hans's son, were his own kinsmen. They all came from nearby places and spoke in familiar accents, and their company brought Sturm welcome relief from the long journeys on horseback, the weeks of waiting for something to happen, and the months of lodging in inns that served overpriced, badly prepared food and wretched wine. These months, the last of his long career, found Jacob Sturm back in the world of his ancestors. Or nearly so, for the appearance of two sovereigns, not one, at Strasbourg in 1552 suggested how much Old Peter Schott's world was slipping away.

In the early morning hours of 30 October 1553 in the great house in Fire Street, Jacob Sturm lay dying. Johann Marbach, who had become Bucer's heir in Strasbourg's Evangelical church, stood at Sturm's death bed, as Sturm had once stood, forty-three years ago, at Geiler's. Marbach left us a portrait of the stettmeister's end. "On 30 October at four o'clock in the morning," he recorded, "I was summoned to Sir Jacob Sturm, who had been ill with a quartain fever for about ten days." As the pastor entered the sickroom, Sturm "lay already in his death agony, and though his tongue was so dry that he could no longer speak, his mind was clear." Marbach began to read from the Bible, and "to every passage he answered, 'yes,' and he prayed with us with folded hands and at the end said audibly, 'Amen.'" By now—it was six o'clock—Marbach asked, "Sir, will you hear some more from God's Word?" The dying magistrate watched, as Marbach read from John: "For God did not send his Son to judge the world but to save it; and whoever believes in Him will not be judged but given eternal life." Sturm closed his eyes, opened his mouth, and in two breaths he was gone.[22] "For myself," the pastor wrote in his grief, "in him I lost my best friend, yes, my father in this city."

That afternoon Ammeister Hans Hammerer of the Cobblers' Guild spoke the terrible news at town hall: "Sir Jacob Sturm, father of the city and an ornament of the republic, has fallen asleep in the Lord (may He grant him a happy resurrection), and we will bury him tomorrow at two o'clock. Mathis Pfarrer says that it is custom for all the magistrates to attend."[23]

Next day they gathered at the Dominicans' whence the school's masters and pupils accompanied them to the Sturms' mansion in Fire Street. From this house, since 1529 home to Jacob and his three unmarried siblings, the cortege—magistrates, civil servants, clergymen, schoolmasters, and pupils—guided the dead stettmeister and scholarch to rest. Through the city's gates they walked and past the Good People's House, where the lepers lived, to a burying ground outside the walls, for the Reformation had banished Strasbourg's dead from its churches. After Marbach preached in German on the text, "For to me to live is Christ, and to die is gain [Philippians 1:21]," in early afternoon on the last day of October 1553, Jacob Sturm was laid to rest, and the magistrates and teachers filed by the open grave and cast clods of earth on him. He lay alone, for his wife was nearly twenty-five years dead, so long that many Strasbourgeois believed that, like his brothers, Jacob Sturm had never married.

A few days later, Jean Sturm eulogized his namesake before the Senate & XXI.[24] The rector's speech, an epitaph for the Reformation movement's glory days, tolled the names of those who had preceded the great stettmeister in death: the ammeisters Daniel Mieg, Batt von Duntzenheim, Martin Herlin,

Hans Lindenfels, Mattheus Geiger, and Claus Kniebis, plus the stettmeisters Hans Bock and Egenolf Röder von Diersburg. Pride of place in the heroic age, however, belonged to Jacob Sturm. The rector noted "what service he performed after the Peasants' War, namely, in changing the religion and suppressing useless rituals and false worship." Then Jean Sturm compared the dead stettmeister to the Greek and Roman statesmen of old—straining, no doubt, his listeners' historical knowledge—and praised his faultless private life, his gentle decency, "his eloquence, his learning, his wisdom," his combination of "sweetness and gravity," and his fine appearance. Above all, the rector associated the dead stettmeister with the founding and growth of the Latin school, far more than with the reconstruction of the church or the political defense of the faith. He recounted Jacob Sturm's steadfast behavior after the Smalkaldic War and in the crisis of the Interim and proclaimed the stettmeister responsible for the fact that "you have your republic; you have your religion; you have your liberty; you have your citizens safe and sound."

As the news of Sturm's death circulated, some were stricken, some were merely saddened, and few were gladdened by the report. At Weimar a preacher replied to the news that "what you wrote me about Jacob Sturm's death shocked and deeply disturbed not only me but also many other honorable people at [the Saxon] court."[25] The historian Johannes Sleidan spoke his grief more simply: "You know how much we lose in him." And Dr. Ulrich Geiger, a longtime agent in Strasbourg's employ, put it most simply of all: "He was the guide and the driver."[26]

NOTES

1. *PC* 4:1016, no. 791.
2. Lenz 2:342 n. 2; *PC* 3:570.
3. *PC* 3:604–6, no. 574.
4. *PC* 5:111, no. 72.
5. Viktor Ernst, ed., *Briefwechsel des Herzogs Christoph von Wirtemberg*, 4 vols. (Stuttgart, 1899–1907), 1:155, no. 165.
6. *PC* 5:169, no. 114.
7. Ibid., 111, no. 72.
8. Ibid., 219, no. 153.
9. Ibid., 252–55, no. 173.
10. Ibid., 308, no. 223.
11. *PC* 4:76, no. 56.
12. *PC* 5:295–97, no. 214; there, too, the remaining quotes in this paragraph.
13. Ibid., 296, no. 214.
14. Baumgarten, ed., *Sleidans Briefwechsel*, 242, no. 116.
15. *PC* 5:306 n. 1, no. 222.
16. *PC* 3:511 n. 3.
17. *PC* 5:320, no. 234.

18. Ibid., 321.
19. Ibid., 326.
20. Alkuin Hollaender, "Straßburgs Politik im Jahre 1552," *Zeitschrift für die Geschichte des Oberrheins*, n.s., 9 (1894): 32 n. 3; and there, too, is Charles's comment.
21. Ibid., 32 n. 3.
22. AST 198, fols. 99^v–100^r; and there, too, the following quote.
23. AMS, XXI 1553, at 30 October 1553.
24. *Ioannis Sturmii Consolatio ad senatum Argentinensem: De morte clarissimi et nobilissimi viri D. Iacobi Sturmij, odae etiam aliquae et epitaphia de eodem* (Strasbourg: Wendelin Rihel, 1553), from which come the following quotes.
25. Cornelius Friedsleben to Dr. C. F. Curio, Weimar, 21 November 1553, in AMS, AA 601, fol. 94.
26. Johannes Sleidan to John Calvin, Strasbourg, 28 December 1553, in *CR* 42:719, no. 1881; *PC* 5:481, no. 386.

15

A LIFE BETWEEN THE AGES

Johann Marbach's funeral sermon and Jean Sturm's eulogy framed posterity's image of their common benefactor. Jacob Sturm was remembered, on the one hand, as the pious Lutheran magistrate and, on the other, as the grave and judicious neo-Roman senator. The passage of centuries smoothed the differences between these images and blended them into a seamless reputation for piety, learning, service, and devotion to duty.

Sturm's historical reputation, as far as it goes, is fully deserved, for he was one of the Reformation's truly remarkable personalities, a figure without compare among all the Empire's urban politicians of his age. Time's leveling effects, however, shaped a reputation which, as the following story shows, was at the time of Sturm's death by no means unambiguous. On 20 January 1554, the lawyer Jacob Hermann of Strasbourg was at Kassel in Hesse on his government's business. When he went in to see Landgrave Philip, Hermann reported, "the prince drew me aside from the statthalter and chancellor, who were also present, into a little turret and asked me all sorts of things about the late Sir Jacob Sturm, Sir Mathis Pfarrer, and the preachers, how they were living." The prince asked especially "whether Sir Jacob Sturm had remained steadfast in our religion to the end."[1]

How is this story to be understood? Was the boundary between the confessions still so fluid, that after thirty years of struggle one of the Smalkaldic League's architects could question the other's steadfastness in their common faith, the stated ground of their long collaboration? Or, should we dismiss the landgrave's remark as a graceless parting shot, a last bit of revenge for the reproaches Sturm flung at him in November 1546, when the Smalkaldic chiefs had turned tail without offering battle, and for Strasbourg's refusal to come forward with yet more money for the war?

There is no reason whatsoever to doubt Jacob Sturm's belief in the Christian faith in the general form in which the Evangelical preachers presented it to his generation. His religious views were Evangelical in the Erasmian-Zwinglian sense of the southern urban reformation; his ecclesiology was particularist and Erastian; and his entire public career unfolded in service to the Protestant cause in and beyond the Empire. Sturm did not believe, however, as many Evangelicals

244

did, that the Christian Gospel would transform the world, at least in his time. Like Luther, he disbelieved in an inner connection between "the liberty of the Christian" and "Christian liberty," understood respectively as Christ's freeing of the individual Christian from the consequences of sin and a Gospel-based relationship of justice among Christians. His aristocratic heritage, his Erasmianism, and his experience of the Peasants' War all disposed him against seeing the Gospel as a kind of godly law and against placing any trust in the religious opinions of ordinary people. Theology apart, his fundamental attitude toward the world in many ways mirrored that of his greater contemporary, Martin Luther, whom he also resembled in his ability to fling principle to the winds when golden opportunity beckoned. Cases in point were Württemberg in 1534, Brunswick-Wolfenbüttel in 1542, and the campaign against the Imperial Chamber Court, affairs in which Sturm sanctioned illegal, even violent, actions that belied his endless pleas for tolerance, understanding, and legality. Why then did he balk at regarding the plight of the Evangelical Messins in a similar light?

Probably because the Messins' case presented once again the aspect of the Reformation movement that Sturm found most dangerous, namely, the proposition that the sensible (or "visible") religious community should find in "the Gospel" or "the godly law" an authorization to ignore or even disrupt civil authority. Landgrave Philip of Hesse and Martin Bucer accused Sturm of listening too much to the lawyers, of legalism, but the matter went deeper than that. Sturm did not flinch from violence, and he sometimes approved it, so long as it was a violence of rulers against one another. He feared, however, the power of religion to legitimize subjects' refusal to obey their rulers. Here lay the potential connection, in Sturm's mind, between the situation in Metz and the great popular disturbances of his age—the Anabaptist kingdom at Münster, Jürgen Wullenwever's regime at Lübeck, and, first and foremost, the great Peasants' War of 1525.

The events of 1525 hung like a great shadow over Sturm's policy and colored his political mentality to the very end. The Peasants' War was the archetypal, shaping event of Sturm's career, and its memory made the common people— unwanted, from Sturm's point of view—actors in the German Reformation's drama long after the movement's heroic days were past. What had occurred once could occur again. No one had better reason to understand this possibility than Sturm did in August 1548, when he faced a coalition of social antagonism and religious enthusiasm far more potent than what Strasbourg had experienced in 1525. It was not a mere tactic, therefore, when Sturm played the "card of 1525," as he did to Chancellor Granvelle at Augsburg in 1548. He knew what could happen, knew it with a vivid precision that the Burgundian, along with almost everyone else around Charles V, could hardly imagine.

From his conversion and his experiences of insurrection, therefore, Jacob Sturm carried a conflicted legacy—loyalty to the Gospel, fear of revolution—

into his long career as a Protestant politician. Out of this past arose the ambivalence toward direct action in the Gospel's name that so irritated his closest and most effective collaborator, Landgrave Philip. Without, perhaps, recognizing its root, the Hessian prince criticized Sturm's ambivalence, his caution, his "listening to the lawyers," long before their final split in 1547.

Jacob Sturm's political ambivalence—loyalty to the Gospel, fear of revolution—went to the heart of Protestant politics in the Empire. During his generation the Reformation movement unfolded in a zone of tension between the habitual sense of wider religious community and the grasp for ecclesiastical autarky, which the particularist past demanded and the events of 1525 urged. The more Protestant politics pressed forward toward a confrontation with the emperor, the more it placed in jeopardy the structures of particularism that were its principal refuge. The politics of confrontation contained a special danger for the burghers, because Protestant political successes weakened the two main protectors of local autonomy, the Imperial monarchy and the regional federations, notably the Swabian League. The Smalkaldic League could not step in to assume this protective role, both because it was geographically too far-flung and because it lacked an adequate mediating force between conservative cities and expansionist princes. The common Evangelical religion was strong enough to bring these disparate authorities together across wide distances, but it was too weak to submerge the differences of interest and of political culture that divided North from South and the aristocracy from the burghers.

Lingering conflicts with their bishops aside, already before the Reformation the free cities' burghers possessed what they wanted: particularist liberty protected from princely aggression by the sprawling, loosely jointed political umbrella that was the Holy Roman Empire. In a sense, the free cities already enjoyed the stable liberty that the Italian city-states had never achieved, local autonomy with external security. Their sole need was greater legitimacy, which the Protestant Reformation supplied by transferring sacral rights from their bishops to their magistrates, who welcomed this particularizing ecclesiastical gift of the Evangelical Gospel, just as they rejected its disruptive, explosive potential. Of the latter they had seen quite enough in 1525.

The Reformation's impact on Sturm's world was nevertheless not simply reinforcing and conservative. It also perturbed that world. Not only did the Reformation movement raise doubts about all traditions, including political ones, but its spread was inevitably caught up into the formation of a new political order. The old Christendom was giving way to a new Europe, a Europe of the great powers driven by dynastic politics, high finance, large armies, and protracted warfare. In the old world, Sturm's Strasbourg had been an important military power; in the new one, it became an important military object. Jacob Sturm lived through this transformation. In 1476, thirteen years before Sturm's birth, Uncle Ott Sturm had won his knight's spurs on the field of Murten, where he and other warriors from the region's small powers had destroyed a whole army of the expansionist Burgundian state. In 1552, the year before his death, Jacob Sturm himself watched the armies of Europe's two greatest powers march under his city's walls, King Henry of France coming eastward to the Rhine, and the Emperor Charles V headed westward to Lorraine. Jacob Sturm was born in a regional metropolis; he died in a frontier city.

One sector alone of Sturm's life remained unburdened by ambiguity and unthreatened by princely aggression, popular turmoil, or great-power politics. In his labors for the schools, Sturm reveals himself as a man of the Renaissance, a disciple both of Wimpheling who taught him the pleasures of scholarship and Erasmus who taught him its uses. For the well-to-do burghers of Sturm's time, Renaissance learning gave access to an entirely new, cosmopolitan culture, the international "republic of letters," which the printing industry and the new academies rooted more solidly in the cities than the universities' culture had ever been. In this Latinate world without boundaries, Jacob Sturm's imagination could range at will, untroubled either by the particularist heritage that gave weight, while weighing down, his political career or by the strife over religion. We can imagine Sturm, home again in Strasbourg's Fire Street after months away at Nuremberg, Regensburg, or some dumpy provincial nest in Thuringia, sitting at night over the schools' business. He pores over the accounts for salaries, books, and the students' food; he reads and replies to letters of recommendation for prospective teachers; he drafts instructions to the rector about discipline and to the warden about housekeeping; and he plans for the library's expansion.

This world of schools and scholars was a world of order, guarded by the restored Latin language, in which patience could do more than merely hold fortune at bay. The world of the church, by contrast, was a communal and public one, in which the beliefs and dreams of ordinary people ever and again threatened to burst the sturdy institutional fences, with or without the collaboration of their clergy. Religion was the central mode of expression and knowledge in Sturm's world; the church's inability to regulate it led to his own break with the religious past; and the failure of its full domestication in the free cities, the most firmly governed societies of the age, must have puzzled Sturm to the end of his days.

The cumulative image of Jacob Sturm of Strasbourg, therefore, displays a man who lived simultaneously in what we perceive as the later Middle Ages, the Reformation, and the Renaissance. To the late medieval era belonged Sturm's devotion to Strasbourg and to his own aristocratic and civic heritage; to the Reformation, his conviction of a biblically bound Evangelical faith; and to the Renaissance, his warm promotion of the republic of letters at Strasbourg. These "eras" of Middle Ages, Reformation, and Renaissance—our constructions, not his—lie braided in his biography, sometimes in partnership, sometimes at loggerheads. Together they shaped Sturm's twisting path between devotion to God and service to mammon.

The only book we possess from Jacob Sturm's library is a Clement of Alexandria printed at Florence in 1550. The volume contains the extant writings of this late second-century convert to Christianity, whose ideas are characterized by serenity and hopefulness; its texts are in Greek, a language accessible to but a tiny elite of scholars; and it was produced in a Catholic city which had been entirely undisturbed by the movement that shook and shaped Jacob Sturm's life.

That seems about right, for in Sturm's day Europe's lay elites were discovering in Renaissance humanism an ecumenical culture of their own, just as the churches were becoming more local, more territorial, and more national. In its dead authorities they found refuge from the disputes about the living authorities of religion and a world of values and symbols insulated by ancient languages from the inconstant and volatile behavior of the common people. Jacob Sturm, who experienced the common people's disruptive potential as intimately and often as any aristocrat of his age, had every reason to prize in Renaissance culture the serene universalism which Reformation religion, with its driving thrust to capture the hearts of the common people, could never supply, but also never disrupt.

Jacob Sturm lived between God and mammon, between the hope of renewed Christian faith and the fear of the uncontrollable powers of the common people and dynastic politics. Nothing symbolizes this dividedness more clearly than do the events surrounding his death. As he lay dying in the great house in Fire Street, Sturm listened to Johann Marbach read to him the holy words about the hope of eternal life. A few days later, Jean Sturm eulogized him as a Roman senator, an "ornament of the republic," a man of "grave sweetness." Because of this man, the rector reminded, the magistrates had their religion, their liberty, and their citizens "safe and sound." At the supreme moments, the crises of military defeat and the Interim, Jacob Sturm's patience had indeed conquered fortune and brought his beloved Strasbourg intact into Europe's new and harder age. Far more than Cosimo de' Medici and others who claimed this title, he was the "father of his country," Strasbourg, whose citizens were the only children he ever possessed.

NOTE

1. *PC* 5:504, no. 404.

EPILOGUE

Jacob Sturm's passage from the world of the late medieval city through the storms of the German Reformation into the age of the great powers tells us something about the larger movements of the times. His career illustrates three important developments in sixteenth-century Europe. First, in Sturm's era Europe was shifting from the decentralized, polycentric, and politically multivalent world of the later Middle Ages to an early modern Europe organized by large national states engaged in the making of wars and empires. In Leopold von Ranke's view, the struggle of Habsburg and Valois, which began during Jacob Sturm's lifetime, formed the first stage of European modernity.

The Protestant Reformation embodied a second major change. Ironically, the second wave of militant, international revolt against the Roman church developed not out of German Lutheranism, the victor in the struggle for leadership of the Protestant Reformation in the Empire, but out of Zwinglianism, the losing party. This meant that in leading Strasbourg away from Zwinglianism and into the Lutheran communion, Jacob Sturm diverted his native city from the main direction of international Protestant development. Very likely, the sleepy provincialism of Strasbourg and many other German cities during the following two hundred years, which contrasts so dramatically with their cultural vitality and openness before 1550, owed something to this shift. No work written by a German-speaker between 1550 and 1750 owns a place today in the international canon of vernacular literatures.

The third movement, Renaissance humanism, compensated to a limited degree for the diversion of German cultural development by the Protestant Reformation. Through the Latin school organized and nurtured by the two Sturms, Jacob and Jean, Strasbourg became a major node of exchange in the international network of Latin letters, but at the same time it ceased to be a leading center of vernacular culture. Jacob Sturm, who loved the serene world of classical learning he had entered with Wimpheling's tutelage and Erasmus's encouragement, understood this all very well. Unlike struggles over religion, disputes about "good letters" posed no threats to the fragile structures of authority.

Behind these cultural changes, the Empire's history experienced great continuity. As badly as the rupture in religion grieved some, and as much as it inspired and elated others, the German Protestant movement was absorbed into the Empire's structure at the cost of only two minor civil wars, one in 1546–47 and the other in 1552. Three years later, and two years after Jacob Sturm's death, the Religious Peace of Augsburg restored the Empire's political structure in 1555 by recognizing the Lutheran faith and the principle of "whose the rule, his the religion" (*cuius regio, eius religio*).[1] This settlement endured for more than fifty years, and its disruption by the Thirty Years' War, though catastrophic in its social effects, proved politically transitory. Reinstated, the Imperial constitution endured until Napoleonic times. Impressive as this continuity is at the Imperial level, on the territorial and local levels the political continuity between late medieval and post-Reformation Germany is more impressive yet. The Protestant Reformation, its theological radicalism aside, contributed substantially to this continuity.

Neither the Reformation's second, Calvinist wave nor the revival of Catholicism in the second half of the sixteenth century, nor yet the events of the Thirty Years' War, altered the Reformation's outcome: the survival of dispersed governance as the Empire's political condition until Napoleonic times. The toughness and resilience of this structure is demonstrated by the ease with which the Empire absorbed the Protestant Reformation, how quickly it restored itself after the Thirty Years' War, and how long it resisted being transformed by the emergence of true great powers, Austria and Prussia, within the Empire. The German-speaking lands remained the "hollow center" of Europe, and to some degree the Empire's dispersed governance became an essential element in the European balance of power.[2] Its very "hollowness," its lack of central power, qualified claims to sovereignty in principle and abilities to mobilize subjects' purses and sons without their consent in particular. "The distinctive genius of the Holy Roman Empire," Mack Walker has written, "was that, in practice as well as in law, to preserve the powerless was to defend one's interests and to uphold the imperial constitution."[3]

It may be argued that this long tradition of political experience in relatively small, nonsovereign units, plus its preservation of plural histories, ill prepared the German-speakers for the nineteenth century. There came an age when the leaders of a new Germany strove to imitate the achievements—industrial capitalism, military conquest, seaborne empires, and absolutist claims to sovereignty—of France and Britain. These states trained their peoples in the schoolrooms of war and empire and melted their plural histories down into integrated, national identities. The peoples of the old Holy Roman Empire long preserved their plural religious and political identities and largely escaped this Western fate. Their descendants did not.

NOTES

1. This formula was actually invented somewhat later by Heinrich Stephan, a professor of law at Greifswald.
2. The phrase "hollow center" comes from Walker, *German Home Towns*, 12.
3. Ibid., 16.

GLOSSARY

Ammeister. The chief magistrate of Strasbourg; six ammeisters, elected for life, officiated in rotation for one year each. A similar office elsewhere might be called "guild master" (*Zunftmeister*) or "burgomaster" (*Bürgermeister*), often translated as "mayor."

Bench (*Bank*). One of two (Rhenish and Swabian) divisions of the Cities' House (*Städterat*) of the Imperial Diet. Speakers of the two benches were, respectively, the senior envoys of Strasbourg and Nuremberg.

Bundschuh. A rural conspiracy originally formed in Alsace in 1493, it reemerged in the lands of the bishop of Speyer in 1513 and may have continued to merge into the Peasants' War of 1525.

Church Assembly (*Kirchenkonvent*). At Strasbourg, the weekly assembly, sanctioned by the magistrates in 1531, of the clergy and (in theory) the churchwardens, at which the city's ecclesiastical affairs and problems were discussed.

Church Ordinance (*Kirchenordnung*). A law introduced in Protestant cities to regulate the church. Strasbourg's was drafted by Jacob Sturm in 1534 and issued in early 1535.

Churchwardens (*Kirchenpfleger*). At Strasbourg since 1531, laymen appointed by the magistrates to oversee the affairs of a parish.

Circles (*Reichskreise*). The ten, later twelve, administrative districts created by the reforms under Emperor Maximilian. Some Circles began to function by the 1530s, mainly in highly fragmented regions such as Swabia, Franconia, and the Rhine Valley.

Cities, Free (*Reichsstädte*). The cities which, by custom or by charter, had no lord but the emperor and who thus possessed the right to sit in the Cities' House (*Städterat*) of the Imperial Diet. Around 1520 they numbered about sixty-five.

Common Man (*der gemeine Mann*). The contemporary phrase for the common people.

Common Penny. *See* Taxation.

Commune (*Gemeinde*). The body of all full citizens (usually male heads of household) of a city, village, or district.

Council, City (*Rat*). The small council, usually the effective governing body of a German city. At Strasbourg it contained six patrician senators and one commoner from each of the twenty guilds (each for two-year terms), and it sat alone as the city's supreme court and together with the privy councils of XV and XIII (*Rat & XXI*) as the city's highest deliberative body.

251

Council, General. The supreme representative body of the church, beginning with the Council of Nicaea (323 A.D.). The Council of Trent, which was convened by Pope Paul III in 1545, met in 1545–49, 1551–52, and 1562–63.

Council, Governing (*Reichsregiment*). A committee of Imperial Estates—actually of their envoys—established to be the Imperial executive body during the emperor's absence from the Empire; first organized in 1501 and again in 1521.

Councils, privy. Small, permanent committees of magistrates who were co-opted for life terms. At Strasbourg the XV handled domestic affairs and the more senior XIII foreign affairs.

Court, Imperial Chamber (*Reichskammergericht*). The supreme court of the Holy Roman Empire, established in 1495, attacked by the Protestants, and suspended in 1543–48. Its judges, named by the emperor, electors, and Circles (*Reichskreise*), were professional jurists trained in Roman law.

Diet, Imperial (*Reichstag*). The parliament of the Holy Roman Empire, an assembly of the Imperial Estates, called by the emperor or his deputy to advise and consent on matters of common concern. It was divided into three houses (*Räte*) of electors, princes, and cities, and its decisions were incorporated into a recess (*Abschied*), which upon confirmation became Imperial law.

Diet, territorial (*Landtag, Landschaft*). The parliament of a territorial principality, consisting of two or more corporately organized estates (*Landstände*) and with widely varying rights.

Diet, urban (*Städtetag*). A separate meeting of the free and Imperial cities, attended by one to three envoys per city; usually held in the South and attended mainly by southern cities, plus Cologne.

Electors (*Kurfürsten*). The seven princes who, following the Golden Bull (1356), elected a king of the Romans and emperor-elect. They were the prince-archbishops of Mainz, Cologne, and Trier, the electors Palatine and of Brandenburg and Saxony, and the king of Bohemia.

Emperor (*Kaiser, imperator*). Ruler of the Roman Empire in the West, the highest nonclerical office in Christendom; also the title of a King of Germany who had been crowned emperor by the pope. Frederick III was the last emperor to be crowned at Rome, and Charles V the last to be crowned by the pope. Although elective to the end (1803), since the fifteenth century the office was de facto hereditary in the Habsburg dynasty (House of Austria).

Estates (*Stände*). The corporately organized subjects entitled to be consulted by the emperor (*Reichsstände*) or a territorial prince (*Landstände*), and who met as the parliament of the Empire (*Reichstag*) or a territory (*Landtag, Landschaft*). The term can also refer simply to the legal status of a person or group.

Guilds (*Zünfte*). Originally corporations of merchants and artisans organized for economic and religious purposes. In many German cities, the guilds gained representation in the civic regime, which meant that guilds as political organizations often came to contain unrelated crafts. Strasbourg had twenty guilds, each governed by a board of fifteen men (*Schöffen*), whose president (*Oberherr*) was normally a privy councilor.

Hansa. The Hanseatic League (the term was first used in 1344) was a federation of trading cities in the trade zones centered on the North and Baltic Seas. Headquartered at Lübeck, its merchants operated from London and Bruges to Novgorod. The Hansa encountered ever stiffer competition from the Dutch cities, which took the lead in the northern trade during the sixteenth century.

Houses (*Räte*). The separate chambers of a parliament or diet, such as the Imperial Diet, which was divided into the electors' (*Kurfürstenrat*), princes' (*Fürstenrat*), and cities' (*Städterat*) houses. Territorial parliaments show a variety of arrangements in the number and social composition of their houses.

Lansquenets (*Landsknechte*). German mercenary infantry, armed and drilled in the Swiss manner. First organized by King Maximilian around 1490, in the sixteenth century they were one of the most sought after mercenary forces.

League, Smalkaldic (*Schmalkaldischer Bund*). A military league formed in 1531 to protect Protestant interests and dissolved after its defeat by Charles V in 1547. Under the dual command of the elector of Saxony and the landgrave of Hesse, it possessed a diet (*Bundesrat*) and a war council (*Kriegsrat*); its member princes, nobles, and free cities were divided into a southern and a northern (or Saxon) circle.

League, Swabian (*Schwäbischer Bund*). A military league of free nobles, prelates, and cities (i.e., those subject only to the emperor), later joined by South and central German princes; founded under Habsburg leadership in 1488 and periodically renewed until 1534.

Prince (*Fürst*). A general term for lay rulers belonging to the upper nobility, also for all those who possessed a customary right to sit in the Princes' House (*Fürstenrat*) of the Imperial Diet.

Prince-bishop (*Fürstbischof*). A bishop who was also, by virtue of being an Imperial vassal, civil ruler of a territory and possessed thereby a seat in the Princes' House (*Fürstenrat*) of the Imperial Diet. A prince-bishop's diocese and his territory were not coterminous.

Recess (*Abschied*). The document in which were recorded the decisions of any assembly, including a body of estates.

Religious matters (*Religionssachen*). Matters touching religion, allegedly distinguishable from "secular" (*weltlich*) matters; the distinction lay behind the Protestants' attacks on the Imperial Chamber Court, though they were equally unable to agree on such distinctions in dealing with their own affairs.

Schöffen. At Strasbourg the three hundred members of the guilds' ruling committees, fifteen per guild, who collectively made up the city's large council. They were called irregularly to approve or reject measures proposed by the magistrates through the ammeister.

School Board (*Scholarchen, Schulherren*). At Strasbourg since 1526, the three magistrates who oversaw the civic schools.

Senate. *See* Council, City.

Stettmeister. The older office of chief magistrate of Strasbourg, in some functions displaced by the ammeister. Four stettmeisters officiated each year in quarterly rotation.

Suits, reformation (*Reformationsprozesse*). Judicial suits before the Imperial Chamber Court and other Imperial courts against Protestant princes and urban regimes that had confiscated or otherwise deprived Catholic clergy of their rights, incomes, and properties.

Taxation. The Imperial Diet, followed by those of the Swabian League and Smalkaldic League, normally granted taxes in units called "months" according to lists (*Matrikeln*) of assessments by alleged ability to pay. The grants were either emergency (*eilende*) or long-term (*beharrliche*) aids. To replace this form, the Imperial Diet experimented with a direct property tax, called the Common Penny, in 1495, 1542, and 1543.

RECOMMENDATIONS FOR FURTHER READING

INTERPRETATION OF THE REFORMATION ERA IN GERMANY

Brady, Thomas A., Jr. "'Special Path'? Peculiarities of German Histories in the Early Modern Era." In *Germania Illustrata: Essays on Early Modern Germany Presented to Gerald Strauss*, edited by Susan Karant-Nunn and Andrew Fix, 197–216. Kirksville, Mo., 1992.

Iggers, Georg G. *The German Conception of History: The National Tradition of Historical Thought from Herder to the Present*. Rev. ed. Middletown, Conn., 1983.

Krieger, Leonard. *Ranke: The Meaning of History*. Chicago, 1977.

Lehmann, Hartmut, and James Van Horn Melton, eds. *Paths of Continuity: Central European Historiography, 1933–1950s*. Cambridge, 1992.

Mommsen, Wolfgang J. "Ranke and the neo-Rankean School." In *Leopold von Ranke and the Shaping of the Historical Discipline*, edited by Georg G. Iggers and James M. Powell, 124–40. Syracuse, N.Y., 1990.

Nipperdey, Thomas. "The Reformation and the Modern World." In *Politics and Society in Reformation Europe*, edited by E. I. Kouri and Tom Scott, 535–52. London, 1987.

Pelikan, Jaroslav. "Leopold von Ranke as Historian of the Reformation: What Ranke Did for the Reformation—What the Reformation Did for Ranke." In *Leopold von Ranke and the Shaping of the Historical Discipline*, edited by Georg G. Iggers and James M. Powell, 89–98. Syracuse, N.Y., 1990.

Ranke, Leopold von. *History of the Reformation in Germany*. Translated by Sarah Austin. London, 1905.

Rublack, Hans-Christoph. "Is There a 'New History' of the Urban Reformation?" In *Politics and Society in Reformation Europe: Essays for Sir Geoffrey Elton on His Sixty-Fifth Birthday*, edited by E. I. Kouri and Tom Scott, 121–41. London, 1987.

Scribner, Robert W. "The Reformation as a Social Movement." In Robert W. Scribner, *Popular Culture and Popular Movements in Reformation Germany*, 145–74. London, 1987.

Sheehan, James J. "What is German History? Reflections on the Role of the *Nation* in German History and Historiography." *Journal of Modern History* 53 (1981): 1–23.

Vann, James A. "New Directions for the Study of the Old Reich." *Journal of Modern History* 58 (1986): supplement, S3–S22.

LATE MEDIEVAL GERMANY

Barraclough, Geoffrey. *The Origins of Modern Germany.* Oxford, 1946.

Dollinger, Philippe. *The German Hansa.* Translated by D. S. Ault and S. H. Steinberg. Stanford, Calif., 1970.

Du Boulay, F. R. H. *Germany in the later Middle Ages.* New York, 1983.

Leuschner, Joachim. *Germany in the Later Middle Ages.* Translated by S. MacCormack. New York, 1978.

Lütge, Friedrich. "The Fourteenth and Fifteenth Centuries in Social and Economic History." In *Pre-Reformation Germany*, edited by Gerald Strauss, 316–80. New York, 1972.

Heimpel, Hermann. "Characteristics of the Late Middle Ages in Germany." In *Pre-Reformation Germany*, edited by Gerald Strauss, 43–72. New York, 1972.

Press, Volker. "The Habsburg Lands: The Holy Roman Empire." In *Handbook of European History, 1400–1600*, edited by Thomas A. Brady, Jr., Heiko A. Oberman, and James D. Tracy, 1: 437–66. Leiden, 1994.

EARLY MODERN GERMANY

Brodek, Theodore V. "Socio-Political Realities in the Holy Roman Empire." *Journal of Interdisciplinary History* 1 (1971): 395–406.

Dahm, Georg. "On the Reception of Roman and Italian Law in Germany." In *Pre-Reformation Germany*, edited by Gerald Strauss, 282–315. New York, 1972.

Ehrenberg, Richard. *Capital and Finance in the Age of the Renaissance: A Study of the Fuggers and their Connections.* London, 1928.

Holborn, Hajo. *A History of Modern Germany.* Vol. 1, *The Reformation.* New York, 1959.

Hughes, Michael. *Early Modern Germany, 1477–1806.* Philadelphia, 1992.

Janssen, Johannes. *A History of the German People at the Close of the Middle Ages.* Vol. 1, translated by A. M. Christie. London, 1896.

Strauss, Gerald. *Sixteenth-Century Germany: Its Topography and Topographers.* Madison, 1959.

GOVERNANCE OF THE HOLY ROMAN EMPIRE

Hartung, Fritz. "Imperial Reform, 1485–1495. Its Course and Its Character." In *Pre-Reformation Germany*, edited by Gerald Strauss, 73–135. New York, 1972.

Kunkel, Wolfgang. "The Reception of Roman Law in Germany." In *Pre-Reformation Germany*, edited by Gerald Strauss, 263–81. New York, 1972.

Press, Volker. "The Holy Roman Empire in German History." In *Politics and Society in Reformation Europe: Essays for Sir Geoffrey Elton on His Sixty-Fifth Birthday*, edited by E. I. Kouri and Tom Scott, 51–77. London, 1987.

Sea, Thomas F. "The Swabian League and Government in the Holy Roman Empire of the Early Sixteenth Century." In *Aspects of Late Medieval Government and Society: Essays Presented to J. R. Lander*, edited by J. G. Rowe, 249–76. Toronto, 1986.

Strauss, Gerald. "The Holy Roman Empire Revisited." *Central European History* 11 (1978): 290–301.

———. *Law, Resistance, and the State: The Opposition to Roman Law in Reformation Germany*. Princeton, 1986.

Vann, James A., and Steven W. Rowan, eds. *The Old Reich: Essays on German Political Institutions, 1495–1806*. Brussels, 1974.

TERRITORIAL PRINCIPALITIES

Blaschke, Karlheinz. "The Reformation and the Rise of the Territorial State." Translated by Thomas A. Brady, Jr. In *Luther and the Modern State in Germany*, edited by James D. Tracy, 61–76. Kirksville, Mo., 1986.

Brunner, Otto. *Land and Lordship: Structures of Governance in Medieval Austria*. Translated by Howard Kaminsky and James Van Horn Melton. Philadelphia, 1992.

Carsten, Francis Ludwig. *Princes and Parliaments in Germany from the Fifteenth to the Eighteenth Century*. 1959. Reprint, Oxford, 1963.

Oestreich, Gerhard. *Neo-Stoicism and the Early Modern State*. Cambridge, 1982.

Schilling, Heinz. "The Reformation and the Rise of the Early Modern State." In *Luther and the Modern State in Germany*, edited by James D. Tracy, 21–30. Kirksville, Mo., 1986.

Stievermann, Dieter. "South German Courts around 1500." In *Princes, Patronage and the Nobility: The Court at the Beginning of the Modern Age, c. 1350–1650*, edited by Ronald G. Asch and Adolf M. Birke, 157–72. London, 1991.

TOWNS AND VILLAGES

Blickle, Peter. *Obedient Germans? A Rebuttal: A New View of German History*. Translated by Thomas A. Brady, Jr. Charlottesville, Va., 1997.

Brady, Thomas A., Jr. *Turning Swiss: Cities and Empire, 1450–1550*. Cambridge, 1985.

———. "The 'Urban Belt': South Germany and Switzerland, 1400–1700." In *Communalism, Representation, Resistance*, edited by Peter Blickle. Oxford, 1996.

Rublack, Hans-Christoph. "Political and Social Norms in Urban Communities in the Holy Roman Empire." In Peter Blickle, Hans-Christoph Rublack, and Winfried Schulze, *Religion, Politics and Social Protest: Three Studies on Early Modern Germany*, edited by Kaspar von Greyerz, 24–60. London, 1984.

Scott, Tom. "Community and Conflict in Early Modern Germany." *European Historical Quarterly* 16 (1986): 209–16.

THE PROTESTANT REFORMATION

Dickens, A. G. *The German Nation and Martin Luther*. New York, 1974.

Dickens, A. G., and John Tonkin. *The Reformation in Historical Thought*. Cambridge, Mass., 1985.

Fischer-Galati, Stephen A. *Ottoman Imperialism and German Protestantism, 1521–1555*. Cambridge, Mass., 1959.

Parker, N. Geoffrey. "Success and Failure during the First Century of the Reformation." *Past and Present*, no. 136 (August 1992): 43–82.

Strauss, Gerald. "Success and Failure in the German Reformation." *Past and Present*, no. 67 (May 1975): 30–63.

The Habsburg Dynasty

Evans, R. J. W. "The Austrian Habsburgs: The Dynasty as a Political Institution." In *The Courts of Europe: Politics, Patronage and Royalty, 1400–1800*, edited by A. G. Dickens, 121–45. London, 1977.

Koenigsberger, Helmut G. *The Habsburgs and Europe 1516–1660*. Ithaca, N.Y., 1971.

Moraw, Peter. "The Court of the German Kings and of the Emperor at the End of the Middle Ages, 1450–1519." In *Princes, Patronage and the Nobility: The Court at the Beginning of the Modern Age, c. 1350–1650*, edited by Ronald G. Asch and Adolf M. Birke, 103–38. London, 1991.

Press, Volker. "The Habsburg Court as a Center of Imperial Government." *Journal of Modern History* 58 (1986): supplement, S23–S45.

———. "The Imperial Court of the Habsburgs: From Maximilian I to Ferdinand III, 1493–1657." In *Princes, Patronage and the Nobility: The Court at the Beginning of the Modern Age, c. 1350–1650*, edited by Ronald G. Asch and Adolf M. Birke, 289–312. London, 1991.

The Emperor Maximilian I

Benecke, Gerhard. *Maximilian I, 1459–1519: An Analytical Biography*. London, 1982.

Waas, Glenn. *The Legendary Character of Kaiser Maximilian*. New York, 1941.

The Upper Rhine Region around 1500

Scott, Tom. "Economic Conflict and Cooperation on the Upper Rhine, 1450–1600." In *Politics and Society in Reformation Europe*, edited by E. I. Kouri and Tom Scott, 210–34. London, 1987.

———. *Freiburg and the Breisgau: Town-Country Relations in the Age of Reformation and Peasants' War*. Oxford, 1986.

Strasbourg before the Reformation

Brady, Thomas A., Jr. *Ruling Class, Regime, and Reformation at Strasbourg, 1520–1555*. Leiden, 1978.

———. "'You Hate Us Priests': Anticlericalism, Communalism, and the Control of Women at Strasbourg in the Age of the Reformation." In *Anticlericalism in the Late Middle Ages and Reformation*, edited by Peter Dykema and Heiko A. Oberman, 167–207. Leiden, 1993.

Chrisman, Miriam Usher. *Lay Culture, Learned Culture: Books and Social Change in Strasbourg, 1480–1599.* New Haven, 1982.

Cowie, M., and M. Cowie. "Geiler von Kaysersberg und Abuses in Fifteenth Century Strasbourg." *Studies in Philology* 58 (1961): 483–95.

Douglass, E. Jane Dempsey. *Justification in Late Medieval Preaching: A Study of John Geiler of Keisersberg.* Leiden, 1966.

Gaier, U. "Sebastian Brant's *Narrenschiff* and the Humanists." *Publications of the Modern Languages Association* 83 (1968): 266–70.

Rott, Jean. "The Library of the Strasbourg Humanist Thomas Wolf, Senior (+1511)." In *The Process of Change in Early Modern Europe: Essays in Honor of Miriam Usher Chrisman,* edited by Phillip N. Bebb and Sherrin Marshall, 33–58. Athens, Ohio, 1988.

Zeydel, E. H. *Sebastian Brant.* New York, 1967.

JACOB STURM

Brady, Thomas A., Jr. *Protestant Politics: Jacob Sturm (1489–1553) and the German Reformation.* Atlantic Highlands, N.J., 1995.

UNIVERSITY LIFE

Oberman, Heiko A. *Masters of the Reformation: The Emergence of a New Intellectual Climate in Europe.* Translated by Dennis Martin. Cambridge, 1981.

———. "University and Society on the Threshold of Modern Times: The German Connection." In *Rebirth, Reform and Resilience: Universities in Transition, 1300–1700,* edited by James M. Kittelson and Pamela J. Transue, 19–41. Columbus, Ohio, 1984.

HUMANISM AND SCHOLASTICISM

Becker, Reinhard Paul. *A War of Fools. The Letters of Obscure Men: A Study of the Satire and the Satirized.* Bern, 1981.

Bernstein, Eckhardt. *German Humanism.* Boston, 1983.

Brann, Noel L. "Humanism in Germany." In *Renaissance Humanism: Foundations, Forms, and Legacy,* edited by Albert Rabil, Jr. Vol. 2, *Humanism beyond Italy,* 123–55. Philadelphia, 1988.

Hoffmann, Manfred. *Rhetoric and Theology: The Hermeneutic of Erasmus.* Toronto, 1994.

Nauert, Charles G. "The Clash of Humanists and Scholastics: An Approach to Pre-Reformation Controversies." *Sixteenth Century Journal* 4 (1973): 1–18.

Overfield, James H. *Humanism and Scholasticism in Germany, 1450–1520.* Princeton, 1984.

———. "Scholastic Opposition to Humanism in Pre-Reformation Germany." *Viator* 7 (1976): 391–420.

Ozment, Steven. "Humanism, Scholasticism, and the Intellectual Origins of the Reformation." In *Continuity and Discontinuity in Church History: Essays*

Presented to G. H. Williams, edited by F. Forrester Church and Timothy George, 133–49. Leiden, 1979.

Rummell, Erika. *The Humanist-Scholastic Debate in the Renaissance and Reformation*. Cambridge, 1995.

Shoeck, Richard J. *Erasmus of Rotterdam: The Making of a Humanist, 1467–1500*. New York, 1993.

Spitz, Lewis W. "The Course of German Humanism." In *Itinerarium Italicum*, edited by Heiko A. Oberman and Thomas A. Brady, Jr., 371–435. Leiden, 1975.

———. *The Religious Renaissance of the German Humanists*. Cambridge, Mass., 1963.

Tracy, James D. *Erasmus: The Growth of a Mind*. Geneva, 1972.

REFORMATION AT STRASBOURG

Abray, Lorna Jane. *The People's Reformation: Magistrates, Clergy, and Commons in Strasbourg, 1520–1599*. New Haven, 1985.

Bainton, Roland H. "Katherine Zell." *Medievalia et Humanistica*, n.s. 1 (1970): 3–28.

Brady, Thomas A., Jr. "Architect of Persecution: Jacob Sturm and the Fall of the Sects at Strasbourg." *Archiv für Reformationsgeschichte* 79 (1988): 262–81.

Chrisman, Miriam Usher. *Strasbourg and the Reform: A Study in the Process of Change*. New Haven, 1967.

Kittelson, James M. "Martin Bucer and the Sacramentarian Controversy: The Origin of his Policy of Concord." *Archiv für Reformationsgeschichte* 64 (1973): 166–83.

———. *Wolfgang Capito from Humanist to Reformer*. Leiden, 1975.

Stafford, William S. *Domesticating the Clergy: The Inception of the Reformation in Strasbourg, 1522–1524*. Missoula, Mont.: 1976.

Tinsley, Barbara S. "Johann Sturm's Method of Humanistic Pedagogy." *Sixteenth Century Journal* 20 (1989): 23–40.

MARTIN BUCER

Burnett, Amy N. *The Yoke of Christ: Martin Bucer and Christian Discipline*. Kirksville, Mo., 1994.

Eells, Hastings. *The Attitude of Martin Bucer toward the Bigamy of Philip of Hesse*. New Haven, 1924.

———. *Martin Bucer*. New Haven, 1931.

Stephens, W. P. *The Holy Spirit in the Theology of Martin Bucer*. Cambridge, 1979.

THE PEASANTS' WAR

Blickle, Peter. *The Revolution of 1525: The German Peasants' War from a New Perspective*. Translated by Thomas A. Brady, Jr., and H. C. Erik Midelfort. Baltimore, 1981.

Cohn, Henry J. "Anticlericalism in the German Peasants' War 1525." *Past and Present*, no. 83 (1979): 3–31.

Sea, Thomas F. "Imperial Cities and the Peasants' War in Germany." *Central European History* 12 (1979): 3–37.

REFORMATION IN THE CITIES

Baron, Hans. "Religion and Politics in the German Imperial Cities during the Reformation." *English Historical Review* 52 (1937): 405–27, 614–33.

Blickle, Peter. *The Communal Reformation: The Quest for Salvation in Sixteenth-Century Germany*. Translated by Thomas Dunlap. Atlantic Highlands, N.J., 1992.

———. "Social Protest and Reformation Theology." In P. Blickle, Hans-Christoph Rublack, and Winfried Schulze, *Religion, Politics and Social Protest*, edited by Kaspar von Greyerz, 1–23. London, 1984.

Grimm, Harold J. *Lazarus Spengler: A Lay Leader of the Reformation*. Columbus, Ohio, 1978.

Guggisberg, H. *Basel in the Sixteenth Century: Aspects of the City Republic before, during, and after the Reformation*. St. Louis, 1982.

Hannemann, Manfred. *The Diffusion of the Reformation in Southwestern Germany, 1518–1534*. Chicago, 1975.

Moeller, Bernd. *Imperial Cities and the Reformation: Three Essays*. Translated by Mark U. Edwards, Jr., and H. C. Erik Midelfort. Philadelphia, 1975.

Ozment, Steven. *The Reformation in the Cities: The Appeal of the Reformation to Sixteenth-Century Germany and Switzerland*. New Haven, 1975.

Scribner, Robert W. "Practice and Principle in the German Towns: Preachers and People." In *Reformation Practice and Principle*, edited by Peter N. Brooks, 97–117. London, 1980.

Strauss, Gerald. *Nuremberg in the Sixteenth Century: City Politics and Life between Middle Ages and Modern Times*. 1966. Reprint, Bloomington, Ind., 1976.

Walton, Robert C. *Zwingli's Theocracy*. Toronto, 1967.

Zophy, Jonathan W. *Patriarchal Politics and Christoph Kress (1484–1535) of Nuremberg*. Lewiston, N.Y., 1992.

THE LUTHERAN PRINCES AND PROTESTANT ALLIANCE

Blaschke, Karlheinz. "The Reformation and the Rise of the Territorial State." Translated by Thomas A. Brady, Jr. In *Luther and the Modern State in Germany*, edited by James D. Tracy, 61–76. Kirksville, Mo., 1986.

Christensen, Carl C. "John of Saxony's Diplomacy, 1529–1530: Reformation or Realpolitik?" *Sixteenth Century Journal* 15 (1984): 419–30.

Hillerbrand, Hans J. *Landgrave Philipp of Hesse, 1504–1567: Religion and Politics in the Reformation*. St. Louis, 1967.

Wright, William J. "Philip of Hesse's Vision of Protestant Unity and the Marburg Colloquy." In *Pietas et Societas: New Trends in Reformation Social History*, edited by K. C. Sessions and P. N. Bebb, 163–80. Kirksville, Mo., 1984.

PROTESTANTS AND RIGHT OF RESISTANCE

Cargill Thompson, W. D. J. "Luther and the Right of Resistance to the Emperor." In W. D. J. Cargill Thompson, *Studies in the Reformation: Luther to Hooker*, edited by C. W. Dugmore, 3–41. London, 1980.

———. *The Political Thought of Martin Luther*. Hassocks, 1984.

Estes, James M. *Christian Magistrate and State Church: The Reforming Career of Johannes Brenz*. Toronto, 1982.

Schoenberger, Cynthia Grant. "The Development of the Lutheran Theory of Resistance, 1523–1530." *Sixteenth Century Journal* 8 (1977): 61–76.

———. "Luther and the Justifiability of Resistance to Legitimate Authority." *Journal of the History of Ideas* 40 (1979): 3–20.

PROTESTANT REFORMERS

Brecht, Martin. *Martin Luther*. Translated by James L. Schaaf. 3 vols. Philadelphia, 1985–91.

Edwards, Mark U., Jr. *Luther's Last Battles: Politics and Polemics, 1531–46*. Ithaca, N.Y., 1983.

Oberman, Heiko A. *Luther: Man between God and the Devil*. Translated by Eileen Walliser-Schwarzbart. New Haven, 1989.

Potter, G. R. *Zwingli*. Cambridge, 1976.

Stephens, W. P. *Zwingli: An Introduction to His Thought*. Oxford, 1992.

THE EMPEROR CHARLES V

Alvárez Fernandez, M. *Charles V, Elected Emperor and Hereditary Ruler*. London, 1975.

Brandi, Karl. *The Emperor Charles V: The Growth and Destiny of a Man and of a World-Empire*. Translated by C. V. Wedgwood. 1939. Reprint, London, 1959.

Fichtner, Paula Sutter. *Ferdinand I of Austria: The Politics of Dynasticism in the Age of the Reformation*. Boulder, Colo., 1982.

———. "When Brothers Agree: Bohemia, the Habsburgs, and the Schmalkaldic War, 1546–1547." *Austrian History Yearbook* 11 (1975): 67–78.

Headley, John M. *The Emperor and His Chancellor: A Study of the Imperial Chancellery under Gattinara*. Cambridge, 1983.

———. "The Habsburg World Empire and the Revival of Ghibellinism." *Medieval and Renaissance Studies* 7 (1978): 93–127.

Jedin, Hubert. *A History of the Council of Trent*, vol. 1. Translated by Ernest Graf, O.S.B. Edinburgh, 1957.

Rodríguez-Salgado, M. J. *The Changing Face of Empire: Charles V, Philip II and Habsburg Authority, 1551–1559*. Cambridge, 1988.

Tyler, Royall. *The Emperor Charles the Fifth*. London, 1956.

ORIGINS AND HISTORY OF THE SMALKALDIC LEAGUE

Brady, Thomas A., Jr. "A Crisis Averted: Jacob Sturm and the Truce of Frankfurt, 1539." In *Krisenbewußtsein und Krisenbewältigung in der Frühen Neuzeit: Festschrift für Hans-Christoph Rublack*, edited by Monika Hagenmaier and Sabine Holtz, 47–60. Frankfurt am Main, 1992.

———. "Jacob Sturm and the Lutherans at the Diet of Augsburg, 1530." *Church History* 42 (1973): 183–202.

———. "Jacob Sturm and the Seizure of Brunswick-Wolfenbüttel by the Schmalkaldic League, 1542–1545." In *Politics, Religion and Diplomacy in Early Modern Europe: Essays in Honor of De Lamar Jensen*, edited by Malcolm R. Thorp and Arthur J. Slavin, 33–51. Kirksville, Mo., 1994.

———. "Phases and Strategies of the Schmalkaldic League: A Perspective after 450 Years." *Archiv für Reformationsgeschichte* 74 (1983): 162–81.

———. "Princes' Reformation vs. Urban Liberty: Strasbourg and the Restoration of Duke Ulrich in Württemberg, 1534." In *Städtische Gesellschaft und Reformation*, edited by Ingrid Bátori, 265–91. Spätmittelalter und Frühe Neuzeit. Tübinger Beiträge zur Geschichtsforschung, vol. 12. Stuttgart, 1980.

Cohn, Henry J. "Church Property in the German Protestant Principalities." In *Politics and Society in Reformation Europe: Essays for Sir Geoffrey Elton on His Sixty-Fifth Birthday*, edited by E. I. Kouri and Tom Scott, 158–87. London, 1987.

Dueck, A. "Religion and Temporal Authority in the Reformation: The Controversy among the Protestants Prior to the Peace of Nuremberg, 1532." *Sixteenth Century Journal* 13 (1982): 55–74.

Elton, Geoffrey R. "England and the Continent in the Sixteenth Century." In *Reform and Reformation: England and the Continent, c. 1500–c. 1750*, edited by Derek Baker, 1–16. Oxford, 1979.

Fischer-Galati, Stephen A. "Ottoman Imperialism and the Religious Peace of Nürnberg." *Archiv für Reformationsgeschichte* 47 (1956): 160–80.

Fraenkel, Pierre. "Utraquism or Co-Existence: Some Notes on the Earliest Negotiations before the Pacification of Nuernberg, 1531–32." *Studia Theologica* 18 (1964): 119–58.

Hagen, Kenneth. "The Historical Context of the Smalcald Articles." *Concordia Theological Quarterly* 51 (1987): 245–53.

Knecht, R. J. *Francis I*. Cambridge, 1982.

Kolb, Robert A. "Augsburg 1530: German Lutheran Interpretations of the Diet of Augsburg to 1577." *Sixteenth Century Journal* 11 (1980): 47–61.

Matheson, Peter. *Cardinal Contarini at Regensburg*. Oxford, 1972.

Potter, D. L. "Foreign Policy in the Age of the Reformation: French Involvement in the Schmalkaldic War, 1544–1547." *Historical Journal* 20 (1977): 525–44.

Tjernagel, Neelak Serawlook. *Henry VIII and the Lutherans: A Study in Anglo-Lutheran Relations from 1521 to 1547*. St. Louis, 1965.

Wicks, Jared. "Abuses under Indictment at the Diet of Augsburg, 1530." *Theological Studies* 41 (1981): 253–71.

Johannes Sleidan and His History

Dickens, A. G. "Johannes Sleidan and Reformation History." In *Reformation Conformity and Dissent: Essays in Honour of Geoffrey Nuttall*, edited by R. Buick Knox, 17–43. London, 1977.

Kelley, Donald R. "Johann Sleidan and the Origins of History as a Profession." *Journal of Modern History* 12 (1980): 574–98.

Vogelstein, Ingeborg. *Johann Sleidan's Commentaries: Vantage Point of a Second Generation Lutheran.* Lanham, Md., 1986.

Anabaptism and Anabaptists

Clasen, Claus Peter. *Anabaptism: A Social History, 1525–1618. Switzerland, Austria, Moravia, South and Central Germany.* Ithaca, N.Y., 1972.

Deppermann, Klaus. *Melchior Hoffman: Social Unrest and Apocalyptic Visions in the Age of the Reformation.* Translated by M. Wren and edited by B. Drewery. Edinburgh, 1987.

Deppermann, Klaus, Werner O. Packull, and James M. Stayer. "From Monogensis to Polygenesis: The Historical Discussion of Anabaptist Origins." *Mennonite Quarterly Review* 49 (1975): 83–122.

Hillerbrand, Hans, ed. *Radical Tendencies in the Reformation: Divergent Tendencies.* Kirksville, Mo., 1988.

McLaughlin, R. Emmet. *Caspar Schwenckfeld, Reluctant Radical: His Life to 1546.* New Haven, 1986.

Vogler, Günter. "The Anabaptist Kingdom of Münster in the Tension between Anabaptism and Imperial Policy." In *Radical Tendencies in the Reformation: Divergent Perspectives*, edited by Hans Hillerbrand, 99–116. Kirksville, Mo., 1988.

Williams, George H. *The Radical Reformation.* Philadelphia, 1962.

INDEX OF PLACES
AND SUBJECTS

INDEX OF PERSONS

NOTE: Members of ruling dynasties and bishops are entered under the English forms of their Christian names. Key to citizenship: (A) = Augsburg; (B) = Basel; (C) = Constance; (M) = Metz; (N) = Nuremberg; (S) = Strasbourg; (U) = Ulm; (Z) = Zurich